MOTHERS WHO DELIVER

SUNY SERIES IN FEMINIST CRITICISM AND THEORY
Michelle A. Massé, editor

Mothers Who Deliver

Feminist Interventions in Public and Interpersonal Discourse

EDITED BY
JOCELYN FENTON STITT
AND
PEGEEN REICHERT POWELL

Cover image entitled "Generations" by Fred Mutebi.
Used by permission.

Published by State University of New York Press, Albany

© 2010 State University of New York

All rights reserved

Printed in the United States of America

No part of this book may be used or reproduced in any manner whatsoever without written permission. No part of this book may be stored in a retrieval system or transmitted in any form or by any means including electronic, electrostatic, magnetic tape, mechanical, photocopying, recording, or otherwise without the prior permission in writing of the publisher.

For information, contact State University of New York Press, Albany, NY
www.sunypress.edu

Production by Diane Ganeles
Marketing by Anne M. Valentine

Library of Congress Cataloging-in-Publication Data

Mothers who deliver : feminist interventions in public and interpersonal discourse / edited by Jocelyn Fenton Stitt and Pegeen Reichert Powell.
  p. cm. — (SUNY series in feminist criticism and theory)
Includes bibliographical references and index.
ISBN 978-1-4384-3223-6 (hardcover : alk. paper)
ISBN 978-1-4384-3224-3 (pbk. : alk. paper)
 1. Motherhood—Political aspects. 2. Mothers. 3. Feminism.
I. Stitt, Jocelyn Fenton. II. Powell, Pegeen Reichert, 1970–
HQ759.M8736 2010
306.874'301—dc22

2009054367

10 9 8 7 6 5 4 3 2 1

Contents

Acknowledgments   vii

Introduction: Delivering Mothering Studies
JOCELYN FENTON STITT AND PEGEEN REICHERT POWELL   1

PART 1
FEMINIST INTERVENTIONS IN PUBLIC DISCOURSE

1. Contrapuntal Delivery and Reception of Hildegard Westerkamp's Electrovocal Performance Work on Mothering, *Moments of Laughter*
ANDRA MCCARTNEY   21

2. The Empty Mirror No More: Mother-Daughter Relationship and Film Spectatorship in Patricia Cardoso's *Real Women Have Curves*
NAN MA   41

3. Cyborg Mothering
SHELLEY PARK   57

4. "Mommyblogging *Is* a Radical Act": Weblog Communities and the Construction of Maternal Identities
LISA HAMMOND   77

5. "The Pencilling Mamma": Public Motherhood in Alice Meynell's Essays on Children
LEE BEHLMAN   99

6. Picturing Mom: Mythic and Real Mothers in Children's Picture Books
   GRETCHEN PAPAZIAN   119

PART 2
FEMINIST INTERVENTIONS IN INTERPERSONAL DISCOURSE

7. More than Talk: Single Mothers Claiming Space and Subjectivity on the University Campus
   JILLIAN M. DUQUAINE-WATSON   145

8. From Postcolonial to Postpartum: Pedagogical Politics of Motherhood
   JOCELYN FENTON STITT   163

9. Constrained Agency: British Heterosexual Mothers of Homosexual Sons
   JANET PEUKERT   191

10. Writing the Script: Finding a Language for Mothering
    LYNN KUECHLE   215

11. From Gestation to Delivery: The Embodied Activist Mothering of Cindy Sheehan and Jennifer Schumaker
    NATALIE WILSON   231

12. Political Motherhood in the United States and Argentina
    MEGHAN GIBBONS   253

    Epilogue: Power in a Movement
    JUDITH STADTMAN TUCKER   279

    List of Contributors   293

    Index   301

Acknowledgments

A conference panel on mothering studies at the Midwest Modern Language Association in 2005 was the inspiration for this collection. We would like to thank our co-panelists at that conference, Jennifer Ahern-Dodson and Carol Poston, for their enthusiasm and for helping us think about the possibilities for mothering studies at the beginning of this project. The contributors to this volume have truly enacted our goal of moving mothering studies beyond recitations of the problems mothers face to discussions of mothers as agents of social change. We thank them for their hard work and dedication to bringing this scholarship to press.

We would like to thank Fred Mutebi for his generosity in allowing us to use his multicolor woodcut print, "Generations," as the cover art for this book. Mr. Mutebi uses his artistry to convey the fragility of the human condition in Africa and to celebrate the natural beauty of Uganda, his homeland. He feels that it is important to reach ordinary people with art that relates with their issues, especially the youth of Uganda. He is the executive director of Let Art Talk, which he founded in 2007. The mission of Let Art Talk is to educate the diverse segments of society by using common terms and creative techniques to encourage constructive change for a positive future. For more information about Fred Mutebi and Let Art Talk, please visit: www.FredMutebi.org

I would like to thank my role models of mother professors, Patsy Yaeger and Anita Norich. The enthusiasm of the students (and the waiting lists for enrollment) for my mothers in popular culture classes at the University of Michigan convinced me that mothering studies was worth exploring. The support of the members of my department at Minnesota State University, Mankato, Maria Bevacqua, Susan Freeman, and Cheryl Radeloff, was crucial. When I tentatively mentioned the topic of mothers in popular culture for my upper-division seminar, their wholehearted approval made possible my further explorations into mothering studies. Teaching "Good Mother/Bad Mother: Interdisciplinary Approaches to Mothers in Popular Culture" in 2006 and 2008 allowed me to learn more about the field and solidify my ideas about pedagogy and mothering. The students in those two classes were a joy to teach. Thanks also to the College of Social and Behavioral Sciences for a course release in 2008 to work on *Mothers Who Deliver.* That release allowed me the time to edit this book, as well as the time to teach my ideal version of "Good Mother/Bad Mother." My mother, Carolyn Stitt, and my aunt, Stephanie Porter (my "othermother" as Patricia Hill Collins puts it), have provided me with numerous examples of empowered feminist mothering. I would like to thank my parents, parents-in-law, and Allison Plocher for providing excellent child care while I was working on this book. To Neil Fenton, thank you for being a patient and an attentive father to our children and for always supporting my work and activism. And to Elizabeth and Ramsey, thanks for always reminding me of what is important.

—Jocelyn Fenton Stitt

I would like to thank my friends and colleagues of Parents@Duke (2002–2004) for all of the work we did together to bring about some of the conditions necessary for empowered caregiving. I would also like to thank Sara Reichert and Betsy Parkinson for modeling the best kind of mothering and for supporting my own mothering in countless ways. Any work I do—as a mother, an activist, and a scholar—is always more rewarding because of my collaborations with Doug, and our best collaboration has been raising Charlie and Elizabeth, who give me hope that the world can change for the better.

—Pegeen Reichert Powell

Introduction

Delivering Mothering Studies

JOCELYN FENTON STITT AND
PEGEEN REICHERT POWELL

For more than thirty years now, there has been growing interest in the subject of mothering. Adrianne Rich's (1976) groundbreaking book *Of Woman Born,* in which she recognized that "We know more about the air we breathe, the seas we travel, than about the nature and meaning of motherhood," began a body of work that has intensified in recent years with the rise of the Association for Research on Mothering and the publication of books, both popular and academic, on the subject of motherhood (11). Questions central to *Mothers Who Deliver* came about through a panel organized at the Midwest Modern Language Association in 2005. That panel asked whether mothering was still marginalized and unknown, as Rich postulated, or a topic whose time had come? What new ideas about mothering and new forms of maternal activism have arisen since feminists first began analyzing motherhood? How can these ideas help us understand earlier women's experiences? How do mothers today understand our identities, our work, and our children?

Our meeting at the conference had the hallmarks of the best kind of feminist encounters: we were strengthened through a recognition of our common experiences of mothering and teaching across generations, we found an audience for an exploration of our differences, and we began to plot how we might intervene in scholarly discourse.[1] Our work in *Mothers Who Deliver*, as it has evolved out of that conference, posits that we are at a point in our collective intellectual history where we can draw from the wealth of knowledge about mothering that has circulated since Rich's first foray into this topic. At the same time, this collection moves us forward into new arguments and new forms of knowledge about mothering.

In short, we believe that mothering studies has come of age. Since the 1970s, feminist scholars have analyzed the history and current conditions of mothering and have documented mothers' difficulties. These works range from psychoanalytic discussions, such as Nancy Chodorow's *The Reproduction of Mothering* (1978) and Daphne deMarneffe's *Maternal Desire* (2004), to philosopher Sara Ruddick's *Maternal Thinking* (1989) to work on race and mothering by scholars such as Hortense Spillers (in her famous 1987 essay "Mama's Baby, Papa's Maybe: An American Grammar Book"), Patricia Hill Collins's *Black Feminist Thought* (1991), and Jennifer Morgan's *Laboring Women: Reproduction and Gender in New World Slavery* (2004), to economic analysis such as Ann Crittenden's *The Price of Motherhood* (2001), to sociological work such as Stephanie Coontz's *The Way We Never Were* (2000), Miriam Peskowitz's *The Truth behind the Mommy Wars* (2005), and Kathryn Edin and Maria Kefalas's *Promises I Can Keep: Why Poor Women Put Motherhood before Marriage* (2005), to media studies such as *The Mommy Myth* by Susan J. Douglas and Meredith W. Michaels (2004), just to name a few. Motherhood's dilemmas and ideological contradictions are spelled out, often chillingly, in these texts.

These texts demonstrate the problem motherhood constitutes in our society and in feminism as well. As the aforementioned texts enumerate, traditional notions of good mothers (White, married, Christian, middle-class, heterosexual) relying on a selfless, naturalized, maternal figure are also part of a racist, heterosexist, and classist duality that pathologizes the mothering of women of color (Roberts 1997; Collins 1991, 2007), queer mothers (Rich 1976; Lewin 1993), young mothers (Perales 1999; Berman, Silver, and Wilson 2007), and working-class mothers (Edin and Kefalas 2005). This cultural framework of traditional motherhood, defined by Patrice DiQuinzio (1999) as "essential motherhood," requires that "all women want to be and should be mothers and clearly implies that women who do not manifest the qualities required by mothering and/or refuse mothering are deviant or deficient as women" (xiii). Feminists have quite rightly resisted this inscription into motherhood, as defined for women in male-dominated societies. Feminist theorizing about motherhood, especially during the early years of the second wave, often postulated the act of caring for children rather than the social construction of motherhood as the originating and primary source of women's oppression.[2]

What we as coeditors, in concert with the contributors to *Mothers Who Deliver*, seek to redress in this volume are a couple of key issues: (1) the multiple ways in which understandings and practices of mothering are obscured by patriarchal constructions of motherhood as an institution; and (2) that mobilizing and theorizing about motherhood remains unfinished business for feminism. Feminism's difficulty reconciling the practice of mothering with the politics of women's liberation is a complex issue. Scholars argue that the individualized subject of our current discourses on "women's rights" is difficult to reconcile with the intersubjectivity experienced by many mothers.[3] Equally important, the intersections of maternal experience with class, race, and sexuality have created a divide between some White middle-class feminists who have historically seen the family as the locus of female oppression and some working-class women and/or women of color who have found refuge and resistance in their maternal praxis (Horn-Miller 2002; Collins 2007; Anderson 2007). As bell hooks (1990) has written, while growing up in her African American community, the work of homemaking was not simply drudgery, "it was about the construction of a safe place where Black people could affirm one another and by doing so heal many of the wounds inflicted by racist domination" (42). This tension between the oppression experienced by mothers and our often simultaneous experience of resistance through our mothering has been difficult to mediate.

The dilemmas surrounding motherhood have led to frustration within the feminist movement. The contradictions between the devalued nature of child care and women's disproportionate shouldering of that work, on the one hand, and the fact that some women (although not all to be sure) seem to authentically desire to care for children, on the other, have generated, according to Elaine Tuttle Hansen (1997), a "growing sense of impasse" (6). "Feminists have demanded and gained new attention for the previously ignored problems of motherhood, but they have not arrived at consensus about how to redefine the concept or adjust the system" (6). In the midst of this forty-year evolution and debate about the values and dangers of motherhood within feminism and the culture at large, we can find one point of consensus: mothers face significant barriers and obstacles.

Despite the fact that roughly 80 percent of U.S. women will have children at some point during their lifetimes (this statistic leaves out adoptive mothers, so the percentage of women actively caring for children is likely to be higher), issues facing mothers are still seen as the marginal problem of a subgroup (Dye 2008). The problems facing mothers and families today are numerous and complex. While this volume is intended to look forward to new solutions and new arguments, we feel it is important to note here the current sociopolitical and economic context in which we are writing.

According to the Save the Children's Mothers' Index, which ranks the world's countries according to maternal and child health, as well as economic and education standards, the United States placed 27th in 2008 (Save the Children 2008); the World Economic Forum placed the United States 31st out of 128 countries using similar criteria in 2007 (Hausmann, Tyson, and Zahidi 2007). The maternal mortality rate is the highest it has been in decades, according to data released by the CDC in August 2007, and is 3.7 times higher for Black women as for Whites (CDC 2007).[4] While the rates in the United States are still relatively low, in a worldwide perspective, an article about the CDC report, published in the *Washington Post*, states that three separate studies "indicate at least 40 percent of maternal deaths could have been prevented" (Stobbe 2007). In part, therefore, maternal death is just the most extreme consequence of the more widespread problem of the inaccessibility of quality health care in the United States. According to the Kaiser Family Foundation, just over half of all Americans carry health insurance through their employer, and 15.4 percent are uninsured. In addition, 10.3 percent of children ages 0 to 18 are uninsured (Kaiser State Health Facts 2007–2008). The implications for these abysmal statistics are clear: mothers and their children are not receiving preventive care, their medical conditions are not being treated, and/or they are going bankrupt to pay for out-of-pocket medical expenses. About half of all families who file for bankruptcy do so after a serious medical problem (Warren 2007).

Not included in the data on maternal deaths are deaths of pregnant women that are the result of violent acts; in fact, domestic violence is the leading cause of death for pregnant women (Curtis 2003; Campbell et al. 2007).[5] Moreover, women's mother status makes them more vulnerable to domestic violence (Romans et al. 2007), and, among immigrant populations, this status makes them more vulnerable to exploitation by traffickers (Miller et al. 2007).[6] Not only are mothers more likely to be the victims of crime, but a woman can be prosecuted *because she is pregnant*, typically in cases involving drug use. Among those accused of these "crimes," mothers of color are prosecuted disproportionately to other populations (Roberts 1997)—possibly up to 70 percent of all cases involve mothers of color (National Advocates for Pregnant Women 2008).

Even when disregarding cases of illness, violence, and prosecution, the problems facing mothers in the United States today are wearisome and overwhelming. Among industrialized countries, the United States is the only one that does not require that workers be offered paid leave to care for families (A Better Balance 2009). While some states are correcting for this major gap, the slow progress on this issue indicates that the work that mothers and other caregivers do is simply not valued to the extent that popular discourse about "family values" would suggest. Moreover, the dearth of flexible work arrangements, the rarity of benefits for part-time workers, and the lack of quality, affordable child care make the United States an extremely difficult place to simultaneously raise a family and hold down a job.[7] In the workplace, being a mother subjects women to a hidden "penalty" that plays out in reduced perceptions of competence and commitment to the workplace and lower pay (Correll, Benard, and Paik 2007). Discrimination against those with family responsibilities is not illegal under federal law and is illegal only in Alaska and in a small number of other counties and cities (Work Life Law 2008).[8] Therefore, although some mothers do "choose" to do unpaid care work full time, as Anne Crittenden (2001) observes, "to most women choice is all about bad options and difficult decisions" (237); moreover, because of this choice, which is made far more by women than by men, "motherhood is the single biggest risk factor for poverty in old age" because of lost wages and lack of retirement savings (6).

As if the decision about whether or not to work outside of the home is not difficult enough, as Susan J. Douglas and Meredith W. Michaels (2004) argue, "both working mothers *and* stay-at-home mothers get to be failures. The ethos of intensive mothering has lower status in our culture ('stay-at-home mothers are boring'), but occupies a higher moral ground ('working mothers are neglectful')" (12). The media seized on this contradiction and reflected it back on mothers, making the case that the "war" was not between mothers and harmful ideologues but among mothers themselves (Douglas and Michaels 2004).

Our work in this volume would be impossible without the work of researchers, scholars, and analysts who have helped us name and understand the context in which we mother. Peskowitz (2005) explains the difficulties faced by all who seek to improve this context for mothers: "It's hard to know who or what to blame when the problem's so big and broad" and when solutions "would lead into every other social issue imaginable" (170). Nevertheless, *Mothers Who Deliver* goes beyond a recitation of the problems facing mothers to an activist agenda of reclaiming a past history of mothers with agency and looking forward to solutions to contemporary problems. While frequently critical texts end with a gesture toward solutions, our panel raised the question, and our contributors explore here, of how to go beyond an analysis of the often difficult conditions of mothering toward new thinking on the subject.

The evolution that our project has undergone suggests at least two important, and related, points: first, the need for women's studies in general, and mothering studies in particular, to move beyond critique and into other productive forms of analysis, and, second, the need for feminists, both inside and outside of the academy, to identify those innovative, forward-looking practices from which we can better understand the knowledge inherent in mothering. In doing so we join a new movement in feminist studies calling for a reconnection of the personal and the political with agendas for social change.

Under the heading "Feminist Criticism Today" in the October 2006 issue of *PMLA*, a consensus seemed to have been reached by the diverse contributors: the "disconnection between inside and outside" the academy, as Susan Gubar (2006) put it, has threatened feminism's relevance to both communities (1714). Toril Moi (2006) notes "an ever-escalating number of articles on how hard it is for women to combine work and motherhood" without an attendant feminist analysis of the situation (1739). Instead, we get self-help books. Moi challenges us to "analyze our own world" and to produce "a feminist analysis of women's lives [that] can make a real difference to those who take it seriously" (1739).

Mothers Who Deliver provides just such an analysis of the conditions of mothering and motherhood in a variety of contexts. It is a collection of essays that focuses on mothering as an intelligent practice, deliberately reinvented and rearticulated by women. The chapters focus on women as *agents* of discourse and of cultural production. Following Andrea O'Reilly following Adrienne Rich, we identify mothering as a potentially empowered practice and experience that is different from the institution of motherhood, which is often oppressive to women in many cultures (O'Reilly 2006). "Mothering," as used in *Mothers Who Deliver*, encompasses intentional acts of nurturing children as done by men or women. This is a rejection of compulsory heterosexuality, of biological motherhood as the epitome of the parent-child relationship, and of motherhood as self-abasement "to make possible other more empowered practices of mothering," as Andrea O'Reilly puts it (2006, 12).

The chapters that follow share a common starting point in viewing mothers as subjects rather than as objects of research, but beyond this methodology our contributors speak from a variety of disciplinary and ideological standpoints. In doing so, we feel that this text delivers on a vision for the future of feminist theory, which will not reveal a unitary theory of mothering practice and subjectivity but, rather, a multiplicity of perspectives:

> Feminist theorists must recognize that, given the hegemony of individualism and essential motherhood, accounts of mothering will inevitably be characterized by inconsistencies and contradictions, and feminist theory will inevitably include multiple accounts of mothering that will contradict each other and nonetheless contribute something important to our understanding of mothering. (DiQuinzio 1999, 247)

Thus *Mothers Who Deliver* distinguishes itself from much writing about mothering today in that it focuses on forward-looking arguments, new forms of knowledge about the practice of mothering, instead of remaining solely within the realm of critique of current ideologies and policies that are detrimental to mothers.

DELIVERY

The concept of "delivery" in our title plays on the physical process of childbirth. Etymologically, the word "delivery" to signify childbirth has been used concurrently with the same word used to signify the act of setting free or rescuing someone. The second definition also inflects our use of the word "delivery" here, through the feeling of being liberated from old ideologies, old arguments about mothering, and moving forward into new understandings of mothers and mothering. Highlighting the delivery of arguments about mothering enables us to foreground women as actors in a scene characterized by the movement of discourse about mothering: mothers are the agents of discourse, responsible for its delivery, rather than the passive recipients of received wisdom.

Delivery as a guiding metaphor in this book also implies delivery as one of the five canons of classical rhetoric. The canons are the five stages of the process of composing discourse.[9] The study of delivery in classical rhetoric deals primarily with the physical performance of discourse, especially in an era when written texts were very uncommon and orators spoke to an audience that was physically present. To study delivery meant to study gesture, facial expression, and vocal management. Today, however, delivery can be extended to a consideration of all means of circulating discourse, and in our multimedia world, the available modes of delivery are vast, if not equally accessible to all.

Therefore, the metaphor of delivery here calls attention to the audience we imagine for our work. It is worth remembering that this book began at a conference, when the enthusiasm of the audience who was physically present and its appreciation for the questions we were raising inspired us to take this project farther. As the collection developed, our audience was sometimes almost eerily present with us, as we imagined the people with whom we were speaking. The concept of delivery here compels us to consider carefully who our audience is, to whom we are speaking, and the most effective way to reach this particular audience. Because the book is focused on moving beyond the critiques of current ideologies surrounding mothering, and moving forward into new arguments about who mothers are and what they do, we envision an audience who is ready for this next step. While we certainly do not assume that our audience is familiar with the entire body of work that has so usefully provided these critiques, we do assume that what will be most persuasive for our readers at this point in history is a collection of arguments that envisions mothers as intelligent agents of the practice of mothering.

Finally, considering delivery in the context of this book raises the issue of the relationship between performance and identity. Perhaps most apparent during political campaigns, delivering a speech is a performance; some people are better at it than others.[10] A politician—any speaker or writer, in fact—must *perform* being a good person in order to persuade her listeners that she *is* a good person. Ever since ancient Greece, the extent to which such a performance could actually change a person's identity has been debated. Feminist theory, especially the work of Judith Butler (1993), provides further insight into the relationship between performance and identity. There is no preexisting social subject outside of discourse, Butler argues, and so identity is produced through the performance of cultural norms of gender, race, sexuality, and so on. Agency is found through the variations of the repetitions of already constituted identity categories (220). The possibilities for radical mothering opened up by Butler's notions of performativity have been recognized by mothering scholars such as Emily Jeremiah (2006), who writes:

> Mothering behaviours, viewed in this light, contain the potential for a disruption of dominant discourses on maternity, which depend upon their enactment for validity and which, therefore,

are vulnerable and open to change. . . . Thus, to vary the repetition of mothering practices is to exert maternal agency. (25)

The metaphor of delivery in our collection, to the extent that it takes into account the relationship between performance and identity, calls attention to the ways in which our contributors, by the very act of circulating their new arguments about mothering, are at the same time enacting new identities as mothers and potentially "disrupt[ing] the dominant discourses on maternity."

The relationship between performance and identity speaks to us as editors as well. The metaphor of delivery in our title highlights for us the fact that putting together this book about mothers as agents, as intelligent practitioners, has enabled us to enact some of the arguments ourselves. The collaborative process, the shared stories about our children that were braided into our conversations about the book, the activities of writing the book and seeing it through to publication—the work of delivering this book to our audience—these have become a part of who we are as scholars and as mothers. The fact that, during this process, our mothering did not exist in a sphere that was distinct from our scholarship has helped us understand in a very immediate, almost visceral, way the arguments that our wonderful contributors have shared with us.

FEMINIST INTERVENTIONS IN PUBLIC DISCOURSE

Our collection is divided into two parts: the first part of this book focuses on arguments about mothering that are circulated via some medium other than interpersonal contact, through technology such as the cell phone and the Internet, as in the chapters by Shelley Park and Lisa Hammond; film in Nan Ma's chapter; children's picture books in Gretchen Papazian's chapter; essays and newspaper columns in Lee Behlman's chapter; and sound performances in Andra McCartney's chapter. In the chapters by Ma and Papazian, the issue of access to arenas such as the film industry and book publishing is an important consideration as mothers attempt to act as agents of the discourse on mothering; in the other chapters, the authors consider how mothers can refigure these media and technology to better serve mothers and their families.

In "Contrapuntal Delivery and Reception of Hildegard Westerkamp's Electrovocal Performance Work on Mothering, *Moments of Laughter*," McCartney explores the arguments about mothering made by Westerkamp in *Moments of Laughter*. She understands the delivery of these arguments to be quite complicated, and she studies the piece from a variety of perspectives: from her own response to a performance of the piece, from her own experience as mother involved in a custody dispute, from feminist studies, from performer, and from other listeners through a reception analysis of listener responses. The multiple, complex set of perspectives enables McCartney to appreciate what she calls the "transgressive power" of the piece to challenge "problematic cultural stereotypes of motherhood."

Ma, in "The Empty Mirror No More: Mother-Daughter Relationship and Film Spectatorship in Patricia Cardoso's *Real Women Have Curves*," takes up feminist film theorist E. Ann Kaplan's challenge to analyze film from the perspective of mothers. Studying the relationship between the mother and daughter in the film, Ma argues that the character of the mother, Carmen, delivers a "new argument about mothering that goes beyond the binary constructions of the mother as either a mouth piece for patriarchal values from whom the daughter wishes to dissociate herself, or as a victim of patriarchal ideologies." She locates her argument at the intersections of race/ethnicity, gender, and class, and she situates the film and its characters within the larger context of mainstream portrayals of Latinos in film. Ma also studies viewers' responses to the films by reading online discussions of the film and its characters, thus taking seriously the role of audience in the delivery of new arguments about mothering.

Located at the intersection of feminist, postmodernist, and queer scholarship, as well as her own lived experience as the mother of two daughters, Park's chapter, "Cyborg Mothering," argues that technology has the potential to "open spaces of critical self-reflection that are necessary to non-self-sacrificing maternal love." "Cyborg Mothering" is a fresh look at technology as part of a purposeful strategy of mothering. Park understands her work as opposing discourses that either do not recognize mothers as users of technology or that repeat tired ideas of the divisiveness of technology in human relationships. She calls technologies such as the cell phone, e-mail, and social networking sites on the Internet "technologies of co-presence." Rather than getting in the way of true intimacy, as some critics contend, Park argues that these technologies "queer time and space" in ways that can transform in positive ways our experiences of intimacy by enhancing our "response-ability," or our ability to respond and receive response from loved ones.

Like Park, Hammond turns to new communication technologies for new arguments about mothering. Specifically, in her chapter "'Mommyblogging *Is* a Radical Act': Weblog Communities and the Construction of Maternal Identities," Hammond studies blogging as a site for the circulation of alternative representations and arguments about mothering. Bloggers, she argues, "contribute to the multiplicity of voices developing new cultural definitions of motherhood, definitions that are both individual and distinct, but also communal in nature, a collective memory through which women rewrite the roles of mothering in contemporary culture." Thus new arguments about mothering are being constructed and delivered at the same time: the very act of writing and reading blogs, and the development of community that ensues, creates new definitions of mothering, enabling new practices and new understandings.

Even though there is a 100-year span between the topic of Hammond's chapter and that of the following chapter by Lee Behlman, the two authors make similar arguments about mothers as writers. In " 'The Pencilling Mamma': Public Motherhood in Alice Meynell's Essays on Children," Behlman discusses the career of Meynell (1847–1922), who was an influential English poet and essayist at the turn of the century. Behlman argues that especially in her essays, which were published in popular newspapers, Meynell "presents public, journalistic writing unproblematically and without compromise as a career for mothers and not as an obstacle to proper motherhood that must somehow be effaced." Behlman also studies Meynell's poems, which, he argues, present "a more directly critical approach to popular notions of 'essential,' sentimental motherhood," critiques that are still relevant today.

Gretchen Papazian's chapter, "Picturing Mom: Mythic and Real Mothers in Children's Picture Books," begins with the argument that books aimed at preschool children are geared toward their mothers too, containing instructions on how to mother. Unfortunately, these instructions are often unrealistic and demeaning to readers. However, as Papazian demonstrates, the picture book itself as the mode of delivery does have the potential to offer alternative, empowering visions of mothering. She illustrates her point by turning to several picture books written by or for African Americans, and she calls for both greater circulation of such books and greater attention to them.

FEMINIST INTERVENTIONS IN INTERPERSONAL DISCOURSE

The second part of this book focuses on the delivery of new arguments about mothering in settings where the mothers are face-to-face with each other or with other audiences. In this context, the content of one's argument—no matter how "truthful"—cannot be isolated from the performance of the argument. Delivery is the embodiment of the message. In this section, the chapters contain discussions about women who embody their arguments, their new ideas about mothering, in a variety of interpersonal ways. Meghan Gibbons and Natalie Wilson discuss traditional forms of activism; Janet Peukert and Jillian Duquaine-Watson write about support groups; Lynn Kuechle talks about finding a language to speak about mothering in public dramatic performances; and Jocelyn Fenton Stitt argues for academics to serve as role models on work/life integration for students.

In "More than Talk: Single Mothers Claiming Space and Subjectivity on the University Campus," Duquaine-Watson notes that although we live in a world dominated by technologies to enhance communication, the single mothers support group on the University of Iowa campus demonstrates the importance of face-to-face meetings. Using participant observation, Duquaine-Watson spent two years meeting with "S.M.A.R.T.: Single Mothers Achieving and Reflecting Together," as well as analyzing data from archives and interviews. She concludes that the work of this group constitutes "more than talk." She argues that "in the tradition of feminist consciousness-raising, S.M.A.R.T. constitutes a political space in which single mothers use language as a multifaceted tool of engagement, a way to deliver support, ideas, and a sense of community that . . . are important to their well-being and that of their children." It is, in fact, a political act for these women to meet and claim space for themselves as mothers and students in higher education, where they are often marginalized.

Stitt's chapter also focuses on mothers in higher education. Faculty mothers are often told to keep their identities as mothers under wraps because of cultural notions that mothers are incompetent and unprofessional. While much has been written about the elaborate games of hiding and disclosure that many faculty mothers feel compelled to participate in, there is little research on the benefit for students in seeing faculty members model integrated professional and personal identities in the classroom. Stitt argues for "the value for ourselves and our students when we allow our teaching identities to reflect our experiences as mothers." She does so by discussing her own experiences as a professor/mother and giving concrete examples of ways to bring mothering experiences and knowledge into the classroom. She also discusses her pilot study of her students' reactions to seeing her mother and teach in the same classroom space.

In "Constrained Agency: British Heterosexual Mothers of Homosexual Sons," Peukert takes an innovative approach to the study of LGBT (lesbian, gay, bisexual, transgendered) identity. Positing the heteronormativity of family life within Britain, Peukert investigates the effects of a son's claiming a gay identity on his mother. She performed one-on-one interviews with twenty-five mothers who were members of the organization Families and Friends of Lesbians and Gays (FFLAG) in the United Kingdom. Peukert's own identity as a mother of a gay son facilitated her research, allowing her both to establish rapport with her interviewees and to see the cultural contradictions in their narratives about their mothering their gay sons. She writes, "I was located in a society where heterosexuality is the expected outcome of 'successful' mothering and a homosexual child points to a fault with the mother." Peukert concludes that although these mothers' openness about their sons' sexuality is progressive, by claiming that they are not at fault for their sons' "gayness," they continue to hold an allegiance to the heterosexual nuclear family. In addition, many of the mothers interviewed constructed a normative gay identity for their son, which included hopes for a "romantic coupling" for their son along the lines of heterosexual marriage. She concludes by noting the "emotional work" performed by her interviewees and herself to reconcile heterosexist assumptions with their sons' gay identities.

We turn in Kuechle's chapter from support groups to the use of public performance to deliver new language about the experience of mothering. "Writing the Script: Finding a Language for Mothering" explores Kuechle's journey from a stay-at-home mother, to a graduate student in communication studies, to her creation of a scripted public performance. Kuechle interviewed five women who varied in age and mothering experiences. Text from these interviews was combined with Kuechle's own observations and the writings of feminist theorists of mothering to create the performance "Extraordinary Ordinary: Mothering in the Face of Unattainable Social Norms." Noting that "we have a limited vocabulary . . . to talk about motherhood" in all of its realities, Kuechle uses this observation as a platform to create that language through the performance itself. "Extraordinary Ordinary" has been performed in a variety of venues, including Kuechle's home university and other local colleges, on the radio, at the 2007 National Communication Association Conference, and at the 2008 Mamapalooza festival in New York, sponsored by the Association for Research on Mothering.

While Kuechle's work involves new ways to talk about the experience of mothering, Wilson's chapter theorizes new ways to discuss and name the activism of mothers. Both chapters point to the silences around the activities and subjectivities of mothers, especially in the public sphere. Wilson looks at the maternal activism of two American women in "From Gestation to Delivery: The Embodied Activist Mothering of Cindy Sheehan and Jennifer Schumaker." The anti-war activism of Sheehan and Shumaker's LGBTQ and disability rights work carried out during the period 2003–2008 deployed three key modes of delivery, according to Wilson. Both women performed an "everymom" public identity, which allowed them to simultaneously occupy the position of "mother outlaw," as defined by Andrea O'Reilly (2004); they used personal experience to redefine the relationship of the mother figure in relationship to citizenship and the state, and they put into practice what Wilson calls "embodied activism," which is "a form of activism that resolutely refuses 'abstract rationalism' and instead foregrounded the ways in which national and international policies and institutions affect mothers and their families." In this chapter, Wilson traces a change from an essentialized maternalist activism used by women in the early twentieth century to a new form of delivery: embodied activist mothering.

Gibbons's chapter, "Political Motherhood in the United States and Argentina," continues this discussion of mothers' public identities and activism by looking at two activist groups: *Madres de la Plaza de Mayo* (mothers of the Plaza de Mayo), which protested the Argentinean military dictatorship during the period 1976–1983, and the U.S. group Another Mother for Peace, which acted in opposition to the Vietnam War during the late 1960s and early 1970s. While foregrounding their identities as mothers made their public activism suspect, Gibbons notes that "by privileging their identities as mothers, both groups had profound impacts on national discourse around their respective issues." The *madres*' protests shone an international spotlight on Argentinean human rights abuses, and the Another Mother for Peace brought "hundreds of thousands" of U.S. women into an ultimately successful political movement to end the Vietnam War, Gibbons argues. Gibbons ends her chapter with suggestions about the ways in which these earlier activist groups' use of strategic essentialism might be useful for contemporary maternal activism.

All of the chapters point the way forward by naming the specific interventions necessary in order to make more productive representations of mothering more widely accessible. They not only showcase new ideas and arguments about mothering but allow us to contemplate new ways of delivering that knowledge to the wider world. None do this more urgently than the concluding chapter of the book by *Mothers Movement Online* editor and publisher Judith Stadtman Tucker. In her epilogue, "Power in a Movement," she describes her activist work to raise awareness of issues facing mothers. The chapter is not a discussion of past activist practices but instead details her impatience to go beyond analysis toward action. Tucker writes, "I'm tired of dissecting the relationship among motherhood ideology, conflicts in feminism, and the politics of organizing mothers for change." Asserting that she is

Introduction 15

"moving on to the next stage," Tucker goes on to outline steps at both the political and organizational level for taking action: in our families, neighborhoods, communities, and nation. Her chapter encapsulates our hopes that this book can bring us closer to real social change.

NOTES

1. We would like to acknowledge and thank Jennifer Ahern-Dodson and Carol Poston, our co-panelists at the conference, for being a part of the early conversations that led to this book.
2. See Snitow (1992) for an overview of the relationship between different waves of feminism in the United States and feminist theory about motherhood. Snitow traces the rise of early "demon" texts (34) that sought to reject motherhood (1963–1975) to critiques and explorations of motherhood within second-wave feminism (1976–1979), as well as later attempts (1980–1990) to look at motherhood more complexly, asking not just what motherhood is but "what women actually *do* when they mother" (39, emphasis in original).
3. Patrice DiQuinzio (1999) writes: "Feminism has to rely on individualism in order to articulate its claims that women are equal human subjects of social and political agency and entitlement. But, I argue, feminism has found it impossible to theorize mothering adequately in terms of an individualist theory of subjectivity" (xii).
4. As a point of comparison, the maternal mortality rate in the United States is 14 deaths per 100,000 live births, with European Union countries such as Spain having 5 deaths per 100,000 and Sweden having 8 per 100,000 (Hausmann, Tyson, and Zahidi 2007).
5. Campbell and colleagues (2007) note that "Pregnancy-associated homicide has emerged as a leading cause of maternal mortality. . . . Two studies concluded that pregnant and recently pregnant women are at 2 to 3 times the risk of homicide compared to non-pregnant women" (258).
6. Miller and colleagues (2007) cite the case of a Guatemalan woman resident in Massachusetts who paid more than $10,000 to be trafficked into the United States. Her "coyotes" would call her and threaten to hurt her children if she did not repay them. Threats to immigrant women can come from traffickers as well as family members who can use undocumented status as a means of control.
7. See Rosanna Hertz's (2004) review essay "The Contemporary Myth of Choice" for an excellent overview of recent scholarship on the lack of choice facing working families.
8. The Work Life Law Web site notes that Cook County (Illinois), Atlanta, Milwaukee, and Tampa have outlawed family responsibilities discrimination (see http://www.worklifelaw.org/FRDFAQ.html 2008).
9. The other four canons are invention, arrangement, style, and memory.

10. The Greek word for delivery comes from the verb that describes what an actor does.

REFERENCES

A Better Balance. 2009. Family leave. http://www.abetterbalance.org/cms/index.php?option=com_ content&task=view&id=29&Itemid=49.
Anderson, K. 2007. Giving life to the people: An indigenous ideology of motherhood. In *Maternal theory: Essential readings*, ed. A. O'Reilly, 761–81. Toronto: Demeter Press.
Berman, R. C., S. Silver, and S. Wilson. 2007. "Don't look down on me because I have one": Young mothers empowered in a context of support. *Journal of the Association for Research on Mothering* 9:1: 42–52.
Butler, J. 1993. *Bodies that matter: On the discursive limits of "sex."* New York: Routledge.
Campbell, J. C., N. Glass, P. W. Sharps, K. Laughon, and T. Bloom. 2007. Intimate partner homicide: Review and implications of research and policy. *Trauma, Violence and Abuse* 8:3 (July): 246–69.
CDC. 2007. Deaths: Final data for 2004. *National Vital Statistics Reports* 56:9 (August 21). http://www.cdc.gov/nchs/data/nvsr/nvsr55/nvsr55_19.pdf.
Chodorow, N. 1978. *The reproduction of mothering: Psychoanalysis and the sociology of gender.* Berkeley: University of California Press.
Collins, P. H. 1991. *Black feminist thought: Knowledge, consciousness, and the politics of empowerment.* New York: Routledge.
———. 2007. The meaning of motherhood in Black culture and Black mother-daughter relationships. In *Maternal theory: Essential readings*, ed. A. O'Reilly, 274–89. Toronto: Demeter Press.
Coontz, S. 2000. *The way we never were: American families and the nostalgia trap.* New York: Basic Books.
Correll, S. J., S. Benard, and I. Paik. 2007. Getting a job: Is there a motherhood penalty? *American Journal of Sociology* 112:5: 1297–1338.
Crittenden, A. 2001. *The price of motherhood: Why the most important job in the world is still the least valued.* New York: Henry Holt and Company.
Curtis, K. 2003. Murder: The leading cause of death for pregnant women. National Organization for Women, April 23. http://www.now.org/issues/violence/043003pregnant.html.
deMarneffe, D. 2004. *Maternal desire: On children, love, and the inner life.* New York: Little, Brown and Co.
DiQuinzio, P. 1999. *The impossibility of motherhood: Feminism, individualism, and the problem of mothering.* New York: Routledge.
Douglas, S. J., and M. W. Michaels. 2004. *The mommy myth: The idealization of motherhood and how it has undermined all women.* New York: Free Press.
Dye, J. L. 2008. *Fertility of American women: 2006.* Current Population Reports, P20–558. Washington, DC: U.S. Census Bureau.

Edin, K., and M. Kefalas. 2005. *Promises I can keep: Why poor women put motherhood before marriage*. Berkeley: University of California Press.
Gubar, S. 2006. Feminism inside out. *PMLA* 121:5: 1711–16.
Hansen, E. T. 1997. *Contemporary fiction and the crisis of motherhood*. Berkeley and Los Angeles: University of California Press.
Hausmann, R., L. D. Tyson, and S. Zahidi. 2007. *The Global Gender Gap Report 2007*. World Economic Forum. http://www.weforum.org.
Hertz, R. 2004. The contemporary myth of choice. *Annas, AAPSS* 596 (November): 232–44.
hooks, b. 1990. *Yearning: Race, gender and cultural politics*. Boston, MA: South End Press.
Horn-Miller, K. 2002. Bring us back into the dance: Women of the Wasase. In *Colonize this: Young women of color on today's feminism*, ed. D. Hernández and B. Rehman, 230–44. Emeryville, CA: Seal Press.
Jeremiah, E. 2006. Motherhood to mothering and beyond: Maternity in recent feminist thought. *Journal for the Association for Research on Mothering* 8:1, 2: 21–33.
Kaiser State Health Facts. 2007–2008. Health insurance coverage of the total population, states (2007–2008), U.S. (2007–2008). http://www.state healthfacts.org/comparebar.jsp?ind=125&cat=3.
Lewin, E. 1993. *Lesbian mothers: Accounts of gender in American culture*. Ithaca, NY: Cornell University Press.
Miller, E., M. R. Decker, J. G. Silverman, and A. Raj. 2007. Migration, sexual exploitation, and women's health: A case report from a community health center. *Violence against Women* 13:5: 486–97.
Moi, T. 2006. "I am not a feminist, but . . .": How feminism became the F-Word. *PMLA* 121:5: 1735–41.
Morgan, J. 2004. *Laboring women: Reproduction and gender in New World slavery*. Philadelphia: University of Pennsylvania Press.
National Advocates for Pregnant Women. 2008. Criminal cases and issues. http://www.advocatesforpregnantwomen.org/issues/criminal_cases_and_issues/.
O'Reilly, A. 2004. *Mother outlaws: Theories and practices of empowered mothering*. Toronto: Women's Press.
———. 2006. *Rocking the cradle: Thoughts on motherhood, feminism and the possibility of empowered mothering*. Toronto: Demeter Press.
Perales, N. 1999. Cultural stereotype and the legal response to pregnant teens. In *Mother troubles: Rethinking contemporary maternal dilemmas*, ed. J. E. Hanigsberg and S. Ruddick, 81–96. Boston, MA: Beacon Press.
Peskowitz, M. 2005. *The truth behind the mommy wars: Who decides what makes a good mother?* Emeryville, CA: Seal Press.
Rich, A. 1976. *Of woman born: Motherhood as experience and institution*. New York: W. W. Norton.
Roberts, D. 1997. *Killing the Black body: Race, reproduction, and the meaning of liberty*. New York: Pantheon Books.

Romans, S., T. Forte, M. M. Cohen, J. Du Mont, and I. Hyman. 2007. Who is at most risk for intimate partner violence?: A Canadian population-based study. *Journal of Interpersonal Violence* 22:12 (December): 1495–1514.

Ruddick, S. 1989. *Maternal thinking: Toward a politics of peace.* Boston, MA: Beacon Press.

Save the Children. 2008. Mother's Day report card: The best and worst countries to be a mother. http://www.savethechildren.org/newsroom/2008/best-worst-countries-mother.html.

Snitow, A. 1992. Feminism and motherhood: An American reading. *Feminist Review* 40: 32–51.

Spillers, H. 1987. Mama's baby, papa's maybe: An American grammar book. *Diacritics* (Summer): 65–80.

Stobbe, M. 2007. Experts: U.S. childbirth deaths on rise. *The Washington Post*, August 24. http://www.washingtonpost.com/wp-dyn/content/article/2007/08/24/AR2007082401321_3.html.

U.S. Bureau of the Census. 2008. *Fertility of American women: 2006 population characteristics.* http://www.census.gov/population/www/socdemo/fertility.html.

Warren, E. 2007. Medical bankruptcy: Middle-class families at risk. Testimony before House Judiciary Committee (July 17). http://www.judiciary.house.gov/hearings/July2007/Warren070717.pdf.

Work Life Law: A Center of UC Hastings College of the Law. 2008. Frequently asked questions about FRD. http://www.worklifelaw.org/FRDFAQ.html.

PART 1

Feminist Interventions in Public Discourse

ONE

Contrapuntal Delivery and Reception of Hildegard Westerkamp's Electrovocal Performance Work on Mothering, *Moments of Laughter*

ANDRA MCCARTNEY

Vancouver composer Hildegard Westerkamp's electrovocal (audiotape and performance) piece *Moments of Laughter* explores the auditory traces of a relationship between mother and child, from birth to seven years of age. Unlike in individualistic models of child development, this is a contrapuntal relationship: in Westerkamp's piece both parts, live vocal and recorded sound narrative, mother and child, woman and sound technology, take emotional and musical shape in dialogue with the other. A reception analysis of listener responses to this work extends the counterpoint into many parts, with some surprising counter-melodies. I use the term counterpoint here in its musical sense of intersecting and developing melodies as well as in its discursive sense of productive dialogue. Westerkamp expresses many different kinds of laughter and other emotional moments of childhood and mothering through this work and leads performers and audiences to consider their emotionally complex relationships to parenting, childhood, and the public sounding of domestic spaces.

The theme of childhood sound making is an important one for Westerkamp. Her master's thesis uses the childhood experience of Christmas music as a case study (Westerkamp 1988a). Her autobiographical performance piece Breathing Room III includes a childhood song, and she refers to the importance of childhood sound making in her presentations. She explores this theme most fully in *Moments of Laughter*, which challenges conventional thinking about compositional choices, distinctions between public and private domains, the roles of children and women, and the importance of children's nonverbal communication. My thinking about the transgressive power of this piece began when I included it in a pilot project about listener responses to Canadian electroacoustic works. Initially I was surprised by some very visceral, even hostile, responses. This led me to continue my analysis, expanding the range of listeners, to learn more about what was behind these strong reactions.

My initial response to the work was complex, including discomfort. Through my experience with a parental custody dispute, and subsequent feminist studies, I had become sensitized to the problematic cultural stereotypes of motherhood. For example, the performer's reading in one recording seemed too sweet, even cloying. When Westerkamp gave me the score, I realized that this reading tone had been chosen by that performer, who may have intended irony. The score seemed to allow great scope for interpretation. Even though the piece had been performed publicly only by professional vocalists (Meg Sheppard, Elise Bedard, and D. B. Boyko), Westerkamp's instructions in the score also made the work accessible to a wider range of performers, including vocal alternatives for amateurs. Aware that the work had been performed several times when it was first composed in 1988, but not since, I decided to perform it. Although I had only attended short workshops on experimental vocal techniques with actor, singer, and vocal coach Richard Armstrong, I had lots of experience singing with groups and vocalizing with young children. I had enjoyed this interaction with my own children as they were growing up, and I continue to enjoy vocal play with babies and toddlers, discovering their vocal range and abilities. I performed the work in a variety of public and private contexts in 1998 and 1999.

This chapter focuses on contrapuntal movements between compositional approach, performative style, and audience responses, including other commentary in dialogue with my own shifting perspective as listener, performer, and researcher. The listener responses were based on sessions conducted with high school, undergraduate, and graduate university students, as well as at concerts where I performed the work.

SCOURING THE CONTEXT

In the score for *Moments of Laughter*, Westerkamp refers to the work of French psychoanalyst and semiotician Julia Kristeva:

Moments of Laughter is dedicated to my daughter, the child whose voice forms the basis for this piece. Her voice has accompanied mine for many years now and has brought me in touch with an openness of perception, uninhibited expressiveness and physical presence that I had long forgotten.

I have made recordings of her voice since she was born and from the age of four on, she has made her own recordings of stories and songs. *Moments of Laughter* utilizes these for the tape portion of the piece, tracing musically/acoustically the emergence of the infant's voice from the oceanic state of the womb: from the sounds of the baby to the song and language of the child. According to Julia Kristeva, moments of laughter are those moments in infancy and early childhood in which the baby recognizes the "other" as distinct from the "self." They are the first creative moments that speak of recognition of self and place. The child expresses these moments with laughter. (Westerkamp 1988b)

Moments of laughter, both for Kristeva and for Westerkamp, are moments of recognition, of self in relation to another, in a particular context or place. Westerkamp asks the female vocal performer of the piece to balance impression and expression, voicing in response to a tape of a very young child making sounds. The performer needs to create through the performance an analogue of a mother's changing relationship with a growing child.

Kristeva describes the baby's desire for connection through sensual moments of voice, music, and light. She says that during the anaclitic period of the first three months, the baby begins to experience discreteness through

> the breast, given and withdrawn; lamplight capturing the gaze; intermittent sounds of voice, of music—all these meet with anaclisis . . . hold it, and thus inhibit and absorb it. . . . At that point, breast, light, and sound become a *there*: a place, a spot, a marker. The effect, which is dramatic, is no longer quiet but laughter. (Kristeva 1980, 283, emphasis in original)

Westerkamp notes that Kristeva's approach is different from that of theorists such as Deleuze, those who describe the recognition of separateness as a violence (Westerkamp 1988b, 119). The moment of recognition of another, for Kristeva, is not a moment of angst, of existential loneliness, but of laughter, an expression of joy that someone, some other, is here to relieve the distress and provide pleasure and security.

> These scattered and funny moments become projected—archaic synthesis onto the stable support of the mother's face, the privileged receiver of laughter at about three months. . . . Oral eroticism, the smile at the mother, and the first vocalizations are contemporaneous. (Kristeva 1980, 283)

As a semiotician influenced by psychoanalytic theory, Kristeva writes of the role of the mother-child dyad as being crucial with regard to its relationship to desire and psychological wholeness. Westerkamp, as a composer, is interested in this desire as it relates to creativity and sociality. Lorraine Code, as an epistemologist, discusses this relationship in terms of its importance to learning: "recognizing nurturant others, learning what she or he can expect of them, comprises the very earliest infant learning" (Code 1998, 236). Code also points out that in traditional developmental psychology and epistemology, this initial learning is devalued, constructed as an early, private, dependent, and inarticulate phase in the development of the child into a mature individual:

> Discourses of development and maturation represent "the child" as a being who unfolds out of an infancy in which he is radically, vitally dependent on nurturant others, to a place of full individual autonomy where he becomes his "own" person, renouncing dependence to emerge as a self-sufficient individual. (Code 1998, 4)

Code challenges this traditional, linear "mastery" model of child development, suggesting an alternative in which the agency of the child is recognized and respected. Westerkamp's approach to this time of initial learning, desire, and creative sound making also challenges the linear developmental model through its emphasis on the continuing construction of identity in both children and adults. We hear the development of the child's voice during the piece. At the same time, dialogically, the mother in the piece (played by the female vocalist in performance) is changed by the experience and constantly shifts identities in response to the sound making of the child. By taking this relationship as a formal basis of the music, Westerkamp also taps into important familial power relations, as will become obvious when I discuss listener responses to this piece.

A TRANSGRESSIVE APPROACH TO SOUND ART

Moments of Laughter transgresses electroacoustic and social norms by bringing domestic sounds, relatively unprocessed or naked, into the public sphere. It transgresses discourses of development by challenging the stereotypical roles of parents and children. The introduction gives an authoritative position to the child, who frames the coming performance. She describes herself as experienced and skilled as a recordist: she has recorded "tons of times." She affirms her connection with her mother, who is also a composer. The girl's voice ends the piece as well. Within the frame is an electroacoustic exploration of several moments at different ages of the girl's life, with the female performer singing scored melodies and improvised vocalizations, contrapuntally with the recorded sounds on tape, the narrative of the mother developing in tandem with that of the child.

There are several layers of counterpoint: between composer, vocalist, and child; between live and recorded sounds; between sonic, verbal, and performative narratives; between sound makers and audience. Initial responses to the piece were gathered during a 1995 project about Canadian electroacoustic works, when an excerpt (about six minutes in length) was played for individuals and undergraduate university classes as part of a larger set of works. I played a recording of the entire piece for a Toronto high school girls' vocal class. I also thought it important to garner responses to live performances, and I decided therefore to perform it. The initial performance was in private, for a friend; the next on CIUT radio, Toronto (Sarah Peebles's *The Audible Woman*). I performed live in Chicago (December 1998), at the miXing sound art festival, and in Kingston, Ontario (Modern Fuel Gallery, March 1999). There were ninety-eight written responses to all of these performances.

The most detailed analyses of the narrative structure of this piece were made by the high school students: ten of these were from the class of Grade 10 girls. Two of the girls described the piece in some detail. Music student Liane (14f, i.e., 14 years of age and a female) said:

> I believe the music was grouped by different stages in the life of the baby, e.g., birth, when [the baby] began to talk. Tells the story of a baby through music. Background music expresses the emotions. Relationship between mother and child:
> 1 = birth
> 2 = speaking—not English

3 = playing
4 = poem
5 = making child laugh
6 = reading a story to child
7 = speaking

This summary includes almost all of the moments indicated in Westerkamp's score, and many of the sections have titles similar to Westerkamp's: "Prologue and Birth" becomes, in this listener's response, "Birth"; "Laughter" becomes "Making child laugh"; "Songs and Stories" becomes "Reading a story to child." This listener clearly apprehended not only the general idea of the piece but also its progression through stages of life, indicated through different approaches to sound. Another student associated these sections with different memories and emotions of her own:

> The music was full of so many mixed emotions. It had the fears of a child and also some of the joys of growing up and learning and developing into a little person.
> I really liked the moment with the baby being washed. It brought back memories of watching my mom wash my little sister. I also remembered having baths with my sisters.
> The part with the dog barking in the background and hearing the sound of the baby's voice brought back memories of my fear of animals as a child. That whole scene kind of reminded me of the fear and anxiety of being [a] child; even though people think it's all carefree, there's really so much to worry about.
> The part where it went nana nana nana reminded me of kindergarten and playing little games with all my friends. Then all the other voices added in, and it sounded like recess at my school.
> The woman's voice talking about words sounded like the child's . . . leading it and trying to get it to say something instead of just meaningless words.
> The part where there was kind of like a choir singing reminded me of my old school, because it was an Anglican school so we had to go to church, so that part in the song represented to me the child being introduced to religion and knowledge because she started speaking and saying numbers.
> When the child was singing it reminded me of when I would learn songs at school and I would feel so excited to go

home and show my parents. (Angel, 15f, North Toronto C. I. vocal class)

Like the previous listener, Angel thinks about the development of the baby, focusing on the child's experiences more than the adult's. She listens to the piece thinking of her own memories and experiences, commenting on religion, education, socialization in kindergarten, and relationships with parents.

I was impressed by the number of drawings that accompanied the teenage girls' responses. There were many more than in other responses. Also, there were many poems, and references to playing with sound in similar ways to those heard on tape. It was heartening to see this level of expressivity among teenage girls—a time when I remember losing touch with my own in the wash of hormones and social pressures.

While the responses of these high school students were exploratory and positive, several listeners described the work as being "too personal." Are the visceral bodily sounds that are represented too personal for some? A short segment of the work imitates (in a very muted form) the sounds of birth, a part of life that is rarely represented in music. Musicologist Suzanne Cusick attributes this silence about birthing to a "cultural horror" of the act of giving birth (1994, 26). She suggests that part of the social discomfort with childbirth is that the breathing and cries of a laboring mother can sound sexual. Some listeners initially interpreted the birthing section as a representation of sexuality, and they were embarrassed by it. Another listener notes that the birth section was very stylized. But if it had been even more visceral, then perhaps it would have caused even greater embarrassment. Beth (23f, music student) interprets the bodily sounds as dangerous: "don't like the breathing—giving birth or doing something she shouldn't to a baby [psycho] while they are in the bath." Live (20f, music student) also hears these sounds as evidence of the mother being a danger to the child: "scaring the poor baby [moans and groans]. Splashing in the bathtub. Mommy had a little too much to drink." The conflation of sexuality and motherhood through the bodily sounds of heavy breathing and panting is a cultural danger zone: Jo Anna Isaak, reading Julia Kristeva, claims that "the figure of the 'mother who knows sexual pleasure' is the most severely repressed 'feminine' figure in Western culture" (Isaak 1983, 205). To make these sounds public is considered by some to be obscene, embarrassing, or potentially dangerous. I would suggest that the act of representing this repressed figure by making these sounds public is radical and transgressive.

Is the call-and-response too close to the sonic play between parent and child that I myself initially considered "too personal" to be music? One controversial aspect of the work is its exploration of nonverbal communication between mother and child. Some listeners like this expression of communication without words (see also Chapman 2007). James (20m, music student) says: "I liked the call/response between voice and baby—playful like a child . . . reminded me of how we learn to associate sounds and what it would be like not to have any associations." James notes how the piece leads him to think about free play with sound. Kapok (16f, music student) likes this part because of the interaction between woman and child: "I particularly like the communication between the performer and child, and the reaction that performer has towards the child. I also like the performer's imitation of the child's noises." Max (21f, music student) says: "I like the variation and call/response between child and woman, very artistic idea. Generally the interaction of sounds really works with this piece. WHOA! The last groan (by woman) is brilliant sounding." Mark Heinrich (24m, music student) locates the musicality of the passage in the presence of the female vocalist: "woman's voice repeating conversations of vocables between baby—turning it into music—and mother." My initial response to this section was "This is what I did with my children. But it is just play, not music." When asked to make similar sounds in a vocal workshop, I did not question their musicality. Putting these sounds, and the sonic relationship between parent and child, in a concert setting challenges assumptions about the musical and social importance of sonic play with children. While practicing, I remember the concentration, improvisation, and interaction that characterized daily sessions of sound making with my children. Because Westerkamp calls for experimentation by the vocalist, it can allow the performer and audience members to make a connection between musical expressivity and the sounds of babies. At the same time, Westerkamp does not want the piece to move into virtuosity and away from a relationship with the child, reminding the performer to balance her voice with that of the child's, to avoid competing with or covering up the child's voice.

Do responses to this work that it is "too personal" refer to Westerkamp's decision to leave the vocal sounds on tape relatively unaltered, and therefore recognizable, not abstracted from their context? Westerkamp decides how much to manipulate particular sounds based on her relationship to the sound, her care for it: she admits that she is more ruthless with the sounds of truck brakes than with the sounds of organisms, and she is even more careful than usual with the sound of her own daughter's voice.

Some listeners share Westerkamp's careful attitude toward the manipulation of sounds. Eve Angeline (27f, listener) says that the recording is

> kind of "dangerous" sounding, about things that are explicitly private [invisible?] in relation to the symbolic order. Voice not particularly altered: I worried about scary alterations of mother/baby voice. Anticipated. . . . *Safety* is important to me . . . i.e., don't want composer to "turn baby into machine."

It is interesting that the first time the child's voice is altered is when the child is two and a half years old. This is the point at which children begin to express themselves more fully with language, entering the symbolic order. At that point, perhaps Westerkamp feels less of a need to protect the child's voice from alteration, since she has moved out of the realm that Eve Angeline describes as "explicitly private" in relation to the symbolic order. Eve Angeline wants the child's voice to remain safely unaltered and anticipates frightening alterations of it. Jane (20f, York undergraduate, electroacoustic music) says "the child seems vulnerable and helpless amid a hostile and potentially dangerous world."

This theme of the innocent child menaced by a hostile world is one that has been used repeatedly in Hollywood films, as Lou (31m, composer) points out: "Kids' voices recorded are a horror show cliché. It's creepy and sentimental." It is not Westerkamp's intention to present such a dramatic context: this is not a story about a child being menaced. Yet nineteen listeners use words such as "scary" and "sinister" in their responses. I believe that this has less to do with Westerkamp's treatment of childhood sounds and more to do with Hollywood's dramatization of them. As Eve Angeline points out, it is the anticipation of a possibly dangerous environment that characterizes her response rather than the perception of one intended by the composer; in Jane's words, it is a "potentially dangerous" world rather than one that is actually dangerous. It is plausible that listeners would anticipate a dangerous environment for the child's voice, since the treatment of a child's voice in a dramatic context such as television or film is often to create an image of innocence that is menaced.

Westerkamp chooses to keep the child's voice safe by only changing it slightly rather than radically, and by doing this she loses some of the musicians, who wish for more manipulation of the voices. Elizabeth (21f, music student) says: "Interesting things are done with the voice. The singing voice in the middle sounds a bit out of place—needs to be a bit more 'abstract' or experimented with." Biff (22m, York music student) comments: "I really think that the vocals would have sounded better altered—like at the beginning." In these responses, there is no concern about the safety of the child's voice but rather a description of it as a resource, something to be experimented with, or altered, or made more abstract, as in traditional electroacoustic music.

Is the simple presence of a child's voice in a public place controversial? Should children (and perhaps women) be seen and not heard? Some listeners in my study reacted very negatively to the voices. Zubian (20m, York music student) says: "Extremely annoying child talking. Excited woman grabs attention. I feel like I'm intruding on the woman and child's privacy. Towards end of piece voice becomes unbearable torture. Shut up lady!" Cora (25f, music student) says: "Can't take this. Can't stand the little girl's voice who sang "I love recording." Both these listeners use very strong language expressing their distaste for the voices such as "unbearable torture" or "I can't stand this." Gwen (15f, music student) writes: "Very interesting . . . shut this kid up already!" (She then crosses out the latter phrase.) Another girl in the same class (using the same pseudonym) is equally ambivalent about the voices:

> I am trying to be open-minded, but I find this song annoying. I feel like I'm at home trying to have some peace and quiet but my family is annoying me . . . the lady reading reminds me of the storytellers on polka dot door (a Canadian television show for children) [so phony]. She has a nice voice! (Gwen2 15f, music student)

While many listeners did not complain about the characteristics of the recorded and live voices, the intensity of many of these comments led me to wonder about their basis. Is it an insistence that the private sounds of a mother and child should remain private, not cross into the public domain of a concert hall where listeners could feel that they are intruding on a private space, spying on a home? I find this challenge to the public-private dichotomy an exciting and important aspect of the piece.

The controversy around the use of a child's voice as the focus of imitation could be a reflection of the cultural denigration of children's activities. In an article on this topic, composer Pauline Oliveros and music theorist Fred Maus have the following interchange:

> [Oliveros]: There is the whole cynical attitude about babies and children that their activities are to be sneered at, not to be taken seriously. "That's just a baby!"

[Maus]: And of course, that's tied in with the way that women are thought about—"That's just a baby," and "That's just the way that women spend their time, watching the baby do these silly things." (Oliveros and Maus 1994, 181)

With a deeply rooted cultural prejudice that babies have nothing to say, particularly before they learn language, it would seem foolish to base a musical piece on an imitation of the baby's sounds. This is similar to the reaction of the traditional art world in 1975 to Mary Kelly's *Postpartum Document*, which was based on her relationship with her child: "The mainstream art crowd denigrated the piece because it was just about a woman and her baby, thereby no fit subject for high culture" (Lippard 1983, xi).

Several listeners expressed concerns about possible gender stereotyping in *Moments of Laughter*. For instance, Jean (42f, composer) said:

At various times in the piece I feel a tension between being very engaged in the sound world being created and at other times am uncomfortable with the sentimentality being expressed. This could have to do with my uncomfortableness with the "mother" culture and how it forces adult women to remain at a child level. This is not necessarily inherent with the work, but I feel that because at times one is able to feel a sense of female power and at other times these references [are] to [a] more sentimentalized female culture, the piece doesn't fully address this cultural problem.

Cora (25f, Queen's University gender and music course) has a stronger reaction, in that she cannot stand hearing the child's voice. This adverse reaction seems to be located in her feeling of not belonging, of not knowing what she is supposed to be feeling, in a feeling of intimidation:

I can't take this. Can't stand the little girl's voice who sang "I love recording." Sounds of giving birth, water, baby. . . . Nature me? My female body, is this where I belong? I guess the combination of these sounds [is] supposed to be . . . peaceful . . . normal . . . soothing. But I can't stand it.

I can't stand [the] abnormally loud [amplified] sound of the water. I prefer sound which is more visual [for me somehow] than this—too artificial sound, which imitates nature. I don't know what I am supposed to be feeling. Not only I can't stand [it], but also I feel intimidated.

Her feelings of intimidation in relation to the piece bring to mind the many descriptions of this piece being "scary" or disturbing among the high school girls' responses. Jen (15f) writes her response as a poem:

> the birth of the child
> the cues and laughter too
> the mind warps of the toddler
> who to the world is new
> the growing process now begins
> the pains of aging, amongst things
> the growling of dogs
> the singing of mom
> she teaches the child
> a new song
> now the child is older
> learnt new interesting things
> the child will grow and love
> into the world a new child it brings
> listen to the laughter
> as it grows
> and again the seeds of life
> it does sew

This poem describes a cycle of life based on giving birth and raising children. What are the "pains of aging" that this young woman mentions? Another student in the class, Amantha (14f), mentions "fear of the unknown," while Kate (15f) says "later in the song, the talking and emotions made me feel scared." For some of these teenage girls, the fearful unknown may be the role of motherhood. On the one hand, they have been told that giving birth is a miracle—three girls used the phrase "miracle of birth." One of them put the word "miracle" in quotes, indicating a degree of skepticism. On the other hand, they see their own mothers' lives, as well as mass media versions of motherhood, and they wonder about how this role would shape their identity. Danae (15f) imagines a mother's identity as being completely linked to the child:

> my bodily fluids immerse you,
> washing and cleansing.
> my blood is your blood
> my body your body
> my heart beating . . . your heart pounding
> mother and child.

Contrapuntal Delivery and Reception   33

This poem was accompanied by a Madonna image. Hope's discussion of motherly identity is more complex:

> Very loving and motherly. Mysterious (a few parts). Calming [in some sections]. Enchanting, very unusual, a little uncomfortable. The moments in a baby's life sound comforting, rewarding, and they cheer you up [the sounds]. One sequence of this composition made me feel sad, and it even made me miss my own mum, even though she is at work. [When the mother is solemnly humming and singing to her baby, as the baby is playing, it sounded as though she was subconsciously watching her daughter grow up.] Dreaming. This part was also a little sad, and it made me feel as though "mentally" I was traveling through time and back. It's hard to explain. When the woman sings, it sounds like those old folk songs in the times of slavery. (Hope, 14f)

Here, Hope describes different parts of the piece in terms of the unknown (mysterious), a construction that makes the unknown seem more enchanting than fearful but still somewhat uncomfortable. She hears the baby's sounds as comfortable and rewarding and at the same time sad. It is interesting that at this point she travels back and forth in time, attempting perhaps to associate the imaginary mother identity she has constructed so far with that of the child: it makes her miss her mum and also identify with the mother watching the child grow up. This description recalls Westerkamp's description of the self as desire in motion, searching for nourishment for her creativity in the mother, then in others. Hope's association of the blues lullaby with the times of slavery is musically accurate and also politically interesting. Even before I considered the significance of using a blues song as a lullaby, it felt right in rehearsal, seeming to express much more than the attempt to help a baby sleep. Blues songs are commonly understood as a musical form that expresses loss, as well as rebellion against the slaves' secondary place in the social and symbolic orders; the choice of that form as a basis for the lullaby could invoke these associations.

The adolescent girls' responses to the piece were often related to their memories of their own childhoods, as well as the anticipation and imaginings of a future role as a mother. But what about reactions by men? I have often wondered, for instance, whether a man could perform this piece. The inclusion of a birthing sequence near the beginning would mean that a man would need, at least at that point, to be "cross-dressing" in a way that I have never heard before. Certainly this would contradict Westerkamp's intent, since she appears quite clear that this is intended for a female vocalist, to explore feminine identity in terms of motherhood. Does a performance by a female vocalist exclude men from the role of audience, or does the piece still speak to them as people who may be parents, and certainly were children, themselves?

Some men do relate to the piece as parents. Albert (28m, composer) says, "I must continue to record Ivan and Lizzie." Larry, another composer (50m), relates as a parent and finds the sounds problematic: "Background sounds trite—no depth [sonically]—just too cute—I lived with my daughter on a boat in B.C. until she was two. These are not the sounds I remember." Brit (40m, composer) is also reminded of his daughter's early life: "memories of my daughter's birth and early months at home." Several other male listeners described the work as a mother-child piece and did not refer to any memories of their own childhoods. These responses (twelve in total) were fairly neutral, interested without expressing a high level of engagement or alienation. Five other responses were clearly alienated, to differing degrees, describing a distance based on lack of understanding, fears of disturbing privacy, or distaste for the voices. Two composers described the piece as being too academic. At the Kingston concert, I also played Westerkamp's piece *The Deep Blue Sea,* which is based on a noncustodial father's parenting experience, both before and after losing custody. A male listener who could not understand *Moments of Laughter* had a much more engaged response to this piece: "A strange, warming, yet sad story. The intonation of the voice and the background sounds blend perfectly to create the mood." This listener wonders if his lack of engagement with *Moments of Laughter* is because of his maleness and lack of maternal instincts. Is it because *The Deep Blue Sea* was based on a man's experience (Brian Shein), read by a man (Norbert Ruebsaat), that it was easier for Chris to identify with the narrative? However, some of the male listeners, quoted earlier, did have more engaged responses to *Moments of Laughter,* so Chris's response seems more idiosyncratic than generally male.

I was surprised that none of the men's responses referred to their own childhoods, or to their relationships with their family members, themes that arose often in the responses of the adolescent girls in particular, as well as some of the adult women. For instance, Morgan (22f, music student) says:

> These sounds are so familiar. I too loved to hear my voice on tape recorder (tape retorter, I called it) when I was small. The baby sounds are like my baby brother. The catches in the voice and breathing to catch air to make a sound, like the baby is not

sure what is going to be effective in making the sound it wants, [are] familiar.

Newton (22f, music student): "Little girls' comments are cute and remind me of when I was young and recorded my own voice and thought it was fun." Two of the adolescent girls also refer to recording their own voices when they were little. Several of the girls mention memories of being a child or caring for children as a babysitter.

For some of the girls, the piece led them to revalue their mothers. Alex (14f) said: "makes you think what a world without a mother to talk to, to be with, just to love and be loved by, would be like." Bab (14f) said:

> I remember when my mum used to teach me patty cake. She also taught me to read. I used to go to my mom if I had a bad dream. This piece brought back the good memories that I had when I was little. It also made me think about life. We have a lot to live for.

The responses from the adolescent girls indicate much greater access to their memories of early family life, or at least their willingness to talk about these memories, than other respondents. Would the same be true of adolescent boys? It also seems that some of the women listeners were able to relate the piece to their own childhood, while the men either related as parents or did not seem to be able to identify strongly with either woman or child. Is this because White, middle-class, Western men are pressured to individuate more clearly, defining themselves as mature adults, to fit their stereotyped gender role?

There were significant differences in listener responses to this piece, based on age and gender. Cultural specificity is another possible limiting factor. Referring to Carol Gilligan's approach to developmental psychology, Code (1998) notes that Gilligan's texts are markedly White, and she contrasts them with developmental stories from other racial and cultural locations. She quotes a striking example related by writer bell hooks in *Bone Black*:

> In traditional southern-based black life, it was and is expected of girls to be articulate, to hold ourselves with dignity. . . . These are the variables that white researchers often do not consider when they measure the self-esteem of black females with a yardstick that was designed based on values emerging from white experience. (hooks 1996, xiii)

Westerkamp is clear that her piece is based on her own experience with her daughter. When she searched for cultural representations of female power, such as the welcoming call in Moment One, she sometimes borrowed expressions from other cultures (in this case an African welcoming call). Other cultural borrowings were a lullaby with a blues sound and a reference to the melodic leaps of pygmy music. Listeners' responses to these cultural borrowings seemed to focus on whether or not they fit. When I discussed the piece with the girls' vocal class, several mentioned that they found the welcoming call frightening. Not understanding its meaning as a welcome, they heard it as a loud and threatening sound. Its reflection of female power as loud and assertive was unfamiliar to them.

Only one listener expressed concerns about cultural appropriation and universality. Larry (50m, composer) said: "I also have trouble with the all too obvious great mother woman child bit—the 'universal representation'—a bit of jazz, black soul—pygmy music to boot." Dympna Callaghan, in her discussion of feminism and the problem of identity, notes:

> The crucial contradiction of the liberal humanist aesthetic is that individual identity and personal experience are paramount aspects of art so long as they provide evidence of a universal human nature on the model of the privileged white male; but they become specious once they mark specificities (gender, race, etc.) that are diametrically opposed to this hegemonic model of identity. (Callaghan 1995, 202)

Westerkamp's cultural borrowings reflect her urge to expand the piece beyond her personal experience, to find powerful women's voices elsewhere, creating a version of motherhood that aspires to greater universality, which attempts to speak to an audience beyond White European women. They are aspects of other *women's* experience, and her attempts at greater inclusivity are clearly considered specious by this listener, who speaks from the privileged position of a White male composer, and who also criticizes the sounds she uses from her personal experience: "trite—no depth [sonically] just too cute. I lived with my daughter. . . . These are not the sounds I remember." Some listeners criticize Westerkamp for being too personal in this piece, for relying too much on her personal experience. This listener criticizes her for attempting to go beyond her personal experience by borrowing aspects of sonic styles from other cultures. Perhaps in both cases the criticism is due to the fact that the experiences of women are the focus of her work in this piece, experiences that mark specificities that differ from the hegemonic male model.

The charge of essentialism—of positing an essential, unchanging feminine identity—is one that tends to arise whenever Westerkamp uses natural or bodily sounds or refers to aspects of women's experiences. In *Moments of Laughter*, the concern about stereotyping arises in response to the birthing sequence, an experience that is limited to (some) women. But sometimes listeners who were concerned about this possible essentialism had changed their minds by the end of the piece. For instance, Blue Green (27f, composer) said: "Great ending! Not sure about [the] beginning. Actually, it set me up for a sentimental scene that was not as predictable as I thought it would be."

While essentialism would posit a fixed, unchanging identity, Westerkamp asks the performer to engage with a range of identities. I believe that the piece is not essentialist, because the vocalist is asked to move through—to perform—a series of different identities in relation to the child's development, culminating in that of the fool, a parodic character. At times the female vocalist is soothing; at other times she is discovering the joys of vocal performance with the child, involved in developing an inner song, teaching the child about feminine identities through storytelling, and clowning to make the child laugh. In the ending, there is a sonic expression of the tension between the woman as earth mother and as clown, expressed by the child: she sings "my mom dug down, down, down to the middle of the earth, to the heart, to the heart," and her final words are: "Hi mum, see you mum, you're a silly fool, mum." Throughout the piece, the performer revels at times in being silly, in playing both child and fool simultaneously, the fool who is childlike. In Westerkamp's work, as in Mary Kelly's *Post-partum Document*, the identities of both child and parent constantly shift. Kelly states:

> In the *Post-partum Document*, I am trying to show the reciprocity of the process of socialisation in the first few years of life. It is not only the infant whose future personality is formed at this crucial moment, but also the mother whose "feminine psychology" is sealed by the sexual division of labour in child care. (Kelly 1983, 1)

Code notes that recognition of this type of reciprocity is unusual in most feminist writing about motherhood, in which primary attention is usually given to the woman as subject:

> In mothering relations throughout their duration, it is difficult to "let go" of a child sufficiently to see her, or him, and act with her in full cognizance of her own agency; to resist treating her as a projection of her mother. Maternal thinkers' sometimes excessive valuing of connectedness can represent such "letting go" as neither right nor desirable. Moreover, in most feminist writing on motherhood, mothers are the "persons" and children are the "others." . . . Engaging with one's child as "the person she or he is," however fluctuating her identity, requires more separateness than the early articulations of maternal thinking allow. (Code 1991, 94)

Throughout *Moments of Laughter*, the adult female performer is directed to balance her sound making with that of the child, engaging sonically with the child's voice as it is at that point. These directions to the performer differ from moment to moment, at times emphasizing connectedness to the child through dialogic improvisation and at other times moving toward more detachment through the use of contrasting musical styles or delivery. Throughout the piece, the performer is never intended to overwhelm the child's voice with her own: she is to aim for balance as much as possible, indicating a respect for the child's voice and position while maintaining different positions in relation to her. This dialogue acknowledges the importance of mother and child to each other as second persons while allowing their identities to shift interdependently.

The performer is both mother and not-mother, as Homi Bhabha says of a character in another production, "the mother's simulacrum at once a symbol of her presence and the sign of her absence" (1992, 61). Remember the teenage girl who said this piece made her miss her mother? This being mother and not-mother simultaneously further complicates the private-public distinction: the performer is a symbol of motherhood, a shifting symbol at that, as well as a sign of (real) absent mothers. I can only agree with Minfe (51f, Indian, individual contact), who says:

> Worthy of more attention. No one has, as far as I know, formulated such sounds of a baby so closely. I would like to interpret with my soprano voice this vocal score. For my fun—would anyone else like to listen to it? I wonder!

Certainly performing this piece was physically, intellectually, and emotionally demanding, as well as fun. Playing or performing it for a variety of listeners made me realize the complex and important issues it explores, especially regarding the strong boundary that still exists between private family life and public performance. No other composer has explored the positions of a mother in relation to a child in quite such a complex musical way. The emphasis on a musical dialogue between performer and tape and the wide range of sounds voiced by the child make it challenging to perform and remind the performer of the value of listening to children's voices. Because it tugs at the walls of the family home, it elicits more emotional responses than other works do (and, in some cases, more hostile responses). In others, listeners thought of their mothers or families with greater appreciation. Each time I presented it, people talked of recording the voices of their children, and some women pored over the score, announcing that they would like to perform the piece. Readers who are interested in learning more about Westerkamp's soundscape work could consult my online monograph about her, *Sounding Places with Hildegard Westerkamp*, at the Electronic Music Foundation (McCartney 2000).[1]

NOTE

1. I thank Canada's Social Sciences and Humanities Research Council for its continuing generous support of this research.

REFERENCES

Bhabha, H. K. 1992. Post-colonial authority and postmodern guilt. In *Cultural studies*, ed. L. Grossberg, C. Nelson, and P. Treichler, 56–68. New York: Routledge.
Callaghan, D. 1995. The vicar and virago: Feminism and the problem of identity. In *Who can speak? Authority and critical identity*, ed. J. Roof and R. Wiegman, 195–207. Urbana: University of Illinois Press.
Chapman, O. 2007. What is sampling? Inclusions, exclusions, and conclusions. *Selected sounds: A collective investigation into the practice of sample-based music*. http://www.selectedsounds.org.
Code, L. 1991. *What can she know? Feminist theory and the construction of knowledge*. Ithaca, NY: Cornell University Press.
———. 1998. Naming, naturalizing, normalizing: "The child" as fact and artefact. In *Toward a feminist psychology*, ed. P. Miller and E. Kofsky Scholnick, 215–40. New York: Routledge.
Cusick, S. 1994. Feminist theory, music theory, and the mind/body problem. *Perspectives of New Music* 32:1: 8–27.

hooks, b. 1996. *Bone Black: Memories of girlhood*. New York: Henry Holt.
Isaak, J. A. 1983. Our mother tongue: The post-partum document. In *Post-partum document*, ed. M. Kelly, 205–206. London: Routledge.
Kelly, M. 1983. Introduction. In *Post-partum document*, ed. M. Kelly, 1–12. London: Routledge and Kegan.
Kristeva, J. 1980. Place-Names. In *Desire in language: A semiotic approach to literature and art*, ed. Julia Kristeva and Leon S. Roudiez, 271–94. New York: Columbia University Press.
Lippard, L. 1983. Foreword. In *Post-partum document*, ed. M. Kelly, ii–xii. London: Routledge and Kegan.
McCartney, A. 2000. *Sounding places with Hildegard Westerkamp*. http://www.emfinstitute.emf.org/materials/mccartney00/. Electronic Music Foundation.
Oliveros, P., and F. Maus. 1994. A conversation about feminism and music. *Perspectives of New Music* 32:2: 174–93.
Westerkamp, H. 1988a. "Listening and sound making: A study of music-as-environment." M.A. thesis, Department of Communications, Simon Fraser University.
———. 1988b. *Moments of laughter*. For female voice and two-channel tape. Commissioned by Vancouver New Music Society. Premiere: March 1988, Vancouver. Meg Sheppard, voice.

TWO

The Empty Mirror No More

Mother-Daughter Relationship and Film Spectatorship in Patricia Cardoso's Real Women Have Curves

NAN MA

> I see the mother-daughter relationship as the dark continent of dark continents. The darkest point of our social order. I don't know one woman who isn't suffering in her relationship with her mother. And, most often, this suffering is expressed through tears and screams. It translates into a silence between mother and daughter, as well as an inability to identify with each other. The daughter tries her best to find an image in her mother that's both similar and different, but she finds herself in front of an empty mirror.
> —Luce Irigaray, "Mothers and Daughters"

At the 2002 Sundance Film Festival, a memorable disrobing scene from Patricia Cardoso's *Real Women Have Curves* delighted audiences and film critics alike. In this scene, a voluptuous Chicana teenager named Ana unabashedly strips down to her undergarments to combat the sweltering heat of a small garment factory. The other female workers at the factory, with the exception of Ana's mother, Carmen, soon participate in the undressing. Meanwhile, Carmen, disgusted with the women's behavior, walks away in frustration. This scene has been lauded by critics as being progressive in its representation of the female body. Elvis Mitchell of the *New York Times* calls the film "a love song to full-figured women everywhere" (Mitchell 2002). Roger Ebert of the

Chicago Sun-Times calls this particular scene "one of the sunniest, funniest, happiest scenes in a long time" (Ebert 2002). However, what many critics have overlooked is that the daughter's radical ideals are achieved at the expense of the alienation of her mother.

This chapter takes the popularity of the film as the point of departure and investigates the possible explanations for why the undressing scene has created such a strong impact on audiences, despite its problematic representation of the mother figure. Drawing on feminist criticism, film theory, and psychoanalysis, I place the film within the broader sociopolitical context of mainstream media portrayals of Latinos and examine the film's construction of the mother-daughter relationship at the intersections of race/ethnicity, gender, and class.[1] Finally, I turn to the numerous viewer responses to the film posted on the Internet and examine the ways in which viewers identify with the film's characters. This chapter does not end with a deconstruction of the mother-daughter bond in the film but is more interested in how issues of race/ethnicity, gender, and class impact the ways mothers and daughters see and speak to one another. I argue that through the character Carmen, *Real Women Have Curves* delivers a new argument about mothering that goes beyond the binary constructions of the mother as either a mouthpiece for patriarchal values from whom the daughter wishes to dissociate herself or as a victim of patriarchal ideologies.[2] Carmen is a complex character whose identity is formed at the intersections of multiple categories of identification (woman, immigrant, working class, middle aged, mother), and she actively negotiates her subjectivity as a mother.

THE MOTHER AND DAUGHTER IN FILM THEORY: CONSIDERATIONS OF GENDER, CLASS, AND ETHNICITY

The focus on gender equality of second-wave mainstream feminism has reaped great gains for women and paved the way for future feminist activism. At the same time, mainstream feminism has been critiqued by Marxist feminists and women of color for universalizing women's experiences through its overlooking of class and race/ethnicity as categories of subject formation. Because so much of the focus of mainstream feminism was on the male-female gender divide, the relationship between women, especially the problematic relationship between mothers and daughters, was left largely unexamined until Adrienne Rich's (1976) groundbreaking book *Of Woman Born: Motherhood as Experience and Institution*. Rich contends that motherhood as an ideological institution constructed by patriarchy forces a violent separation between a girl-child and her mother through the denigration of the mother. As Rich notes, "The first knowledge any woman has of warmth, nourishment, tenderness, security, sensuality, mutuality, comes from her mother. . . . But institutional heterosexuality and institutional motherhood demand that the girl-child transfer those first feelings of dependency, eroticism, mutuality, from her first woman to a man, if she is to become what is defined as a 'normal' woman" (1976, 219). Hence, patriarchal ideologies mandate the rejection of the mother as part of a woman's subject formation.

In her essay "The Case of the Missing Mother: Maternal Issues in Vidor's *Stella Dallas*," film scholar E. Ann Kaplan substantiates Rich's statement by recounting her own feelings of alienation when she first joined the feminist movement in the late 1960s. Kaplan feels that when she first joined the feminist movement she had no place to address the issues that were important to her as a mother. She attributes her sense of isolation to the fact that the early feminist movement was a "movement of daughters" (Kaplan 2000, 466). Kaplan reminds us that what early feminists overlooked was their own unwitting repetition of "the patriarchal omission of the Mother" (2000, 466). In other words, mothers were perceived as agents of patriarchy from whom young feminists felt a need to disassociate themselves in order to claim their own legitimacy as independent, progressive advocates of women's rights. Specifically, Kaplan laments the repressive, one-dimensional, patriarchal models of representation of the mother found in most Hollywood films that push the mother to the margins of film narratives, denying her the right to be a desiring, independent, and complex subject (2000, 467–468).

How might race/ethnicity and class complicate the notion that the only way for mothers and daughters to communicate is either through screams or silence because there are no role models for daughters and mothers to identify with, as the quotation from Luce Irigaray in the epigraph suggests? What roles do these vectors of difference play in the already complicated mother-daughter relationship? In particular, how are the differences between an immigrant mother and her Americanized daughter produced and articulated? What kinds of subjectivities are constructed for these women by the media? In her work on mothering and the meanings of motherhood for women of color, Patricia Hill Collins illuminates what has remained in the shadows of mainstream feminist theory: the intersections of race, ethnicity, and class as categories impacting the analysis of gender and motherhood. Collins points out that much theorizing by mainstream feminists concentrates on the totalizing dichotomies of public and domestic spheres, male domination and female subordination, and male autonomy and female dependence. This particular strand of theorizing, however, assumes a universal womanhood that fails to consider the differences in race, class, and sexuality among women. As Collins argues, for the racialized woman, "the subjective experience of mothering/motherhood is inextricably linked to the sociocultural concern of racial ethnic communities. . . . This type of motherwork recognizes that individual survival, empowerment, and identity require group survival, empowerment, and identity" (1994, 47). For the sake of survival, the woman of color oftentimes has to choose the integrity and cohesiveness of her family or racial ethnic group over her own autonomy as a woman.

In a similar spirit, Lisa Lowe has argued in *Immigrant Acts: On Asian American Cultural Politics* that the racialized woman occupies a multiply determined subject position that is "materially in excess of the subject 'woman' posited by feminist discourse, or the 'proletariat' described by Marxism, or the 'racial or ethnic' subject projected by civil rights and ethno-nationalist movements" (1996, 163). For the woman of color, actions and thoughts are at once impacted by the often competing and conflicting demands of gender expectations, economic necessities, and racial-ethnic divisions. Thus in a discussion pertaining to mothering, we must keep in mind that "mothering is not just gendered, but also racialized" (Glenn 1994, 7).

Patricia Cardoso's film adaptation of Josephina Lopez's well-received autobiographical play, *Real Women Have Curves*, invites us to pay close attention to the ways in which race/ethnicity and class complicate the mother-daughter relationship. I argue that the film's complicated mother-daughter relationship can only be understood by attending to the multiple registers of differences that the film weaves together. In the film, Carmen's traditional view of femininity is heavily critiqued and dismissed by her daughter Ana's feminist approach to beauty and the female body. However, to simply argue that the daughter is progressive and that the mother is backward is to once again reenact the patriarchal dismissal of the mother with which some feminisms have been complicit, as Kaplan has argued. Moreover, although the film ultimately reinscribes patriarchal power structures, that reinscription is prompted by the economic struggle faced by the working-class family of color, as well as by a political motivation to create alternative representations of Latino men rarely found in mainstream Hollywood cinema. That is, because the film straddles multiple categories of identification, it cannot be read through simple binary oppositions. *It is within patriarchy that the mother and daughter have to negotiate their subjectivities and their relationship with each other.* In this process of negotiation, both mother and daughter become liminal figures, taking charge to meet the demands and challenges of their simultaneous roles as mother, daughter, and worker who contribute to the family economy. Lastly, because the film registers multiple categories of difference, the film spectator is invited to identify with multiple subject positions. From more than 100 viewer commentaries about the film posted on the Internet,[3] I find that viewers do not only identify with the film's central character, Ana, but also with Carmen, Ana's older sister, Estela, and the female workers at Estela's struggling garment factory.

THE MOTHER AND DAUGHTER IN *REAL WOMEN HAVE CURVES*: CONSIDERATIONS OF GENDER, CLASS, AND ETHNICITY

Real Women Have Curves is set in the predominantly Latino neighborhood of Boyle Heights in East Los Angeles. The film portrays the joy and hardship of the everyday life of the Garcia household, where three generations live under one roof. Much of the film focuses on the conflicts between the headstrong immigrant mother, Carmen (Lupe Ontiveros), and her equally headstrong American-born daughter, Ana (America Ferrera). Ana's desire for self-definition and her mother's resistance to Ana's independence create the tension that motivates the film's plot. Ana's dream to go to college is challenged and put on hold by Carmen's wish for Ana to become a productive member of the family by finding employment, getting married, and eventually having children.

In the opening sequence, Ana is standing on the porch of her house. Immediately, Ana's position as a liminal figure is established: she is literally standing at the threshold of the house, at once attached to the house and outside of it. As Ana scrubs the windows of her home, her image is reflected on the glass. In the film, women's images are often seen as reflections in windows and mirrors, or as filtered images through screen doors. The mirror holds important symbolic meaning in how one understands oneself to be a subject in Lacanian psychoanalysis. During the mirror stage, the child, "held tightly as he is by some support . . . nevertheless overcomes, in a flutter of jubilant activity, the obstruction of his support and, fixing his attitude in a slightly leaning-forward position, in order to hold it [his image in the mirror] in his gaze, brings back an instantaneous aspect of the image" (Lacan 1977, 12). Hence, the mirror stage encompasses both a recognition and a misrecognition as the child, who, at this moment, lacks coherent motor skills but nevertheless identifies with the unified figure in the mirror.

More importantly, the mirror stage also inaugurates the separation of the child from his or her mother (symbolized by the support that holds the child in Lacan's argument).

As the child enters the symbolic stage, he or she becomes more separated from the mother through the acquisition of language and learning the meaning of the pronoun "I." For the boy-child, the separation becomes complete and final through his rejection of his mother as "lack," the one who does not possess the phallus. However, when the child is a girl, the separation from the mother becomes more complicated. Linda Williams's discussion of Lacan offers a lucid explanation for this complexity: "According to Lacan, through the recognition of the sexual difference of a female 'other' who lacks the phallus that is the symbol of patriarchal privilege, the child gains entrance into the symbolic order of human culture. This culture then produces narratives which repress the figure of the lack that the mother—former figure of plentitude—has become" (Williams 1984, 5–6). Therefore, the female child encounters the paradox of having to identify with her mother as part of her own socialization process (she learns her role as a female by studying her mother's role) and having to reject her mother as "lack" at the same time—she must identify with and learn from the one she rejects.

The opening scene of the film sets up the first confrontation between mother and daughter. Pretending to be sick, Carmen wants Ana to stay home to cook for the men in the house, but Ana wants to attend her last day in high school and defies Carmen's wishes. This scene can be viewed as a case of failed communication between mother and daughter, and the reason for failure can be attributed to the lack of role models as prescribed by Irigaray in the epigraph. However, we soon learn in the film that Carmen's actions are based precisely on her beliefs that her work as a wife and mother has meaning, and that she can be a role model to Ana. When Carmen's husband tries to convince Carmen to allow Ana to continue her school education, Carmen objects to his suggestion with authority: "I can teach her [Ana]. I can teach her to sew. I can teach her to raise her children and take care of her husband." Carmen's statement might be interpreted as Carmen's internalization of her role as a wife and mother within a patriarchal family structure—she believes that marriage and reproduction are the sole purposes in a woman's life. When I watched this film in an undergraduate class, many of the students laughed during this scene; their laughter was triggered by Carmen's naiveté and her stubbornness in equating what she can teach Ana and what a college education has to offer. However, I would like to suggest another reading of Carmen's speech. That is, by equating domestic work with formal school education, Carmen expresses the values she sees in her own work. She is obviously not embarrassed by the domestic labor that she performs and perceives a woman's work as being an invaluable contribution to her family.

It is the film's reinscription of patriarchy that makes the mother-daughter relationship so volatile at times. Even though women take center stage in the film, the male characters are positioned as voices of reason and authority. Both Ana and Carmen operate within a patriarchal familial and social structure. They have to perform domestic duties such as cooking and cleaning while holding jobs outside of the household to contribute to the overall family income. Ana aligns herself with the male figures in her life, who are depicted as warm, wise, understanding, and supportive, characteristics that contrast sharply with the demanding and often unsympathetic and unyielding Carmen. At school, Ana heeds the advice of Mr. Guzman (George Lopez), who recognizes her as a "smart woman." At home, Ana is her grandfather's prized grandchild—he claims her as his "gold" and motivates her to go forward with the pursuit of her own gold. When Ana's sister, Estela, sinks into financial difficulty as four seamstresses unexpectedly quit Estela's small and struggling garment factory, Ana turns to their father for help—his money eventually helps save Estela's factory. It is also with the ultimate consent of her father that Ana leaves home for college, which causes further mother-daughter estrangement and isolates Carmen as the only family member who hinders Ana from pursuing a college education. Ironically, Carmen also has to resort to a male figure to make her arguments for keeping Ana at home. She makes Ana feel guilty by implying that by going away to college, Ana will abandon her grandfather to loneliness.

It is here that I would like to return to the famous disrobing scene mentioned at the beginning of this chapter. I argue that patriarchy is not only maintained through the construction of the mother-daughter relationship in the film but also through the representation of the female body, which severs the mother-daughter bond. During this pivotal scene of the film, in which four voluptuous women strip down to their undergarments and compare their cellulite, the celebration of the full-figured female body is engendered through the vilification and ultimately the silencing of the mother. While this scene can be viewed as subversive and resistant to traditional Hollywood's interpretation of the perfect female body as being slender and blemish free, it is also in this scene that Carmen becomes the voice of patriarchy and is thus ostracized by her daughters and the other two female workers. When Ana,

Estela, Pancha, and Rosali begin to disrobe, Carmen protests vehemently, saying that Ana and Estela look terrible because they are overweight, and that all of the women have no shame. Although Carmen herself is plump, she thinks that it is no problem because she is already married. Carmen becomes the policing voice of patriarchal values, designating the female body as the most prized feature to attract the opposite sex. In contrast, Ana becomes the spokesperson of feminist philosophy when she remarks that she is more than just her body. Carmen finally walks away angrily, while the other women achieve solidarity and begin a dance of celebration in their undergarments.

In an interview about the mother-daughter relationship, Irigaray notes that what the discussion on the mother-daughter bond lacks is "the singular image of one woman who is also a mother" (Irigaray 2000, 18). Marianne Hirsch, in *The Mother-Daughter Plot: Narrative, Psychoanalysis, Feminism*, also notes that the mother is often portrayed in relation to and from the perspective of the child and is thus perceived as lacking any subjectivity of her own: "[I]n her maternal function, she remains an object, always idealized or denigrated, always mystified, always represented through the small child's point of view" (1989, 167). As reflected in the disrobing scene, the mother-woman cannot coexist, and the daughter's progressive, feminist image is only achieved through the denigration and rejection of the mother.

The disrobing scene, what has been lauded by critics as a progressive representation of the female body, reenacts the marginalization of the mother as many mainstream Hollywood films have done in the past. *However, despite the film's reinscription of patriarchal values, the complexity of the mother-daughter relationship and the film's popularity cannot be fully accounted for by a gendered reading alone.* As Collins notes, "Placing the experiences of women of color in the center of feminist theorizing about motherhood demonstrates how emphasizing the father as patriarch in a decontextualized nuclear family distorts the experiences of women in alternative family structures with quite different political economies" (1994, 46). In the film commentary with Patricia Cardoso, Josephina Lopez, and George Lavoo in the DVD version of the film, Lopez points out that "it's very important to show a positive portrayal of Latino men." According to Lopez, by not making sexism the film's focus, the film is able to bring out the complexities and nuances of the struggles faced by Latino women, in particular, Ana's struggle to gain a college education. Director Patricia Cardoso also remarks that many male viewers, after watching the film, have thanked her for her "good portrayal of men," since Latino men have often been portrayed as greasers, abusers, or gangsters in mainstream cinema. In addition, George Lavoo, the co-writer and producer of the film, recounts his experiences marketing the film script to financiers. Some financiers specifically asked him to add more violence and make the male characters more aggressive than what the script intended. Therefore, even though the film keeps intact a patriarchal social structure, from the commentaries we can see that the maintenance of patriarchy is perhaps less important to the film's overall achievement with its alternative forms of representation of Latino men, who show a tender and supportive side in the film that is rarely found in mainstream Hollywood cinema. By not focusing on sexism alone, we also acknowledge that the struggle of the racialized woman is not merely against sexism.

In her study of colonized women and the central role that they play in shaping family structures as a way to resist imperial domination, Mina Davis Caulfield reminds us that "[c]olonized women are not interested so much in combating the domestic dominance of their husbands . . . as in insuring the inclusion of men in domestic networks of mutual support. . . . We must avoid seeing people who exist under conditions of severe oppression simply as victims. Sufferers everywhere don't simply suffer; they fight back" (1974, 84–85). This is not to say that patriarchal oppression should not be recognized and criticized, but we need to be aware that the patriarchal structure maintained by the film diegesis may be the product of neocolonialism under which Third World immigrants or working-class families are subjected to economic exploitations by the dominant culture, and the female characters' primary concern may not be so much the dismantling of traditional patriarchal ideology as much as acquiring economic means in a collective effort to survive in a capitalist society. By providing the Garcia family's ethnic, cultural, and economic background, the film helps the viewer develop an understanding, on the one hand, of the mother, who has worked diligently as a seamstress for almost thirty years and wishes for her daughter what she sees as sources of stability—gainful employment, marriage, and children—and, on the other hand, of the daughter who, because of her parents' hard work, can dream of a college education and independence. Therefore, despite the film's reinscription of a patriarchal familial and social structure, I find the agency that the women do exercise and the roles they negotiate for themselves within patriarchy still worthy of examination.

What kind of agency does the mother have in the film? What kind of subjectivity is constructed for Carmen in contrast to Ana? In her analysis of Vidor's film *Stella Dallas*, Kaplan concludes, "[W]hat it is to be a Mother in patriarchy—it is to renounce, to be on the outside, and to take pleasure in this positioning" (2000, 476). Here Kaplan is speaking of the ending of *Stella Dallas*, in which the working-class mother, Stella, relinquishes her own intimate relationship with her daughter Laurel in order to help Laurel gain an entry into upper-class society, all the while having to pretend to take pleasure in her renunciation. The mother thus becomes the spectator of her own oppression (as an outsider looking in), willing to deny her own needs and desires for the sake of her child. Kaplan concludes that mainstream Hollywood cinema constructs four paradigms for the representation of the mother figure: the self-effacing, loving "Good Mother," who is the caretaker of the family; the selfish and malicious "Bad Mother," or "Witch," who is condemned for her deviance from the feminine ideal; the altruistic "Heroic Mother," who uncomplainingly suffers for her family's sake; and the "Silly, Weak, or Vain Mother," who is often the killjoy figure in comedies (Kaplan 2000, 468). In *Real Women Have Curves*, Carmen does not neatly fit into any of the four paradigms described by Kaplan. On many levels, Carmen does seem less liberated and more confined in her role as a woman than Ana. For example, whereas Ana is seen walking on the streets of L.A. and taking buses from her Latino neighborhood to the wealthy Beverly Hills (a motion in itself that signifies Ana's chance at upward mobility), Carmen is mostly seen in the domestic space of the home and the feminine space of the garment factory. Whereas Ana shows an indifference to children and openly talks about safe sex, Carmen wishes that St. Antonio would help both of her daughters get married. Despite these generational differences, which in themselves carry social and cultural implications, Carmen, like Ana, is also a complex liminal figure who not only plays the role that traditional patriarchy has prescribed for her but also subverts or maximizes the potential of that role by carving out a voice for herself within the limitations of the film's overall patriarchal structure.

Inside the household, Carmen possesses a great deal of dignity. She finds listeners in her husband, her father-in-law, and her older daughter, Estela, when she tells stories about the soap opera she watches. In one scene, the family members (tellingly, with the exception of Ana, whose back is turned against Carmen) sit around Carmen as she talks about a new soap opera, making her the focal point. In this scene, the camera shot shifts back and forth between Carmen and Ana. The viewer not only sees Ana's reaction to her mother's story but also sees the animated way in which Carmen tells the story. It is Carmen who possesses the voice of the storyteller in the film. She brings gossip from the market to entertain her female coworkers at the garment factory. She consoles Pancha, a worker at the factory who did not have money to bury her father, by validating Pancha as a good daughter.

The film shows Carmen as the bearer of tradition in her wishes for Ana to get married and have children, but it also shows Carmen pushing those traditional boundaries. That is, she herself is undergoing a transformation in the film. Carmen steps outside of her role as the authoritative, know-it-all mother when she tells Ana about what she believes is an unexpected pregnancy during middle age, not realizing that she is starting menopause. Carmen's confiding in Ana shows that Carmen is comfortable sharing her worries about her body with Ana, worries that she is not inclined to share with anyone else in the family. Carmen unwittingly expresses the values that she sees in Ana's ability to talk openly about sexuality and the female body without treating them as taboos, a direct result of Ana's school education. Therefore, Carmen not only undergoes the "change of life" biologically, but culturally she also begins to adapt to her life in America, which is illustrated by her asking Ana, her Americanized daughter, for help.

Although the film's ambiguous ending may leave the viewer wondering whether or not the mother-daughter conflicts are ever resolved, it does hint at the two women's transformation through their attempts to understand one another. On the day Ana leaves for college, Ana's reflection again appears, this time, in a mirror, echoing Ana's reflection in the window in the first scene of the film. Unlike in the beginning, however, where Ana is cleaning the window (as discussed, a symbolic gesture to have a clearer view of herself), in this scene, Ana is washing her face instead. It is a baptismal moment in which Ana recognizes that her life has taken a new turn. In addition, we also see a reflection of Carmen in the mirror. When Ana knocks on Carmen's door to say good-bye, Carmen looks at herself (albeit for a brief moment) in her bedroom mirror while holding a picture of Ana in her hand. Carmen's gaze into the mirror also reflects the earlier scene in which Carmen and her husband discuss Ana's future in their bedroom, where Carmen insists on teaching Ana herself. The early mirror scene with Carmen looking into the mirror suggests Carmen's desire to make Ana into her own reflection. In the scene at the end of the film, however, Carmen's recognition of herself in the mirror marks the beginning of her own entrance into the symbolic order as she begins to accept the separation between her and Ana. In other words, whereas in order for Ana to develop into a "real woman" she has to recognize her mother's concerns and motivations through their working together at the factory, Carmen begins to develop into her own person by recognizing that she and her daughter are different.

As the car taking Ana to the airport leaves the house, Carmen goes to the window to catch a last glimpse of Ana. The camera then cuts to Ana turning around in the car and looking at her house through the car window. Although the shot/reverse-shot sequence does not match the women's eye line perfectly, and their gazes are filtered by the windows between them, the film ultimately hints that the women have started to recognize and return each other's gaze. As Williams has instructively stated, "Instead of destroying the cinematic codes that have placed women as objects of spectacle at their center, what is needed, and has already begun to occur, is a theoretical and practical recognition of the ways in which women actually do speak to one another" (1984, 7). It is in this farewell scene between Ana and Carmen with their imperfectly matched gaze at each other that the film acknowledges that, despite their differences, the women "do speak to each other" through their gaze.

REAL WOMEN HAVE CURVES AND VIEWER RESPONSE

Because of the film's popularity with the audience (it won the Dramatic Audience Award at the Sundance Film Festival), it is crucial to examine viewer responses to the film. After reading over 100 online postings (there were 99 postings on the Internet Movie Database and 46 postings on Yahoo!Movies; these postings range from a few lines to over 1,000 words of commentary and analysis), I find that spectators do indeed identify with the multiple registers of difference that the film brings together. For example, many viewers say that they can relate to the film, and many express an appreciation for the film's representation of Latinas. One viewer with the screen name "garcia3892" writes, "This movie is one of the few movies out there that tells the story about Mexican-American women the right way" (garcia3892 2004). Another viewer, "Heather T," writes the following passage:

> The cinematic accomplishments by Latina and Latin American women filmmakers has [sic] overwhelmingly challenged cultural and gender stereotypes, as well as introduced non-Latino audiences to the experiences of a community rooted in Latin America. *Real Women Have Curves* is no exception. Latinos have long been struggling with society's guidelines on what is beautiful. In the U.S., with such limited choices to turn to for Spanish language media, its [sic] not difficult to see what exec-

utives consider beautiful. Many Latin television stars fit into similar categories, i.e., fair skin and blonder hair leads [sic] the way. In *Real Women Have Curves*, Ana embodies what young Latinas face on a daily basis, from the pressure of conforming to generations of subservience to dealing with society's unfair measures of beauty. (Heather T 2004)

While viewers such as "garcia3892" and "Heather T" laud the filmmaker's effort to dismantle racial and gender stereotypes, not all viewers identify with Ana. Some viewers are more interested in what happens to Estela and her factory, while others show empathy for Carmen. For instance, viewer "enigma88" writes, "I spent more time being irritated and wishing the movie featured more of an in-depth picture of her mother or sister—much more likeable characters despite their obvious flaws" (enigma88 2003). Because the film narrative emerges from the interlocking of multiple identity categories, viewers are invited to participate in a fluid, nonlinear process of identification. We learn to identify with both the daughter and the mother by refusing to reject the mother as the villain in the film. For Ana and Carmen, the mirror is no longer empty, because each woman has begun to see an image of herself that is both similar and different, both connected and separate from each other. In turn, the film spectator can refuse to take part in the denigration and dismissal of the mother that mainstream Hollywood cinema invites by not reading the film through simple binary constructions but through its multiple registers of difference.

My own approach to the film participates in the methodologies of feminism's third wave, as defined by Leslie Heywood and Jennifer Drake in *Third Wave Agenda: Being Feminist, Doing Feminism*. Whereas "postfeminists . . . define themselves against and criticize feminists of the second wave" (1997, 1), third-wave feminism is "a movement that contains elements of second wave critique of beauty culture, sexual abuse, and power structures while it also acknowledges and makes use of the pleasure, danger, and defining power of those structures" (1997, 3). Third-wave feminism also recognizes that feminism's second wave consisted of multiple branches of feminist thoughts, and hence "a third wave goal that comes directly out of learning from these histories and working among these traditions is the development of modes of thinking that can come to terms with multiple, interpenetrating axes of identity, and the creation of a coalition politics based on these understandings" (Heywood and Drake 1997, 3). Instead of criticizing and rejecting the second-wave model altogether, third-wave feminists see a need for the young generation of feminists to pay homage to the legacy of the second wave, using it as a constructive model for political activism while learning from its blind spots. A new generation of feminists can stop the process of the "patriarchal omission of the Mother" by acknowledging the achievements of the feminists of our mother's generation. That is, young feminists can create a mirror for both the mother generation and the daughter generation of feminists that is not empty by recognizing the differences and similarities between the generations.[4]

NOTES

1. For a discussion of Latino images in film, see Frank Javier Garcia Berumen's *The Chicano/Hispanic Image in American Film* (1995), Charles Ramírez Berg's *Latino Images in Film: Stereotypes, Subversion, Resistance* (2002), and Clara Rodriguez's *Heroes, Lovers, and Others: The Story of Latinos in Hollywood* (2004). For a discussion of the rise and development of Chicana/Chicano cinema, see Linda Rosa Fregoso's *The Bronze Screen: Chicana and Chicano Film Culture* (1993), Chon A. Noriega and Ana M. Lopez's *The Ethnic Eye: Latino Media Arts* (1996), and Chon A. Noriega's *Shot in America: Television, the State, and the Rise of Chicano Cinema* (2000).
2. For my analysis, I define patriarchy as a state-enforced, socially sanctioned value system in which men acquire dominant subject positions and women become figures of subordination. I am especially interested in the ways in which this hierarchy delineates and reinforces stringent gender roles within familial relations and the domestic space of the home. For example, in *Real Women Have Curves*, Ana's father is installed as the breadwinner who has the economic power to save his older daughter Estela's business from going bankrupt. Even though the women in the film also work, they do not seem to have this monetary power. Moreover, the women are seen working both outside and within the household, whereas the men's workplace remains outside of the domestic realm. Therefore, one of my critiques of the film is that it still engages in a masculinist discourse. However, it is also within this masculinist discourse that women's agency is located. In a later section of this chapter I discuss in more depth how the film's reinscription of patriarchal familial structures is complicated by and contingent upon issues of race and class.
3. For my analysis, I read viewer comments for this film from the Internet Movie Database and Yahoo!Movies.
4. I thank Professor Carole-Ann Tyler of UC Riverside for reading several drafts of this chapter and giving me invaluable feedback. I also thank my mother, who taught me the complexities and values of motherwork long before any theoretical text could.

REFERENCES

Berg, C. R. 2002. *Latino images in film: Stereotypes, subversion, resistance.* Austin: University of Texas Press.

Berumen, F. J. G. 1995. *The Chicano/Hispanic image in American film.* New York: Vintage Press.

Caulfield, M. D. 1974. Imperialism, the family, and cultures of resistance. *Socialist Revolution* 20:4: 67–85.

Collins, P. H. 1994. Shifting the center: Race, class, and feminist theorizing about motherhood. In *Mothering: Ideology, experience, and agency,* ed. E. N. Glenn, G. Chang, and L. R. Forcey, 45–65. New York: Routledge.

Ebert, R. 2002. Real women have curves: A review. *Chicago Sun-Times,* October 25. http://www.rogerebert.suntimes.com/apps/pbcs.dll/article?AID=/20021025/REVIEWS/210250310/1023.

enigma88. 2003. Disappointed. *Internet Movie Database,* October 5. http://www.imdb.com/title/tt0296166/usercomments?start=40.

Fregoso. L. R. 1993. *The bronze screen: Chicana and Chicano film culture.* Minneapolis: University of Minnesota Press.

garcia3892. 2004. It's real. *Internet Movie Database,* August 22. http://www.imdb.com/title/tt0296166/usercomments?start=20.

Glenn, E. N. 1994. Social construction of mothering: A thematic overview. In *Mothering: Ideology, experience, and agency,* ed. E. N. Glenn, G. Chang, and L. R. Forcey, 1–29. New York: Routledge.

Heather T. 2004. Real women have curves (may contain spoilers). *Internet Movie Database,* May 10. http://www.imdb.com/title/tt0296166/usercomments?start=20.

Heywood, L., and J. Drake. 1997. Introduction. In *Third wave agenda: Being feminist, doing feminism,* ed. J. Drake and L. Heywood, 1–20. Minneapolis: University of Minnesota Press.

Hirsch, M. 1989. *The mother/daughter plot: Narrative, psychoanalysis, feminism.* Bloomingdale: Indiana University Press.

Irigaray, L. 2000. Mothers and daughters. In *Why different? A culture of two subjects: Interviews with Luce Irigaray,* ed. L. Irigaray and S. Lotringer, 17–27. New York: Semiotext(e).

Kaplan, E. A. 2000. The case of the missing mother: Maternal issues in Vidor's Stella Dallas. In *Feminism and film,* ed. E. A. Kaplan, 466–78. Oxford: Oxford University Press.

Lacan, J. 1977. The mirror stage as formative of the function of the I as revealed in psychoanalytic experience. In *Ecrits: A selection,* trans. Alan Sheridan, 1–7. New York: W. W. Norton & Company.

Lowe, L. 1996. *Immigrant acts: On Asian American cultural politics.* Durham, NC: Duke University Press.

Mitchell, E. 2002. Sweatshop or college? Guess which one mom's pushing. *New York Times,* October 18. http://www.nytimes.com/2002/10/18/movies/18REAL.html?ex=1155355200&en=16e12cce1edbb955&ei=5070.

Noriega, C. A. 2000. *Shot in America: Television, the state, and the rise of Chicano cinema*. Minneapolis: University of Minnesota Press.
Noriega, C. A., and A. Lopez. 1996. *The ethnic eye: Latino media arts*. Minneapolis: University of Minnesota Press.
Rich, A. 1976. *Of woman born: Motherhood as experience and institution*. New York: W. W. Norton.
Rodriguez, C. 2004. *Heroes, lovers, and others: The story of Latinos in Hollywood*. Oxford: Oxford University Press.
Williams, L. 1984. Something else besides a mother: Stella Dallas and the maternal melodrama. *Cinema Journal* 24:1: 2–27.

THREE

Cyborg Mothering

SHELLEY PARK

As new communication technologies transform everyday life in the twenty-first century, personal, family, and other social relations are transformed with them. As a way of exploring the larger question—How exactly does communication technology transform love and how love is lived?—this chapter examines the cell phone, e-mail, instant messaging, social networking, and other communication technologies as electronic extensions and modifications of maternal bodies connecting (cyber)mother to (cyber)children. Such transformations of maternal bodies, I suggest, open a space for new and liberating forms of maternal love.

There is a notable lacuna in feminist, postmodernist, and queer scholarship pertaining to these issues. The past two decades have witnessed the emergence of a rich body of feminist scholarship on mothering alongside an equally burgeoning body of postmodernist scholarship on digital technologies and a rapidly proliferating and challenging body of literature in queer theory. However, there has been little dialogue between feminists theorizing motherhood, on the one hand, and cultural theorists (including feminists and queer theorists) investigating the transgressive potential of our posthuman, postmodern condition, on the other hand. Here I wish to begin to put these areas of scholarship into dialogue by exploring how mothering in the postmodern world is inescapably (for me, at least) intertwined with technology in ways that are both the effect of and affected by queer domestic space and critically reflective love.

The space I inhabit is located at a particular intersection of feminism, postmodernism, and queerness. I am the mother of two daughters whom I hope will become independent, autonomous, self-supporting, and fulfilled young women. I am a primary breadwinner in my family. I have a career and friendships that are important to me, and I do not define myself simply as a mother. I am a divorced mother who is attempting to live well in a complicated, extended, blended family. I am a joint custodial parent who is on friendly, albeit not intimate, terms with my ex-husband. He and I (try to) parent cooperatively, making large decisions together while allowing for individual parenting styles and sharing certain economic resources, while not others. I have a same-sex partner. She and I negotiate living among several homes, sharing some, but not all, domestic chores and sharing certain economic resources, while not others. This is a lived reality that demands taking account of different strands of cultural theory in order to provide an adequate analysis of different facets of my struggles and aspirations as a mother.

In the last several years, after ending a long marriage, I have been immersed largely in trying to think through ways of loving my now teenage daughters consistently while—as a joint custodial parent—only occupying shared material space with them half of the time. An important way in which I retain consistent contact with my daughters is to inhabit virtual space with them during the times during which we do not share material space. I talk with them on the cell phone; I e-mail and instant message them; and I visit their My Space and Facebook accounts. Indeed, given the proclivity of my daughters to be attached to a cell phone or computer even when we are in the same physical domicile, I often meet them in virtual space even during the weeks I am living under the same roof as they. Sometimes, as I will argue here, technology enables a co-presence that physical proximity does not.

Given the number of commuting parents, divorced parents, diasporic families, and wired teenagers who exist in our postmodern era, I think it unlikely that I am the only mother who relies on technology to care for her children. For feminists and queers interested in both mothering and technology, important questions arise, namely: Is mothering transformed by our uses of technology, and, if so, how? Can technology liberate us from the patriarchal institution of motherhood, and can it be used to subvert the heteronormative paradigm of family, or does it simply reinforce gendered relations of oppression?

Without minimizing the legitimate feminist concerns about the ways in which technology may reproduce relations of oppression under patriarchal capitalism (see, e.g., Edley 2001; Gurley 2001), my focus here will be on some of the ways in which cellular and digital technologies might help us disrupt patriarchal, heteronormative practices of motherhood. New communication technologies do not, I argue, merely reproduce existing gender and domestic relationships; they also transform those relationships. Transformations in those relationships, in turn, engender new uses and conceptions of technologies. Indeed, if we take seriously, as I think we should, cyberfeminist Donna Haraway's claim that postmodern humans are cyborgs (1991), then the distinction between human animals and machines breaks down in ways that invite us to revise the questions we ask about technology. Thus instead of inquiring about the oppression engendered by the production and consumption of communication technologies, here I sketch the ways in which technology functions as an extension and a modification of human embodiment, transforming our experiences of intimacy and our ability to create, maintain, and transform responsible, loving relationships with others. More specifically, I will argue that digital and other technologies queer cultural processes of reproduction by queering the temporal and spatial structures of mothering and that this, in turn, transforms the meaning and experience of maternal love.

As this overview suggests, my interest here is not in how communication technologies enable mothers to bridge the much discussed gap between work and home but is instead in how these technologies enable us to decompartmentalize and transform our private lives themselves. This is particularly important for queer families, such as my own, who do not inhabit material domestic space in normative ways. When separating from my husband several years ago, we agreed to an unconventional living arrangement wherein our young daughters remained in one home which we as custodial parents time-shared, along with a rental apartment in which we lived alternatively as noncustodial parents. Although we have recently divorced and split property, we continue to alternate custody on a biweekly basis (with flexibility as needed), maintain a joint bank account for basic children's needs, consult one another on parenting issues, and maintain a fluidity between and amidst homes. Our homes now number four—his, mine, his girlfriend's, and my girlfriend's. Navigating multiple homes and diverse styles of caregiving and domesticity is an intentional, cooperative effort that gives all of us—including my now teenage daughters—access to both city and suburban amenities, as well as time alone when needed. As Judith Halberstam (2005) suggests, queerness may be less a matter of sexual identity than it is "an outcome of strange temporalities, imaginative life schedules, and eccentric economic practices" (1).

Such queerness is not without its challenges. Despite wanting to teach my daughters the value of queering domestic configurations, I continue to find it difficult to live *as a mother* outside of the nuclear family and maintain consistent physical proximity to my daughters. How does one "leave" her children and still mother?

Mothering at a distance, I am learning, requires queer uses of time and space; inhabiting time and space queerly is made possible by communication technologies—or what I call here "technologies of co-presence." In the following section, I begin my argument for embracing the ideal of cyborg motherhood by drawing on the canonical cyberfeminist work of Haraway and the queer theoretical work of Halberstam to sketch the notion of cyborg motherhood as an evolution of non-normative motherhood. Following this, I explore the importance of technologies of co-presence as extensions and modifications of maternal bodies in families that diverge from the heteronormative paradigm of the nuclear family. Borrowing feminist philosopher Kelly Oliver's (2001) notion of "response-ability," in the third section I suggest that technologies of co-presence enhance the subjectivity of both mother and child by increasing their mutual ability to respond to one another—especially, although not exclusively, in queer time and space. I conclude that insofar as cyborg identities open spaces of critical self-reflection that are necessary to non-self-sacrificing maternal love, we should embrace the potential of cyborg mothering.

MOTHERING AS/WITH TECHNOLOGY

Haraway (1991) asks how our "natural" bodies can be "reimagined—and relived—in ways that transform the relations of same and different, self and other, inner and outer, recognition and misrecognition into guiding maps for inappropriate/d others" (3–4). Her answer lies in viewing ourselves as "hybrids of machine and organism" or, in other words, as "cyborgs." Cyborgs, Haraway suggests, live intimacy in ways that embody an oppositional politics, that transgress the boundaries of mind and body, culture and nature, and abandon "the polarity of public and private," in part, by reconfiguring "social relations in the . . . household" (151). Urging us to embrace "the skilful task of reconstructing the boundaries of daily life, in partial connection with others, in communication with all of our parts," including those parts that find pleasure in reason and technology, Haraway concludes her famous cyberfeminist manifesto with a rejection of cultural feminism's celebration of an idealized femininity, claiming that she would (and we should) "rather be a cyborg than a goddess" (181).

In an essay contemplating technology and gender, queer theorist Halberstam (1998) concurs with Haraway's recommendation, rejecting a feminism predicated on a "goddess-given right to birth children" as ultimately rooted in a patriarchal story about women's essential connection to nature and moral superiority to men (478). Disparaging the notion that there is "some 'natural' or 'organic' essence of woman that is either corrupted or contained by any association with the artificial," Halberstam claims that "femininity is always mechanical and artificial—as is masculinity" (478). The female cyborg, a fusion of femininity and intelligence, as described by Halberstam, "thinks gender, processes power, and converts a binary system of logic into a more intricate network. As a metaphor, she challenges correspondences such as maternity and femininity or female and emotion. As a metonym, she embodies the impossibility of distinguishing between gender and its representation" (479).

While I am less optimistic than Haraway (1991) about the cyborg as "a creature in a post-gender world" (150), I agree with Halberstam (1998) that "gender is a technology" irreducible to "natural" bodies and that "[g]ender emerges within the cyborg as no longer a binary but as a multiple construction dependent upon random formations beyond masculine and feminine" (480). Viewing ourselves as cyborgs certainly does blur the distinctions between mind and body, culture and nature, and public and private in ways that both complicate and multiply our notions of gender, in part by denaturalizing them and, related to this, by throwing into question assumptions about women's "place." In so doing, it complicates and multiplies our notions of mothering by rejecting any residual essentialist ideas about mothering as rooted in "natural" or "instinctual" female practices of caregiving performed in particular bodily ways or in particular material spaces. Mothering, like gender itself, is a technology (a social artifice produced by shifting power relations), not an essential identity tied to natural bodies. One way to see this is to recognize the ways in which technologies (machines) are integrated into the practices of mothering in ways that transform the maternal body, its location in time and space, and its engagement with others, making possible resistant forms of maternal agency.

As Haraway (1991) notes, "communications technologies and biotechnologies are the crucial tools for recrafting our bodies," tools that "embody and enforce new social relations" (164). Among the social relations transformed by these new technologies are the relations of sexuality and of reproduction (168–69). Sexuality, as conceived by sociobiology, Haraway notes, becomes an instrumental activity emphasizing a genetic calculus as well as desire-satisfaction (169). This is sexuality as repro-sexuality: an "interweaving of heterosexuality, biological reproduction, cultural reproduction, and personal identity" (Warner 1991, 9). The straight personal identity supported by sociobiological accounts is closely interwoven with biological reproduction; it is, as queer theorist Michael Warner (1991) has contended, a "breeder identity"—a self-understanding and conception of one's sexual identity closely tied to one's status as procreative (9). Breeder identities combine with medical technologies in the postmodern era, however, in ways that transform reproductive relations, making clear the social nature of such relations. As Haraway (1991) observes, these technologies—sonograms, amniocentesis, in-vitro fertilization, and so forth—permeate the boundaries of women's bodies via photographic and biochemical means, undermining claims about the "naturalness" of reproductive bodies and identities (169).

Biomedical technologies are not, however, the only technologies that reveal mothering as artifice. Also noteworthy are the wide variety of domestic technologies producing and satisfying maternal desires. As both feminists and queer theorists have suggested, "reprosexuality involves more than reproducing. . . . [I]t involves a relation to self that finds its proper temporality and fulfillment in generational transmission" (Warner 1991, 9). Generational succession requires us to feed and clothe and teach and nurture our offspring so that they can, in turn, reproduce our values as well as our genes. This is closely linked to Halberstam's recent critique of temporal norms as followed by "bourgeois families." These temporal norms include not only the "time of reproduction" (women's "biological clock"), but also the "normative scheduling of daily life . . . that accompanies the practice of childrearing" ("family time") and "generational time within which values, wealth, goods, and morals are passed through family ties from one generation to the next" ("the time of inheritance") (Halberstam 2005, 5).

These cultural processes of reproduction—and with them the temporal and spatial structures of mothering—are also intertwined with technologies (machines) that reveal mothering—a specific gendered identity—as a technology (an artifice produced by relations of power). In *The Cyborg Mommy: User's Manual*, performance artist Pattie Belle Hastings (2002) focuses on the postpartum technologizing of mother and child. In the introduction to her ongoing multimedia work, Hastings (2006) suggests that in contrast to "movies and fiction that depict the cyborg as a futuristic, superhuman, or technological monster . . . it is actually your average mother and housewife that are among the first so-called cyborgs." The machine, she observes, has "extended the body of the mother for centuries"; mothers have "tended the stove, cranked the washer, peddled the sewing machine, and vacuumed the house." Today, mothering occurs in an environment in which "microchips are embedded in everything from toys and greeting cards to thermometers and baby monitors," leading to a situation in which mothering relationships are increasingly "mediated, complicated, and enhanced by machine" (Hastings 2002, 79).

It would be easy to interpret this environment as being oppressive and reproductive and domestic technologies as being invasive (see, e.g., Edley 2001; Friedan 1963; Rakow and Navarro 1993). Nonetheless, I wish to suggest, following Haraway and Hastings, that the cyborg stands as a potentially utopian figure. As Hastings suggests, the Cyborg Mommy is liberated and not merely oppressed: "As machines and bodies increasingly become fused, Cyborg theory celebrates" as well as "criticizes and condemns the process—the machine/body relationship is at once liberating and oppressive" (Hastings 2002, 79). To see the liberatory potential of cyborg mothering, however, it is fruitful to focus on a particular type of technology, namely, communication technologies such as cell phones, e-mail, instant messaging, and social networking sites such as My Space and Facebook. I term these *technologies of co-presence* in order to emphasize the ways in which these technologies allow us to be present to and with others in ways not tied to the physical facticity of the body. These technologies thus permit us, as mothers, to inhabit space and time differently—in ways that enable resistance to bourgeois family norms (especially self-sacrificial forms of mothering) and suggest different forms of intimacy between family members.

TECHNOLOGIES OF CO-PRESENCE: QUEERING SPACES AND BODIES

Cultural theorist Mark Poster distinguishes between a modernist (enlightenment) understanding of machines as tools or prosthetic devices enabling humans to have greater control over (natural) reality and postmodern understandings of machines as, instead, reconfiguring our reality and transforming who we are. Speaking specifically of the Internet, he says:

> The Internet is more like a social space than a thing, so that its effects are more like those of Germany than those of hammers: the effect of Germany upon the people within it is to make

them Germans (at least for the most part); the effect of hammers is not to make people hammers . . . but to force metal spikes into wood. . . . The problem is that modern perspectives tend to reduce the Internet to a hammer. In this grand narrative of modernity, the Internet is an efficient tool of communication, advancing the goals of its users, who are understood as pre-constituted instrumental identities. (Poster 2001, 177)

Poster's analogy is useful for thinking about the distinctions between two paradigms of technology; however, it may underplay the ways in which tools themselves are misunderstood as mere extensions of the human will. It is no more a "preconstituted instrumental identity" that uses a hammer than it is a preconstituted subjectivity that uses the Internet. Technological tools—including the bottle washers, vacuums, and washing machines used by Hastings's cyborg mommy, as well as Poster's hammers—do not merely *extend* the embodied will of their users, they also *mediate* and *transform* human agency and social norms. As Betty Friedan argued, the domestic gadgetry imported into suburban U.S. households in the mid-twentieth century produced (in addition to being produced by) new norms of good housekeeping and good mothering (Friedan 1963). As such, these tools played an important role in transforming (bourgeois) women's desires, goals, and identities. In this sense, Hastings is right: cyborg mothers—mothers whose agency can only be understood as being inextricably intertwined with domestic technologies—have been around a long time.

There is, however, something qualitatively new about the ways in which communication technologies, such as the Internet, transform our human subjectivity. This is captured, in part, by Poster's emphasis on the Internet as a *space* rather than a *thing*. It is further unpacked by Allucquére Rosanne Stone's (2001) distinction between relationships with technology that are characterized by playfulness and those characterized by work. Like Poster, Stone rejects a conception of computers as tools extending the human will, arguing that this framework for thinking about digital technologies is rooted in "a human work ethic" that renders invisible the beliefs and practices of many playful cyber communities, including many programmers, hackers, and discussion groups (12–14). Following anthropologist Barbara Joans's distinction between those who play with technology ("Creative Outlaw Visionaries") and those who build and sell it ("Law and Order Practitioners"), Stone suggests that the paradigm of computers as tools only makes sense from the latter group's perspective. Visionaries, however, are "thoroughly accustomed to engaging in nontrivial social interactions through the use of their computers—social interactions in which they change and are changed, in which commitments are made, kept, and broken, in which they may engage in intellectual discussion, arguments, and even sex" (Stone 2001, 15). Thus visionaries "view computers not only as tools, but also as *arenas for social experience* (Stone 2001, 15, emphasis in original). Unlike the Law and Order Practitioners, who view computers as little boxes containing information, Visionaries understand that "inside the little box are *other people*" (16).

Recognizing communication technologies as opening new social spaces requires us, Stone argues, to "rethink some assumptions about presence."

> Presence is currently a word that means many different things to many different people. One meaning is the sense that we are direct witnesses to something or that we ourselves are being directly apprehended. . . . Another meaning is related to agency, to the proximity of intentionality. The changes that the concept of presence is currently undergoing are embedded in much larger shifts in cultural beliefs and practices. These include repeated transgressions of the traditional concept of the body's physical envelope and of the locus of human agency. (Stone 2001, 16)

Intimacy, as sociologist Gill Valentine (2006) notes, has been typically assumed to require physical proximity: "The word 'close' is a synonym for intimate, and literal closeness is often assumed to be essential for familiarity and commitment" (367). Yet as the number of families "living apart together" (Holmes 2004, 181) indicates, physical distance need not bring an end to intimacy (Valentine 2006). For Valentine, as for Poster and Stone and other theorists of technology, viewing technology as an arena for social experience enabling familial and other forms of intimacy is closely linked to the advent of the Internet:

> The Internet expands the opportunities for daily meaningful contact between family members locked in different time-space routines at work, school, traveling, and so on. In this sense online exchanges and daily Internet use are adding a new dimension, rearticulating practices of everyday life and lived spaces. (Valentine 2006, 370)

While there may be an element of truth to this, I am less inclined than they to insist upon an essential difference between new digital communication technologies and earlier "tools of networking," such as the telephone. What is important for thinking about transformations in the way love is lived is, I think, Stone's point about presence in shared social spaces. The telephone and the Internet, it seems, allow for intentional social interaction between agents—including intimate and transformative engagement between family members—that is not grounded "in the physical facticity of human bodies" (Stone 2001, 17). Women have long used the telephone as a vehicle for sustaining relationships across cities, countries, and continents; it is largely men who have traditionally viewed the phone as merely a vehicle for transmitting information (Rakow and Navarro 1993; Honey 1994). It is in order to capture the array of technologies that may be understood as "arenas for social experience" for at least some users that I speak here simply of "technologies of co-presence."

What all technologies of co-presence have in common is that they restructure—to a greater or lesser degree—our experiences of ourselves as agents in space and time. As Poster (2001) notes, "the vectors of space and time are drastically reconfigured" by the computer. Bodies move almost instantaneously through space and time with/in the technological vehicle; "the simultaneity of e-mail and chat modes on the Internet completely erases spatial factors and implodes time" (26). It would be inaccurate to indicate that the telephone "erases space" or "implodes time" in the same ways as the Internet; nonetheless, as the Bell telephone slogan "reach out and touch someone" indicated, the phone does allow us to move through space and time with/in it. This experience of moving through space and time becomes intensified with cellular phone technologies that allow us to reach out (and be reached) wherever we may be. The cell phone may thus be envisioned as "an entry-level, cyborg technology" (Clark 2003, 15).

For some, like cultural studies theorist Paul Virilio, the technologies by which space and time are transgressed give rise to dystopian anxieties (see Virilio 1986, 1995). In *La vitesse de liberation*, Virilio worries that online chat groups and other social spaces may promote forms of eroticism that threaten to destroy loving relationships and undermine fundamental social institutions such as the family:

> The end of the supremacy of physical proximity in the megalopolis of the postindustrial era will not simply encourage the spread of the single-parent family. It provokes a further more radical rupture between man and woman, threatening directly the future of sexual reproduction . . . the Parmenidean rupture between masculine and feminine principles broadens to allow remote acts of love. (Virilio 1995, 130)

Virilio's dystopian vision highlights the heteronormative anxieties underlying concerns about social spaces ungrounded by relations of physical proximity. As Poster notes, it is not the family—much less love itself—that is endangered by relationships without physical presence. What is threatened is a particular historic arrangement, namely, the heterosexual, nuclear family (Poster 2001, 115). At the same time technologies of co-presence undermine the normativity of the nuclear family formation, however, they enable, promote, and respond to new forms of love and families. In queering time and space, technologies of co-presence make room for queer love and queer families. As Halberstam (2005) notes, the models of temporality and place-making practices that emerge within postmodernism allow for creative, non-normative organizations of community, identity, embodiment, and agency (6). This includes new forms of relationships between mothers and children and new forms of maternal identity, maternal embodiment, and maternal agency.

RESPONSIBILITY FOR BOUNDARIES

In contrast to Virilio's claim that technologies of co-presence threaten the reproductive family and thus humanity's future, Haraway (1991) argues that coming to terms with our cyborg identities includes rejecting the dichotomy between us (as vulnerable subjects) and machines (as threatening objects). It thus allows us to accept our pleasure—including maternal pleasure—in machine skills and technological communications not as a sin (or some sort of false consciousness) but simply as an aspect of embodiment:

> The machine is not an *it* to be animated, worshipped, and dominated. The machine is us, our processes, an aspect of our embodiment. We can be responsible for machines; *they* do not dominate or threaten us. We are responsible for boundaries; we are they. (Haraway 1991, 180, emphases in original)

What does it mean for a cyborg mother to be responsible for boundaries? How do boundaries oppress and/or liberate us? And how can boundaries assist or detract from our ability to love and be loved? In addressing these questions in a postmodern era, feminists studying technology have largely focused on the virtual boundary between the public and private spheres. There has, moreover, been considerable ambivalence about this boundary. On the one hand, feminists have long been critical of the distinction between the public and the private, sensing that women's oppression is closely linked to their relegation to the (devalued) private sphere and their (unpaid) responsibilities therein. Insofar as a variety of technologies of co-presence (e-mail, the Internet, instant messaging, cell phones, pagers, and so forth) have permitted the blurring of boundaries between the public and private spheres, these technologies free us from rigid constraints on where we must be when. They enable us to be at work while at home and at home while at work. On the other hand, many feminists are also simultaneously wary of this blurring of boundaries between work and home, sensing that it "extend[s] work and one's availability into all periods of time and into all places," thus making it difficult to be present to those with whom one is (at work or at play) in physical proximity (Rakow and Navarro 1993, 148; see also Edley 2001; Gurstein 2001).

What has gone largely unnoticed in this debate over dismantling or protecting the boundary between the public and private aspects of our lives is the way in which there are also boundaries *within* the public and, as I discuss here, *within* the private aspects of our lives. These too are boundaries that communication technologies permit us to transgress, and these transgressions require equal attention and responsibility.

It is somewhat surprising, given widespread feminist awareness that the nuclear family is a somewhat mythical creature, that so little feminist attention has been given to the geographical and emotional boundaries that exist within the private sphere. In addition to the lack of geographical proximity to our extended kin networks, the postmodern era has witnessed a proliferation of commuter relationships between adult partners and between parents and children in the case of separation and/or divorce. The way in which people are "doing" family has changed radically in recent decades (Morgan 1999), as have "traditional patterns for delivering love and care" (Valentine 2006, 368). The postmodern family, as feminist philosopher Cheshire Calhoun (1997) notes (and Virilio [1995] fears), is a family configured by affectional choices rather than biology or proximity. This both requires and enables intimacy to be lived differently.

I have been suggesting here that technologies of co-presence can transform our lived experiences of intimacy, providing us with a means of embodying love in queer space and time. It has simultaneously extended our responsibilities and our abilities to respond to others with whom we are in a relationship. It is, I think, the extended responsibilities (here as with work) that may be experienced as oppressive. The extension of our abilities to respond, however, may be experienced as liberating.

Like several of the "remote mothers" interviewed by Rakow and Navarro (1993), I originally refused to purchase a cell phone because of resistance to additional responsibility. I emphatically did not want to be accessible to others—at work or at home—all of the time. In retrospect, however, this stance manifested a particular standpoint of privilege—namely, the standpoint of being an administrator with staff who could competently handle matters in my absence and take messages for me and the standpoint of being a primary breadwinner in a family that included a husband with flexible work that accommodated my children's needs during the weekdays. My stance also reflected my ability to respond in physically embodied ways to the needs of others (colleagues and children) who might need my reply. It was permissible to be out of (virtual) touch sometimes because most of the time I was within (physical) reach: as an administrator, I was in the office for extended periods of time every weekday, and as the member of an intact nuclear family, I was at home with my children almost every night and weekend.

The embodiment of my work and family life has since shifted significantly, however. After stepping down from administration, I volunteered to work at a satellite campus and began to commute between cities and campuses on a regular basis. Around the same time, I chose to separate from my husband, and we mutually agreed to a joint custody arrangement wherein we, as co-parents, time-shared a family home (where our children consistently lived) and an apartment (where we each lived separately on alternating weeks when we were not with our children in the family home). On some of my noncustodial weeks, I lived not in the apartment but with my new partner at her home. Hence, in addition to commuting between two workplaces, I was regularly commuting among three homes. These lived divisions within my public sphere and especially within my private sphere could only be transgressed by embracing a cyborg identity and, in particular, the identity of a cyborg mother.

I frequently refer to my cell phone as my electronic umbilical cord, and this is, indeed, how I experience it—as an extension of my body that sustains and nourishes my relationship with my now teenage daughters. Sometimes this is a frustrating part of my identity—for example, when I am awoken from sleep by the phone's ring in the middle of the night because of a child angered by frustrations or frightened by nightmares, or when I am called away from my work because a child has missed her school bus or forgotten a needed item. Their father is sleeping in the same house as they, and working in the same city, but I, several miles away, am the one being interrupted. Like the breastfeeding mother, I resent at these moments feeling like the only parent to sustain my children and thus the only parent deprived of time to sleep or work. On the other hand, the umbilical cord, unlike perhaps the breast, is a two-directional connection for which I am grateful. Yes, my daughters have greater access to me, but I too have greater access to them. A greater responsibility to be available, yes, but also a greater knowledge of their lives, a stronger and more consistent connection to them than I would otherwise enjoy. When my daughter phones me (cell phone to cell phone) from the school bus on her way home, she is considerably more enthusiastic and informative regarding her day at school than she is in a face-to-face dinner conversation. Indeed, as my daughters have become teenagers, family meals have largely become a thing of the past: my youngest daughter is apt to be involved in an after-school activity of some sort; my elder daughter remains glued to her computer, chatting with friends in virtual space.

Oliver comments on the connection between responsibility and what she calls "response-ability" (the ability to respond) as the foundation of personal subjectivity. She says:

> We are obligated to respond to our environment and other people in ways that open up rather than close off the possibility of response. This obligation is an obligation to life itself. . . . Subjectivity is founded on the ability to respond to, and address, others. . . . Insofar as subjectivity is made possible by the ability to respond, response-ability is its founding possibility. The responsibility inherent in subjectivity has the double sense of the condition of possibility of response, response-ability, on the one hand, and the ethical obligation to respond and to enable response-ability from others born out of that founding possibility, on the other. (Oliver 2001, 15)

If, as Oliver contends, subjectivity is response-ability—the ability to respond and to enable responsiveness from others (91), then my subjectivity is enhanced by the various electronic umbilical cords without which it would be difficult for me to respond to and enable response from my daughters. As Clark (2003) indicates, cyborg technologies "impact what we feel capable of doing, where we feel we are located, and what kinds of problems we find ourselves capable of solving" (34). By technologies of co-presence, I become potentially capable of mothering, of feeling—indeed being—close to my daughters and caring for them, despite physical distance. I can—regardless of where I am physically located—sing lullabies to my daughters when they have nightmares, kiss them good night when they miss me, empathize with them about romantic breakups, remind them and be reminded about important tasks and events, hear or read about the highlights and low moments of their days, and share with them my important moments and daily routines as well. I can be present in their lives and they in mine. Technologies of co-presence allow me to open up the possibility of responses delivered in *both* directions, and my identity as a cyborg is thus essential to my maternal subjectivity and not merely an adjunct to it.

CHOOSING LOVE, CHOOSING FAMILY

While technologies of co-presence do serve to enable "presence at a distance," they should not be seen "merely as imperfect attempts to recreate real world relationships" (Clark 2003, 184). Such technologies also enable new forms of personal contact, presence, and relationship than may be forged in relationships of physical proximity. They allow us to not only reconfigure domestic space and time, for example, but also to transform familial intimacy—and, in particular, maternal love—itself. Cyborg mothering is thus a practice that enables us to resist self-sacrificing ideals of motherhood. Such practices are especially important in the context of the "new momism" that insists on standards of perfection for mothering that are both unrealistic and debilitating for women (Douglas and Michaels 2004; see also Warner 2005). Technologies of co-presence do not require—from mothers or others—that we respond *without thinking* to all calls on our time and attention. Instead, they enable the critical distance necessary for love that is reflective and transformative.

To see the importance of distance to the feminist transformation of maternal identity and practice, it is useful to consider the reasons mothers leave their children—for work, for sexual freedom, or for other autonomous pursuits. Examining the story of Lilith, a woman who chose to leave her husband and children, sociologist Petra Büskens (2004) asks, "What happens to motherhood when it occurs outside the conventional nuclear or single-parent family?" (106). Her answer is that mothering, as a practice, is reinvented. The act of leaving, Büskens suggests, "can be understood as one way of resisting the totalising institution of self-sacrificing/desexualizing mothering" (109). By leaving her familial home, a mother "opens up the space to be something other than a mother," creating a room—and perhaps even a *home*—of her own. Once she has established her own autonomy, Lillith reestablishes a connection with her children, ultimately inviting her teenage daughter and sons to share this space with her, but as contributing members of a shared household manifesting *mutual* care and responsibility. By "altering the terms and spaces from which she mothers," according to Büskens, she "repositions the whore within the madonna, or the woman within the mother," thus deconstructing notions of selfless, asexual, instinctual mothering (109). In view of Lillith's return to mothering, Büsken contends, Lillith is best understood not as leaving her *children* but, rather, as leaving "the hegemonic *institution* of mothering" (2004, 116, emphasis added). Leaving, for Lillith and others like her, may be most accurately viewed as "a *strategic withdrawal on the mother's behalf geared to disrupt and reorganise the terms on which parenting is conventionally organized*" (2004, 117, emphasis in original).

Cyborg mothering may likewise be seen as a strategy for reorganizing the terms of mothering. Communication technologies—or technologies of co-presence, as I have been calling them—make it possible for mothers to live autonomous lives outside the confines of the nuclear family on an intermittent or a more permanent basis. Doing so need not require "leaving" one's children but instead intentionally and consciously reorganizing the terms on which, and spaces and times in which, mother and child are present to one another.

According to bell hooks (2000), love is a choice. Love is not, however, always experienced that way. Love may often feel involuntary and beyond our control as captured by the phrase "falling into love." Or it may feel obligatory, as though we have no option but to love another, as a mother feels obliged to love her children. For cyborgs, however, love is more clearly a choice. The would-be cyborg lover does not just fall, against her will, into her lover's arms. She makes conscious decisions, for example, to say this rather than that in her electronic correspondence and to send or not send her flirtatious messages. Similarly, the cyborg mother does not just instinctively respond to her child's cry. She makes conscious decisions to turn the baby monitor, cell phone, online indicator, or other communication device on or off. And each time a communications device beckons her, she must make a conscious decision to answer or not answer the call. Cyborg love is thus more likely to be experienced as the practice of freedom. Through various circuits and send and delete buttons and on and off switches, we can, in Oliver's (2001) words, "choose to close ourselves off to others or we can choose to try to open ourselves toward others" (220).

In addition to choosing whether to open ourselves to others, we choose how to open ourselves to others. And we leave records of our choices—their traces are on voice mail, message machines, e-mail archives, and social networking "bulletins" and "walls." These traces do not guarantee, but they do make it more likely that we will be vigilant about our choices on each occasion that we make them. The secret lover hesitates to leave a message on her lover's answering machine, for fear it will be overheard and in that hesitation has the opportunity to reflect on what she is doing. The cyborg mother chooses her tone of voice and words to her child to more carefully reflect loving concern when she reprimands or cautions her child via electronic communication than she might in the exasperation of the in-person moment. Moreover, where vigilance is not practiced at the moment of decision making, the historical record left enables learning through post-partum analysis and interpretation. As Oliver, following hooks, also suggests, it is "only through vigilant reinterpretation and elaboration of our own performance" of opening ourselves toward others that we can maintain a loving attitude: "love is not something we choose once and for all. Rather, it is a decision that must be constantly reaffirmed through the vigilance of self-reflection" (2001, 220–21).

This is, then, the liberating aspect of loving from afar. As Oliver (2001) notes, space is not empty, and thus distance need not be experienced as "unbridgeable, empty, or alienating" (213). It is "the gaps or spaces between" the lover and the beloved, the mother and child, that open up possibilities for "communication and communion" that may exist, but are not as readily discernable, when we are in close proximity or enmeshed in relationships that seem "natural" rather than voluntarily constructed (221). Insofar as cyborg identities enable this form of subjectivity, we would do well to embrace, rather than resist, them. Technologies of co-presence are not artificial and inadequate bridges between subjects. Instead, they make possible extensions and transformations of ourselves that engage in the critical self-reflection necessary to loving one another consciously and intentionally across emotional and cognitive, as well as geographical and temporal, boundaries.

REFERENCES

Büskens, P. 2004. From perfect housewife to fishnet stockings and not quite back again: One mother's story of leaving home. In *Mother outlaws: Theories and practices of empowered mothering*, ed. A. O'Reilly, 105–22. Toronto: Women's Press.

Calhoun, C. 1997. Family's outlaws: Rethinking the connections between feminism, lesbianism, and the family. In *Feminism and families*, ed. H. L. Nelson, 131–50. New York: Routledge.

Clark, A. 2003. *Natural-born cyborgs: Minds, technologies, and the future of human intelligence.* Oxford: Oxford University Press.

Douglas, S. J., and M. W. Michaels. 2004. *The mommy myth: The idealization of motherhood and how it has undermined women.* New York: Free Press.

Edley, P. 2001. Technology, employed mothers, and corporate colonization of the lifeworld: A gendered paradox of work and family balance. *Women and Language* 24:2: 28–35.

Franklin, M. 2001. Inside out: Postcolonial subjectivities and everyday life online. *International Feminist Journal of Politics* 3: 387–422.

Friedan, B. 1963. *The feminine mystique.* New York: Dell.

Gurley, P. 2001. *Wired to the world, chained to the home: Telework in daily life.* Vancouver: University of British Columbia Press.

Halberstam, J. 1998. Automating gender: Postmodern feminism in the age of the intelligent machine. In *Sex/Machine: Readings in culture, gender and technology*, ed. P. Hopkins, 468–83. Bloomington: Indiana University Press.

———. 2005. *In a queer time and place: Transgender bodies, subcultural lives.* New York: New York University Press.

Haraway, D. 1991. *Simians, cyborgs, and women: The reinvention of nature.* New York: Routledge.

Hastings, P. Belle. 2002. The cyborg mommy: User's manual. Excerpted in *Art Journal* 59:2: 78–87.

———. 2006. Cyborg mommy. http://www.icehousedesign.com/cyborg_mommy/ home.html.

Holmes, M. 2004. An equal distance? Individualisation, gender, and intimacy in distance relationships. *Sociological Review* 10: 180–200.

Honey, M. 1994. The maternal voice in the technological universe. In *Representations of motherhood*, ed. D. Bassin, M. Honey, and M. M. Kaplan, 220–39. New Haven, CT: Yale University Press.

hooks, b. 2000. *All about love: New visions.* New York: William and Morrows.

Morgan, D. 1999. Risk and family practices: Accounting for change and the fluidity in family life. In *The new family*, ed. E. B. Silva and C. Smart, 13–30. London: Sage.

Oliver, K. 2001. *Witnessing: Beyond recognition.* Minneapolis: University of Minnesota Press.

Poster, M. 2001. *What's the matter with the Internet?* Minneapolis: University of Minnesota Press.

Rakow, L., and V. Navarro. 1993. Remote mothering and the parallel shift: Women meet the cellular telephone. *Critical Studies in Mass Communication* 10:2: 144–57.

Stone, A. R. 2001. *The war of desire and technology at the close of the mechanical age.* Cambridge, MA: MIT Press.

Valentine, G. 2006. Globalizing intimacy: The role of information and communication technologies in maintaining and creating relationships. *Women's Studies Quarterly* 34:1, 2: 365–93.

Virilio, P. 1986. *Speed and politics: An essay on dromology.* Translated by P. Camiller. New York: Verso.
———. 1995. *La vitesse de liberation.* Paris: Galilee.
Warner, J. 2005. *Perfect madness: Motherhood in the age of anxiety.* New York: Riverhead.
Warner, M. 1991. Introduction: Fear of a queer planet. *Social Text* 29: 3–17.

FOUR

"Mommyblogging *Is* a Radical Act"

Weblog Communities and the Construction of Maternal Identities

LISA HAMMOND

We readers and authors of parenting blogs are looking for a representation of authentic experience that we're not getting elsewhere. We sure as hell aren't getting it from the parenting magazines. If you want to find out how to make nutritious muffins that look like kitty cats, you can read those. But a parenting magazine will never help you feel less alone, less stupid, less ridiculous. This is the service I think parenting blogs provide—we share our lopsided, slightly hysterical, often exaggerated but more or less authentic experiences. If one blogger writes about, say, her bad behavior at the doctor's office, then maybe at some point, some freaked-out new mother is going to read that and feel a little better—less stupid, less ridiculous—about her own breakdown at the pediatrician's.
—Alice Bradley, *Finslippy* (qtd. in Camahort 2006)

How could I tell you how healing it's been both on the internet and in my real life to find women I really love?
—Melissa Summers, *Suburban Bliss*

When Melissa Summers's son Max started preschool, she was not concerned about his adjustment; after all, he is a bright boy who throws himself happily into social situations.[1] On the contrary, Summers had "big plans" for herself, ranging from yoga and browsing in the bookstore and volunteering in both of her children's classrooms to something very simple, staring "at the emptiness of my house." In fact, those five hours of freedom each week for a woman who stays home with two small children sounded like cause for celebration. While Summers watched other mothers crying as they left their children, she repressed her desire for champagne because her son's preschool was "a religious based program in a church and in public I like to pretend I'm like the other mothers." Or at least when she is face-to-face with them. Back home at her computer, though, it is another story: "Only to you, Internet," she writes, "do I admit to the joy I feel. I may fake a tear or two, but really . . . I'll be light-headed with all the freedom."[2] Summers is the author of *Suburban Bliss: Birth Control via the Written Word*, a Weblog, or blog, about her life—a type of journal published on the Internet. And "Only to you, Internet" is a huge audience, one writers everywhere would envy; *Suburban Bliss* receives an average of 4,041 hits daily and has surpassed 2 million hits.[3] While Summers's account of maternal ambivalence is not especially unusual today, her very public expression of it is. For many "ordinary" women, such conversations happen quietly, with close friends. While Summers's crocodile tears in public indicate her awareness of the potential judgment inherent in such overt expressions, her choice to reveal that ambivalence to the global audience she personifies as intimate, accepting, and cozy—"Only to you, Internet"—is in fact surprisingly new in the American culture of motherhood. While Summers might not characterize her blog's intent or purpose in this language precisely, she is one of many women bloggers who appear to be writing specifically to debunk contemporary mythologies of motherhood and to create alternate individual and community conceptions of maternal identity.

While discussions and redefinitions of motherhood are abundant today, authors such as Adrienne Rich (*Of Woman Born*, 1976) and Anne Lamott (*Operating Instructions: A Journal of My Son's First Year*, 1993) are widely regarded in much scholarship as the mothers or grandmothers of the contemporary conversation about visions of realistic motherhood—and these "seminal" texts are less than thirty-five years old, in many cases barely older than the young mothers who might read them today. Certainly there are older foundational texts of mothering literature, including Charlotte Perkins Gilman's "The Yellow Wallpaper" (1892) and Kate Chopin's *The Awakening* (1899), but often these portraits of maternal identity are extreme, with female characters driven to insanity or suicide by the strict and unfulfilling roles of women, wives, and mothers in their cultures. On the other extreme, of course, exists a plethora of cultural messages about the job of mothering, not only in the parenting magazines loudly proclaiming from grocery store checkout lanes everywhere that a mother's largest parenting problem might be how to while away a lazy summer afternoon tie-dyeing T-shirts, but also in the dozens of books offering parenting advice, their covers illustrated with hazy, airbrushed paintings of contemplative expectant mothers or laughing families rolling in the grass together. As Andrea Buchanan (2004) writes in "The Secret Life of Mothers: Maternal Narrative, Momoirs, and the Rise of the Blog," "What is a mother to do when the writing she wants to read isn't there? When the only discussion about maternal ambivalence is the one in the glossy magazine about whether to get the Bugaboo or the Frog stroller?"

For many of those mothers, blogs like Summers's *Suburban Bliss*, Heather Armstrong's *Dooce*, Michelle Lamar's *White Trash Mom*, Liz's *Mom-101*, Jenn Satterwhite's *Mommy Needs Coffee*, Alice Bradley's *Finslippy*, and Eden Marriott Kennedy's *Fussy* offer the middle ground that Buchanan notes has been so sorely missing. These mothers, whom Buchanan (2004) characterizes above all as "resourceful," "who do not find themselves in what they read have begun to create their own narrative and to publish it in a place where anyone with access to a computer can find it: the Internet." Online, Summers's and other writers' experience of rejoicing in their limited personal time free of their children, or other obviously less-than-June Cleaver maternal behaviors, is increasingly common and accepted, despite the trolls lurking in judgment, always ready to criticize a mother's choices by leaving nasty comments. Blogging offers a venue for mothers to represent their lived experiences of mothering as a means of building a more realistic vision of maternal roles, one that resists assigning judgments and feeding the guilt that has permeated the literature of mothering from the beginnings of the twentieth century.

What resonates about Summers's experience for many of those readers is her openness about "the simple fact that raising a child is not fun all the time. It's not always profound and awe inspiring"[4]—but her writing about it is always honest, usually funny, and often poignant. Although most bloggers have a far more modest audience, Summers is only one of thousands of women today routinely taking advantage of the easy availability of blogging software to write daily about the experience of motherhood for all the world to read. These women read and write in a quest for authentic narratives of being mothers, and in choosing to represent their lives through technology—and to represent those lives widely and publicly—they actively rewrite maternal narratives, refusing to accept simplistic or stereotypical notions of mothering and instead creating more complex representations of women's lives. Certainly women have sought in literature before alternative visions of their lives, but blogs allow for a fundamentally new technology of approaching the literature of mothering, opening doors to defining motherhood through multiple lenses, through a literal community of women who choose the blogs that speak best to their own understanding of being a mother—and if a woman cannot find that vision, then she can create it herself.

EVOLVING GENRES:
BLOGS AND BUILDING SHARED CULTURAL IDENTITY

Women have always sought communities in which to parent—for instance, it is a commonplace that the contemporary playdate is often as much an opportunity for mothers to socialize and seek support as it is a chance for children to play together, sometimes more so. However, finding the right women in a limited geographic area can prove difficult, leaving a mother who parents differently isolated. Blogging and reading blogs provide a fundamentally new means of representing an individual experience of mothering and at the same time offer to the public that new conception of mothering. While this type of writing may not require advanced technology skills, it does require a sharp eye for observation and the ability to make observations without prescriptively writing mothering for the audience. Indeed, resistance to idealized notions of perfect mothers seems the most common trait among the many blogs written by women to represent their lives and experiences as mothers.

A certain elite group of bloggers (those women who often started out simply as ordinary mothers with a computer and a new baby) has gone on to make a living blogging (Armstrong's *Dooce*) and publishing books based on those writings (Mimi Smartypants's *The World According to Mimi Smartypants* and Catherine Newman's *Waiting for Birdy*). It is important to note here, however, that many of these women who have become prominent bloggers, featured in national news media, were not, in fact, professional writers, nor did they begin blogging with aspirations of national readership. Summers herself has been featured in articles published in the *New York Times* and the Chicago *Tribune* and appeared on the *Today* show, but she notes about *Suburban Bliss*, "Traffic is of course something a personal blogger loves . . . but I loved writing this site when I had 8 people reading it."[5] The phenomenon of publishing one's personal musing or the details of one's private life online is an interesting one, deeply immersed in the assumption that the writer seeks an audience—otherwise why publish one's work on the Internet? Madeleine Sorapure (2003) writes about online diarists that "these writers obviously and intentionally are creating public documents. Even if no one other than the author reads the diary, it is available on the Web for others to read, and is to some extent put on the Web precisely for others to read" (9). Like Summers, many of these women simply write because they want to, need to, for very small audiences and for their own purposes. Sometimes, though, because of how connections are forged in the blogosphere, at times those audiences grow both wonderfully and unexpectedly. Lena Karlsson (2007) notes in "Desperately Seeking Sameness: The Processes and Pleasures of Identification in Women's Diary Blog Reading" that what she calls a "diary blog" "is deeply personal, emotion-laden, and thrives on readerly attachment—readers are invited to enter into and identify with the thoughts and feelings of others; it runs and runs in installments with no end in sight, just like the feminine genre par excellence, the TV soap" (139). As readers stumble across blogs in the random and not-so-random webs of Google searches and listings of favorite blogs and then form attachments with the authors of the new sites they have discovered, they build connections that enable communities to develop online that can literally change contemporary culture.

Melissa Summers, the author of *Suburban Bliss,* in many respects provides an excellent example of how ordinary women keeping a blog and participating in the blogosphere's culture of interaction can not only find support for their own visions of mothering but also gain national prominence in doing so, advocating publicly for more diverse and positive models of mothering. In her blog, Summers positions herself as being outside the realm of "ordinary" parenting, ambivalent about the accepted wisdom of what a mother should be, but still seeking a community. She writes, for example, about joining a local chapter of an organization for stay-at-home mothers, despite her self-proclaimed "general disdain for large groups of women," in addition to her "general distrust of mothers, especially mothers who stay at home because it's 'The Best Thing'. Because I don't actually believe there is such a thing." Summers joined, however, "because, just like in every group, there are always some nice people. There may even be people who have a realistic view of motherhood. People who are maybe as frazzled and overwhelmed by the job as I am."[6] In seeking this "realistic view of motherhood" both online and face-to-face, Summers resists identification with romanticized notions of mothering, instead focusing on "my strict policy of not sugar coating the hardest parts of raising small children."[7] Bloggers often represent their experiences online for the possibility that individual women's stories function as an ameliorative balm to widespread images of idealized motherhood. For example, the editors of *Mommybloggers*, a Web site created to highlight the diversity of women's blog writing about motherhood, describe their intent specifically as "inclusive," explaining that

> Mommybloggers does not intend to create a flawless polished image of what a perfect mother looks like. Many mothers, for fear of seeming like bad mothers, hesitate to share their disasters, mishaps and insecurities. We will not perpetuate judgements about what is and what is not good mothering. We want to share humor, insights, fears, joys and frustrations through our stories—your stories—as we learn more about the power of mommyblogging. ("What Mommybloggers" n.d.)

Crafting "our stories—your stories" through blogs, sharing those narratives online, creates a vast possibility for social change within the communities of the Web.

Because blogs are an ideal medium for sharing personal narratives, they are often compared to journals or diaries and indeed do serve a function similar to these more conventional genres of self-expression, but in fact they are a uniquely new genre of contemporary writing.[8] With their episodic nature, regular dated entries, sometimes brief and other times longer, blogs resemble their paper and print cousins, the diary or the journal, and, to a lesser extent, the memoir or autobiography, and each of these genres can be made to serve the same primary function of allowing the author the opportunity to define an individual identity, literally to write a self into being. But diaries and journals and even autobiographies written explicitly for publication lack the wide public access, immediacy of reaching an audience, and opportunity for an audience to participate in the narrative creation of the written self. While that creation of identity is often more fragmented and less unified than more traditional autobiographical genres, each entry posted builds on previous ones to create over time a portrait of the author akin to that presented in the traditional literary genre of the memoir. Nancy K. Miller (2002) in *But Enough about Me: Why We Read Other People's Lives* notes that "[w]hat seems to connect memoir writers and their readers is a bond created through identifications" (2). The act of reading one mother's life can create a bond, allowing the reader to understand the cultural role of mothers, the individual author's understanding of how those roles manifest themselves in her own life, and the reader's own relationship with these roles, the common elements of their lives as mothers.

Shared cultural identity builds slowly in traditional print genres, as a book may take a year or more to appear in print, and then reader and writer often have no interaction outside the act of reading itself. On the Internet, however, Weblogs allow for an immediate experience of community, unlike their paper counterparts, most especially in the ways they can serve as a foundational element for community formation, and, consequently, for the formation of a community identity, a shared identification of the author with readers. Unlike diaries or journals, which generally are private or read by a limited number of known or approved readers, or memoirs and autobiographies, which typically are written to be shared in print form with a wider audience, blogs are published online for any reader with both Internet access and the desire to seek out such writings. And a blogger need not have any particular technical expertise to publish her ideas about motherhood—many blogging programs exist that allow a writer to create and maintain a blog as quickly and easily as one might send an e-mail, with no complex technical apparatus necessary. Although a number of serious bloggers who have now achieved status as nationwide writers do make use of sophisticated design and publishing platforms, as does Armstrong in *Dooce,* many women blog in low-tech ways, practicing instead of technical skills the knowledge of textual construction of an individual identity within a community of readers. Whether a new mother blogging mostly with her friends and family in mind or a professional writer who makes her living blogging, most bloggers seek to expand their audiences, and many writers employ specific features of blogging software and conventions of blog readerships to seek out readers and, indeed, to involve them in growing communities of women writing online about motherhood.

Specifically, the inclusion of reader comments and blog rolls (listings of blogs the author reads regularly and recommends) facilitates the construction of communities of women writing about motherhood in ways that print memoirs cannot reproduce. Because blog software allows the author to choose whether to provide spaces in which readers may comment on what they read, a writer may post a blog entry and receive comments within minutes. Often readers will comment on other readers' comments, as well as on the original post, and it is not uncommon for the blog author to engage readers in the comment areas as well. The commenting function of blogs thus allows for the immediacy of a response that shapes the writing of the next element of the narrative; the author forms relationships with her readers. As Laurie McNeill (2003) notes in "Teaching an Old Genre New Tricks: The Diary on the Internet," "The reader of an online diary therefore actively participates in constructing the narrative the diarist writes, and the identities he or she takes on in the narrative" (27). The author's ability to interact with her readership creates a constantly evolving negotiation of her role as mother and her place in Internet parenting cultures. Equally important, however, is the way that the inclusion of blog rolls creates online communities of women whose shared experiences of birth and motherhood reinforce each other, building an understanding of the maternal role that allows participants as both readers and writers to shape those roles. These communities often focus on something more specific than general parenting at large, such as pregnancy loss, or adoptive families, or ethnic identifications. The author of one blog, finding another that resonates for her personally, links to that blog on her site; since most serious bloggers use software to determine where traffic originates from, such links are often reciprocated. In some cases, reciprocal links and reading result in firm friendships, even at times transcending online spaces and moving "IRL," "in real life." Such practices mirror conventions of print publications; as McNeill (2003) observes, reciprocal links "not only connect readers and diarists, but also act as legitimating forces—the online diary community's version of print-culture practices of celebrity endorsements or book-jacket blurbs" (34). Cynthia G. Franklin (1997), in *Writing Women's Communities: The Politics and Poetics of Contemporary Multigenre Anthologies*, explores the ways in which print anthologies constitute "sites in which cultural identities are being constructed" (4); maternal identities, then, may be defined even more rapidly, and indeed, may flourish on the Internet, which provides mothers who write with an ideal venue in which to create authoritative maternal voices as both individuals and community members. Effectively, women blogging about mothering and those who read these women's blogs contribute to the multiplicity of voices developing new cultural definitions of motherhood, definitions that are both individual and distinct but also communal in nature, a collective memory through which women rewrite the roles of mothering in contemporary culture.

The notion that autobiographical writings might be a site of community is not a new idea; Sidonie Smith and Julia Watson (1996), in *Getting a Life: Everyday Uses of Autobiography*, explore the political ramifications of autobiography, deconstructing the term itself in its emphasis on the traditional (male) notion of "the imagining of 'autobiographical' and of individual lives as 'representative' of a community of lives" (5). In a postmodern resistance to the representative life, Smith and Watson continue, in "everyday occasions autobiographical narrators move out of isolation and loneliness into a social context in which their stories resonate with the stories of others in a group" (15). Envisioning autobiographical writing as a single person's story obscures the ways in which such texts function as a social construct of personal *and* communal identity—whether the author intends such a reading or not. Often, however, women writing personal narratives write with deliberate intent to construct what some critics have called virtual communities, or discourse or interpretative communities, and these constructions of community are inherently political. In her introduction to *Women's Life Writing and Imagined Communities*, Cynthia Huff (2005) discusses Benedict Anderson's conception of nation as imagined community, noting that "any imagined community, including one that is seemingly innocuous, is not without political dimensions nor are its foundations beyond questioning" (9). An imagined community of mothers is often one created by media images—how mothers are represented on television programs and commercials, for example—or through political contexts, as has been the case with the now ubiquitous political demographic of the soccer mom, but women blogging about their experiences as women and mothers often refuse to accept these pat cultural definitions of their roles. John M. Swales's (1990) discussion of the term *discourse community* best defines the way bloggers create discourse communities; defining characteristics of such communities, Swales notes that they must have not only "common public goals" but also "participatory mechanisms" designed for community exchange (24-25). Thus the blog itself becomes a self-authenticating genre of such expression; mothers in blog discourse communities must have not only the desire and ability to create a blog, link to others, and engage in an interchange with other mothers/readers, they must also have the desire to explore their identities as women and as mothers and have some sense of the community of mothers to which they wish to belong.

"MOMMYBLOGGING IS A RADICAL ACT!": CHANGING THE WORLD ONE WOMAN AND ONE WORD AT A TIME

As blogging about motherhood has begun to attain wide-ranging recognition, including media coverage in the *New York Times* (see Hochman 2005), women bloggers have attempted to identify the political community created by their seemingly individual and personal efforts. Since 2005, for example, women have gathered for the national BlogHer convention, with the number of attendees and participants growing from more than 300 women and men to over 1,000 in 2008. Katie Couric invited a group of "Mommy Bloggers" to participate in an informal discussion broadcast on You Tube, which in three months of being posted in April 2008 had been viewed 25,104 times.

Elisa Camahort (2006) describes an incident at the BlogHer 2005 conference that provoked considerable discussion in the community of women bloggers:

> During last year's closing session of BlogHer an attendee told her fellow attendees that if they "stopped blogging about themselves they could change the world." When I heard that I interpreted it to be directed at all of us who blog about our lives and the events therein big and small, but some (maybe most) of the MommyBloggers in the room felt the remark was directed at them. Seems that more than a few MommyBloggers felt there was a distinction being drawn by some other bloggers between people blogging about "important" stuff, and people "just" blogging about their feelings, their families and the joys and struggles of parenting.

After this comment, Camahort tells the story of one prominent blogger, Alice Bradley, the author of *Finslippy*, who "held up her hand, waited patiently until we got a microphone to her, stood up, and said loud and clear: 'MommyBlogging *is* a radical act!' " Bradley, asked to elaborate on this declaration, explained that blogging provides "a representation of authentic experience that we're not getting elsewhere," a sharing of "our lopsided, slightly hysterical, often exaggerated but more or less authentic experiences":

> We sure as hell aren't getting it from the parenting magazines. If you want to find out how to make nutritious muffins that look like kitty cats, you can read those. But a parenting magazine will never help you feel less alone, less stupid, less ridiculous. . . . If one blogger writes about, say, her bad behavior at the doctor's office, then maybe at some point, some freaked-out new mother is going to read that and feel a little better—less stupid, less ridiculous—about her own breakdown at the pediatrician's. (qtd. in Camahort 2006)

Bradley's conception of the purpose of blogs here moves beyond seeing each individual blogger's site as solely a personal voice; instead, each blog has the capability of reaching a reader who feels isolated and changing that reader's life by offering her "authentic experience." Effectively, Bradley poses the genre of the blog as an alternative to traditional media outlets for mothering information, specifically parenting magazines, a direct manifestation of the feminist notion that the personal is political. That Bradley has chosen to represent blogging as a personal act with political implications points directly to the power of the Weblog to redefine maternal roles in self-defined communities of women—communities that have grown to spread a wide support network for mothers across the country and even worldwide.

Summers echoes Camahort's and Bradley's conviction that in small personal acts of blogging, women are writing a larger community, one that not only provides personal friendships but also one that serves a political function in the redefinition of the roles of mothering. Summers, who attended the BlogHer conference as well, describes meeting members of her blogging community at the convention in a post titled "It's like a yearbook entry: 'Stay Sweet!' " She asks, "How could I tell you how healing it's been both on the Internet and in my real life to find women I really love?" Speculating that perhaps "in the last two years since I've had this Web site I've become more comfortable with myself," she attributes this in part to the community of women readers, those who read and support her site. Through this Internet community, she concludes, she has been able to redefine her conceptions of mothering:

> Instead of being filled with self-loathing (though I still have all that) I've come to realize that motherhood can look different and still be fine. In my case, motherhood looks incredibly whiney and needy and sometimes funny. Like I said earlier, I bare my soul to the Internet and these people still like me. I have the same benefit from my real-life friends reading this Web site. Maybe that makes me more comfortable just being?[9]

Although Summers jokingly concludes this preface to her description of her yearbook community with "[p]robably I need more therapy," in fact she continues to outline the various reasons other bloggers have become so important to her: Alice, author of *Finslippy*, and Mrs. Kennedy, the nom de plume of Eden Marriott Kennedy, author of *Fussy*, are "supportive and kind and not judgmental and they love their kids and can sometimes be just as annoyed as I am by the job of raising them. They're not afraid to admit that and they aren't upset when I admit that too." Employing the metaphor of the yearbook as a means of describing the closeness of the community these women have formed—and not just these two women but many whom Summers reads regularly and met at the convention—Summers, like Bradley, locates the power and authority of blogging communities in their ability to offer alternative perspectives of a mother's life; this power is literally life altering, transforming not only the blog as a document written regularly in response to those readers but also transforming the lives of the authors.

Despite the closeness of the community of which these women have become a part, still some uneasiness exists about the redefinition of personal identity into community identities, however important. A great deal of this uneasiness comes from attempts by outsiders to disrupt those communities, which often have clearly defined codes of conduct. But comments are an option—a blogger may choose to permit them or not, and comments may also be mediated in various ways, such as a process requiring site administrators to approve comments before they appear on the site. As Lena Karlsson (2005) notes, because an author may choose whether to allow comments on her site, "a certain amount of authorial control is retained" (224). At the outset, bloggers often exercise such "authorial control" by limiting their communities, inviting in particular types of readers, and thereby defining their identities in ways that make clear the subject matter of the site, but they also do so by restricting the readership, defining those audiences that will likely refuse to accept the values of the site and its community, and may possibly transgress those values. For example, both Summers and Kennedy, in their descriptions of their sites, state up front their refusal to accept those readers who do not value the codes of the community. While both invite e-mail correspondence from readers and allow comments, neither are willing to tolerate trolls, those readers who are not part of the community and who intentionally disturb the atmosphere of the site with pointless arguments designed only to irritate, not to explore issues under discussion. In one version of her biography, Summers writes in *Suburban Bliss*:

> I love e-mail and most of what I get makes me happy inside. Some of what I get is nasty and mean and that's fine too, except don't be surprised if I publish your nasty e-mail in it's [sic] entirety. Before you hit that send button ask yourself if you want the world to see what you've written. The internet breeds very brave anonymous people. Beware if you want to be "brave" you'll have to stand up for what you "believe."[10]

Similarly, Kennedy includes "a picture of an old lady flipping you off," explaining that "It's her philosophy that I'm allowed to write about anything I want on my Web site, and if you don't like it you can go ~~fuck yourself~~ somewhere else."[11] Although Kennedy cleans up her language, changing "go fuck yourself" to "go somewhere else," by emending the text with a visible strikethrough, she makes clear her unwillingness to accept adversarial reader comments. In fact, after one "particularly stupid exchange in my comments with a person who was nuts," Kennedy explains that she developed a T-shirt for bloggers that reads "Writing well is the best revenge":

> No rational commenter could take it, this crazy person would always come back and have the last word and it was infuriating for everyone. I finally realized that the only way I could win was to follow up with a terrific post, and then another, and another, and another. That was the only way to get revenge on this jerk, to be the better writer/blogger. (qtd. in Satterwhite 2006)

Orloff (2006) notes that Kennedy has sold 500 of her T-shirts, a visible identifier of community members should they meet face-to-face and a clear indication of her success in reaching readers.[12] In some respects, however, bloggers like Summers and Kennedy define their communities as much by excluding trolls as they do by inviting in like-minded members, an indication that, however valuable Weblog communities may be, they are also conflicted to a certain extent.

The community of "mommy bloggers" is one that must routinely deal with such challenges; as a group, these women are marginalized by the very definition of their writing into the genre of Weblogs about motherhood, in many cases because they do not see their writing as being so narrowly defined. Summers expresses a vexed identity as a mommy blogger, so much so that even when meeting Alice Bradley and Mrs. Kennedy she feels uncomfortable making a direct claim about their importance to her: "For all the weeping I do, I don't know why it's so hard for me to say how Alice and Mrs. Kennedy are now among my best friends. I feel silly saying that . . . but it's true."[13] More significantly, however, when nominated for a BlogMechanics Best of the Blogs award, specifically the Best Mommy Blog, Summers at first resists identification with the very category: "When I wrote about being nominated for this award I thought, 'Is this really a Mommy blog?' and I felt kind of uncomfortable with that name." The term, she continues,

> conjures up images of happy motherhood. Tales of the wonderment in the journey of Mommy-Hood. I think of "Mommy

Blog" and I think of stories of when the baby ate and how the baby slept and I definitely don't think of all this Fucking Swearing I Do ALL THE FUCKING TIME. But again, whatever.[14]

In a similar way, in several interviews Kennedy resists the image of mothers evoked by the term *mommy blogger*, contesting the label and "being shoved into the mommy blog ghetto" (qtd. in Orloff 2006). She explains,

> I hate it. People have used it against me—both offhandedly and ferociously—to infantilize my brain and my blog and my life, non-parents who seem to think that being a mother makes you a second-class citizen; they feel perfectly free to use that term in the most demeaning way possible. It's so bloody stupid to be so prejudiced against women who are audacious enough to talk about what their lives are like as they raise young children—and do you ever see these assholes go after the dads? I could go on all day about this. (qtd. in Satterwhite 2006)

Summers and Kennedy depict a conflicted sense of identity with those communities, as do many of the authors of so-called "Mommy blogs." And such resistance makes perfect sense in light of one high-profile media incident in 2005, an event that at once brought nationwide recognition to one community of women writing about motherhood and at the same time represented a public dismissal of their efforts, damning without even faint praise.

On January 30, 2005, David Hochman published an article on the front page of the Styles section of the *New York Times*. The piece, titled "Mommy (and Me)," ostensibly provides an overview of the growing popular phenomenon of blogs written by parents about their lives and their children, but in fact harshly criticizes these parents who blog, characterizing them as narcissistic; indeed, in the line most quoted by bloggers in the flurry of commentary following the article's publication, Hochman writes that "The baby blog in many cases is an online shrine to parental self-absorption." Ironically, Hochman does discuss briefly respected print predecessors to baby blogs, explaining that "[e]xposing the dark underbelly of parenthood is not exactly new. Books like Anne Lamott's *Operating Instructions: A Journal of My Son's First Year* and Andrea J. Buchanan's *Mother Shock: Loving Every (Other) Minute of It* have made it clear that raising children is not all sunshine and sippy cups." Despite the established cultural phenomenon he cites here of attempting to represent mothering as more than the blissful 1950s-inspired "sunshine and sippy cups," Hochman continues that "[w]hat is remarkable is that being a parent has inspired so much text and that so many people seem eager to read it." Hochman's article does in fact fail to explore any of the elements that attract over 40,000 readers a day to blogs belonging to authors such as Heather Armstrong, the woman who contributed the word "Dooced" to the vernacular—someone fired for what was written on her blog; instead he focuses on his assertion that, for bloggers, "there is not a tale from the crib (no matter how mundane or scatological) that is unworthy of narration," diminishing the accomplishment of these widely read women by labeling them members of "a generation of parents ever more in need of validation" to overcome their "anxiety and uncertainty." Even Hochman's attempt at the end of the article to find positive uses for baby blogging fails in the means he chooses to express it, as he writes that "perhaps all the online venting and hand-wringing is actually helping the bloggers become better parents and better human beings."

The article immediately generated considerable commentary by bloggers and a flood of responses by their readers, most in defense of their communities and with a sense of outrage at Hochman. In their refusal to allow Hochman to define the linguistic purposes of their communities, and in their readers' support of their sites and condemnation of Hochman's rhetoric, the bloggers created a clear picture of the discourse community of women redefining their lives, first as women and then in their roles as mothers and partners. Most of the bloggers featured in the article expressed both some satisfaction with the national media coverage (the theory no doubt being that there is no such thing as bad publicity) and some dissatisfaction with the article's tone. Armstrong, of *Dooce*, sums up these two extremes in her comment on seeing the article early the morning it was published:

> I had a hard time containing my glee—not because I and some of my fellow women writers were made out to be selfish, resentful, overreacting pigs in search of validation; funny that none of us were informed that the article would run with that notion when we were interviewed—but that my child's green eyes were staring at me from the pages of a national paper.[15]

Bradley's post that morning in *Finslippy* welcomes new readers directed to her site after reading the article but also comments on the fact that Hochman spelled two of the bloggers' names incorrectly, including hers, ironically naming her as Alice *Brady*: "Of course I'm all for being mentioned in the (vaguely damning) *New York Times* article, but um,

Mr. Hochman? It's BRADLEY."[16] In his article, Hochman (2005) quoted one of Summers's comments in *Suburban Bliss*, that her son "likes cars and tutus with equal passion. . . . I think he might be gay"; Summers's response to his article employs her characteristic combination of humor with just a touch of anger; she explains that although "I'm absolutely flattered and Max will one day be totally horrified to be mentioned in this article as being GAY," "I'm also a little stunned by the tone of the piece." Perhaps, though, she "shouldn't be surprised":

> I guess I find it vaguely insulting to have this site called an "online shrine to parental self-absorption." Because all blogs are not lessons in self-absorption. We, as parents should be condemned for indulging in writing about our experiences as parents, since SURPRISE! parenting takes up 200% of our lives.
> In the end what this article shows me, once again, is that we can't win no matter what we do. If we aren't worried about our kids, we're neglectful. If we think (and write) about the things our kids do we're called hand-wringing obsessives [sic]. Hooray *New York Times* for capturing the essence of mothering![17]

If the very "essence of mothering" is that of failing—either neglectful or obsessive, self-centered or a "helicopter" parent—then it is no wonder that women like Summers and Bradley feel a need to create an alternate identity for mothers, or that many of the bloggers' readers rallied around these authors in support of their writing, their honesty, and their refusal to allow themselves to be forced into the artificial double bind of mothering constructed by such media coverage.

Although many readers simply posted a brief note expressing support of the bloggers they read, Summers's post reflects a clear pattern of reader commentary that goes beyond the nurturance that is a routine part of such communities to a recognition of the political implications of Hochman's comments as a dismissal of the women whose writing he describes. Even though the article did feature two male bloggers as well, the focus of the article was clearly on "Mommy," and many respondents read the article as an explicit commentary on mothers' parenting styles, exclusive of male parental figures, as did the author of *Laid Off Dad*, who in the comments to *Suburban Bliss* remarks about "Mommy (and Me)," "Nice title, too. Apparently writing about parenting is a penis-free zone."[18] Jen Lawrence, the author of the blog *MUBAR* (Mothered Up Beyond All Recognition), contributes the most overtly political reading of Hochman's article, posting an entry titled "The Politics of Blogging" to comment on what she sees as "elements of good old mother judgement [*sic*]." Responding to a persistent theme throughout the article that questions why any person would either want to write or read baby blogs, Lawrence explains that

> I started writing not because I was mourning the "me me me me-ness" of pre-parenthood but because I was shocked at the lack of support for new moms. And while I felt "the system" failed me big time, the voices of other women who once felt just like me carried me through the hard times. And I thought—maybe sharing my experiences would be helpful for someone else.
> Because it is cool to receive an e-mail or comment from a like-minded soul. I also write as a political act, to try to point out when marketing companies make mothers out to be a bunch of crudely drawn sterotypes [*sic*], or when the media judges mothers more harshly than her non-mother counterparts.[19]

For Lawrence, the issue focuses on why mothers are judged more harshly, as a function of their willingness to subsume their personal identity to their maternal role; why, she asks, "does society feel it has the right to police a parent's level of self-sacrifice?"

Lawrence rightly sees Hochman's interpretation of mommy blogs as simply yet another highly visible, unflattering media portrayal of mothers, worthy of comment and rebuttal but "not troubling [in] itself," more or less a blip on the radar. Within a couple of weeks the reaction to Hochman's article had largely died down, and the women returned to their usual subject matter. The article continues to be referenced periodically, including during the discussion at the "MommyBlogging Is a Radical Act" session at the 2006 BlogHer conference in San Jose, California, but in effect the publication of "Mommy (and Me)" resulted in two opportunities for these women: the introduction of new readers to their sites, and a clear expression of the rationale for blogging, both as individuals and as members of the community derisively dismissed as mommy bloggers. In one summative post from *BloggingBaby*, a commercial blog network hosting blog postings discussing parenting advice, contemporary media coverage, and even information about travel and celebrity babies, Sarah Gilbert goes so far as to thank Hochman

> for inspiring me to jump from blog, to blog, to blog all week, to discover amazing writers I hadn't been reading and rediscover ones I hadn't visited in a while, to hear all these mothers and fathers coming together in a melodic chorus about

community and voice and the power of writing it all down. And I have to say, thank God that these things weren't written in someone's journal to be discovered 80 years from now in an attic, thank the Internet that I can read them today. I'm a better parent, and a better writer, for all of you. (Gilbert 2005)

Gilbert's observation that blogs allow for the expression of these radical redefinitions of motherhood to occur in a public forum rather than in private diaries that may or may not be discovered years after the fact points to the crucial ways that the developing genre of the blog is changing our understanding of how women define their identities, how they redefine motherhood.

REDEFINING MOTHERHOOD

For many women writing about motherhood, blogging represents a personal act of expression, a means of recreating the self in a new role. For others, the scope of one's blog becomes much larger; a number of women with a more explicit professional intent have created careers through blogging, supporting themselves and their families through their individual blogs, or serving as editors and writers for blogging networks. Webzines featuring these writers as well as many others include Ariel Gore's *Hip Mama*, the now-defunct *Salon Magazine*'s Mothers Who Think features, and *Literary Mama: A Literary Magazine for the Maternally Inclined*. Each of these three magazines has resulted in print anthology publications as well. Not only are blogs and the Webzines with which they are at times associated changing how we read motherhood, but, effectively, blogs are becoming a powerful force in shaping the book publishing industry's response to women's demand for more diverse, meaningful texts on mothering.

In "The Secret Life of Mothers: Maternal Narrative, Momoirs, and the Rise of the Blog," Andrea Buchanan (2004) explains that blogs represent a "proliferation of shared experience," "a powerful way to unite women who might not otherwise feel as though they had anything in common"; women writing motherhood in this new genre "are real mothers struggling to create a narrative out of the often disjointed, complex, and simultaneously occurring events of their lives." While many of the thousands of women blogging their lives—as women *and* mothers—may not initially see the act of writing as a political one, nevertheless as their words join the multiple voices of the communities of women writing motherhood, they add their distinctive and original perspectives to a new understanding of the many roles of mothers. This multiplicity of narrative lives offers fruitful ground for exploration, a fundamental cultural rewriting of maternity in the words of hundreds and thousands of ordinary women who have chosen to do something extraordinary. For those women who become fully immersed in the Weblog communities of mothers—those who post over a period of years, who read and comment on each other's blogs, and especially the very visible few who achieve national prominence through media coverage and attendance at BlogHer—the redefinition of motherhood becomes much more conscious, an overt recognition of Alice Bradley's declaration that writing about motherhood is a "radical act." The richness of this multivoiced community continually creates new representations of motherhood, a depiction that reflects the vexed nature of mothering, how it is simultaneously funny and fearful, lonely and redemptive, mind-numbingly repetitive and unimaginably enriching. As this community continues to grow and thrive, so can we expect our understanding of motherhood to continue to evolve, allowing mothers an unprecedented voice in our literature and history.

NOTES

1. Since blogs are updated in reverse chronological order, referring to a blog's main page will take the reader to the most recent entry. In order to easily allow the reader to reference an individual blog entry, I have chosen to cite such posts in this Notes section. The entire blog itself is cited in the References at the end of this chapter, but in-text citations in the Notes section will include the author's name, the title of the blog posting, and its permalink—in other words, the constant link at which the post continually resides. Summers, "It's Like a Yearbook Entry: 'Stay Sweet!,' " http://www.suburbanbliss.net/suburbanbliss/2005/08/its_like_a_year.html.

    Most of the blogs I cite here are well-established sites, likely to remain available online as permanently as any Internet site is likely to be permanent, but given the rapidly changing and at times ephemeral nature of the Internet, I cannot guarantee that cited pages will continue to be available. Readers seeking Web sites no longer online may wish to consult the Wayback Machine at the *Internet Archive*, http://www.archive.org, for archives dating back to 1996.
2. Summers, "It's Like Motherhood without the Kids," http://www.suburbanbliss.net/suburbanbliss/2004/05/its_like_mother.html.
3. Summers's Web site statistics are compiled by SiteMeter; as of August 6, 2006, *Suburban Bliss* had received 2,025,324 total visits. See http://www.sitemeter.com/?a=stats&s=sm9suburbanbliss. More recent statistics are not posted publicly.

4. Summers, "My Own Job," http://www.suburbanbliss.net/suburbanbliss/2004/05/my_own_job.html.
5. Summers, "The Universe: Reacting to Trolls with Philosophy," http://www.suburbanbliss.net/suburbanbliss/2006/02/the_universe_re.html.
6. Summers, "Worst Playgroup Ever," http://www.suburbanbliss.net/suburbanbliss/2004/10/i_joined_my_loc.html.
7. Summers, "Bumpy Transition," http://www.suburbanbliss.net/suburbanbliss/2005/06/bumpy_transitio.html.
8. See Blood (2002) for a discussion of the origins of the blog, including the first incidents of national media coverage (4). She dates blog precursors as early as 1993, but Zuern (2003) cites 1995 as "the arrival of the Web as a fertile environment for the development of innovative forms of self-representation with potentially global audiences: personal home pages, online diaries and photo albums, Weblogs or 'blogs' " (vi). As of this writing in 2008, the National Institute for Technology and Liberal Education (NITLE) estimates the existence of 2,869,632 blogs worldwide ("NITLE Weblog Census" n.d.).

Blood (2002) notes that blogs most commonly "resemble short-form journals" with the author's "daily life" as the subject (6); Julie Rak (2005) discusses the difficulty of comparing online genres of life writing with conventional print and paper structures such as the diary and the journal, discussing from a 2003 issue of *Biography* several articles, a number of which I cite here. The concept of blogs has changed considerably since that issue, yet blogs are still routinely described as journals or diaries, suggesting a more substantial comparison than Rak implies.
9. Summers, "It's Like a Yearbook Entry: 'Stay Sweet!,' " http://www.suburbanbliss.net/suburbanbliss/2005/08/its_like_a_year.html.
10. Summers, "Biography," http://www.suburbanbliss.net/about.html, 29 July 2006.
11. Kennedy, "Hello and Welcome to *Fussy!*," http://www.fussy.org/about.html.
12. A number of well-known bloggers have significant commercial investments in their blogs, which generally develop over time as the site becomes more popular; many display ads as a means for paying for the bandwidth required to host their sites, which can run to thousands of readers, and a number sell items printed with their blogs' banners or icons. Summers, for example, has opened her own Café Press shops to sell T-shirts, bumper stickers, and coffee mugs with her "Momtini" logo, a pacifier dipped in a martini glass.
13. Summers, "Even Worms Can Reproduce . . . but Can They Write about It?," http://www.suburbanbliss.net/suburbanbliss/2005/01/even_worms_can_.html.
14. Summers, "Even Worms Can Reproduce . . . but Can They Write about It?," http://www.suburbanbliss.net/suburbanbliss/2005/01/even_worms_can_.html.
15. Armstrong, "*NY Times*, Gateway Drug to *Playboy*," http://www.dooce.com/archives/daily/01_31_2005.html.

16. Bradley, "Welcome to *Finslippy*. I'm Mrs. Brady," http://www.finslippy.typepad.com/finslippy/2005/01/welcome_to_fins.html.
17. Summers, "A Near Miss," http://www.suburbanbliss.net/suburbanbliss/2005/01/i_guess_david_h.html.
18. Comment to Summers, "A Near Miss," posted by Laid Off Dad, http://www.suburbanbliss.net/suburbanbliss/2005/01/i_guess_david_h.html#comment-3669734.
19. Lawrence, "The Politics of Blogging," http://www.tomama.blogs.com/mubar/2005/01/thanks_to_andi_.html.

REFERENCES

Armstrong, H. B. n.d. *Dooce*. http://www.dooce.com.
Blood, R. 2002. *The Weblog handbook: Practical advice for creating and maintaining your blog*. Cambridge, MA: Perseus.
Bradley, A. n.d. *Finslippy*. http://www.finslippy.com.
Buchanan, A. J. 2003. *Mother Shock: Loving Every (Other) Minute of It*. Emeryville, CA: Seal Press.
———. 2004. The secret life of mothers: Maternal narrative, momoirs, and the rise of the blog. Guest blogger on M. J. Rose's *Buzz, balls, and hype*. November 21. http://www.mjroseblog.typepad.com/buzz_balls_hype/2004/11/guest_blogger_a.html.
Camahort, E. 2006. BlogHer '06 session discussion: MommyBlogging is a radical act! *BlogHer: Where the women bloggers are*. May 20. http://www.blogher.org/node/5563.
Chopin, K. [1899] 1993. *The Awakening and selected stories*. Edited by N. Baym. New York: Modern Library.
Franklin, C. G. 1997. *Writing women's communities: The politics and poetics of contemporary multi-genre anthologies*. Madison: University of Wisconsin Press.
Gilbert, S. 2005. The mommy bloggers respond to their *NYT* judgment. *Blogging baby*. February 6. http://www.bloggingbaby.com/2005/02/06/the-mommy-bloggers-respond-to-their-nyt-judgment/.
Gilman, C. P. [1892] 1996. The Yellow Wallpaper. In *The Yellow Wallpaper*, ed. E. R. Hedges. New York: Feminist Press.
Hochman, D. 2005. Mommy (and me). *New York Times*, January 30. http://www.nytimes.com/2005/01/30/fashion/30moms.html?ex=1110949200&en=b84bd923d8149c3c&ei=5070.
Huff, C. 2005. Towards a geography of women's life writing and imagined communities: An introductory essay. In *Women's life writing and imagined communities*, ed. C. Huff, 1–16. New York: Routledge.
Karlsson, L. 2005. Consuming lives, creating community: Female Chinese-American diary writing on the Web. In *Women's life writing and imagined communities*, ed. C. Huff, 219–39. New York: Routledge.

———. 2007. Desperately seeking sameness: The processes and pleasures of identification in women's diary blog reading. *Feminist Media Studies* 7:2: 137–53.

Kennedy, E. M. n.d. *Fussy.* http://www.fussy.org/.

Lamar, M. n.d. *White trash mom.* http://www.whitetrashmom.com.

Lamott, A. 1993. *Operating instructions: A journal of my son's first year.* New York: Pantheon.

Liz. n.d. *Mom-101.* http://www.mom-101.blogspot.com/.

McNeill, L. 2003. Teaching an old genre new tricks: The diary on the Internet. *Biography* 26:1: 24–47.

Miller, N. K. 2002. *But enough about me: Why we read other people's lives.* New York: Columbia University Press.

Newman, C. 2005. *Waiting for Birdy: A year of frantic tedium, neurotic angst, and the wild magic of growing a family.* New York: Penguin.

NITLE Weblog Census. n.d. *National Institute for Technology and Liberal Education.* http://www.blogcensus.net/.

Orloff, P. 2006. Eden Marriott Kennedy: That's Mrs. Kennedy to you. *The Santa Barbara Independent*, April 6. http://www.independent.com/living/2006/04/eden_marriott_kennedy.html.

Rak, J. 2005. The digital queer: Weblogs and Internet identity. *Biography* 28:1: 166–82.

Rich, A. 1976. *Of woman born: Motherhood as experience and institution.* New York: W. W. Norton. Reprint, 1995.

Satterwhite, J. n.d. *Mommy needs coffee.* http://www.mommyneedscoffee.com/.

———. 2006. Mommybloggers dish with Mrs. Kennedy. *Mommybloggers.* July 10. http://www.mommybloggers.com/2006/07/mommybloggers_dish_with_mrs_ke_1.html.

Smartypants, M. 2005. *The world according to Mimi Smartypants.* New York: Avon.

Smith, S., and J. Watson. 1996. Introduction to *Getting a life: Everyday uses of autobiography*, 1–24. Minneapolis: University of Minnesota Press.

Sorapure, M. 2003. Screening moments, scrolling lives: Diary writing on the Web. *Biography* 26:1: 1–23.

Summers, M. n.d. *Suburban bliss: Birth control via the written word.* http://www.suburbanbliss.net.

Swales, J. M. 1990. *Genre analysis: English in academic and research settings.* Cambridge: Cambridge University Press.

What Mommybloggers are all about. n.d. *Mommybloggers.* http://www.mommybloggers.com/aboutus.html.

Zuern, J. 2003. Online lives: Introduction. *Biography* 26:1: v–xxv.

FIVE

"The Pencilling Mamma"

Public Motherhood in Alice Meynell's Essays on Children

LEE BEHLMAN

In the middle of her career, Alice Meynell (1847–1922), the influential English poet, essayist, and *fin de siècle* literary *salonnière* who would twice be nominated for poet laureate, began to publish a landmark series of essays on children in the London evening newspaper, the *Pall Mall Gazette*. These "Wares of Autolycus" essays (1893–98) initially appeared unsigned, but her authorship, which was already well known among the London literary set, was revealed to a wider public when these and other works were later revised and collected in two well-received volumes, *The Children* (1897) and *Childhood* (1913).[1] As Linda M. Austin has recently noted, with these essays Meynell emerged as "the leading observer of children and child development in the daily and weekly newspapers of the 1890s" (Austin 2006, 249), but what is most striking about these essays are the ways in which Meynell frames her own position as a literary, professional, and maternal observer of children. In writing for a broad newspaper-reading public, Meynell delivers a distinctive new *fin-de-siecle* persona of a professional woman writer at work within the ostensibly maternal domestic space, making use of the materials set before her, the behavior of her seven children. An image of this ideal in practice appears in her son Everard's memoir: "At her place at the library table . . . the pencilling mamma would sit at her work, the children at scrap-books on the floor or perhaps editing a newspaper under the table" (quoted in Meynell 1929, 88).[2] In Meynell's essays on children, this "pencilling mamma" depicted by her son is far from indifferent to the children's play; rather, she has both a professional *and* maternal eye trained on their activities (including, in this case, editing a family newspaper), even as she works on her own copy.

What Sharon Hays has called, in a contemporary context, the "cultural contradictions of motherhood" between the "historically constructed images of warm, nurturing mothers on the one side and cold, competitive career women on the other" was in its infancy in the 1890s, when middle-class women were only beginning to leave the home and join the workforce in large numbers (Hays 1996, 16). But female professional writers (along with female philanthropists) were a special case, for a tension between their unusually public careers and their private roles as mothers was long established by Meynell's time. As much as a century earlier, such figures as Anna Letitia Barbauld and Felicia Hemans—among the first women writers who could support themselves through their writing—endorsed what Patrice DiQuinzio terms "essential motherhood," or motherhood as "a function of women's essentially female nature" (DiQuinzio 1999, xiii). Hemans in particular negotiated the claims of traditional motherhood by promoting private domestic virtues as patriotic ones, providing a space for traditional mothers to support the nation without actually leaving the home or otherwise threatening patriarchy.[3] What is distinctive about Meynell's approach is how she presents public, journalistic writing unproblematically and without compromise as a career for mothers and not as an obstacle to proper motherhood that must somehow be effaced, thus delivering new arguments about mothering and professional women. Her son Everard again provides a telling description, in this case of Meynell's attitude of equanimity in both her maternal affections and her professional life:

> [We were] exquisitely fondled, but with economy, as if there were work always to be resumed. We were at once the most befriended of children, yet the most slighted; *we fitted into the literary life and business of the household.* (qtd. in Meynell 1929, 88, emphasis added)

In this chapter, I will show how Meynell presents a version of herself to her broad newspaper-reading public through observations of her own (unnamed) children, and how she uses them to draw conclusions about children in general. In doing so, she defines a persona at once intellectual, professional, and affectionate, one in keeping with her son Everard's descriptions. Meynell establishes her observing mother persona through a variety of discursive strategies, including using aesthetic language and other stylistic devices common to her art criticism, adopting terms from late-nineteenth-century science, including evolution and eugenics, and presenting herself as an advocate for children against an ignorant, misperceiving public. Of course, even as she delineates the observing mother, she limns out in remarkable detail the objects of her examination, the special qualities of children, most notably their distinctive beauty and use of language. I will explore mid-chapter how Meynell refigures childhood through the observing mother's gaze. As I will show, Meynell is attuned to all the paradox, irony, and difference that lie across the gulf between mothers and children, which is also the gulf between her present self and the past that produced her. Her essays display remarkable confidence as they redefine both mothers and children, a quality that her critics sometimes found unsettling.

In order to place Meynell's public representation of motherhood in her essays in the context of her full career, in the final section of this chapter I will compare these works with Meynell's roughly contemporaneous poems about motherhood, which have recently received sustained critical examination. In such poems as "Cradle Song at Twilight" (1896) and "The Modern Mother" (1902), Meynell presents a more directly critical approach to popular notions of "essential," sentimental motherhood. As I will demonstrate, Meynell's essays are distinctive not only for their indirection but for their lack of expressed anxiety on the subject of a mother's responsibility and her nature.

ON MEYNELL'S PUBLIC USE OF THE PERSONAL

It is useful first to note what Meynell's journalistic essays are not: these are not stories in any conventional sense but rather brief works of well-wrought observation and opinion. Nor are they conventional autobiography: Meynell does not write about the specific situation of being the mother of seven children, and she carefully avoids use of the first-person personal pronoun.[4] Individual, unnamed children are described in separate essays in order to flesh out claims about the behavior or appearance of children in general, but we are not introduced to the family as a whole. When the parents appear, they are often referred to simply as "a father" or "a mother," or, in one case, "maternal authority" (Meynell 1897, 4).[5] Meynell does, though, incorporate anecdotes drawn from her life, as when she describes her daughter's recuperation from a thirty-foot fall off a high banister, or when she describes the changes in the coloration of her son's face when he has a tantrum[6]; these references also function as *exempla* for the state of children in general.

Meynell often scatters knowing references to her public status as a successful writer-mother in these essays. In "Fellow Travellers with a Bird, II," for example, she winkingly reports on a letter written by her young daughter condemning the quality of a recent piece of writing. She wrote:

> My dear mother, I really wonder how you can be proud of that article, if it is worthy to be called a article, which I doubt. Such a unletterary article. I cannot call it letterature. I hope you will not write any more such unconventionan trash. (Meynell 1897, 5, original spelling)

Another detail of the writing life intrudes as Meynell describes how the same girl "was wont to bring a cup of tea to the writing-table of her mother" (Meynell 1897, 6).[7] Such gestures are not, I argue, attempts by Meynell to ward off the claim that she was an undutiful mother—indeed, though her household management was well known among friends to be unusually lax for a woman of her time and class status, she displayed little self-consciousness about this (Badeni 1981, 85–86).[8] Instead, Meynell seeks to place the writing life comfortably within the domestic scene.

Talia Schaffer's writings on Meynell's life and career provide a useful point of comparison for my own reading of Meynell's self-presentation as a public, writing mother in her essays on children. Schaffer has produced a memorable depiction of Meynell as a self-conscious manipulator of her public identity, but in very different contexts: she argues that both in her public writings and in her private dealings with male admirers such as Coventry Patmore, George Meredith, and Francis Thompson, Meynell fashions a seductively demure, restrained feminine persona, a real-life Angel in the House to be admired by her general audience and famous writers alike. Schaffer writes:

> As Meynell became famous, silence and loneliness became her essential claim to power, precision, and enviability. . . . Her silence also established her modesty and her desire for personal and family privacy, an appropriate feminine attribute for the household Angel. (Schaffer 2002, 48–49)

In Schaffer's analysis, Meynell sculpts a bodily absence and silence that her male audience could project its fantasies upon, and "Meynell apparently encourage[d] these misattributions," because "the figure of the

Angel . . . carried a particularly erotic charge for Victorian writers, and by producing the frisson, Meynell drastically increased her popularity while simultaneously working through some of her own psychological concerns" (Schaffer 2000, 167). For Schaffer, Meynell was "[o]bsessed with the notion of self-revelation, yet deeply wedded to the idea of self-concealment," and thus she revealed tidbits of her private life only "obliquely" in her poems and essays (Schaffer 2002, 14). As I have already shown, Meynell does indeed present details of her private life in the essays, and they do both rely upon and provoke further interest in her celebrity status. But although I agree that Meynell is a master of carefully limited self-presentation, I do not find her to be producing—in the childhood essays, at least—a "silent" and "lonely" persona for readers to project their erotic and domestic fantasies upon, nor does Meynell's mother-figure in these essays emerge as a passive Angel.[9] Rather, her carefully crafted reticence about details of her family life, her oblique revelations of private details, and especially her projection of analytical distance work instead as gestures against the kind of sentimental maternal self-disclosure that was common in Victorian women's writing about children. Meynell's characteristic reserve fends off rather than invites stereotypical readings of her as a servile mother-ideal; her self-management is not tantamount to self-erasure.

This is not to assert that Meynell is offering a fully worked-out theoretical treatment of professional writing motherhood. Nor are these essays works of feminist memoir in any conventional sense. Instead, as I will demonstrate, Meynell's achievement lies in delivering an argument about professional motherhood, mainly through the medium of a distinctive critical *voice* that assesses children's essential nature.

READING CHILDREN:
MEYNELL'S CRITICAL VOICE AS OBSERVING MOTHER

Throughout her writings on children, Meynell does not present herself to her public as an expert on this or any other subject but as an open-minded inquirer after mysteries; she is a professional writer, but an amateur child psychologist, suggesting that authoritative claims about children made by writers of the past as well as by the new class of psychological professionals may be suspect. As she concludes in "Fellow Travellers with a Bird, II," examining children closely must result in "the rejection of most of the conventions of the authors who have reported them" (Meynell 1897, 4).[10] Meynell's observing mother thus functions as a late-Victorian variant of the well-established European essayistic tradition of humane, skeptical, and empirical observation invented by Montaigne. She revels in children's unsusceptibility to classification systems: "To attend to a living child is to be baffled in your humour, disappointed of your pathos, and set freshly free from all the pre-occupations. You cannot anticipate him" (Meynell 1897, 1).[11]

Meynell seeks to counter long-standing claims and assumptions about children with her individual examples, as she moves from anecdotes to general conclusions. Throughout the essays she confronts two distinct conventional modes of treating children: the first, older mode treated children simply as proto-adults—unformed creatures who represent nothing in themselves but the potential to mature. In "That Pretty Person," she observes that for writers in previous centuries, "childhood was but borne with, and that for the sake of its mere promise of manhood" (Meynell 1897, 9).[12] Citing John Evelyn's diary in a passage reminiscent of the famous opening section of John Stuart Mill's *Autobiography* (1873), Meynell describes how he mourned his two-year-old son by hailing his great promise in classical languages, not for any intrinsic qualities. The second, more recent conventions about children derive from Wordsworth and other Romantic-era writers, who idealized childhood as a state of prelapsarian innocence and unadulterated creative power. In many respects, Meynell retains Romantic notions about childhood innocence and primal creativity, but she attempts in several essays to mark out what she takes to be Romantic excesses. In the essays "Authorship" and "Letters," she uses quoted evidence from her own children's writings to puncture the Wordsworthian balloon, demonstrating that while children are often creative, they are also overly imitative, easily confused, have little sense of plot or character, and generally make terrible writers (1897, 21–23). They may be avatars of the adult imagination, but they cannot harness that imaginative power in their writing; they are also, she observes, very bad spellers (1897, 21–23). She is, here and elsewhere, appreciative of her children's virtues and successes but also attuned to the ways in which their abilities diverge from even her own high opinion of them. Her goal is to clear away lazy thinking about children that other writers may be susceptible to, thus impressing upon the reading public the sense that she is a sensible, accurate reporter on her own household. Such public exposure could lead to embarrassments for her own children: her son Everard wrote of feeling "shame" at being "made a character" in Meynell's essay "A Boy" (qtd. in Meynell 1929, 153).

Gradually, over the course of her 1890s essays on children, Meynell does use evidence based on her own children to draw conclusions about their qualities, including their almost preternatural unpredictability and physical grace. Several of the reviewers of *The Children* (1897), her first volume of collected essays on the subject, observed that Meynell's essays were part of a recent trend of writers treating childhood as, in Meynell's words, a "state adorned with its own conditions" (Meynell 1897, 9). The reviewer for the *Bookman* wrote, "In Mrs. Meynell we have one of the best exponents of the new idea that, as far as possible, childhood's individuality should be as openly recognised as are the ambitious moods of the middle life and the search for repose that commonly marks declining years" (Anon. 1897b, 573).[13]

One factor that distinguishes Meynell's reading of the special "condition" of childhood from her contemporaries is her unusual emphasis on their beauty. Using her own children as examples, she painstakingly searches their features to delineate their striking physiognomies. She argues forcefully that the child's concrete loveliness is the greatest of all human beauties, much brighter than the conventional beauty of adult females. In "Children in Midwinter," perhaps Meynell's most important essay on children, she proposes that the women addressed by male poets in Elizabethan love sonnets were compared to flowers by default because of a well-kept "secret": the poets knew that any woman "could not endure to be compared with a child" (Meynell 1897).[14] It was simply no contest.

Meynell goes further to delineate children's beauty by taking an approach similar to her aesthetic essays on the seasons and on individual colors; that is, she lets loose a rapid flow of inventive synaesthetic imagery. Children, she claims in one especially evocative passage, have their own unique climate:

> Children are so flowerlike that it is always a little fresh surprise to see them blooming in winter. Their tenderness, their down, their colour, their fulness—which is like that of a thick rose or of a tight grape—look out of season. Children in the withering wind are like the soft golden-pink roses that fill the barrows in Oxford Street, breathing a southern calm on the north wind. The child has something better than warmth in the cold, something more subtly out of place and more delicately contrary; and that is coolness. To be cool in the cold is the sign of a vitality quite exquisitely alien from the common conditions of the world. It is to have a naturally, and not an artificially, different and separate climate. (Meynell 1897, 6)

In describing the child's "alien" biosphere positively, Meynell alludes to qualities of light, color, texture, and temperature, creating the kind of impressionistic movement of sensations that Ana Parejo Vadillo has discovered in Meynell's essays on London (a technique she frequently deployed in her art criticism) (Vadillo 2005, 96–109).[15] Like a *flaneur* on the London streets, Meynell's writing mother enjoys the "climate" that surrounds her in the persons of her own children.

What's more, children have, for Meynell, a unique aesthetic sensibility of their own. They have, she writes in "Toys," "a simple sense of the unnecessary ugliness of things, and . . . they reject that ugliness actively."[16] This is why children are usually so disappointed by cheaply made, mass-produced "dolls of commerce." Adults impose their "own sense of humour on children (as usual), and in its most ignoble form" when they "give them grotesque toys" (Meynell 1913, 3, 2).[17] Such violations of children's aesthetic sensibility are, for Meynell, affronts against their dignity. One of the distinguishing features of her writing on children is the defense she offers children against adults who fail to take their measure not just as aesthetic objects but as experiencing subjects. The main transgressors include sentimental writers who underestimate children's emotional complexity, moralistic writers who create crude, boring caricatures of children's mental lives, and contemporary "nonsense" writers and other fantasists who offer them distractions but not edifying entertainment.

In several of the 1890s "Wares of Autolycus" essays that were collected in Meynell's later volume on children, *Childhood* (1913), she critiques the exaggerated simplicity of children's writers such as Mrs. Fenwick, with her "Bad Family" and "Good Family" stories, and she attacks the notion that children genuinely believe in fairies or that such belief is necessary for their enjoyment of fantasy. Rather, most children, like adults, gain pleasure from *pretending* to believe.[18] The fact that children are coerced into clapping for Tinkerbell at the end of stage productions of *Peter Pan* draws Meynell's ire: she calls it "a game of men and women at the expense of children, a cumbersome frolic at best and an artificial, a tyrannous use of the adult sense of sentimental humour against the helpless." "I could with better conscience," she concludes, "use my superior physical strength against them than exploit them for love of my own condescension" (Meynell 1913, 32).[19]

In addition to her use of very positive aesthetic language and her critiques of adult condescension, Meynell deploys a range of scientific language to further emphasize that children are distinct from adults.[20] In "The Child of Tumult," for example, her son's tantrum reveals a child's unique temperament: "there is unequal force at work within a child, unequal growth and a jostling of powers and energies that are hurrying to their development and pressing for exercise and life. It is this helpless inequality—this untimeliness—that makes the guileless comedy mingling with the tragedies of a poor child's day" (1913, 130–31). Meynell presents children as susceptible to scientific understanding but also as unstable or in flux. Linda M. Austin has observed the "impersonal and scrupulous neutrality" of Meynell's observations on children, comparing them to the "detachment of contemporary psychologists such as William T. Preyer and James Sully," and, indeed, Meynell uses the "nervous" discourse of late-nineteenth-century psychology (though without claiming scientific expertise) to maintain a sense that children's behavior is conceptually graspable but nevertheless unpredictable from moment to moment (Austin 2006, 250).[21]

As if any one scientific discourse were insufficient for her purpose, Meynell's observing mother also invokes several other such discourses in her writing, as when she uses the racialized language of contemporary eugenics and anthropology to describe children in "The Man with Two Heads." Here her daughter's susceptibility to fear "is one of the points upon which" she resembles the Japanese, that "extreme Oriental" who in a childlike fashion "runs from the supernatural and laughs for the fun of running" (Meynell 1897, 18).[22] Children are not only compared to a racial other, they are also credited with exemplifying the Darwinian spirit of the age.[23] In "That Pretty Person," an extended examination of childhood through a Darwinian lens, Meynell writes that "[c]hildhood is but change made gay and visible, and the world has lately been converted to change," and that while "[o]ur fathers valued change for the sake of its results," "we value it in the act" (Meynell 1897, 11). Because change is the very condition of modern life, children become the avatars of modernity, their very nature a principle of Darwinian flux that will produce a eugenically improved race.[24] Meynell's shifting, kaleidoscopic use of all of these scientific discourses constitute a return, through a very different route, to the impressionistic treatment of children evident in the aesthetic language of the aforementioned "The Child in Midwinter"; indeed, her variant use of scientific discourses seems to be for the sake of this broader and more consequential impressionistic aesthetic. By their very nature, children would seem to require (and to some extent, elude) many different essays at definition. Like Wallace Stevens's blackbird, they emerge through multiple views as a moving target, a protean force of nature.[25]

Throughout her essays on children, Meynell shifts between enunciating the alien nature of the child through aesthetic and scientific language, which allows for precise description but placing the child at a remove, and the perspective of an adult woman who is, after all, a grown-up child and knows something about the experience. In other words, Meynell holds a double awareness of the strangeness of our own childhoods to us and the fact that at some point they became us. In fact, the distance that we feel from children, the sense that they are part of a familiar but nevertheless remote past, is an ironic sensibility that childhood itself produces. Near the end of "The Child in Midwinter," Meynell writes:

> [W]ith some children, of passionate fancy, there occurs now and then a children's dance, or a party of any kind, which has a charm and glory mingled with uncertain dreams. Never forgotten, and yet never certainly remembered as a fact of this life, is such an evening. When many and many a later pleasure, about the reality of which there never was any kind of doubt, has been long forgotten, that evening—as to which all is doubt—is impossible to forget. *In a few years it has become so remote that the history of Greece derives antiquity from it. In later years it is still doubtful, still a legend. . . . It had so long taken its place in that past wherein lurks all the antiquity of the world.* (Meynell 1897, 8–9, emphasis added)

We develop our sense of historical time as children, when the dubiety of past events contributes to their sense of remoteness, and vice versa. In theorizing our sense of time, Meynell thus links factual uncertainty with the impression of temporal distance.[26] To put it another way, Meynell writes about a distant childhood party like Pater wrote about La Giocanda, for both produce a sense of profound antiquity: as Pater wrote, "All the thoughts and experience of the world have etched and moulded there, in that which they have of power to refine and make expressive the outward form, the animalism of Greece, the lust of Rome" (Pater 1980, 98).[27] The gap between the elusive childhood past and the adult observer provides the opportunity (and a subject) for Meynell's inquiry. As Emily Harrington has helpfully observed, "Meynell's writing . . . distinguishes between detachment and distance. Whereas detachment severs bonds, distance makes room for them. Distance allows one subject to see another's difference clearly" (Harrington 2004, 186).

What is unusual here, of course, is that this distanced, post-Romantic observer is a self-identified mother taking notes on her own children. The innovativeness and potency of this new formulation of motherhood are evident in some of the responses to Meynell's essays on children by her contemporaries. Both Max Beerbohm and the reviewer for the Chicago *Dial* expressed concern that Meynell's intellectual distance would threaten the sacred parent-child bond. Beerbohm (1962) writes, "[t]o me there seems some danger in the prevalent desire to observe children in their quiddity, to leave them all to their own devices and let them develop their own natures, swiftly or slowly, at will" (81). That a mother such as Meynell "observes" children in her characteristic way suggests to Beerbohm that she will take no conventional and productive motherly role in guiding their upbringing. For the reviewer for the *Dial*, because Meynell is "[a] mother herself, and a woman of refined delicacy of perception, she cannot be without sympathy, yet she can rarely regard the child as other than a very interesting circumstance." "We do not," he concludes, "feel warmed on reading" these essays (Anon. 1897c, 337). These writers are complaining, against all evidence, that Meynell's essays demonstrate a lack of maternal "warmth" because she sets details of her maternal care alongside their supposed opposite, analytical rigor. In her essays, the private domestic sphere appears unapologetically as a place of professional opportunity.

These writers are, in effect, arguing that Meynell is alienated both from her own children and from her proper, private role as mother because she has adopted the position of a detached essayistic observer. This is a fully predictable criticism that Meynell's essays seem surprisingly unconcerned with, and it is particularly surprising because during the same period in which she was writing and publishing her essays on childhood, Meynell elsewhere was confronting this claim far more directly. In her poetry of the 1890s and later, she delivers sympathetic portrayals of mothers who are alienated from their ostensibly natural roles as mothers, not because they have successfully entered the public sphere as writers, nor because they have chosen, in Beerbohm's terms, simply to "observe children in their quiddity," but because of a crushing claustrophobia caused by their confinement to the domestic space. Their desire for escape from the conventions of maternal sympathy is frustrated at every turn. In the final section of this chapter, I will seek to make sense of these apparently divergent approaches to motherhood in Meynell's *ouvre*.

ALIENATED MOTHERHOOD IN MEYNELL'S POETRY

In a series of short poems that has recently received sustained critical attention, including "Cradle-Song at Twilight" (1896),"The Modern Mother" (1902), and "Maternity" (1913), Meynell repeatedly presents mothers or maternal substitutes who are repulsed or exhausted by the needs of small children (Meynell 1955). In "Cradle-Song at Twilight," for example, a child will not be lulled to sleep in his "nurse's" arms. As he hangs there, this substitute-figure (where is the true mother?) realizes that she longs for "other playfellows," and as she ponders her "unmaternal fondness" for a man outside the domestic sphere, she looks down at the child with his "alien eyes" (28).

At first glance, this compact Gothic scenario may seem like an indictment of an indifferent servant distracted by wayward thoughts of a lover, but in the context of Meynell's other motherhood poems, it becomes clear that women's alienation from children is not a phenomenon to be condemned but a social reality meriting sympathy. In "The Modern Mother," for example, the child's overheated kiss is a burden "[u]nhoped, unsought!" as the mother prefers only a "slight . . . brief caress" to such attentions (Meynell 1955, 31). In "Maternity," a poem about the death of an infant in childbirth—a common topos for nineteenth-century women poets—the maternal narrator directs our attention away from the pathos of the child's death itself (ten years earlier): "'Ten years ago was born in pain / A child, not now forlorn. / But oh, ten years ago, in vain, / A mother, a mother was born'" (Meynell 1955, 56). The poem refocuses our attention on the mother's unending pain. Meynell's speaker embraces the notion of a mother's profound connection to her child, but it is expressed through its rupture, across the distances of memory and mortality.[28] In swerving from the common female elegiac gestures of celebration and consolation for the lost child, Meynell both affirms maternal feeling—that bloody root is still exposed—and seems to suggest that the connection may be impossible to maintain or express in the present tense.[29]

Angela Leighton (1992) has noted how Meynell's poetic depiction of alienated mothers constitutes an unprecedented critique of the most powerful constraint placed on women's emotional lives, the expectation of "natural" or essential maternal sentiment:

> It is particularly on the subject which generally inspired bad poems in the best nineteenth-century women poets that Meynell rises above the norm. She writes almost the first serious, adult poems, by any poet, about biological motherhood. The experience to which she dedicated some thirteen years of her own life, but about which she felt considerable emotional ambivalence, elicits from her a number of unsentimental poems about mothers and children which are unrivalled in their unobtrusively suggestive skepticism. (Leighton 1992, 256–57)

As Leighton's analysis suggests, Meynell's poetry marks a cultural turn, for as the margins of female domesticity were being violated by women increasingly working outside the home, so the domestic space was itself becoming an unfamiliar, even alien, landscape.[30] Maria Frawley has called this sense of alienation an early manifestation of modernist anxiety about women's changing roles in society: "Meynell helped to establish," Frawley writes, "what might be thought of as the discourse of modern maternity, one characterized by a refusal of the sentimental and a corollary attention to the anxieties of motherhood" (Frawley 1997, 32). Yet while both Leighton's and Frawley's approaches work well in highlighting the often disturbed emotional environments in Meynell's poems, neither is useful for an analysis of the different emotional climate of the essays on childhood.

With Meynell's essays on childhood and her motherhood poems, we have in hand two very different but equally significant responses to Victorian motherhood. As several critics have shown, with the poems, Meynell takes a direct approach, introducing speakers who are self-estranged and alienated from the demands of traditional motherhood. The poems present, in early form, the kind of protest against the constraints of motherhood that came to its fruition decades later in Adrienne Rich's *Of Woman Born* (1976), where Rich describes the institution of motherhood as fundamentally contradictory, "alienat[ing] women from our bodies by incarcerating us in them" (Rich 1976, 13). On the other hand, with the essays on childhood, composed over roughly the same period and having received little critical attention up until now, we have a very different approach to what Rich calls "the dangerous schism between "private" and "public" life for women" (13), in this case by *merging* them in the voice of a public, observing mother who retains an emotional connection to her children. In fact, these approaches have much in common and work quite well together. Each targets contradictions within popular notions of motherhood as private, essential, and unintellecutal, and while the poetry makes a direct frontal attack on these conventions, the essays equally explode them by demonstrating what a public motherhood can look like. The essays put into practice an alternative mode of motherhood that accommodates and indeed enables a woman writer's career. Set against her poems on motherhood, Meynell's essays seem the consummation of an ideal—a successful public and professional motherhood—that her poems' speakers could not even imagine.

NOTES

1. Many of the *Wares of Autolycus* columns were rewritten and included in Meynell's later essay collections, including not only *The Children* and

Childhood but also *The Colour of Life* (1896), *The Spirit of Place* (1898) and *Ceres' Runaway* (1909). The revisions were often extensive: P. M. Fraser has noted Meynell's "habit of re-using the same basic materials in different contexts, modified to suit not only her own inclination, but also such external factors as limitations of space and change of context," which resulted in a "rather fluid body of material" (Meynell 1965, 9, 11). In this chapter I will be addressing the later versions of these essays that were included in the aforementioned collections, but I will include references to the original published versions where possible. Meynell's changes were usually either cosmetic or involved adding emphasis to points already made.

2. The term "pencilling mamma" was, as Viola Meynell notes, drawn from a poem about Meynell by George Meredith (Meynell 1929, 88).

3. Barbauld's "On Female Studies" (1787; published 1826), for example, asserted "the primacy of motherhood as women's social role," though Barbauld was never a biological mother herself (McCarthy and Kraft 2002, 474). Several of Hemans's books of the 1830s addressed the domestic affections in a national context, including *Songs of the Affections, with Other Poems* (1830), *Hymns on the Works of Nature, for the Use of Children* (1833), and *Scenes and Hymns of Life, with Other Religious Poems* (1834). On conventional femininity in Romantic-era women poets, see Armstrong 1995, Leighton 1992, Ross 1989, and Stephenson 1993. On Hemans and domestic patriotism, see Lootens 1994.

4. This is in contradistinction to another popular writer on children who was a contemporary of Meynell's, William Canton (1845–1926). Canton wrote cheerful poems and essays about his daughter Winifred in *The Invisible Playmate: A Story of the Unseen* (1894) and *W. V. Her Book* (1896). Two reviewers of Meynell's *The Children* made extended comparisons between her book and Canton's books; see the anonymous review in the *Spectator* (Anon. 1897a) and psychologist James Sully's review in "The Child in Recent English Literature" from the *Fortnightly Review* (1897). Maria Frawley notes that "It is worth recalling that Meynell rarely wrote directly about motherhood but accessed it instead via representations of childhood . . . " (Frawley 1997, 41).

5. From "Fellow Travellers with a Bird, II," which appeared in its original form as "The Young Child," a "Wares of Autolycus" essay in the *Pall Mall Gazette*, dated Wednesday, September 9, 1896.

6. For both examples, see "The Child of Tumult," which first appeared in the *Pall Mall Gazette* on Wednesday, October 20, 1897, and was revised for publication in *Ceres' Runaway* (1909). Meynell's biographer, June Badeni, has noted that the essay "The Boy" was about her son Everard, and that "The Child in Tumult" and "The Child of Subsiding Tumult," both published in *Ceres' Runaway*, were about her son Francis (Badeni 1981, 140).

7. For a discussion of more such homely details, see Tuell on the unreprinted *Pall Mall Gazette* article "The Nursery," dated Wednesday, December 1, 1897 (Tuell 1925, 143–44).

8. In his memoir, her son Francis writes that she was not "qualified or interested" in housework (Meynell 1971, 27). Francis provides several affection-

ate anecdotes demonstrating Meynell's professional focus. For example, he writes of two new deliveries, "My mother's many child-bearings were never allowed to be a hindrance to her work. (A letter written by the poet and editor W. E. Henley when I was born illustrates this. He congratulates her equally on 'the newcomer' and on an essay which she had lately sent to him)" (27).

9. In a recent essay on Meynell and Coventry Patmore's prosody, Yopie Prins challenges the notion that we can achieve an adequate sense of a "real" Alice Meynell by reading her biography against her work. Prins argues for a nonautobiographical lyric persona that is produced in Meynell's poetry: she locates in her work "a detachable form of intimacy: not her own passion, but a disciplined affect that produces passion as its effect" (Prins 2005, 277).

Recently, scholarly writing on Meynell seems to have receded somewhat from speculation about connections between Meynell's literary production and her life. F. Elizabeth Gray certainly draws on Meynell's biography in writing about her Catholic notion of "ideal womanhood" in her 2007 essay, but the biography informs the reading only to a very limited extent. The same is true of Linda M. Austin's complex analysis of Meynell's use of a "Physio-Psychology of Memory" (2006) and other recent essays by Maria Frawley (1997 and 2000) and Linda Peterson (2006).

10. The reviewer of *The Children* for the *Critic* praised Meynell's critique of commonly accepted ideas about children: "Indirectly, we are delicately made conscious, as we read, of the stupidity which results from taking anything for granted in this world" (Anon. 1897d, 22). For another warning against assuming too much about children, see "The Child of Tumult," where Meynell notes, "But even the naughty child is an individual, and must not be treated in the mass. He is numerous indeed, but not general, and to describe him you must take the unit, with all his incidents and his organic qualities as they are" (Meynell 1910, 27).

11. "Fellow Travellers with a Bird, I" from *The Children* appeared in an earlier form in the *Pall Mall Gazette* for April 13, 1894; parts of this essay were later used in another "Wares of Autolycus" essay, "The Nursery," in the *Pall Mall Gazette* for Wednesday, December 1, 1897.

12. This essay, "That Pretty Person," first appeared in the *Pall Mall Gazette* on Friday, January 17, 1896.

13. Similarly, the reviewer for the *Spectator* claimed (incorrectly) that writers had been focusing on childhood as an independent condition for only "within the last fifteen years, to push the period to its furthest limit" (Anon. 1897a, 173).

14. "Children in Midwinter" originally appeared as "Children in January" in the *Pall Mall Gazette* on Friday, January 10, 1896.

15. Among Meynell's writings on art criticism was *Children of the Old Masters*, a book-length examination of images of the Christ-child in the Middle Ages and the Renaissance. Here she judges the frequent depictions of Italian *bimbi* to be "artificial" because they are "ultra-childish," "exaggerated [in their] infancy," and are placed "in a posture of indirect grace that living

childhood never assumed . . . " (1903, 8). In her essays on childhood, Meynell seeks to do justice to the "natural" beauty of children through her own painterly descriptions.
16. In "Real Childhood," a piece of second-person singular reportage and one of the few essays in which Meynell seems to be reflecting on her own childhood, she amusingly recalls rejecting the bonnets of female relatives on aesthetic grounds (Meynell 1897, 36).
17. An earlier version of "Toys" appeared untitled in the *Pall Mall Gazette* on Friday, March 9, 1894.
18. For Meynell's critique of Mrs. Fenwick in *Childhood* (1913), see "Children's Books of the Past"; for Meynell on fantasy, see "Children's Books of the Present" and "Fairies."
19. Meynell does concede parenthetically that with *Peter Pan*, "Sir J. Barrie has written the most adorable "pretending" story ever written about a child" (Meynell 1913, 32).
20. In *Mary: The Mother of Jesus*, Meynell notes sardonically that children were becoming an increasingly popular subject for both doctors and "women, especially in America" (1912, 34).
21. See also a striking passage in "The Young Child" on how an infant sees: "An infant never meets your eyes; he evidently does not remark the features of faces near him. Whether because of the greater conspicuousness of dark hair or dark hat, or for some like reason, he addresses his looks, his laughs, and apparently his criticism, to the heads, not the faces, of his friends" (Meynell 1897, 31). Maria Frawley has remarked on the striking resemblance between such details and the "rhetoric of behavioral understanding" (Frawley 1997, 35), common in recent books on children by such authors as T. Berry Brazleton and Penelope Leach.
22. See also "Fair and Brown" (Meynell 1897, 33–35), where Meynell compares Southern European beauty standards for children with those of England and Northern Europe.
23. In one essay, though, Meynell presents a child-centered explanation of human behavior *against* a Darwinian one. In "Under the Early Stars," she explains that both the general human lust for the hunt and adults' specific sleeping habits have their root in childhood practices, not evolutionary inheritance: "The habit of prehistoric races has been cited as the only explanation of the fixity of some customs in mankind. But if the enquirers who appeal to that beginning remembered better their own infancy, they would seek no further" (Meynell 1897, 16).
24. Meynell makes an interesting counterintuitive claim at the end of this essay, that because moderns recognize that life is constantly in flux, they are, paradoxically, less in a rush to get places: "But impatience of the way and the wayfaring was to disappear from a later century—an age that has found all things to be on a journey, and all things complete in their day because it is their day, and has its appointed end" (Meynell 1897, 13).
25. Lee Margaret Jenkins has applied the term "epistemological pluralism" to Stevens's 1917 poem "Thirteen Ways of Looking at a Blackbird" (published

in 1923). The term applies well to Meynell's treatment of children in her essays (Jenkins 2007, 39).
26. In an intriguing passage from an undated letter to John Freeman, Meynell addresses the extent of both children's memories and her own: "What I think children have is a sense of the remote past. If I can trust my memory, they have not the sense of the actual going-by of time such as you have, and as I—strange to say—have experienced only lately" (Meynell n.d.). Meynell also connects childhood with a sense of antiquity in "Under the Early Stars" (Meynell 1897, 16–17).
27. With regard to Pater's influence on Meynell's writing, the record is unclear. While Talia Schaffer states that "Meynell's writing was deeply influenced by the ideas of Walter Pater" (Schaffer 2000, 171), June Badeni quotes a 1909 letter from Meynell, stating that "I am the only literary person alive who has never read Pater at all" (Badeni 1981, 199). Given the resemblances in style between Meynell's aesthetic writing and Pater's, it is difficult to believe that he did not bear at least an indirect influence on her work.
28. In *Godiva's Ride* (1993), Dorothy Mermin posits a mid-Victorian logic of erotic replacement in poetry about dead children, in which a "mother's lament for a dead child is the feminine equivalent of a man's lament for a dead beloved . . . " (Mermin 1993, 74).
29. Another notable Meynell poem from this period that associates motherhood (as well as fatherhood) with death is "Parentage" (1896), which puns on the word "bear" in the sense of both carrying a child and feeling the weight of suffering in its conclusion: "And she who slays is she who bears, who bears" (Meynell 1955, 26).
30. Nicole Fluhr, too, has noted recently that there was a marked change in sensibility at the turn of the twentieth century, when "New Woman writers reevaluated maternity, variously questioning the nature and existence of a maternal instinct, representing mothers' ambivalence toward or distaste for maternity . . . " (Fluhr 2001, 243). Although Meynell cannot be categorized as a New Woman writer, her poems on motherhood are among the first to signal a reevaluation of maternity, putting into question the naturalness of the maternal instinct.

REFERENCES

Anon. 1897a. Review of *The children* (1897), by Alice Meynell. *Spectator* 78 (January 30): 173–74.
Anon. 1897b. Review of *The children* (1897), by Alice Meynell. *Bookman* 4 (February): 573–74.
Anon. 1897c. Review of *The children* (1897), by Alice Meynell. *Dial* (June 1): 337–38.
Anon. 1897d. Review of *The children* (1897), by Alice Meynell. *Critic* 28 (August 7): 72–73.

Armstrong, I. 1995. The gush of the feminine: How can we read women's poetry of the Romantic period? In *Romantic women writers: Voices and countervoices*, ed. P. R. Feldman and T. M. Kelley, 13–32. Hanover, NH, and London: University Press of New England.

Austin, L. M. 2006. Self against childhood: The contributions of Alice Meynell to a psycho-physiology of memory. *Victorian Literature and Culture* 34: 249–68.

Badeni, J. 1981. *The slender tree: A life of Alice Meynell*. Padstow, UK: Tabb House.

Beerbohm, M. 1962. *The incomparable Max*. New York: Dodd, Mead, & Company.

DiQuinzio, P. 1999. *The impossibility of motherhood: Feminism, individuality, and the problem of mothering*. New York and London: Routledge.

Fluhr, N. M. 2001. Figuring the New Woman: Writers and mothers in George Egerton's early stories. *Texas Studies in Literature and Language* 43(3): 243–66.

Frawley, M. 1997. Modernism and maternity: Alice Meynell and the politics of motherhood. In *Unmanning modernism: Gendered re-readings*, ed. E. J. Harrison and S. Peterson, 31–43. Knoxville: University of Tennessee Press.

———. 2000. "The tides of the mind": Alice Meynell's poetry of perception. *Victorian Poetry* 38(1): 62–76.

Gray, F. E. 2007. Catholicism and ideal womanhood in *fin-de-siecle* women's poetry. *English Literature in Transition, 1880–1920* 50:1: 50–72.

Harrington, E. 2004. *Lyric intimacy: Forms of intersubjectivity in British women poets, 1860–1900*. PhD Diss., University of Michigan.

Hays, S. 1996. *The cultural contradictions of motherhood*. New Haven, CT, and London: Yale University Press.

Jenkins, L. M. 2007. *Wallace Stevens: Rage for order*. Brighton: University of Sussex Press.

Leighton, A. 1992. *Victorian women poets: Writing against the heart*. Charlottesville and London: University Press of Virginia.

Lootens, T. 1994. Hemans and home: Victorianism, feminine "Internal Enemies," and the domestication of national identity. *PMLA* 109:2: 238–53.

McCarthy, W., and E. Kraft, eds. 2002. *Anna Letitia Barbauld: Selected poetry and prose*. Peterborough, Ont.: Broadview.

Mermin, D. 1993. *Godiva's ride: Women of letters in England, 1830–1880*. Bloomington and Indianapolis: Indiana University Press.

Meynell, A. 1896. *The colour of life, and other essays on things seen and heard*. London and New York: John Lane.

———. 1897. *The children*. Repr., Whitefish, MT: Kessinger, 2004.

———. 1898. *The spirit of place*. London and New York: John Lane.

———. 1903. *Children of the old masters*. London: Duckworth.

———. 1910. *Ceres' runaway & other essays*. New York: John Lane. First published in London, 1909.

———. 1912. *Mary: The mother of Jesus: An essay*. London: Philip Lee Warner.

———. 1913. *Childhood*. London: Batsford.

———. 1955. *The poems of Alice Meynell 1847–1923: Centenary edition.* Westminster, MD: Newman Press.

———. 1965. *The wares of Autolycus: Selected literary essays of Alice Meynell.* Edited by P. M. Fraser. London: Oxford University Press.

———. n.d. Letter to John Freeman, July 18. Berg Collection of English and American Literature, New York Public Library.

Meynell, F. 1971. *My lives.* London: Bodley Head.

Meynell, V. 1929. *Alice Meynell: A memoir.* New York: Charles Scribner's Sons.

Pater, W. 1980. *The Renaissance: Studies in art and poetry. The 1893 text.* Edited by D. L. Hill. Berkeley and Los Angeles: University of California Press.

Peterson, L. 2006. Alice Meynell's *Preludes*, or preludes to what future poetry? *Victorian Literature and Culture* 34: 405–26.

Prins, Y. 2005. Patmore's law, Meynell's rhythm. In *The fin-de-siecle poem: English literary culture and the 1890s*, ed. J. Bristow, 261–84. Athens: Ohio University Press.

Rich, A. 1976. *Of woman born: Motherhood as experience and institution.* New York: W. W. Norton.

Ross, M. 1989. *The contours of masculine desire: Romanticism and the rise of women's poetry.* New York and Oxford: Oxford University Press.

Schaffer, T. 2000. *The forgotten female aesthetes: Literary culture in late-Victorian England.* Charlottesville and London: University Press of Virginia.

———. 2002. Writing a public self: Alice Meynell's "unstable equilibrium." In *Women's experience of modernity, 1875–1945*, ed. L. W. Lewis and A. L. Ardis, 13–30. Baltimore, MD: Johns Hopkins University Press.

Stephenson, G. 1993. Poet construction: Mrs. Hemans, L.E.L., and the image of the nineteenth-century woman poet. In *Reimagining women: Representations of women in culture*, ed. S. Neuman and G. Stephenson, 61–73. Toronto: University of Toronto Press.

Stevens, W. 1923. Thirteen ways of looking at a blackbird. *Harmonium.* New York: Knopf.

Sully, J. 1897. The child in recent English literature. *Fortnightly Review* 67: 218–28.

Tuell, A. K. 1925. *Mrs. Meynell and her literary generation.* Repr., St. Clair Shores, MI: Scholarly Press, 1970.

Vadillo, A. P. 2005. *Women poets and urban aestheticism: Passengers of modernity.* New York: Palgrave.

SIX

Picturing Mom

Mythic and Real Mothers in Children's Picture Books

GRETCHEN PAPAZIAN

> Read to your bunny often,
> It's twenty minutes of fun.
> It's twenty minutes of moonlight,
> And twenty minutes of sun.
> [. . .]
> Read to your bunny often,
> And . . .
> Your bunny will read to you.[1]

Rosemary Wells's (1997) *Read to Your Bunny* is a small, brightly colored book with a jaunty rhyme and plump, cutely clad bunnies as characters. It very clearly looks like a children's picture book. Yet its words (excerpt above); the author's end note ("Reading to your little one is just like putting gold coins in the bank"); the state of Georgia's appropriation of the book for its "best start" hospital program and the governor's note to readers ("We hope you will read this book with your child and help him or her develop a love for reading"); and the just-in-case-it-isn't-clear-yet request from the imagined child on the end papers ("Read to me from birth-two-three" [*sic*]): *All* are addressed to an adult—to the parent. In other words, while *Read to Your Bunny* seems like a book for children, it talks to grown-ups. It tells them how to interact with their child. It offers advice on how to parent. In this, it draws attention to the ways in which children's picture books work to instruct parents in parenting, constructing both parents and parenting.

That picture books are instructive is not a new idea. Indeed, in 1658, John Comenius composed the progenitor of the modern picture book, *Orbis Sensualism Pictus*, to teach his students Latin. Although historians claim that the purpose and sensibility of children's literature have shifted "from instruction to delight" (Demers and Moyles 1982, xi), few would deny that children's literature still teaches. While some books merely offer inexperienced readers information, most do far more. Picture books in particular serve a vital and formidable social purpose as they show the very youngest children how to be members of a culture.[2] Yet as a book like *Read to Your Bunny* highlights, picture books also deliver ideas to the adults who must physically read these books in order for them to do their ideological work on children.

The work that picture books do on adults is the focus of this chapter. The chapter aims to expose not only the lessons in and about mothering that the contemporary picture book teaches but also the possibilities of the mode of delivery. The argument begins by drawing attention to the ways in which the contemporary, popular picture book marks parenting as mothering and then denies mothers power and agency. The argument advances by asserting that, despite this construction, which depends on a particular White middle-class sensibility, the mode of delivery—the picture book itself—has the potential to envision and produce a more empowered, liberated "mother." The chapter then shows how the genre already offers such instruction in less marketed, less conventional books. Taking a set of African American picture books as its example, the chapter demonstrates that the picture book's potential to construct empowered, empowering, realistic notions of mothers has, in fact, been realized. The chapter concludes with a call for more of such images, as well as more attention to them, as the proliferation and delivery of these lessons in real motherhood remain inadequate. Before launching into these claims, though, I establish two contexts for them: (1) the scholarship concerning adults as readers of children's literature, and (2) the relevant feminist explication of contemporary notions of mothers.

CONTEXT 1:
ADULTS AS READERS OF CHILDREN'S LITERATURE

We understand the modern picture book to be for the very youngest of children, but we sometimes forget that an adult always reads these books to a child, and thus the books are always read by both child and adult. In fact, among the fifty-plus studies that, since the 1970s, have looked at sex roles in picture books, only two—Susan Murr's 1997 dissertation and David Anderson and Mykol Hamilton's 2005 study of representations of fathers—mention parents as an audience for these books. The neglect perhaps speaks to the complexity of the issues surrounding adults reading children's literature. For example, Peter Hunt (1991) claims that adults cannot read children's literature in the same way children do because a child's reading is always a "developing one" (74). Adults cannot read like children because part of a child's reading is learning to read—learning how to process information in particular, culturally normative ways. From this perspective, which also seems to be the perspective of a book like *Read to Your Bunny*, the adult's relationship to (as well as role in) a children's book is merely to facilitate the child's learning-to-read process.

However, others argue that adults are readers of books for children—not merely a medium through which the child experiences such texts. In her influential work on audience-address, Barbara Wall (1991) maintains that many children's books speak to the child and the adult simultaneously and on equal terms, using what she calls "dual address" (compared to the more conventional single or double address). Inspiring both a special issue of *Children's Literature* (1997) and an anthology (Beckett 1999), Wall's work engendered the term "cross-writing." The term explains and encompasses "authors [who] and works [that] transgress the usual demarcations separating children's from adult literature" (Myers 1997, 119–120). It is a useful concept for thinking about the adult readers of children's literature, for it not only gives such readers a place in the text, but it suggests a dissolution of the arbitrary generic boundaries between the categories "children's literature" and "adult literature."[3]

Nonetheless, this chapter is less interested in the text's reader address and more interested in the actual readers of (so-called) children's literature, and the readers this chapter is most interested in are parents. More specifically, it is interested in new parents—adults who have not had much experience in their lives with children; these are adults who authors such as Wells and the state of Georgia believe require books such as *Read to Your Bunny*. Again, the oddity of this book is that it is a children's book, and yet the addressee is an adult.[4] One might understand this as a practical matter. The representation of who reads to whom and how parent and child relate through books must, if it is to be realistic, take this form.

Yet Jacqueline Rose's (1984) powerful and influential theories about the "impossibility of children's fiction" question this inevitability. For

Rose, there is no child in children's literature. The child that appears in this literature is no more than a construct of the adult imagination. In other words, children's fiction does not so much represent children and childhood as it offers instruction in how to be a child according to adult notions. As in Hunt's formulation, although to different ends, the child reader becomes like a text—that is, an object produced, created, fabricated, imagined, and delivered by and through the children's literature industry. Rose thus asserts that, as a form, children's literature reveals that relationships between children and adults are impossible because adults believe they can know (and thus write) the child and childhood (Rose 1984, 1). To put it another way, the children's literature that exists does not so much tell stories about children as it evidences adults' failure to know and understand the child as anything beyond adults' own construction.

Following this logic, one might further suggest that children's literature evidences the difficulty adults have relating to, interacting with, and/or knowing how to act with real, as well as imagined, children. This chapter argues that being a parent—especially a new parent— compounds the difficulty (or impossibility) of which children's literature speaks. As the example of *Read to Your Bunny* indicates, children's texts address this inexperience, offering instruction in how to be a parent alongside their instruction in how to be a child. They address new parents' inexperience by imagining the parent and parenting into being, just as they imagine the child and childhood into being.

But here, by "parent," I really mean mothers, for in our culture, "parent" and "parenting" seamlessly slide into "mother" and "mothering." The phenomenon evidences itself quite plainly in the picture book. The point here, though, is that picture books offer not only a particular image of who a mother is/should be, but in doing so they also provide guidelines for how to be a mother. And, these days, many mothers—particularly new mothers, and perhaps particularly White middle-class mothers—need such imperatives, for so very many women (particularly, many White middle-class women) are inexperienced with children, having grown up in a world of small, nuclear families and having experienced adulthood as something separate from family and babies. In many ways, then, the picture books highlighted in this chapter serve a real need. They create an idea of what a mom is, what her roles are, how she should act and feel, and how she should interact with and feel about her child.

Hunt's formulation about how and why children "read" children's literature thus applies to adults too. Adults (mothers in particular) stand as developing readers; as new parents, they become (like children) texts. The art, the medium, the mode of culture delivery, produces "mothers" as much as it produces "children," and this not only merits but requires critical attention. While picture book representations of girls have changed over the past thirty years in response to changing ideas of girlhood,[5] representations of women have remained unchanged.[6] In the world of the contemporary picture book, women cook, clean, and nurture. This is worrisome in terms of the effects that such representations may have on children who are learning how to be members of their culture. It becomes proportionately problematic when one adds the effects that such representations might deliver to the picture book's other major audience: parents—especially new parents, who are trying to sort out their identity and roles as parents at the very moment they encounter these books.

CONTEXT 2: CONTEMPORARY MYTHICAL MOTHERHOOD

The second-wave feminist movement fundamentally changed notions of womanhood and women. It created opportunities for women to choose different sorts of paths—paths that involve power, education, career, and a type of success beyond the home with its repetitive chores and caretaking duties. This is not to say that the home is void of empowering, creative, and/or fulfilling aspects, but the "home" and the identity it confers are not for all women—or for all men, for that matter. In any event, the point is that our moment has structured a new understanding of female identity. And the question has become: Where does the role of mother fit into this identity?

The literature on this topic is expansive, revealing our particular moment's anxiety about mothers, as well as about mothering. The problem supposedly producing the anxiety has been encapsulated in the so-called "mommy wars" staged in the press of the 1980s, 1990s, and 2000s between working mothers and stay-at-home mothers.[7] More useful, though, is feminist work on motherhood. Over and over again, scholars, journalists, and social critics assert that contemporary notions of the mother, mothering, and motherhood rely on, at their core, a set of myths. Nancy Chodorow and Susan Contratto (1989) explain that, according to these myths, "mothers have exclusive responsibility for infants"; the relationship between mother and child is characterized as one of "closeness, oneness, and joy . . . the quintessence of perfect understanding"; and the mother herself is characterized as a person who does not have "her own life, wants, needs, history, other social relationships, [or] work. She is known only in her capacity as a mother" (90).

Shari Thurer (1994) articulates the myth using slightly different terms, asserting, "There is but one correct way to mother. . . . You know [it]: the mother . . . is always loving, selfless, tranquil; [she] finds passionate fulfillment in every detail of childrearing" (xiii). Paula Caplan (2000) appends "mothers don't get angry" to the set of myths (70). And Susan Douglas and Meredith Michaels (2004) find that, according to normative structures, mothers are "fun-loving, spontaneous, and relaxed, yet at the same time, scared out of [their] minds that [their] kids could be killed at any moment"; "No woman is truly complete or fulfilled unless she has kids"; "Women remain the best primary caretakers of children"; "To be a remotely decent mother, a woman has to devote her entire physical, psychological, emotional, and intellectual being, 24/7, to her children" (3–4). These notions, Douglas and Michaels suggest, support and perhaps even generate the myths "that motherhood is eternally fulfilling and rewarding, that it is *always* the best and most important thing [women] do, that there is only a narrowly prescribed way to do it right, and that if [a woman does not] love each and every second of it, there's something wrong with [her]" (3–4, emphasis in original). While we recognize such myths as mythical—of the fabulous, the fantastical, the imaginary—we also cherish them and even embrace them.

Ultimately, in fact, the myths stand as the measure against which our moment holds mothers and their mothering. While seemingly paradoxical, this is how myth itself functions, according to theorist Roland Barthes (1972), whose work exposes myth as a type of speech that naturalizes history, factualizes culture, and ultimately engenders ideology. And so we find the "myths of motherhood" reflected in and disseminated by nearly every contemporary image of mothers and mothering. Douglas and Michaels (2004) show this quite vividly in their examination of the past thirty years of child-rearing advice, mass-media images of and stories about mothers, and legislation and social policy that speaks to (and does not speak to) the lives, concerns, and situations of women and mothers. To this constellation of mythmakers and myth propagators, this chapter adds the seemingly unlikely source of the children's picture book. The medium delivers the message; it is part of the constellation that produces mothers and motherhood.

The picture book constructs images of and ideas about mothers and motherhood, shaping not only children's but also women's (and men's) understanding of what it means to be a mother. Thinking about the effects of this shaping on adults is important, because most adults do not pay attention to it; they see children's literature as a thing of, about, and for children. Thus the effects of children's literature on adult readers become not only insidious but remain unchecked. It is essential to explore the ways in which children's literature shapes notions of parents, parenting, mothers, and mothering, because women are reading these books at the exact moment they are immersed in figuring out how to be a mother, and at the exact moment they are making a shift from being a woman to being a mom. In addition, given the chaos of adding a child to a life, these may be the only books they are reading at this particular moment.[8]

The section that follows will show that many picture books, especially those for and/or about babies, engender ideas of mothers and mothering that support the myth of motherhood articulated by Chodorow and Contratto (1989), Thurer (1994), Caplan (2000), and Douglas and Michaels (2004). It will then look at how other picture books, especially discipline-oriented ones for and/or about toddlers and preschoolers, seem to counter or push against the myth while they actually reinscribe it. Moving beyond the "all-white world of children's literature" to picture books by and/or about African Americans, the chapter will investigate texts that draw on histories and circumstances outside of those that work to produce the so-very-White "myth of motherhood." In looking to these texts, one needs to be careful not to appropriate one cultural group's experience and equate it to the history and circumstances of another. Too, one needs to be careful not to underestimate the specific structures of oppression that may have compelled these images. At the same time, there is no denying that these images offer less mythical, alternative, and empowering notions of mothers and motherhood.[9] In this, they not only dispel the sovereign power of the motherhood myth but they suggest the potential and possibility of many kinds of motherhood.

PICTURING MOTHERS

The picture books for/about the very youngest of children are the ones that most frequently present an image of parenting as a female occupation and as the only female occupation; mothering as a sacrifice of the self; motherhood as eternally fulfilling; and mothers as attentive, loving, and tranquil. This mother and the mother-instruction that accompanies it are almost perfectly exemplified in Margaret Wise Brown's 1942 *The Runaway Bunny*.[10] *The Runaway Bunny* begins with a young bunny's declaration that he will run away. As he imagines the places he will go to find independence and the ways he will hide from his mother, the mother bunny tells him she will follow and find him. Always. While the book speaks to a child's simultaneous desire for and fear of autonomy, it codes the mother as warm, loving, selfless, and patient. She stands for safety and security. Further, it suggests that mothers are—or should be—fun. Mama bunny plays the game, and she can imagine being a tree, a tightrope walker, and even the wind. The story ultimately maintains that (good) mothers accommodate their child's behavior, and that mothers' only responsibility is to attend to their child. Brown's perennially popular *The Runaway Bunny*'s idea of mothering might attest to its period's thinking more than today's. However, as Raymond Williams's (1961) notion of the "selective tradition" suggests, our current moment's selection of *The Runaway Bunny* as a "classic" and a childhood favorite exposes both the current moment's attempt to characterize and understand the previous moment (the book's period) and the current moment's interests, values, and ways of thinking (64).

Supporting this is the fact that Brown's mother (and type of mothering) appears in more or less the same fashion in more contemporary picture books. Robert Munsch's (1986) *Love You Forever*, Barbara Helen Berger's (1997) *A Lot of Otters*, and Stoo Hample's (2006) *I Will Kiss You (Lots & Lots & Lots)* stand as examples from the three most recent decades. *Love You Forever* is a particularly interesting case because it acknowledges the difficulties of parenting and the complicated feelings many mothers have in response to their children. The book offers a mother's "difficulty" for every stage of childhood, but it ultimately dismisses the mother's frustrations in favor of the all-loving, tranquil, fulfilled-by-motherhood idea of the mother. The book is so invested in this idea of motherhood that it has the mother repeatedly *crawl* into her child's room to substantiate it. The mother even drives across town with a ladder after the child is grown to evidence her love and find fulfillment in mothering as she rocks and sings to her sleeping "boy." While the repetition highlights the book's lessons in motherhood, its reversal in the end as the son mothers the mother when she is too old and too feeble to mother him sharpens the point to a razored edge: mothers' love will be rewarded and returned in the form of the child's love.

Obviously this image of motherhood—and it is an image of motherhood not parenthood—feels good.[11] In identifying the mother (and the mother-reader) as the embodiment of pure, unconditional love, the text reassures and calms. It also gives the woman an identity, a role, a meaningful place in the world. This mother does not work for anything as crass as money; she works for love. And, in fact, she is love. The identity may offer comfort—especially to new parents, who may be caught up in difficult questions of how to and who will care for the new person in their lives. The identity is encouraging—especially to the new mother, who may be facing the identity crisis that seems to come with motherhood these days. Of course, if instead of seeing herself in such images the mother finds herself harried, impatient, or even depressed, then she fails as a mother. If the woman does not feel all-consuming, selfless love for her child, if her emotions are more complicated or even ambivalent, or if she harbors wishes and ambitions for herself, then she is not a good or is not a good-enough mother.

In setting aside the feelings of guilt, remorse, and self-recrimination that the all-and-only-love image of the mother inspires, we expose yet another issue: Why is this particular parenting role most frequently affiliated with women and defined as mothering? It is a role that others in a child's life (others such as men/fathers, grandparents, day care providers) could, should, and often really do occupy. Picture books like Molly Bang's (1983) *Ten, Nine, Eight*, Alexandra Day's (1986) *Good Dog, Carl*, Vera Williams's (1990) *"More More More," Said the Baby*, Sam McBratney's (1994) *Guess How Much I Love You*, Susan Meyers's (2001) *Everywhere Babies*, and Martin Waddell's (2005) *Sleep Tight, Little Bear* argue this point by placing fathers and grandparents in the all-love role. Disquietingly, though, when the father/man is put in the role, he frequently becomes an animal (a dog in *Good Dog, Carl*, for example), and he often "becomes" a woman. In *Sleep Tight, Little Bear*, for example, the parenting bear, though male, participates in what Alleen Pace Nilsen (1971) deems the inexplicable "cult of the apron" that haunts images of women and girls in picture books. In Bang's *Ten, Nine, Eight*, the father-who-mothers becomes a person of color, perhaps suggesting that the mythical mother can only be White. In short, many of the books that try to dispel the idea that women mother fall short in their efforts.

In the end, *The Runaway Bunny/Love You Forever* image dominates the lovey-dovey baby picture book. The primary messages for the adult reader are that parenting is a (White) female occupation, parenting is (or should be) women's only occupation, mothering is a sacrifice of the self, motherhood is eternally fulfilling, and mothers are always and endlessly attentive, loving, patient, and composed.

Picture books that deliver a more realistic vision of the mother do exist. Indeed, there is a whole group of books for and/or about toddlers and preschoolers that seems to push against the myth of motherhood. They portray mothers as disciplinarians, as people with voice, as people with power over others, as people who have boundaries. For example, in Maurice Sendak's (1963) *Where the Wild Things Are*, David Shannon's (1998) *No, David!*, Mem Fox's (2000) *Harriet, You'll Drive Me Wild*, and Sarah Weeks's (2004) *If I Were I Lion*, mothers lose their patience with their children and their naughty behavior. Sendak's Max's mother sends her wild boy to his room, and both Shannon's and Weeks's mothers put their child in a time-out. Fox's mother even loses her temper and shouts at her child: After a day of patiently enduring her child's rambunctious behavior, the mother, who "[does not] like to yell," eventually loses it. "There was a terrible silence. Then [she] began to yell. She yelled and yelled and yelled." Here is a realistic mom: a somewhat harried mom who loves her child but who is also a person.

Although representations of angry women are not typical in American culture, they are common in picture books. In their study of the medium, Anderson and Hamilton (2005) found, to their surprise, that mothers expressed anger and disciplined children more frequently than fathers.[12] In other words, negative feelings and forceful behaviors become acceptable for women in "the context of mothers working with young children" (149). Women are not allowed to be angry, but mothers can be—or so the picture book appears to suggest.

While picture books such as *Where the Wild Things Are*, *No, David!*, *If I Were a Lion*, and *Harriet, You'll Drive Me Wild!* present images of mothers with power and sharp emotions, they ultimately take away such powers and emotions, recuperating them through and into the myth of motherhood. *Where the Wild Things Are*, *No, David!*, and *If I Were a Lion* literally erase or fragment the mother, failing to offer an image of her or picturing her only in bits and pieces. *Harriet, You'll Drive Me Wild!* gives the mother physical presence but it holds her responsible for the child's behavior. For example, it shows the mother reading a newspaper at the breakfast table while Harriet goofs around, toppling orange juice and creating other small disasters. In their endings, and thus finally and conclusively, all four books clearly undermine the more real mother they seemed to construct. The final moment of each book even undercuts each mother's frustration: Max's dinner is "still hot"; David gets a hug and "Yes, David . . . I love you!"; the wild-child of *If I Were Lion* is forgiven; and Harriet receives a hug and an apology. The mothers' power dissolves, and the all-loving, selfless ideal reclaims motherhood. Ultimately, then, even the sort of book that appears to push against the myths of motherhood only reinscribes them: erasing or fragmenting the woman to make her a mother, finding fault in her mothering to explain the child's shortcomings, and obliterating the mother, her needs, her voice, and her authority in deference to the (imagined) child's needs.

One might argue that the selfless, all-giving, all-loving, ever-patient mother is necessary for the child. The texts under discussion here are, after all, for and about children. They are part of a body of literature that aims to address children's needs. Children need to be able to make mistakes; they need to be able to safely test boundaries; and they need to know that they will always be loved—no matter what. They need to learn that they can find comfort from their fears and upsets in other people—or so theorists of child development assert, and so children's literature and those who produce it endorse.

Chodorow and Contratto's (1989) observations on the formation of the ideal mother raise questions about these assumptions. Chodorow and Contratto mark them as assumptions and assert that the child's so-called needs may be as artificial as the myths of motherhood. The myths of motherhood, they argue, emerge in response to "fantasied and unexamined notions of child development," notions that characterize the child as a "passive reactor to drives or environmental pressures," notions that characterize the child's "needs" as indisputably legitimate rather than potentially unrealistic or unreasonable (95, 82–83). These notions deny the child agency and intentionality, while they necessitate particular ways of tending that child, ways that support, respond to, and validate the imagined child's imagined needs. Motherhood, as it is defined in both the popular imagination and children's literature, embodies these ways of caring for children. And so the myths of motherhood emerge out of an invention, a fabrication, or, to reinvoke Rose's terms, impossibility (Rose 1984). Motherhood itself becomes, like childhood and children's literature, impossible: unattainable and insufferable.

Yet Chodorow and Contratto's (1989) discovery allows for another possibility. If "motherhood" depends on imagining children in particular ways, then motherhood might be imagined differently if children were imagined differently. Focusing on motherhood and childhood as products of desire discloses them as mythical. Focusing on motherhood and childhood as products of a desire that is motivated by a power dynamic intended to support a particular kind of authority allows that they could be imagined in ways that serve different groups' desires and needs. Focusing on motherhood and childhood through such a lens allows mothers, mothering, and motherhood to be imagined in ways that might be more in line with real women's lived experiences and that might accord agency.[13]

In truth, images of such alternative mothers and motherhoods already exist. In children's literature, for example, in picture books by and about people of color—but particularly, in those by and/or about African Americans—we find a body of texts drawing on histories and circumstances outside of those that work to produce the very American, very White "myth of motherhood." Evelyn Nakano Glenn (1994), Annelise Orleck (1997), Stanlie James (1999), Patricia Hill Collins (1993,

1994, 2000), Trudelle Thomas (2004), and Andrea O'Reilly (2004) point out that the conversation surrounding the myths of motherhood focuses almost exclusively on the experiences of one group: White middle-class women. This body of scholarship also argues that the African American mother, her mothering, and her motherhood express a different ideal. This ideal stands as a source of growth, hope, status, and power for African American women and the African American community. Moreover, because it is an ideal, and because the ideal responds to "issues that mainstream families have only recently become attentive to, such as combining work and family roles, single parenthood, and extended family relationships" (Glenn 1994, 6), it stands as a model that other American women might be able to adapt to their efforts to negotiate contemporary motherhood.

The model that emerges from African and African American traditions and circumstances does not assume that mothering takes place within the private confines of the nuclear family, nor that the mother has nearly exclusive responsibilities for child rearing; it does not assume strict sex roles, where men do X and women do Y; and it does not assume that to be a "good" mother a woman must make motherhood her sole occupation (Collins 1993, 43–44). Instead, African American motherhood assumes that women are economically independent from men; that vesting one person with full responsibility for "mothering" a child is, at best, foolish and, at worst, dangerous; that "mothering" builds community (both by bringing the young into the culture and by involving the community in child rearing); and that "mothering" can be a form of social activism. In all of these ways, African American motherhood offers freedoms and power to women, for unlike the White myths of motherhood, it does not sacrifice the woman for the child; it does not sacrifice the woman for society.

This is not to imply that African American motherhood is without burdens. In fact, African American motherhood is a fundamentally contradictory institution. O'Reilly (2004) explains that, because African American women "raise children in a society that is at best indifferent to the needs of black children and the concerns of black mothers," African American motherhood must concentrate on "how to preserve, protect, and more generally empower [African American] children so that they may resist racist practices that seek to harm them" (171). African American mothers find themselves in a conflicted position; they have power and are even a source of power within the African American community, but their power is continually challenged, questioned, and/or undercut by institutionalized forces of racial, class, and gender oppression. Thus while African American motherhood can stand as an example of a strong, empowered vision of the mother, African American mothers' "ability to cope with the intersecting oppressions of race, class, gender, sexuality, and nation," as Collins (2000) puts it, "should not be confused with transcending the injustices characterizing these oppressions" (195). In other words, African American efforts to compensate for oppression and injustice do not rectify, excuse, or overcome these oppressions or injustices. Such forces remain, and they remain problematic.

That African American motherhood is entangled in a system of oppression does not, however, negate the fact that the mother it culturally and textually envisions is a strong, confident, powerful, complex individual. African American children's picture books not only evidence this version of the mother, but they promote her ways of being and thinking to and for adult readers. In contrast to the more widely available and heavily promoted White myth of motherhood, they offer some mothers a less-fraught, more-tolerable way of imagining their own motherhood. For other mothers, this representation of motherhood additionally confirms a lived experience. For this latter group, the African American picture book's envisioning of the mother is both a window and a mirror. And, for both groups, it performs the work of African American mothering itself; it offers support to women as mothers and thus helps them resist the forces that seek to marginalize, disempower, or otherwise harm them.

One of the key differences between picture books that construct the (White) myths of motherhood and picture books that imagine mothering through African American traditions and experiences is that, in the latter, mothers work. While most African American picture books do not make an issue of it, the fact that mothers work clearly impacts both the ways mothering happens and how the mother and her roles are understood. For example, in Williams's (1992) *Working Cotton*, which depicts a migrant family's experience picking cotton, the mother works while she watches the children. Her doubled responsibility means she does not pick as much cotton as Daddy, and yet the book marks the adults as equal in their work, noting, "Mamma sing; Daddy hum," and giving Daddy care of the baby on the trip home. Here, work and mothering are not mutually exclusive, and "mothering" does not belong exclusively to women.

Jacqueline Woodson's (2004) *Coming on Home Soon* envisions the mother and mothering similarly, while it adds the idea that the working mother's absence can benefit the child. Mama, who loves her daughter "more than anything in the world," leaves her temporarily with her grandmother because "They're hiring colored women in Chicago." Ada Ruth misses her mother while she is gone, but the book carefully offers a mother stand-in through the figure of the grandmother. The grandmother does not replace the mother herself, as one person can never substitute for another, but she mothers Ada Ruth in her own more-than-adequate way. Thus as in other African American picture book imaginings of the mother—such as Valerie Flourney's (1985) *The Patchwork Quilt* and (1995) *Tanya's Reunion*; Cynthia DeFelice's (1997) *Willy's Silly Grandma*; Angela Johnson's (1994) *Mama Bird, Baby Birds* and (2000) *Down the Winding Road*; Jeannette Caines's (1977) *Daddy* and (1973) *Abby*; Nikki Grimes's (2004) *A Day with Daddy*; Natasha Tarpley's (2002) *Bippity Bop Barbershop*; Mary Hoffman's (1991) *Amazing Grace* and (1995) *Boundless Grace*—the mother's absence is depicted as an opportunity for establishing and developing splendid, full relationships with other family members.

Coming on Home Soon also uses the mother's absence to help Ada Ruth learn to comfort herself. In constructing a world in which a child successfully negotiates her mother's absence, *Coming on Home Soon* suggests that a mother's career does not harm the child; instead, it offers the child opportunities for both richer relationships with other people and personal growth. Understanding the child and her needs thus gives the woman, the mother, the woman reader, and the becoming-a-mother reader a certain freedom to keep and/or take up roles in addition to "mother."

African American picture books not only suggest that working mothers' multiple roles can enrich the lives of both child and mother, they also insist that working mothers' work generates pride and even authority for both. For example, in Joyce Carol Thomas's (1998) *I Have Heard of a Land*, the pioneer mother stakes a claim, plants crops, leads prayer groups, helps build a cabin, and tends her children. Her accomplishments are gratifying (to her) and inspiring (for the child and adult reader), as the text emphasizes in its final line: "Her possibilities reach as far as her eyes can see and as far as our imaginations can carry us."

Dolores Johnson's (1999) *My Mom Is My Show-and-Tell* displays the proud mother even more prominently. When David worries that his mother will embarrass him during her career presentation at his school, she tries to tease him out of his worries, reject them as worthy of concern, and reason them away. When her efforts fail, though, she enacts her pride and self-assurance, joyfully dancing into the school building. David is horrified, but later he proudly introduces her: "She's the best teacher and the best mother in the world. And if you pay real good attention she'll . . . even dance for you." Here the book models a child who has learned to take pride in his mother's job, her mothering, and her quirks. Even more importantly for this chapter's concerns, the book presents a mother who has agency, who is confident in and comfortable with herself and her authority. This mother purposefully embarrasses her child and helps him confront his own fears because *she* knows that *she knows* what is best for him.

Such unqualified authority for women is not unusual in African American picture books. In fact, unlike the discipline books discussed earlier, most African American picture books readily grant the mother the power to discipline. For example, in Patricia McKissack's (2000) *The Honest-to-Goodness Truth*, "Mama punished [Libby] double. For not tending to Ol' Boss, Libby couldn't go play. . . . And for lying, she had to stay on the porch for the rest of the day." Mama then goes about her business. No apologies, no remorse. In Eloise Greenfield's (1972) *Good News*, Mama does not apologize for her impatient words or try to compensate for not having the time to do what her son wants her to do. These mothers do not hesitate to disagree with, chastise, or even shame the child. They are confident in their authority. They hold the power to act on the child's behalf; to help the child learn safe, kind, culturally, and socially acceptable ways to behave; and to expose the child to disappointment and stings to help him or her better weather life.

This version of the mother has the added benefit of according the child authority, responsibility, and respect. This version of the mother exists because it assumes that the child has agency and intentionality. So the mother in Woodson's (2001) *The Other Side* respects her child's efforts to make friends with their White neighbor, despite her own misgivings. So the child in Johnson's (1990) *When I Am Old With You* exists "old-ly" *with* his or her "other mother"; they are equals. So the child in McKissack's (1986) *Flossie and the Fox* outwits a fox. So Debbi Chocolate's (1995) *On the Day I Was Born* celebrates the child's birth from the child's point of view. So in contrast to a book like *Read to Your Bunny*'s injunction to the parent, Sandra and Myles Pinkney's (2006) *Read and Rise* tells the *child* to "read and rise." In short, giving the mother authority—allowing her to be self-sufficient, independent, and accomplished, as well as nurturing and caring—necessitates a different understanding of the child. The parent's duty is to guide and assist the child, but the child acts for and by himself or herself; she or he is not a simple reflection of the parent and/or parenting practices. The relationship between the parent and child becomes interactive, and both mother and child gain power and status.

In children's picture books by and/or about African Americans, we find a construction of the mother, mothering, and motherhood that works much differently from the "myths of motherhood." The picture book medium delivers the possibility of a mother—and a woman—who is self-sufficient, independent, accomplished, nurturing, caring, and satisfied; who is proud; and who has authority. This mother, this woman, is a strong, confident, powerful, complex individual who engages in a range of activities and pursuits. This construction offers a more palatable alternative to the impossible, insufferable myths; it confirms many women's lived experience. And it accomplishes the work of "mothering"—namely, preserving, protecting, and empowering a group (mothers, in this case) within a society that can be dismissive, hostile, and otherwise oppressive.

CONCLUSION

Although the African American picture book's construction of the mother is, like other constructions, an ideal, mythic and impossible, its impossibility is in the realm of the optimistic and the protective rather than the insufferable and the destructive. It tends toward empowerment, community, and a complementary relationship between the woman and the mother. It counters the (White) myth's push toward isolation and divisiveness, toward the erasure and annihilation of the woman in favor of the mother. The African American model of motherhood unquestionably emerges as a defensive maneuver in response to painfully hostile and oppressive social conditions, yet it also defies these conditions, imagining a woman—a mother—who effectively negotiates the work and family complexities of her life, who remains whole as she negotiates the work and family complexities of her life.

Unhappily, as the selection of picture books employed in this chapter reveals, the (White) mythic mother overshadows this mother. The mother delivered to women—the mother delivered by the publishing industry, by bookstores, by the culture industry generally—remains the mythic one. While one must determinedly seek books such as the ones in the latter part of the chapter, nearly all of the books in the earlier part of the chapter are standard childhood fare. Many are canonical. Most are readily available in big-box bookstores. They are popular. And, as Raymond Williams (1961) has taught us, the popular is a significant index of any moment's "structure of feeling": its felt sense of the quality of life; its culture; its sense of what is ordinary, normal, standard.

However, one of the great beauties of the popular is that it is unstable; it changes. Studies of gender, sex roles, and children's picture books have had an impact on representations of children.[14] Nancy Larrick's (1965) call to action, "The All-White World of Children's Books," resulted in an increase in the number of books published by and about non-White cultures and experiences. Such changes bode well for future representations of adults, of parents, and particularly of mothers.

Thinking about the adult in children's literature and the adult as a reader of children's literature exposes and speaks to a number of concerns. It shows that adults are constructed, just as children are, in and by children's picture books. That is, the views, opinions, actions, and ways of thinking of the adults reading children's literature are affected by what is in these books. How adults take up parenting roles and how they learn their relationship to children are affected. These effects can be insidious, especially in the case of new mothers who may be trying to reshape their sense of self at the very moment they are reading these books. These effects remain unchecked because most adults see children's literature as a thing of, about, and for children. But adults are reading these books. And the children who are being read to will also, one day, be adults.

Many of the current representations embody, encourage, and deliver notions of parent and child that are oppressive, disrespectful, and limiting to both. Many of the current representations encourage and embody the impossibility of a relationship between adult and child, the impossible relation between adult and child. And, if children's literature is about the relation between child and adult, representations of adults—especially representations of parents—are as significant as representations of the child. Exposing these representations (and rethinking them in terms of other versions, versions that are informed by other histories and experiences) creates possibility—possibility for parents and parenting, mothers and mothering, child and childhood, and possibility for better, more viable, more respectful interaction and relations between adulthood and childhood. Keeping those other versions available, and making those other versions more available, can only work to deliver such possibilities, to make such possibilities realities.

NOTES

1. Wells (1997). I have not included page numbers for the quotations from the picture books because most of these books are both unpaginated and short enough for any reader to find the quoted material easily.
2. Nodelman (1988) elaborates on this point. Nodelman's theories of how picture books work also inform all of the picture book analysis in this chapter.
3. There is a long-standing debate in the field about how to define children's literature. The oft-cited remark by C. S. Lewis stands as one piece of evidence: "I am almost inclined to set it up as a canon that a children's story which is enjoyed only by children is a bad children's story" (1982, 11).

More exhaustively, Shavit spends an entire chapter explicating the "Ambivalent Status of [all children's] Texts" in her seminal *Poetics of Children's Literature* (1986).
4. Wells and Scholastic, in fact, continue to capitalize on this, most recently publishing (in 2006) *Raising a Child Who Is Ready to Learn (My Shining Star)*. Although it is sold in the picture book section of the bookstore, *Booklist* reviewer Julie Cummins notes that it is clearly "directed to adults" (Cummins 2006).
5. From this conviction grows a great body of scholarship that more specifically explores how picture books represent and construct gender and gender roles. There are over fifty articles that discuss sex roles in children's picture books. The most influential, cited, and recent include the following: Weitzman, Eiffer, Hokada, and Ross 1972; Engel 1981; Kolbe and LaVoie 1981; Collins, Ingoldsby, and Dellmann 1984; Davis 1984; Dougherty and Engel 1987; Williams, Vernon, Williams, and Malecha 1987; Dellmann-Jenkins, Florjancic, and Swadener 1993; Kortenhaus and Demarest 1993; Creany 1995; Miller 1996; Oskamp, Kaufman, and Wolterbeck 1996; Turner-Bowker 1996; Murr 1997; Chatton 2001; Poarch and Monk-Turner 2001; Sarvis 2004; Anderson and Hamilton 2005. Much of this scholarship finds connections between the ways gender and gender roles are represented in picture books and the attitudes and behaviors of actual children.

Encouragingly, the sequence of studies done from the 1970s through the present reveals progress in terms of balancing the number of males and females that appear and in terms of representing girls in more active and less stereotypical roles. The foundational and highly influential study done by Weitzman and colleagues in 1972 found that, in award-winning picture books published from 1967 to 1971, male characters appeared in 92 percent of all pictures (261 times), while females appeared in 8 percent of all pictures (23 pictures). Further, while the males were shown involved in and/or initiating adventures and exciting activities, the females were generally depicted as watching, waiting, and helping. By the mid-1980s, scholars such as Dougherty and Engel claimed that the percentage of female characters had risen to 43 percent, and that their roles were more active. In the mid-1990s, research (e.g., Oskamp and colleagues) showed that 43.3 percent of the pictures represented females, and that male and female actions were more similar than different. For the 2000s, Hamilton, Anderson, Broaddus, and Young (2006) found little further progress in the number of female characters portrayed.
6. See Kortenhaus and Demarest 1993; Oskamp, Kaufman, and Wolterbeck 1996; Murr 1997; Poarch and Monk-Turner 2001; Bersh 2003; Sarvis 2004.
7. For an overview of the Mommy Wars and what is at stake in them, see Peskowitz (2005).
8. This is not to suggest that picture books are the *only* point of influence over women's efforts to redefine themselves when they become mothers. Obviously they have lived in the world and have been exposed to notions of mothers, mothering, and motherhood from multiple sources throughout

their lives, even if they have not consciously attended to these images and ideas. Further, in addition to picture books, many parents are reading (or are only reading) advice books (such as William and Martha Sears's (2003) *The Baby Book*, Penelope Leach's (1997) *Your Baby and Child*, or the *What to Expect* series). While these books quite clearly code parenting as mothering, a study of these books and their construction of motherhood remains to be done. Finally, as Douglas and Michaels (2004) point out, new mothers also read (and often only read) magazines during this period. In fact, Douglas and Michaels argue, the various advice columns in women's magazine are often "avidly read because they [are] about raising kids, [have] a user-friendly format, and [allow readers] to compare" their behaviors and their child's to that of others (61).
9. International picture books can also create such images. For example, the 2004 Korean book *Guji Guji* by Chen presents a model of a mother who is both a mother and her own person. It offers a version of mothering that depends on women having interests and engagements outside of their children. It envisions a woman who is important to the functioning of her society in both her mothering and her other pursuits.
10. Although *The Runaway Bunny* features a slightly older child, I include it here with the "baby books" because of the way it represents the parent-child relationship.
11. Anderson and Hamilton's (2005) work on fathers in picture books supports this contention. Their study reveals that not only are fathers underrepresented in parenting roles, but also even when fathers appear, mothers are more likely to be portrayed as affectionate and nurturing. Murr's (1997) findings on parent behaviors in picture books concur with this finding.
12. They hypothesize that "mothers would more often express the stereotypically feminine emotions of happiness and sadness and would more often be disobeyed, whereas fathers would more often mention money, express anger, and discipline their children" (Anderson and Hamilton 2005, 146).
13. Children and childhood are entirely another matter, as Rose's (1984) work brings to the fore. As children do not usually produce public representations of themselves, childhood is only ever produced in relation to adults' imaginings.
14. See note 4.

REFERENCES

Anderson, D. A., and M. Hamilton. 2005. Gender role stereotyping of parents in children's picture books: The invisible father. *Sex Roles* 53:3, 4 (February): 145–51.
Bang, M. 1983. *Ten, nine, eight*. New York: Scholastic.
Barthes, R. 1972. *Mythologies*. London: Jonathan Cape.
Battle-Lavert, G. 2003. *Papa's mark*. Illustrated by C. Bootman. New York: Holiday House.

Beckett, S. L., ed. 1999. *Transcending boundaries: Writing for a dual audience of children and adults*. New York: Garland.
Berger, B. H. 1997. *A lot of otters*. New York: Putnam.
Bersh, L. C. 2003. Exploring female images in the Caldecott Award book 1980–2003. PhD Diss., University of Alabama.
Brown, M. W. 1942/1991. *The runaway bunny*. Illustrated by C. Hurd. New York: Harper & Row.
Caines, J. 1973. *Abby*. Illustrated by S. Kellogg. New York: Harper & Row.
———. 1977. *Daddy*. Illustrated by R. Himler. New York: Harper & Row.
Caplan, P. J. 2000. *The new don't blame mother: Mending the mother-daughter relationship*. New York: Routledge.
Chatton, B. 2001. Picture books for preschool children: Exploring gender issues with three- and four-year-olds. In *Beauty, brains, and brawn: The construction of gender in children's literature*, ed. S. Lehr, 57–78. Portsmouth, NH: Heinemann.
Chen, C. 2004. *Guji guji*. La Jolla, CA: Kane/Miller.
Chocolate, D. 1995. *On the day I was born*. Illustrated by M. Rosales. New York: Scholastic.
Chodorow, N., with S. Contratto. 1989. The fantasy of the perfect mother. In *Feminism and psychoanalytic theory*, 79–96. New Haven, CT: Yale University Press.
Collins, L. J., B. B. Ingoldsby, and M. M. Dellmann. 1984. Sex role stereotyping in children's literature: A change from the past. *Childhood Education* 60 (March–April): 278–85.
Collins, P. H. 1993. The meaning of motherhood in Black culture and Black mother-daughter relationships. In *Double stitch: Black women write about mothers and daughters*, ed. P. Bell-Scott, B. Guy-Sheftall, J. J. Royster, J. Sims-Wood, M. DeCosta-Willis, and L. P. Fultz, 42–60. New York: HarperPerennial.
———. 1994. Shifting the center: Race, class, and feminist theorizing about motherhood. In *Mothering: Ideology, experience, agency*, ed. E. Nakano Glenn, G. Change, and L. Rennie Forcey, 45–66. New York: Routledge.
———. 2000. *Black feminist thought: Knowledge, consciousness, and the politics of empowerment*. 2d ed. New York: Routledge.
Creany, A. D. 1995. The appearance of gender in award-winning children's books. In *Eyes on the future: Converging images, ideas, and instruction: Selected readings from the annual conference of the International Visual Literacy Association*, ed. D. G. Beauchamp, J. M. Hunter, and R. E. Griffin, 18–22. ERDS # ED 391 510. 289–298.
Cummins, J. 2006. Review of *My shining star*. *Booklist* (May 15): 48.
Davis, A. J. 1984. Sex-differentiated behaviors in non-sexist picture books. *Sex Roles* 11 (July): 1–16.
Day, A. 1986. *Good dog, Carl*. New York: Simon & Schuster.
DeFelice, C. 1997. *Willy's silly grandma*. Illustrated by S. Jackson. New York: Orchard.

Dellmann-Jenkins, M., L. Florjancic, and E. B. Swadener. 1993. Sex roles and cultural diversity in recent award-winning picture books for young children. *Journal of Research in Childhood Education* 7:2 (Spring–Summer): 74–82.
Demers, P., and G. Moyles. 1982. Preface. In *From instruction to delight: An anthology of children's literature to 1850*, ed. P. Demers and G. Moyles, xi–xii. New York: Oxford University Press.
Dougherty, W. H., and R. Engel. 1987. An 80s look for sex equality in Caldecott winners and honor books. *The Reading Teacher* (January): 394–98.
Douglas, S. J., and M. W. Michaels. 2004. *The mommy myth: The idealization of motherhood and how it has undermined all women.* New York: Free Press.
Edwards, A. 2000. Community mothering: The relationship between mothering and the community work of Black women. *Journal of the Association for Research on Mothering* 2:2 (Fall–Winter): 66–84.
Eisenberg, A., H. Eisenberg Murkoff, and S. Eisenberg Hathaway. 1984. *What to expect when you're expecting.* New York: Workman.
Engel, R. 1981. Is unequal treatment of females diminishing in children's picture books? *The Reading Teacher* 34 (March): 647–52.
Flourney, V. 1985. *The patchwork quilt.* Illustrated by J. Pinkney. New York: Dial.
———. 1995. *Tanya's reunion.* Illustrated by J. Pinkney. New York: Dial.
Fox, M. 2000. *Harriet, you'll drive me wild!* Illustrated by M. Frazee. New York: Harcourt.
Frasier, D. 1991. *On the day you were born.* New York: Harcourt.
Glenn, E. N. 1994. Social constructions of mothering: A thematic overview. In *Mothering: Ideology, experience, agency*, ed. E. Nakano Glenn, G. Change, and L. Rennie Forcey, 1–32. New York: Routledge.
Greenfield, E. 1972. *Good news (formerly "Bubbles").* Illustrated by P. Cummings. New York: Coward, McCann, & Geoghegan.
Grimes, N. 2004. *A day with daddy.* Illustrated by N. Tadgell. New York: Scholastic.
Hamilton, M., D. Anderson, M. Broaddus, and K. Young. 2006. Sex stereotyping and under-representation of female characters in 200 popular children's picture books: A 21st century update. *Sex Roles* 55: 757–65.
Hample, S. 2006. *I will kiss you (lots & lots & lots).* Cambridge, MA: Candlewick.
Hoffman, M. 1991. *Amazing grace.* Illustrated by C. Binch. New York: Dial.
———. 1995. *Boundless grace.* Illustrated by C. Binch. New York: Dial.
Hunt, P. 1991. *Criticism, theory, and children's literature.* Cambridge, MA: Basil Blackwell.
James, S. 1999. Mothering: A possible Black feminist link to social transformation. In *Theorizing Black feminism: The visionary pragmatism of Black women*, ed. S. James and A. P. Busia, 44–54. New York: Routledge.
Johnson, A. 1990. *When I am old with you.* Illustrated by D. Soman. New York: Orchard.
———. 1994. *Mama bird, baby birds.* Illustrated by R. Mitchell. New York: Scholastic.

———. 2000. *Down the winding road.* Illustrated by S. W. Evans. New York: DK.

Johnson, D. 1999. *My mom is my show-and-tell.* New York: Marshall Cavendish.

Kolbe, R., and J. C. LaVoie. 1981. Sex-role stereotyping in preschool children's picture books. *Social Psychology Quarterly* 44: 369–74.

Kortenhaus, C., and J. Demarest. 1993. Gender role stereotyping in children's literature: An update. *Sex Roles* 28:3, 4: 219–32.

Larrick, N. 1965. The all-White world of children's books. *Saturday Review* (September 11): 63–65.

Leach, P. 1997. *Your baby and child: From birth to age five.* Rev. ed. New York: Knopf.

Lewis, C. S. 1982. On stories. In *On stories and other essays on literature by C. S. Lewis,* ed. W. Hooper, 3–20. New York: Harvest Books.

McBratney, S. 1994. *Guess how much I love you.* Illustrated by A. Jeram. Cambridge, MA: Candlewick.

McKissack, P. 1986. *Flossie and the fox.* Illustrated by R. Isadora. New York: Dial.

———. 2000. *The honest-to-goodness truth.* Illustrated by G. Potter. New York: Atheneum.

Meyers, S. 2001. *Everywhere babies.* Illustrated by M. Frazee. New York: Harcourt.

Miller, M. B. 1996. Where are the working mothers in children's literature? *Initiatives* 58:1: 47–50.

Munsch, R. 1986. *Love you forever.* Illustrated by S. McGraw. Buffalo, NY: Firefly.

Murkoff, H., and S. Mazel 2008a. *What to expect the first year.* New York: Workman.

———. 2008b. *What to expect the toddler years.* New York: Workman.

———. 2008c. *What to expect when you're expecting.* 4th ed. New York: Workman.

Murr, S. 1997. Parent behaviors displayed in children's literature: Content analysis of picture storybooks 1946–1995. PhD Diss., Texas Woman's University.

Myers, M. 1997. Canonical "orphans" and critical *ennui*: Rereading Edgeworth's cross-writing. *Children's Literature* (Special Issue on Cross-Writing Child and Adult) 25: 116–36.

Nilsen, A. P. 1971. Women in children's literature. *College English* 32:8 (May): 918–26.

Nodelman, P. 1988. *Words about pictures: The narrative art of children's picture books.* Athens: University of Georgia Press.

O'Reilly, A. 2004. A politics of the heart: African-American womanist thought on mothering. In *Mother outlaws: Theories and practices of empowered mothering,* ed. A. O'Reilly, 171–92. Toronto: Women's Press.

Orleck, A. 1997. Tradition unbound: Radical mothers in international perspective. In *The politics of motherhood: Activist voices from left to right,* ed. A. Jetter, A. Orleck, and D. Taylor, 3–22. Hanover, NH: University Press of New England.

Oskamp, S., K. Kaufman, and L. A. Wolterbeck. 1996. Gender role portrayals in preschool picture books. *Journal of Social Behavior and Personality* 11:5: 27–39.

Peskowitz, M. 2005. *The truth behind the mommy wars: Who decides what makes a good mother?* Emeryville, CA: Seal Press.

Pinkney, S. L. 2006. *Read and rise.* Illustrated by M. C. Pinkney. Foreword by M. Angelou. New York: Scholastic.

Poarch, R., and E. Monk-Turner. 2001. Gender roles in children's literature: A review of non-award-winning "Easy-to-Read" books. *Journal of Research in Childhood Education* 16 (Fall–Winter): 70–76.

Rose, J. 1984. *The case of Peter Pan, or the impossibility of children's fiction.* Philadelphia: University of Pennsylvania Press.

Sarvis, J. T. 2004. Gender roles in children's literature: An historical perspective 1970–2003. PhD Diss., Loyola University, Chicago.

Sears, W., and M. Sears. 2003. *The baby book: Everything you need to know about your baby from birth to age two.* Rev. and updated ed. Boston, MA: Little, Brown and Company.

Sendak, M. 1963. *Where the wild things are.* New York: HarperCollins.

Shannon, D. 1998. *No, David!* New York: Scholastic.

Shavit, Z. 1986. *Poetics of children's literature.* Athens: University of Georgia Press.

Tarpley, N. A. 2002. *Bippity bop barbershop.* Illustrated by E. B. Lewis. Boston, MA: Little, Brown.

Thomas, J. C. 1998. *I have heard of a land.* Illustrated by F. Cooper. New York: HarperCollins.

Thomas, T. 2004. "You'll become a lioness": African-American women talk about mothering. In *Mother outlaws: Theories and practices of empowered mothering,* ed. A. O'Reilly, 215–28. Toronto: Women's Press.

Thurer, S. L. 1994. *The myths of motherhood: How culture reinvents the good mother.* Boston, MA: Houghton Mifflin.

Turner-Bowker, D. M. 1996. Gender stereotyped descriptors in children's picture books: Does "curious Jane" exist in the literature? *Sex Roles* 35:7, 8: 461–88.

Waddell, M. 2005. *Sleep tight, little bear.* Illustrated by B. Firth. Cambridge, MA: Candlewick.

Wall, B. 1991. *The narrator's voice: The dilemma of children's fiction.* New York: St. Martin's Press.

Weeks, S. 2004. *If I were a lion.* Illustrated by H. Soloman. New York: Atheneum.

Weitzman, L., D. Eiffer, E. Hokada, and C. Ross. 1972. Sex role socialization in picture books for preschool children. *American Journal of Sociology* 77: 1125–50.

Wells, R. 1997. *Read to your bunny.* New York: Scholastic.

———. 2006. *Raising a child who is ready to learn (My shining star).* New York: Scholastic.

Williams, J., J. Vernon, M. Williams, and K. Malecha. 1987. Sex role socialization in picture books: An update. *Social Science Quarterly* 68: 148–56.

Williams, R. 1961. The analysis of culture. In *The long revolution*, 57–70. London: Chatto & Windus.
Williams, S. A. 1992. *Working cotton*. Illustrated by C. Byrd. New York: Harcourt.
Williams, V. B. 1990. *"More more more," said the baby*. New York: HarperCollins.
Woodson, J. 2001. *The other side*. Illustrated by E. B. Lewis. New York: Putnam.
———. 2004. *Coming on home soon*. Illustrated by E. B. Lewis. New York: Putnam.

PART 2

Feminist Interventions in Interpersonal Discourse

SEVEN

More than Talk

Single Mothers Claiming Space and Subjectivity on the University Campus

JILLIAN M. DUQUAINE-WATSON

In an increasingly high-tech world, communication is often delivered via computers, cellular telephones, e-mail, personal data assistants, and other electronic devices. Given the convenience and proliferation of these contemporary technologies, it is not surprising that many mothers rely on them to find information, participate in discussion forums, and form social relationships with other mothers. Indeed, a quick online search reveals hundreds of mothering-related blogs, Web sites, Listservs, and other e-based communities. In the modern world, then, many mothers may find themselves tempted by technologies, particularly as electronic modes of communication can foster interaction with large numbers of other mothers all over the world and transmit information easily and economically. Consequently, the idea of sitting down with other mothers for face-to-face dialogue may seem more than a little old-fashioned.

Yet as I demonstrate in this chapter, the seemingly outmoded technology of oral interchange can be an important way for mothers to connect with and deliver support to one another. In particular, I discuss "S.M.A.R.T.: Single Mothers Achieving and Reflecting Together," a support and discussion group for women who are engaged in sole parenting. The group is facilitated by the Women's Resource and Action Center (WRAC), the women's center on the University of Iowa (UI) campus in Iowa City, Iowa. I draw on data collected during a two-year research project that focused on the experiences of single mothers attending college. I conducted in-depth interviews with twenty-two UI single-mother students as well as interviews with WRAC staff members, board members, and participants in S.M.A.R.T. In addition, I engaged in participant observation with the S.M.A.R.T. group during the 2003–2004 academic year and conducted archival research on the history of WRAC at the Iowa Women's Archive.

Based on this research, I argue that what happens within the S.M.A.R.T. group is more than talk. Instead, within the post-welfare reform U.S. political climate as well as the "chilly" climate of higher education, this particular support and discussion group constitutes a unique form of delivery that stands in marked contrast to more high-tech modes of communication. The group facilitates discussion among single mothers and enables them to connect with one another in meaningful ways, share their challenges, and, of equal importance, claim subjectivity in an institutional space in which they are often marginalized. Thus, in the tradition of feminist consciousness-raising, S.M.A.R.T. constitutes a political space in which single mothers use language as a multifaceted tool of engagement, a way to deliver support, ideas, and a sense of community that, as the examples in this chapter demonstrate, are important to their well-being and that of their children.

A TYPICAL S.M.A.R.T. GROUP MEETING

Monday, March 28, 2004. I am fifteen minutes late getting to group. As I push open the front door to the Women's Resource and Action Center, the muffled voices of members of the S.M.A.R.T. group drift down from the second floor. I shake off the raindrops that cling to my hair and begin to climb the steep staircase, my left hand sliding along the oak banister that is original to the 1910 structure as I make my way to the top. Creaks announce each step, and by the time I arrive on the landing, the faces of four toddlers are peering anxiously through the doorway of a small but comfortable space that has been dubbed the "kids' care room." One of them asks, "Did that girl come?" Realizing they are referring to my ten-year-old daughter, I shake my head and reply, "No, she stayed home tonight." Disappointed by my response, they return to their play.

I step to the right and continue down the carpeted hall for several yards before turning left into a spacious but drafty room with faded ochre walls. Navigating through a maze of books, backpacks, coats, and other personal items scattered across the floor, I head for the nearest end of the sofa and sit down directly under the autographed poster of Dolores Huerta. Five women are already in the room. "Kate,"[1] the group facilitator, is on the far end of the couch, near the window. "Charlotte" has taken her usual place next to Kate and smiles a friendly "hello." Seated on the floor and near the radiator, "Brenda" is surrounded by the remnants of a Subway dinner. "Lauren" occupies the dark brown chair, the one you literally sink into when you sit in it, and she has tucked her feet beneath her as she struggles to pull her sweater more tightly around her upper body. "Mary" sits closest to the door and is still wearing her coat.

Two apple pies from the supermarket bakery have been placed on a worn end table next to where Kate is sitting. Paper plates, napkins, forks, and a cutting knife have been borrowed from the WRAC kitchen. One of the pies is nearly gone. I am prepared to apologize for my tardiness, but the discussion continues uninterrupted, with group members balancing paper plates on their knees as they converse between bites. The discussion centers on the idea of a group outing. Brenda expresses frustration that she "never get[s] to have alone time anymore" since her child's father stopped taking their son every other weekend. Lauren brings up the idea of a "girls' night out" and asks, "When are *we* all going out?" Kate pulls out a flyer advertising the upcoming "family free night" at a local mall and suggests that everyone meet there for free carousel rides, ice skating, and admission to the children's museum. Lauren, somewhat frustrated, says she thinks that would be a great idea but then makes it clear that a girls' night out, without children, is what she really wants. And needs.

Brenda returns to the topic of her son's father, "William." Group members are well aware of her history with him. Over the course of the semester, we have learned about it, little by little, at our Monday night meetings. For nearly five months, the couple had been involved in a bitter custody battle over their son. The whole situation had taken her by surprise. Although Brenda said William had initially "been real excited about the pregnancy," he abandoned her midway through her second trimester. He reappeared right before Brandon was born and, according to Brenda, "stuck around for a little over a week" before disappearing again. The next time Brenda heard from William was through his lawyer. Brandon was a little over two-and-a-half years old at the time, and William was suing for full custody of the boy. Ultimately, William was denied custody but awarded visitation, a right he exercised for just over two months before vanishing again. Brenda was left with over $20,000 in legal bills. Brandon was left without a father.

After Brenda finishes sharing with the group, Kate silently passes her the box of Kleenex. She takes one and wipes her nose. After a few moments of silence, there is some discussion of the family court system, including child support recovery and how difficult it can be to track down a "deadbeat dad." Mostly, however, group members try to comfort Brenda and help her formulate some possible ways of dealing with the situation. As the discussion wanes, Lauren, who has been mostly silent, returns to the idea of a girls' night out and asks, "So when are *we* all going to go out?" Mary pulls out her planner, and since nobody can afford child care, the group settles on a child-inclusive potluck for the following weekend at Kate's house.

HISTORY OF THE SINGLE MOMS' GROUP AT WRAC

Currently located in a two-story, well-worn Victorian house that appears quaint and old-fashioned amidst the brick and concrete university buildings that surround it, the Women's Center was founded in March 1971 by members of the Women's Liberation Front (WLF), a group of students and community members alike who had ties to Students for a Democratic Society (SDS) and other student and radical political movements. Founders believed the center would serve as a vehicle for challenging sexism both within and beyond the walls of the academy. Operated via a collective decision-making process, the fledgling center offered educational programming, numerous support and discussion groups, a feminist library, office space for the local chapter of the National Organization of Women (NOW), the Rape Victim Advocacy Program, and other women-centered organizations in the community, and it sponsored a fast-pitch softball team and other forms of women-centered amusement and recreation.

It was not until nearly five years later that a support and discussion group for single mothers began with a notice in the January 1976 issue of the *WRAC Newsletter*:

> A support group for unmarried mothers is being organized. The first meeting will be held January 19 at 7 p.m. This group is for women who have never been married; who have made the decision to raise a child alone; who sometimes doubt their capabilities as mothers. Hopefully, we, as single mothers, can provide one another with information and support. It is important for us to retain our rights as single women while being good mothers. It is possible! We need reassurance. We can give

this support to each other. If there is a need for this group, the only way to fulfill it is through participation. Child care will be provided. If you need transportation, or any further information, call the WRAC at 353-6265. Thank you. (*WRAC Newsletter* 1976b)

This description, though brief, reveals much about WRAC's understanding of and attitude toward single motherhood. First and foremost, the announcement acknowledges the power of the cultural definition of the "good mother" and indicates that while single mothers may, at times, "doubt their capabilities," they most certainly can be "good mothers." In addition, it makes it clear that the center is willing to support single mothers by dedicating resources to the group, including child care, transportation, and meeting space, something particularly important given the "competition for space" among WRAC groups at the time (Silander 2002). The announcement also hints at the political nature of single motherhood, particularly the need for single mothers to retain their rights. Finally, it suggests that single mothers could not only find support and reassurance by participating in the group but also provide the same to other women who have "made the decision to raise a child alone." Thus the notice served as a call to action of sorts, positing single motherhood as an important political identity. Within the first month, so many women joined the group that WRAC listed the "Unmarried Mothers" as one of its regular, "ongoing" groups (*WRAC Newsletter* 1976c). By March, only two months after the original announcement appeared, the group had secured a permanent slot in the WRAC schedule (*WRAC Newsletter* 1976d).

It is unclear where the idea for the single mothers' group originated. Publicity and discussion relating to a conference, "The Single Parent Family," held February 11–14, 1976, in the UI student union, may have generated interest among WRAC staff and clients and thus led to the formation of the group (*WRAC Newsletter* 1976a). It seems more likely, however, that the group grew directly out of the needs and interests of early WRAC volunteers.

Single mothers had been prominent among those who founded the center, including a single, lesbian mother who rented the Quonset hut that served as the original UI Women's Center (Silander 2002). Members of the WLF helped turn the living room, kitchen, two bedrooms, and bathroom of the structure into "one large telephone-reception-sitting-party room, one kitchen, one playroom, one crashing room, a bathroom, and some closet space" (*Ain't I a Woman* 1971). In addition, single mothers involved in the WLF drew attention to the specific issues they faced as sole, custodial mothers, particularly in relation to day care and the demands of being a "struggling student with a young child" (Sand 2002). In fact, the issue of child care was so central to members' analysis of women's economic, social, and political oppression that it was listed first on their list of demands intended to bring about revolutionary change:

> WE DEMAND THAT A SYSTEM OF DAY CARE CENTERS BE ESTABLISHED. These centers should be open 24 hours a day. They must be staffed equally by men and women. They must meet the needs of children and must be controlled by the parents and children who use them. (*Ain't I a Woman?* 1970; *The Daily Iowan* 1970)[2]

In addition, their ninth demand offered a clear position on marriage:

> WE DEMAND AN END TO THE MARRIAGE CONTRACT which presupposes the submission of the female to the male. Marriage and the nuclear family is the acceptable living situation today. Because of this the single woman is severely limited and children are treated as property of their parents. All people (including the young) must be treated as individuals with individual social and economic rights. (*Ain't I a Woman?* 1970; *The Daily Iowan* 1970)

Together, the demands illustrate a clear support for women who are mothers, including those who chose not to be "severely limited" by the ideal of the nuclear family.

This is not to suggest that WRAC's early years were free from conflict where motherhood and child care were concerned. On the contrary, there were intense debates surrounding these issues. For example, there was a tendency to automatically assign mothers to the child care cell as others involved with the center "pressured [them] to join groups based on their relationship to children and motherhood" (Silander 2002). In addition, women who did not have children resented the fact that, in keeping with the center's principles of collective support and action, they were expected to donate time and money to child care efforts (Silander 2002).

Despite these tensions, WRAC has continued to provide child care and to support single mothers through the single mothers' support and discussion group. The group has been offered almost continuously since it began in 1976. While there was a one-and-a-half year gap from the spring of 1978 until the group resumed in the fall of 1979, the single mothers' group ran consecutively for twenty years, from the fall of 1979 through the fall of 1999. Then, after a one-semester hiatus, the group started up again in the spring of 2000 and has been offered continually since that time. In fact, since 1976, WRAC has offered the group not only during the academic year but also during eighteen summer sessions.[3] After my research on S.M.A.R.T. ended in 2004, the group maintained a presence in the community, at times meeting as part of WRAC's formal lineup of support and discussion groups and other times adopting a more loosely structured approach and organizing meetings and other activities outside of WRAC's space. The presence and longevity of the single mothers' group indicate not only high demand for it over the years but also WRAC's ongoing commitment to the group, providing a group facilitator, space, and other resources essential to the groups' continuation.

The WRAC staff and board members I interviewed were quite knowledgeable about the single mothers' group, and several discussed the group's name changes that have occurred in the past decade. Dubbed "Mothers without Partners" during the mid-1990s, it was renamed "Single Hip Mamas" shortly after the turn of the century, then "S.M.A.R.T.: Single Mothers Achieving and Reflecting Together" during the 2003–2004 academic year. Staff and board members also addressed the philosophical reasons behind those changes and provided a list of the various single mothers who facilitated the group over the years. Regardless of name changes and group facilitators, however, the goals of the group have remained fairly consistent. As staff member "Amelia Breaux" explains, these include "helping single moms build relationship[s] and have peers and peer support and be able to draw strength from that by sharing all the stuff that is part of your life . . . being able to have that sense of not being the only one, that other people have lived through this, and that together we have more wisdom than we have separately."

SUPPORT FOR THE SINGLE MOTHERS' GROUP

I conducted research as a participant observer in the S.M.A.R.T. group during the 2003–2004 academic year, attending weekly meetings from August 2003 through May 2004. The group met on Monday evenings from 6–7:30 p.m. in WRAC's large group room. A total of eight single mothers participated. Not all participants, however, were present at every session. In fact, a typical meeting was likely to include only three or four participants. There were two occasions when the group facilitator, Kate, was the only one to show up besides myself. Four participants, Kate, Lauren, Charlotte, and Mary, comprised the core of the group and attended almost every meeting, missing only on rare occasions. Brenda's attendance was sporadic. She did not participate during the fall semester. During spring, she would come for two or three sessions and then be absent for a week or two before returning. Three women, Stacy, Kelsey, and Wendy, each attended a single meeting during the research period.

Given that the number of participants is small and attendance is sporadic, it would not be surprising if WRAC discontinued the group. Such a decision might even make sense from a resource management perspective. For example, the meeting space might be used for other groups or events that would serve a greater number of clients. In addition, wages paid to child care workers who oversee the kids' care room during S.M.A.R.T. meetings might be allocated to other expenses, especially given the shoestring budget of the center.

It seems unlikely, however, that these things will happen, particularly given the support for the group expressed among WRAC board members and staff. "Karla Anderson," a WRAC Advisory Board member for over five years, spoke of the pride she felt in being part of an organization that provided that type of support. She said it "makes me really proud to be affiliated with the center, to know that we provide that service . . . I think the single moms group serves an incredible need and one that is obviously not being served elsewhere in our community." Staff member "Jennifer Trainor" also indicated strong support for the group and articulated an understanding of the political nature of single motherhood. When I asked Jennifer if she thought it was important for the group to continue, she responded by pointing to the changes wrought by the welfare reform of the mid-1990s and particularly her belief that the "need is even greater . . . as other services and [programs] are being cut and changed. Things like the Family Investment Program . . . social services and daycare funds." Another staff member, Amelia, believes the group helps single mothers connect with one another, helps them "build relationships and have peers and peer support." In addition, she situates the challenges UI single-mother students face within broader political frameworks pertaining to single motherhood:

> The whole of welfare reform is just forcing single mothers away from their children and into the workforce, into crappy jobs that don't pay enough to live on, with no child care, no

transportation, no health care. . . . [At the university] there's inadequate child care, it's too expensive, it's substandard in some cases . . . many faculty have a negative attitude about students who are being both parents and students, whether it's single parents or parents who are partnered.

In the post-welfare reform era, the challenges facing single mothers are, as Amelia's statement indicates, substantial. Scholars and critics alike have demonstrated that passage of the Personal Responsibility and Work Opportunities Reconciliation Act of 1996 (PRWORA) essentially dismantled the social safety net that had formerly provided much-needed support to needy families, the majority of whom were single mothers and their children (Abramovitz 1996; Kingfisher 1996; Mink 1998, 1999; Sidel 1998; Albelda and Withorn 2002). At the federal level, PRWORA reduced available cash grants, placed strict time limits on receipt of aid, and altered both the Food Stamps program and child care funding. It also gave individual states the right to impose stricter sanctions as they deemed appropriate. Finally, PRWORA dramatically reduced opportunities for participation in postsecondary education and training programs. In doing so, it blocked an important avenue out of poverty for poor women (Adair 2001; Center for Women Policy Studies 2002; Zhan and Pandey 2004), leaving many quite literally "shut out" of institutions of higher education (Polakow et al. 2004). In fact, from 1996 to 1998, college enrollment among welfare recipients declined 20 percent nationally (Cox and Spriggs 2002). At some institutions, decreases have totaled 50 percent and higher among students receiving public assistance (Applied Research Center 2001; Kates 1998; Kahn and Polakow 2000; Marx 2002).

Even with the barriers posed by welfare reform, some single mothers do make the decision to pursue postsecondary education. Yet the challenges they face are significant. In addition to struggling financially, they encounter sometimes insurmountable challenges in relation to child care and frequently find it difficult to balance the diverse and often competing demands they face as single mothers, college students, and, in many cases, employees. While many single mothers must grapple with issues pertaining to finances, child care, and time constraints, those attending college also face the unique challenge of a "chilly" climate that marginalizes them in both subtle and obvious ways (Duquaine-Watson 2007).

An understanding of these issues has prompted WRAC staff to take specific action to help ensure continuation of the S.M.A.R.T. group. During the center's early years and into the 1990s, child care was often a challenge. The center relied on volunteers for this task, typically students who would or would not show up, depending on illness, homework, work schedules, and other commitments. Thus it was not unusual for a volunteer to cancel or simply to not show up. Furthermore, although volunteers frequently claimed they liked being around children, few had experience in early childhood education or training in CPR and first aid. To address this situation, child care became a regular item on the agenda at weekly WRAC staff meetings throughout the 2001–2002 academic year. Staff members drafted a job description that included, according to Amelia, "a decent amount of experience doing child care, they have to be trained in First Aid and CPR, and we especially like it if their certification in those is current but we will pay for our child care workers to attend a course if their certification has lapsed." Staff also determined a formula for caregiver-to-child ratio and made it a priority to clean, paint, and reorganize the kids' care room and clean out the toy closet, discarding old or broken toys or those that presented a choking hazard. They also placed toys into storage tubs based on age-appropriateness. The center then advertised for two child care positions, taking applications before interviewing prospects and eventually hiring two work-study students who are scheduled for every Monday evening during S.M.A.R.T. meetings.

These changes in child care have been quite successful. Child care was available for every meeting of S.M.A.R.T. during the course of this research. And the children who participated in kids' care have given it positive reviews. Brenda says that her son "loves the kids' care room and the other kids and the staff." One Monday evening when she considered staying home to catch up on her sleep rather than attend S.M.A.R.T., her son begged, "Please, oh please can we go? I really want to play with the mommies' kids!" My ten-year-old daughter also gave me feedback on the child care provided at WRAC after attending kids' care while I conducted participant observation in the S.M.A.R.T. group. She gave the workers, toys, and other kids an enthusiastic "two thumbs up! *Way* up!"

WRAC staff has also made a concerted effort to ensure that there are volunteers on hand to facilitate the group. Despite beginning the 2003–2004 academic year without a facilitator for the group, WRAC's group services coordinator says she "got the word out that we really needed someone" by calling and e-mailing people across the UI campus. Kate, a former participant in the group, applied for the position and completed the group facilitator training, thus enabling the center to offer the group during both the fall and spring semesters.

THE IMPORTANCE OF LANGUAGE: CONNECTION, SUPPORT, STRUGGLE, AND RESISTANCE

As important as these forms of support from WRAC staff are, they are not the only reasons for the continuing presence of the single mothers' group among the center's annual group offerings. Fundamental to the group's success is the participation of single mothers and the support they provide to one another. I requested one-on-one interviews with all of the women who participated in the single mothers group during the 2003–2004 academic year. Four of them, Kate, Brenda, Lauren, and Mary, agreed to be interviewed for this project.

The women who participate in S.M.A.R.T. are not all that different from the other single mother students at UI. They have arrived at single motherhood in various ways, including through divorce, unintended out-of-wedlock pregnancy, and intended out-of-wedlock pregnancy. They also face many of the same challenges as other single mother students, including time constraints, child care, economics, and a "chilly" institutional climate.

However, unlike their peers, they have made the decision to participate in S.M.A.R.T. In doing so, particularly through sharing stories, experiences, and feelings with other group members, these women rely on language as a means of both seeking support from and offering support to one another. Thus they have been able to effectively address two of the primary needs of single mother students at UI—both those who participated in S.M.A.R.T. during the course of this research and those who did not—identified as important to their success as parents *and* students: the need for meaningful social interaction with their peers and the need for information about resources that exist both at UI and in the broader community.

Language, though, is about more than connection. In addition, and as bell hooks (1989) has argued, language can be a source of empowerment, enabling marginalized groups to claim space and subjectivity. For single mothers, language is also, as Kingfisher (1996) contends, a political act, an "everyday" form of engagement through which they actively participate in

> producing, reproducing, and contesting identity, ideology, institutional arrangements, and policy. . . . Language is the primary means by which we share our lives with others. It provides the means to typify and categorize experiences in ways that have meaning for ourselves subjectively and for others objectively in

the same category of experience. . . . The use of language in interaction is a key location for the ongoing interpretation and construction of the social world, and is a significant and fundamental way we create meaning. . . . Meaning, then, is not only imposed on individuals but also bestowed by them. (4)

Through participation in S.M.A.R.T., then, single mother students use language in a variety of ways. It allows them not only to connect with one another but also to make meaning of their experiences and actively engage with, interpret, and analyze cultural and institutional ideologies. Of equal importance, participation in the group fosters dialogue that enables these women to formulate and communicate a sense of identity and self that centers on belonging, inclusion, and understanding, something that stands in marked contrast to the marginalization and stigmatization many of them experience within the broader university. For Brenda, this is the primary reason she began participating in the group shortly after her son was born, and it has continued to bring her back year after year. As she described it, "The single moms' group is the only place I've ever been where I've been around women [on this campus] who get it. They just get it. They know what I'm talking about, what I'm going through." For Kate, participation in the group was spurred by frustration concerning what she perceives as a lack of attention to the issues facing single mother students on the UI campus. She believes that "the university [does not] even think about single mother students . . . many instructors don't even consider that we are here on this campus." Mary, like Brenda, regarded participation in S.M.A.R.T. as a way to connect with other people on campus who could understand both the challenges and rewards of being a single mother student, who would "know something about how it can be hard and how it can be great to be a single mother because they had that experience as well." For Lauren, it was important that the group was peer-facilitated, as she had "had enough of people who don't know what it's like [to be a single mother] trying to tell me how to raise my kids and what I need to be doing." Building connections with other single mother students was also one of the principal reasons she joined the group. Yet she desired those connections not only for herself but also for her children. As she explained, "I want them to be connected to more people than just me, to have more in life than just me and my paycheck to count on."

Through participation in the group and the resulting relationships and sense of community, the women support one another in numerous ways. They offer suggestions about resources in the community as well as "insider information" about their experiences as individuals who have relied on those resources. These include federal programs for day care and housing, state-sponsored programs, and local initiatives through churches, secular groups, and the university. Yet the way in which the women support one another extends beyond simply sharing information about resources. The women also inform one another about exactly who to contact at a particular agency or organization because, according to group members, locating resources is only half the battle. Actually securing things they need or qualify for can be a different story altogether and may depend, at least in part, on who they talk to at an office.

This was certainly the case for Lauren. She had moved to Iowa City from Utah with her two young daughters in late December 2003, eager to begin graduate school at UI. She was supposed to start the previous August, but due to an illness that left her hospitalized for several weeks, she had to wait until January to begin classes. The postponement left her in a difficult situation. She had filed for Section 8 housing assistance in Iowa City more than six months earlier and had been approved for a move-in date of August 1. However, when her illness forced her to wait until January, she was considered to have "declined" her housing assistance and, consequently, she was placed at the bottom of a very long waiting list. Lauren did not receive a letter informing her of the changes in her Section 8 status until days before moving to Iowa City. Thus she arrived in the city and had to put down $1,300 to cover security deposit and rent. It drained her finances, including her credit cards, and she was left without money for phone, food, or bus fare. She admitted that she and the kids "hadn't eaten much" the past few days.

As Lauren described her situation to the other members of S.M.A.R.T., they were silent, nodding their heads every now and again. While none of them had been in her exact situation, several had personal experience dealing with agencies, and all of them, to varying degrees, spoke of struggling to meet the basic needs of themselves and their children. When Lauren finished, the silence of S.M.A.R.T. group members ended almost immediately as they began to create not only a list of places Lauren could go for assistance but also exactly who she should talk to at each place. Kate told her that she needed to appeal the Section 8 decision, and that if she told them about her illness, it "should be fairly easy to get it back. But make sure you go on Monday. That's when Maggie works, she takes the walk-ins then, and she's really great. She's understanding and is willing to work with you." Someone took out a piece of paper and a pen and began to write down various names, phone numbers, and addresses for Lauren. By the time the group finished, the list had grown to nearly twenty service sites, including the county crisis center, a church that is known in the community for providing emergency assistance, the food bank, the free lunch program, WIC, the Free Medical Clinic, the Salvation Army, the director of the UI Family Services Office, and others. I later learned that after the meeting, Mary had given Lauren and her children a ride home so they would not have to walk in the January cold. In addition, and claiming that she "had been dying for some French fries anyway," Mary had taken Lauren and the kids to McDonald's and bought them all dinner.

The following week, Lauren reported that she was still working to get her housing assistance back but had talked with Maggie at the office and had a "wonderful experience with her. She was laid back and not at all like some social service workers." Through the county crisis center, she had gotten bus passes for herself and her daughter as well as two bags of groceries. Although it was not "quite enough to feed us for the week," Lauren was certainly appreciative of the fact that "at least we can eat now and won't have to go to bed hungry every night." In addition, one of the local churches provided Lauren's family with hats, mittens, and coats, something they desperately needed, as they had "underestimated how cold it would be in Iowa." She had also visited several free meal sites throughout the community, indicating that "if someone wanted to, they could probably eat free lunch and dinner every day of the week in Iowa City." Within a few weeks, she had gotten her Section 8 reinstated as well. While the recommendations provided by other members of S.M.A.R.T. did not solve the various challenges facing Lauren, they have been crucial in helping her connect with resources and programs that have made a real difference in helping her secure food, affordable shelter, and warm clothing for her family. Thus, and as this example demonstrates, group participants rely on language to make knowledge claims—particularly as knowledge is gained through experience—and to deliver that knowledge in ways that can have a positive impact on the lives of other group members and their children.

CONCLUSION

Throughout this chapter, I have discussed a low-tech, rather unique means of delivering information about mothering: a support and discussion group for single mothers. Like all modes of delivery, the S.M.A.R.T. group has some limitations. Perhaps the most obvious is the groups' low participation rate. The total number of participants over the

2003–2004 academic year was rather small, only eight women, and of that total number, only four attended the group on a regular basis—Kate, Charlotte, Mary, and Lauren. Others, like Brenda, attended sporadically, or, like Stacy, Kelsey, and Wendy, they attended only a single meeting. Because of these variations in attendance patterns, it was difficult for the facilitator to make plans for any given session, as she never knew who was going to show up. As a result, the group lacked a formal structure or agenda, and it was difficult to know who was going to be there from one week to the next. Furthermore, it is difficult to measure the impact of the single mothers' support and discussion group, particularly in ways that yield any quantitative data. And such data, of course, may be significant in helping others understand the importance of the group and vital in helping WRAC secure funding from both public and private sources, which is crucial to the future of the women's center overall and to the S.M.A.R.T. group in particular.

While it is important to consider these limitations, it is equally important to listen to the single mother students who participate in S.M.A.R.T. and attempt to understand the significance that the group holds for them. Clearly, those who were interviewed think the group is valuable. It provides an opportunity to make connections with others who share similar experiences and to support one another by sharing resources, including information, food, and friendship. Most indicated that they would like more single mothers to attend because, as Brenda explained, "there are so many on this campus and in Iowa City, and it would be great to just share more information or different perspectives on parenting or whatever." However, Mary pointed out that a smaller group "allows everyone to hear what one another are saying and everyone to have an opportunity to talk." In addition, while the "open membership" status of the group often means that attendance changes from one session to the next, group members liked this flexibility and lack of structure. For Kate, this was an especially important aspect of the group. For her, it is important to "have a place . . . where it's not totally structured, where it's okay to walk in half an hour late if you have to or leave early if you have to. Or to miss a group meeting if you're too tired and don't feel like doing another thing that day because you've already gone to all of your classes and taken care of the kid and all of that." Thus what some might critique as a lack of structure is, in fact, what participants consider one of the strengths of the group and something that enables their ongoing involvement in S.M.A.R.T.

There is no doubt that digital communications have become increasingly common and even preferred for many individuals and groups. The S.M.A.R.T model represents, in many ways, a move against this trend in that it seeks to remove technological barriers between participants rather than add to them. And yet it is crucial to remember that talk is not a mere default setting to which all humans revert. Face-to-face interaction and exchange is the original and most primary art of inter-relation. But it takes, in all senses of the word, *practice*. This recognition of the importance of practice—that is, a particular type of delivery that leads to products such as insight, community, and solidarity—throws a light on what is really happening in a S.M.A.R.T session. Those of us who seek to support mothers might do well to resist the lure of the high-tech world and remember that nothing can replace what happens when individuals sit down together in a physical space to share their thoughts, laughter, tears, and experiences as they forge meaningful, supportive connections with other mothers. And while mothers from all walks of life may benefit from these types of connections, they may be especially important for single mothers and other groups who find themselves economically, politically, or otherwise marginalized.

NOTES

1. Throughout this chapter, I use pseudonyms in order to maintain confidentiality.
2. The demands were printed simultaneously in the UI student newspaper, *The Daily Iowan*, as well as the feminist underground magazine, *Ain't I a Woman?*
3. Information on the WRAC support and discussion group for single mothers was gathered from monthly *WRAC Newsletters*, January 1975–July 2004.

REFERENCES

Abramovitz, M. 1996. *Regulating the lives of women: Social welfare policy from colonial times to the present*. Rev. ed. Boston, MA: South End Press.
Adair, V. C. 2001. Poverty and the (broken) promise of higher education. *Harvard Educational Review* 71: 217–39.
Albelda, R., and A. Withorn. 2002. *Lost ground*. Boston, MA: South End Press.
Applied Research Center. 2001. *Welfare reform as we know it*. Oakland, CA: Applied Research Center.
Center for Women Policy Studies. 2002. *From poverty to self-sufficiency: The role of postsecondary education in welfare reform*. Washington, DC: Center for Women Policy Studies.
Cox, K. C., and W. E. Spriggs. 2002. *Negative effects of TANF on college enrollment*. Washington, DC: National Urban League Institute for Opportunity and Equality.

DiCarlo, M. 2002. Introduction. In *At the Center: Celebrating thirty years of activism and communities*, ed. Women's Resource and Action Center, 1–4. Iowa City: Women's Resource and Action Center.

Duquaine-Watson, J. M. 2007. Pretty darned cold: Single mother students and the community college climate in post-welfare reform America. *Equity & Excellence in Education* 40: 229–40.

hooks, b. 1989. *Talking back: Thinking feminist, thinking Black*. Boston, MA: South End Press.

Kahn, P., and V. Polakow. 2000. *Struggling to stay in school: Obstacles to postsecondary education under the welfare-to-work restrictions in Michigan*. Ann Arbor: Center for the Education of Women, University of Michigan.

Kates, E. 1998. *Closing doors: Declining opportunities in education for low-income women*. Waltham, MA: Welfare Education Training Access Coalition, Heller School, Brandeis University.

Kingfisher, C. P. 1996. *Women in the American welfare trap*. Philadelphia: University of Pennsylvania Press.

Kostick, S. 2002. Interview. In *At the center: Celebrating thirty years of activism and communities*, ed. Women's Resource and Action Center, 35. Iowa City: Women's Resource and Action Center.

Marx, F. 2002. *Grassroots to graduation: Low-income women accessing higher education. Final report: Evaluation of the Women in Community Development Program, Women's Institute for Housing and Economic Development*. Boston, MA: Center for Research on Women, Wellesley College.

Mink, G. 1998. *Welfare's end*. Ithaca, NY: Cornell University Press.

Mink, G., ed. 1999. *Whose welfare?* Ithaca, NY: Cornell University Press.

Polakow, V., S. S. Butler, L. S. Deprez, and P. Kahn, eds. 2004. *Shut out: Low income mothers and higher education in post-welfare reform America*. Albany: State University of New York Press.

Sand, G. 2002. Interview. In *At the Center: Celebrating thirty years of activism and communities*, ed. Women's Resource and Action Center, 25–31. Iowa City: Women's Resource and Action Center.

Sidel, R. 1998. *Keeping women and children last: America's war on the poor*. New York: Penguin Books.

Silander, A. 2002. Interview. In *At the Center: Celebrating thirty years of activism and communities*, ed. Women's Resource and Action Center, 11–18. Iowa City: Women's Resource and Action Center.

Ain't I a Woman? 1970. (July 10). To meet the needs of women.

Ain't I a Woman? 1971. (April 30). Women's Center.

The Daily Iowan. 1970. (October 1). Women's demands.

WRAC Newsletter. 1975. (August). Feminist c-r and support groups.

WRAC Newsletter. 1976a. (January). The single-parent family is coming.

WRAC Newsletter. 1976b. (January). Unmarried Mothers Support Group.

WRAC Newsletter. 1976c. (February). Ongoing groups at the WRAC.

WRAC Newsletter. 1976d. (March). Groups at WRAC.

Zhan, M., and S. Pandey. 2004. Economic well-being of single mothers: Work first or postsecondary education? *Journal of Sociology and Social Welfare* 31: 87–113.

EIGHT

From Postcolonial to Postpartum

Pedagogical Politics of Motherhood

JOCELYN FENTON STITT

During my first time on the academic job market I received lots of advice. Since I had ignored the imperative not to have children before finishing graduate school, getting a tenure track job, and achieving tenure, my advisors were anxious to protect me from any potential bias I might experience as a mother. Over and over I heard how I could avoid discrimination by appearing childless: women with children were not taken seriously. No one at my institution would have such backward views, it was implied, but others might. Mentors offered tips such as remove any rings that might signify a relationship, screen calls so that interviewers would never hear a child in the background, and never mention that I had a family during a campus visit. I obeyed, with an odd feeling I still cannot quite describe. This feeling comes close to shame mixed with anger and sorrow, shame that I had let my mentors and myself down by having a child in graduate school, and sorrow and anger that I let this discourse shape how I felt about my early years as a mother.

The same semester that I was on the job market, I had an international student from the Netherlands enrolled in a course I was teaching on Caribbean women writers. She added a wonderful dimension to the class since she had studied Dutch-speaking Caribbean authors at her home university and was able to provide a comparative dimension to our class discussions. In the middle of the course she came to my office and told me that she might have to leave the United States early since

163

her son was not able to cope with public school. He had a learning disability that when coupled with English as a foreign language made him the subject of teasing and harassment by his American peers. If my student could not keep her son in school, then she could not attend university. I understood her dilemma keenly—I had also been an international student, and I knew how difficult negotiating culturally different institutions can be. Indeed, my success at handling this cross-cultural experience was something I had been told to play up; my British master's degree was an asset and experience with cultural capital that could help me gain a tenure track job.

Beyond the international dimensions of this situation, I had the experiential knowledge that without supervision for one's children, one's work and education are impossible. I also had some knowledge of what resources for schooling and child care existed in our town, since as a mother living in the community I regularly read all of the local parenting magazines. I remembered an article on a local Waldorf school that welcomed students with learning disabilities and had also recently hosted some international students. With the shaky authority of a brand-new Ph.D. and the permission of my student, I called the school, introduced myself as Dr. Stitt from the university, and explained the situation to the director. Would they be interested in having a foreign student for the next eight weeks? Would it be possible for tuition to be waived?—his mother was an international student who would be returning home soon. The director seemed delighted and offered to set up a meeting with my student and her son. In short, they agreed to accept him and waive tuition, since they were excited by the cultural diversity he would bring to the school. My student met with me later and told me that I had saved her semester, and, just as important, had allowed her son to have a positive experience in the United States. While helping this student and her son was one of the highlights of my year, no one, including myself, thought that my experience and knowledge as a mother might be just as worthwhile as my international master's degree in terms of helping students. This anecdote never became part of a rehearsed answer for a "tell us about a difficult situation you had with a student," or "tell us about your experiences with student diversity," during a job interview, since it brought up the forbidden subject of my motherhood. Indeed, I have never discussed it with anyone until I began writing this chapter.

I did not anticipate that trying to embody mother and professor would be this hard and complicated, or this fascinating and engrossing. The politics of speaking from the subject position of a mother within the university classroom involves exploring new intellectual territory while at the same time making myself vulnerable to criticism about revealing personal aspects of myself in a professional space. In writing this chapter, I find myself in the same position as Sara Ruddick, one of the founders of mothering studies, when she wrote in *Women's Studies Quarterly* twenty-five years ago. Ruddick (1983) notes that speaking about mothering presents challenges for anyone, "certainly any feminist," because of the deep ambivalence many people have about their own mothers, or about "being or not-being mothers in a society which either insults maternal work, or sentimentalizes it beyond recognition while, at the same time, perniciously identifying Womanhood with Motherhood" (4). In addition to the difficulty of speaking about mothering at all, Ruddick explains that, within academic discourse, "It is hard to speak specifically . . . about maternal thinking—about particular metaphysical attitudes and habits of mind. . . . We seem either to know what it is already or believe that there is nothing new to learn" (6). It is especially difficult to theorize and present issues associated with mothering and working within the academy for fear that these revelations will reflect poorly on our professional identities.

While I will touch upon the subject of the professional identity of academic mothers in relationship to colleagues, this chapter largely focuses on a topic that has not received as much attention: the value for ourselves and our students when we allow our teaching identities to reflect our experiences as mothers.[1] To begin, I focus on attitudes toward professors who are mothers. I do so not because other barriers do not exist to women's employment in academia generally, but because when speaking specifically of the issues of parenting and professing, as Rachel Hile Basset (2005) argues, "obstacles to successfully combining parenting and work result almost entirely from attitudes entrenched in the academic culture, not from the exigencies of the work itself" (1). I give an overview of some issues related to identity politics in teaching, move to the more specific politics of being a mother in the university, and end with suggestions for pedagogical practices that deliver new knowledge stemming from my experiences of performing mother and professor in the classroom. I conclude with a discussion of why bringing together the personal and the professional in the classroom, despite the risk of negative perceptions by colleagues, provides many benefits to students.

THE "NO-UTERUS RULE"

Ironically, when so much of scholarly discourse examines the role of social forces in determining individual agency, academic mothers often feel that it is up to them to make the best of difficult work situations in silence. After giving birth to my daughter, I was advised to "never complain, never explain" about any difficulties I might have in child rearing and being a professor; in effect, I was to pass for being childless. It seems others were given this same advice. Amita Vyas, an assistant professor at George Washington University, stated in an interview with the *Chronicle of Higher Education* that her friendship with two other professors who are mothers was crucial to her, since "You can't really talk about this at any other place because you don't want it to come out that you are complaining or can't handle things" (Wilson 2005a, A10). Janet Hinson Shope (2005) calls this the "no-uterus rule" in academia, where visible signs of femaleness, such as pregnancy or discussing caregiving responsibilities, cause "administrators, department chairs, and colleagues to question one's allegiance to the institution and intellectual life" (56). The knowledge of this bias against seeing mothers as committed professors is undoubtedly the reason my advisors counseled me against discussing my private life during interviews.

Additionally, there are excellent reasons women generally may not want to flaunt their motherhood at work. Cultural beliefs in the United States reveal that mother status is incommensurate with intellectual activity and competence in a variety of professions, not just academia.[2] Shelley J. Correll, Stephen Benard, and In Paik (2007) designed an experiment to test bias against mothers in hiring. They discovered that job applicants perceived to be mothers (but with identical CVs to other candidates) "were judged as significantly less competent and committed than women without children," and were offered starting salaries of "$11,000 (7.4 percent) less than offered to nonmothers," (1316). Mothers were offered employment at a much lower rate: 47 percent of mothers were recommended for hire, in contrast to 84 percent of non-mothers (1316). Discrimination against mothers was found in both the laboratory conditions of their study as well as in an audit study, where resumes and cover letters were sent to actual companies, with variations on names indicating a specific sex, and references within the resume belonging to either the PTA of an elementary school or to a university alumni organization. The audit study found that "childless women received 2.1 times as many callbacks as equally qualified mothers" (Correll, Benard, and Paik 2007, 1330). Finally, Correll, Benard, and Paik (2007) found that working fathers were seen as being more committed to their jobs and were offered higher salaries than childless men (1317).

Emily Toth (1997), known for her academic advice as Ms. Mentor, advises being closeted as a mother. Picking up on these cultural norms that stigmatize working mothers, Toth states, "It is indeed strange that motherhood, like homosexuality, has to remain in the closet until tenure" (120). Toth tells her readers that "Bearing, nursing, and raising children is difficult in the best of times, and hiding the fact that one is doing so is even harder, if not downright peculiar. Yet that is exactly what Ms. Mentor must advise you to do . . . a woman seen with a baby is believed to be 'un-serious.' Viewing herself as a mom first, she's thought likely to drop her career at any moment" (119). In reading this passage, I had to stop and ask myself: Who is doing the viewing here? First a woman is seen by a colleague with her child. Then the mother's presumed vision of herself as primarily a mother (the simple act of appearing in the flesh on campus with one's child is apparently enough to signal this) is transmitted psychically to the colleague, who decides the mother is likely to "drop" her work. In other words, holding a child means dropping one's work. Simply being present as a mother and a professor is enough to completely jeopardize a professional identity. The mother's subjectivity is erased here in Toth's vision of an irreconcilable presence—a professor mother holding her child on campus.

Robin Feldman, a tenured professor at the University of California's Hastings College of Law and a mother of five, describes her greatest challenge in getting back on the tenure track after being at home with her children for four years, as "convincing others that she was serious as an academic" rather than juggling child care and work responsibilities (Fogg 2008). The idea that women are seen as rational individual subjects in the workplace *unless* they have children must surely be qualified by the racism, sexism, homophobia, and classism experienced by some working women, but Toth's advice and Feldman's experiences demonstrate Patrice DiQuinzio's (1999) notion that in contemporary U.S. culture, "women can be subjects of agency and entitlement only to the extent that they are not mothers, and that mothers as such cannot be subjects of individualist agency and entitlement" (13). I find it difficult to interpret the extent to which Toth is mirroring the ideologies of the workplace to best advise her readers, or whether she believes these herself.

However, the assumption that when women think of themselves primarily as mothers they are disqualified from having a professional life is unchallenged in Toth's work generally. Instead of theorizing that valuing one's affiliational ties equally or more than one's role as a worker might constitute a feminist response to exploitation under capitalism, Toth (1997), advising another mother about her multiple roles, puts the job first, scolding, "being an academic means being a workaholic" (168). Advising another young female professor to participate in the social rituals of older female faculty members, she states, "The older women are doing the stuff your mom did, but by becoming an academic you've rejected your mom's Sterile, Boring Life as a Housewife. You don't want to be thrown back into that Drivel" (81). Her advice reflects a daughter's nightmare fantasy of the "drivel" of her mother's life rather than a more complex notion of the pleasures and difficulties of mothering, as discussed by many contributors to this volume.

While Toth addresses how working mothers are seen by colleagues, an equally important question is this: How are we seen by our students? A 2004 study involving 122 Princeton undergraduates found that after reading profiles of consultants where only their parental status and gender were changed, working mothers are not only "viewed as less competent and less worthy of training than their childless female counterparts, they are also viewed as less competent than they were before they had children" (Cuddy, Fiske, and Glick 2004, 711.) The authors of this study dryly note that working fathers do not suffer from this same perception (713). They characterize their findings as "particularly disquieting," since these Ivy League students are likely to hold positions of authority and to become working parents themselves (713). Perhaps most distressing, the majority of the students were raised by working mothers, a factor that previously has been thought to "produce more egalitarian attitudes about gender roles" (713). It seems that an elite education and egalitarian family roles are not enough to change cultural stereotypes about working mothers.

Might there then be some value to our students in bringing both of our identities into the classroom? How might stereotypes of working mothers be changed in the minds of students if they saw their professors as both professionals and mothers? I do not want to discount Toth's overall contributions to advising women within the academy, which she does wittily and well, especially since she writes so convincingly of our need for mentors. As a feminist mentor and academic, Toth (1998) counsels that in an academic world, where "to most of our male coworkers, we are women first and scholars second," (46) "the smartest thing we can do is to reach out to other women" (47). This includes the importance of female role models in the classroom:

> We have to conform in dress and behavior and speech—but we should not compromise on our research interests or in our treatment of our students who deserve the best. The women students, in particular, still rarely get to see a woman intellectual in action. Anne Firor Scott, the only woman professor I saw in graduate school, showed me how to teach as a woman: not as a tweedy, pipe-smoking, elbow patched lecturer, but as

the leader of a community of fascinated, engaged scholars and critical spirits. I'm grateful to her every day when I step into the classroom. (Toth 1998, 47)

I want to embrace Toth's astute analysis that to have role models who look like us or share some of our experiences in the university opens up a space where students can imagine themselves doing intellectual work. Scott embodies the identities of a scholar and a woman in both physical ways (she is recognizably female) but through her pedagogy as well: promoting her students' ownership of the class and intellectual ideas through her role as a leader, not a lecturer.

It is within the context of mentoring and role models that I argue for bringing aspects of our maternal identities and experiences into the classroom. As a graduate student in a very large department (with over sixty faculty members), I knew of only a handful of women who had children. Several of these women told me after the birth of my own daughter that their decision to wait until after tenure meant that they experienced secondary infertility and were unable to have another desired child. Statistics back up my graduate school observations. In 2000, 42 percent of academic women ages thirty-eight to forty-two had children in their home, compared to 72 percent of their age cohort who hold bachelors degrees in the United States (Wilson 2005b, A16). According to a study by Nicholas Wolfinger, "female professors are 41 percent less likely than female doctors and 24 percent less likely than female lawyers to have children," while male professors are "21 percent less likely than male physicians and 12 percent less likely than male lawyers to have children," likely because the higher income of physicians and lawyers means they can afford child care (Wilson 2008).[3] Other statistics are more alarming: only 56 percent of women with children pre-tenure go on to earn tenure, as opposed to 77 percent of fathers, of whom it has been said that fatherhood "tends to enhance [their] academic prospects" (Wilson 2005b, A16).

D. Lynn O'Brien Hallstein (2006) notes the internalization of negative myths about mothers, even by feminist mothers themselves: "If academically informed feminists are truly coming out of the closet about mothering, then we must recognize our own internalized matrophobia in the same way that gays and lesbians have worked on purging their own internalized homophobia (or, as another example, as many Blacks have made attempts to move away from their own internalized racism)" (104). However, the use of the terms "passing" (Rusch-Drutz 2006, 272) or "coming out of the closet" (Toth 1997; Hallstein

2006; Segal 2006) to name the hiding and disclosure activities of professors who feel the stigma of their motherhood usurps terminologies that contain their own histories and meanings while not adequately describing the condition, in my view. While one might occlude one's identity as a mother, lesbian, or person of color to avoid negative stereotyping, some of the myths of motherhood sentimentalize and idealize it in a manner that rarely happens for sexual or racial minorities. To simply appropriate terms from minority experiences can oversimplify the power differentials that characterize very different, although sometimes overlapping, situations. Being a mother does not fit well with "passing," which suggests pretending to be an identity you are not, especially with regard to race. "Coming out" also implies a core identity that is revealed (or not) to others. Any generalization I might make about mothers will have its exceptions, but I might venture that mothers have a portion of their lives where they are not mothers and then a portion where they are. Some mothers, like myself, might have three or more decades of being a non-mother. I had a complete adult identity before I became a mother. I taught college students and produced scholarship without having a child, so being that same person in the classroom or in my writing now would not be a lie, exactly. Without being prescriptive, though, my experience of becoming a mother while being a professor radicalized me and changed my subjectivity.[4] There are continuities with my previous self, but the act of mothering, of caring for my children, has changed me. Performing the act of mothering will continue to change me; I am not the same mother I was two years ago, and I will be a different mother two years from now. Becoming a mother has both intensified my oppression as a woman and given me great joy. What I would like to share with my students is the dilemma of cultural contradictions I embody, given the low status of mothers within our society, the stigma associated with mothers within my profession, my encounters with and resistance to traditional notions of motherhood, my individual experience of my relationship with my children, and the relatively high cultural capital afforded to college professors. I do not claim an essentialized identity or pedagogy gained through giving birth, but rather I wish to acknowledge that my presence in the classroom brings all of these overdetermined categories to bear on my professional persona. If academics who are mothers are indeed in the minority (especially after tenure, as statistics seem to suggest), then this provides another strong reason for modeling our dual identities in the classroom, since students may not have the chance to see this embodied pedagogy elsewhere.

FROM POSTCOLONIAL TO POSTPARTUM

Born in the United States but trained in the academic field of postcolonial studies, I was prepared for the complicated nature of what it means when outsiders to non-Western cultures teach and research those subjects in the academy.[5] I finished college and started graduate school during the height of debates over what is known as "identity politics" within literary, cultural, and feminist studies. Issues of identity politics within teaching, broadly, consist of debates over how people's identity affects their ability and authority to teach and write on others different from them. In other words, does one have to be a cultural/racial/gender insider to have the legitimacy to deliver knowledge? Many of these debates focused on, to cite the title of an important anthology edited by Katherine Mayberry (1996), *Teaching What You're Not*. This tension reflected the growing realization of the ways in which a variety of disciplines from anthropology to literary studies co-opted the cultural traditions of marginalized groups (Spivak 1991). Academics from dominant groups reserved the power of naming and defining legitimate cultural practices and aesthetics for themselves while marginalizing members of oppressed groups. Indeed, one of the central insights of postcolonial theory is about the ways colonial education aimed to create subjects who could mimic, but never quite master, their colonial rulers' culture (Bhabha 1994).

While aware of the many issues of authority and authenticity raised by my gender (women are minorities among the tenured faculty) and race (my ancestry is not from the Caribbean, my area of research), I was trained in the tradition espoused by Nellie McKay (2005) in her influential essay "Naming the Problem That Led to the Question 'Who Shall Teach African American Literature'; or, Are We Ready to Disband the Wheatley Court?" While contested and controversial, McKay's article firmly defines African American, and, by extension, other subjects such as Caribbean studies, women's studies, and postcolonial studies as academic fields that scholars gain access to through study rather than through personal characteristics. Countering the "angry rhetoric" and "essentialism" of some scholars within the field, McKay (2005) writes, "There is nothing mystical about African American literature that makes it the sole property of those of African descent" (24). McKay is not arguing that just anyone can be an authority on African American literature, but that authority comes from accountability to previous generations of scholars and a conscientiously undertaken study rather than racial authenticity. Paraphrasing Toni Morrison, McKay argues that the African American literary tradition "can be learned" (24).

As a PhD candidate in a joint program in English and women's studies, my academic and pedagogical training all emphasized that my particular interests, postcolonial women's literature, did not require a female or a postcolonial identity to be a scholar of this work. The program prepared me for challenges to my authority as a young female scholar and to justify my interest in postcolonial and Caribbean literature. Mentors gave me help in establishing a position within the field, suggested that I gain an experiential connection to the culture (such fieldwork is not common in literary studies), and helped me organize two trips to the Caribbean in order to perform archival work and to see contemporary cultures in action.

Yet the academic job market has not caught up with these theoretical rejections of identity politics. "Ethnic" expectations and limitations cut both ways: newly minted scholars of color who are not specialists in any sort of ethnic literature often find themselves interviewed, hired, or pressured after accepting a job to teach the literature of their heritage based on essentialist ideas about the "ease" with which scholars can teach what they are. Hiring practices fueled by nebulous ideas about "diversity" collapse experience with expertise in troubling ways. This seems as professionally dangerous, if not more dangerous, to young scholars of color, as are essentialist hiring practices to those scholars trained in "ethnic" studies who are perceived as ethnically "not diverse." Barbara McCaskill (2005) theorizes that the flip side of questioning White scholars' authenticity or authority to teach African American studies is a "fixed, impervious, unadulterated genealog[y] of scholarly entitlement. African American researchers have no place in eighteenth-century British literature. . . . Like rungs on the Great Chain of Being, some larger and some longer than others, to each race or nation is his or her literature" (116).

I was prepared to teach what I am not, so much so that when as a new graduate student I was offered an opportunity to teach a one-credit course in the Women's Studies Department, I chose to teach a course on representations of mothers in film and television. I was not a mother. I had no immediate or even medium-range plans to become a mother. Mothers were harried creatures with mini-vans and sticky juice cups. Although this course would change my personal and professional identities, I must confess that I chose the topic less out of an interest in motherhood, per se, and more because many key feminist film theorists in the 1980s wrote about mothers in film. Unbeknownst to me, the Association for Research on Mothering was founded in 1998, two years before I taught "Good Mother/Bad Mother: Representations of Mothers in Film and Television" for the first time. I started participating in the current rise of mothering studies without knowing that such a field existed. My dissertation examined constructions of the family under colonialism in the Caribbean, and I thought that students might enjoy learning about this theme through popular culture. My approach was to have the students read some of these key feminist film theorists, such as Linda Williams, Laura Mulvey, and E. Ann Kaplan, and view some of the films they discussed, such as *Stella Dallas* and *Mildred Pierce*. I also included the work of two female directors from the 1990s, Julie Dash and Nancy Savoca, and their films, *Daughters of the Dust* and *24 Hour Woman*, respectively.

My status as a daughter who was not a mother aligned with that of my students, who in those first two years of my teaching this course were mostly female and did not have children. Positioning the class as a method for us (outsiders) to understand the complex figures that are mothers corresponds to Kaplan's (1990) notion that "feminists have focused on the Mother largely from the daughter position" (126). As we moved through the class, however, I worked to contextualize and historicize the films within women's social roles during the period. I found myself in the role of mother translator—of trying to get my students to see things from the mother characters' perspectives.

Other aspects of my training in postcolonial/African diaspora studies let me see that although there were commonalities between the portrayal of the conflicts between mothering and working outside the home experienced by the characters played, for example, by Joan Crawford in *Mildred Pierce* and Rosie Perez in *24 Hour Woman*, other issues, such as historical context, race, education, and class, served to individuate these representations, making difficult any generalization about a unitary mothers' perspective. What my students and I learned was that an examination of the times when narratives were told from mothers' points of view served to highlight a general cultural absence of mothers' perspectives, broadly conceived. Indeed, my personal removal from the identity category of mother allowed me to see what issues I might need to bridge between feminist theory, the representation, and students' own experience. This, I think, underlines the idea that there is definite value in having instructors "teaching what they are not."

This experience, for me at least, confirmed the validity of the position taken by McKay and others about identity politics. Although I was not yet a mother, my training in feminist theories of subjectivity and identity allowed me to see the wisdom of Kaplan's observation, that within both feminist theory and society at large, mothers' subjectivities are represented largely inaccurately by non-mothers. Kaplan (1990) notes about the 1970s U.S. feminist movement, "Our complex Oedipal struggles prevented us from seeing the Mother's oppression (although we had no such problems in other areas), and resulted in our assigning the Mother, in her heterosexual, familial setting, to an absence and silence analogous to the male relegation of her to the periphery" (126). Through historical and sociological readings, such as *The Way We Never Were* by Stephanie Coontz (2000), I began to understand that the categories of "good" and "bad" mother I had used to organize the course were ways of overestimating mothers' power in a patriarchal society. In recognizing that most discourses about motherhood were produced from the subject position of children, albeit adult children, I understood that many of our most resonant cultural portrayals of mothers, from the mammy figure, to the all-giving June Cleaver, to the "no more wire hangers" Joan Crawford of *Mommy Dearest*, represent a profound displacement and psychological fantasy about individual mothers' power instead of a critique of the influence of larger social structures such as racism and sexism on mothers' agency. These representations tell us much about children's issues with the mother figure but little about mothers' desires.

Thinking of representations of mothers as largely displaying the fantasies of children parallels Edward Said's (1978) formulations of the ways in which representations of the colonized were in part created as a mythology necessary for rule by Europeans. Toni Morrison (1992) makes a similar argument in *Playing in the Dark* about the figuration of Black characters within White American literature:

> I came to realize the obvious: the subject of the dream is the dreamer. The fabrication of an Africanist persona is reflective; an extraordinary meditation on the self; a powerful exploration of the fears and desires that reside in the writerly conscious. It is an astonishing revelation of longing, of terror, of perplexity, of shame, of magnanimity. It requires hard work not to see this. (17)

Morrison's notion of an "Africanist" representation as being largely about the "fears and desires" of White writers has an analogue, I think, in what I call "motherist" representations. "Motherist" representations are largely about fantasies of mothers from children's perspectives, rather than from mothers' lived realities.

While researching the material for this chapter, as I realized the connections between postcolonial theory, Kaplan' idea of the cultural erasure of mother's perspectives, my idea of motherist representations, and what I remembered of Morrison's notion of Africanist representations, I returned to *Playing in the Dark*. I was surprised to find that Morrison's first subject of critique, Willa Cather's *Sapphira and the Slave Girl*, hinges on Cather's unsettling representation of a slave *mother*. Believing that her husband is about to commit adultery with Nancy, a young slave woman, the White mistress Sapphira arranges for her nephew to seduce/rape Nancy. A complication noted by Morrison, but largely ignored in *Sapphira*, is that Nancy is the daughter of Sapphira's loyal slave and caretaker, Till. The fact that Till knows of this arrangement to harm her daughter is never presented within the novel as an obstacle to Sapphira's plans. Morrison observes that both Cather's and Sapphira's own failure to take the slave mother's subjectivity into account "could only prevail in a slave society where the mistress can count on (and an author can believe the reader does not object to) the complicity of a mother in the seduction and rape of her own daughter. . . . That assumption is based on another—that slave women are not mothers; they are 'natally dead,' with no obligations to their offspring or their own parents" (Morrison 1992, 21). This "Africanist" representation wholly leaves out the subjectivity of Till. This lack also constitutes what I would call a motherist representation, compromising others' fantasies about mothers' subjectivities, rather than how mothers might interpret their own experience.

It is here, with Morrison, that I can see a way to move forward by making connections between postcolonial and mothering theory. The feminist postcolonial theorist Gayatri Spivak (1991) suggests the difficulties, indeed, the potential "impossibility of restoring the history of empire and recovering the lost text of mothering *in the same register of language*" (165, emphasis in original). To put it another way, the "narrative of capitalism and colony" and "the mother-daughter story . . . cannot occupy a continuous space" (168) because the first is cross-cultural and the second is "within the same cultural inscription" (159). This is certainly true in Cather's novel: slavery, capitalism, and colonialism exist in a narrative that erases the subjectivity of the mother and makes impossible the mother-daughter story of Till and Nancy. But Morrison's (1987) own novel *Beloved* and historian Jennifer Morgan's (2004) *Laboring Women: Reproduction and Gender in New World Slavery*, just to name two examples, illustrate that slavery, colonialism, and capitalism of necessity exist in the same cultural inscription. Women's reproductive capacities were essential for the profitability of New World colonies. This is where my course on mothers in popular culture now begins: by retracing images of motherhood in the New World, we can see how the "good" mother came to be constructed as White, married, and middle class, and the "bad" mother was racialized, unmarried, and of lower class status. This hinge between the colonial and the maternal, which Spivak questions but which I am convinced exists, constitutes my current research project.

ENGAGED PEDAGOGY: PROFESSING AS A MOTHER

As the introduction to *Mothers Who Deliver* asserts, our goal is to go beyond a rehashing of the difficulties facing mothers to deliver new ways of theorizing about and creating change around cultural scripts of mothering. While the statistics about the negative perceptions of professional mothers and our rarity in academe may be disheartening, I would argue that they also reveal that those of us who are parenting and professing may be able to perform a unique service for our students. Remarkably, there has been little formal research on the possibilities of professors modeling work/life balance for their students.[6] Instead of formal research, I rely on the narratives of other feminist professors who seek to make the link between theory and practice in their classrooms, as well as my own research on my students' reactions to my bringing my daughter to class.[7] bell hooks (1994), for one, argues for using pedagogical strategies such as personal narratives in the classroom in order to move students and professors beyond a hierarchical relationship to knowledge and into a transgressive boundary pushing relationship where deep learning can occur. Performing such an engaged and embodied pedagogy causes me to experience intense feelings of vulnerability in the classroom as I decenter myself as the source of knowledge and reveal a personal and more intimate side of my life. hooks acknowledges these fears as real but encourages us to confront them in the service of an "engaged pedagogy":

> When professors bring narratives of their experiences into classroom discussions it eliminates the possibility that we can function as all-knowing, silent interrogators. It is often productive if professors take the first risk, linking confessional narratives to academic discussions so as to show how experience can illuminate and enhance our understandings of academic material. But most professors must practice being vulnerable in the classroom, being wholly present in mind, body, and spirit. (hooks 1994, 21)

While I have touched upon some of the difficulties of mothering and being an academic, equally important perhaps is that the pleasure of mothering and our experience of the mothering relationship can make us better scholars and teachers. If the "don't explain, don't complain" ideology renders invisible the difficulties of being a professor and a parent, then it also forces me to be silent about the knowledge gained from mothering and my pleasure in it. It can also obscure the lives of others who might serve as role models. I remember well from my graduate student days a department party for newly admitted students. One of the senior professors in the department, Anita Norich, brought her adopted two-year-old daughter to this party. Watching her mingle with colleagues, staff, and graduate students while mothering her toddler and speaking to her in Yiddish gave me a sense of an embodied mother with a professional identity. By embodied I mean less an essential bodily identity (such as gestating woman) than the public physical performance of a social role. While Ms. Mentor's advice and the statistics I quoted earlier have often filled me with anxiety over mothering in the academy, I will never forget watching the pleasure this professor took in speaking with her daughter, helping her get fruit salad, and holding her while talking to various members of the department (details I remember over ten years later!). This performance of mothering and professional collegiality allowed me to see the fusion of these two identities. That I was not yet a mother did not lessen the impact of my noticing this professor's integration of work and family. Our differences, such as that I am not Jewish, were less important than seeing this professor's multiple identities in concert. Seeing her enjoying her daughter on this occasion and several others served as an example of the power of embodied mothering to exorcise myths about professional women: that they are not nurturing, that combining work and family is too hard and should not be attempted, and that one cannot be a scholar of national prominence and cut up cantaloupe for a toddler.

So what happened when I decided to ignore Ms. Mentor and other academic advisors, and publicly declare my mother status by teaching courses on mothering as a new assistant professor? While my desire to continue to teach and research on the topic of mothering after my initial foray had to do with my own puzzlement and anger about the difficulties of motherhood, and my decision to discuss my children in the classroom stemmed from a decision not to accept the Ms. Mentor norms of appearing childless in order to present a false professional front, I was surprised to realize that my students were hungry for these conversations. Unlike my elite research graduate institution, at my regional state university many of the students are already encountering the issue of work/family balance in their own lives. I experienced a strange ripple effect from teaching a course on mothers in pop culture during my first and third years at my present position. Coupled with my determination to discuss in all of my classes the fact that I had children (and the fact that I was visibly pregnant one semester), student parents—even those who were not taking classes from me or in my department—began to seek me out during office hours. As Jillian Duquaine-Watson discusses in chapter 7 of this volume, the campus climate for student parents is often not a welcoming one. Although I had my first child during my last year of graduate school and experienced some of the same hostility aimed at undergraduate parents, I did not realize the extent to which student parents are often marginalized on campus before I began speaking as a mother within the classroom.

Students who are not yet confronting parenting and working (or who do not intend to) still passionately want to discuss how to manage the future lives they see for themselves. They imagine themselves involved in similar balancing acts, performing multiple roles such as making time for activism and community work while employed. Becky Ropers-Huilman (2004) usefully points out that the use of the word "balance" when discussing work and family implies a rushing back and forth to maintain even distribution of weight, whereas thinking of "blending" the key "threads" of one's life, whatever they may be, "is complementary . . . to make not a fractured worker, but rather a coherent and fully human being." It is this perspective of bringing together the chosen "threads" of my life that I hope to model for students, rather than advocating that they have children. One of my students commented that when another professor brought his/her child to class "it reminded me that teachers are a lot like me to [sic] they have obligations and things in life besides teaching." That, I think, is a powerful message about the scope of people's lives beyond work, and that our students have lives outside of our classes too.

While I have found no studies of the effectiveness of professors modeling work/life balance or "blending" for their students, several feminist academics have written personal essays on this topic. Reflecting on her own graduate school experience, Lucia Martinez (2006) notes that although her mentor, "a wonderful young Latina professor," was an inspirational figure who was successful professionally and also had two children while achieving tenure, the mechanics of her life remained obscure: "I heard her discuss her children, and sigh about what must have been her frustrations with balancing a successful career and a happy family. As an observer, sometimes those two things seemed incompatible, but I never really asked her for specifics—how, exactly, she was managing." Like me, Martinez did not lack for mentors, but no one talked specifically about strategies for having a family while building an academic career. As Martinez ruefully notes, "Those details my Latina professor and I never discussed. I am living them." Her conclusion, similar to my own, involves removing the mask of infallibility, endless energy, and unlimited time and "speaking more openly to students about what it means to the individual behind the faculty title to be overloaded with service obligations." In particular, when the question of work/family balance came up during an invited speaking engagement with a group of students on the subject of Latinas in the academy, Martinez honestly replied that her presence with the group meant that she could not have breakfast with her son, "that he had cried and cried as I left. That was on top of not having been home much that week due to other extracurricular commitments, and I listed some of those commitments." Martinez's sharing of her personal negotiations with her professional life led to "one of the best discussions I have ever had with a student organization" and a greater understanding on the part of students of the ways in which gender, ethnicity, and mothering construct her personal and professional choices.

The blogger "Bitch Ph.D." (2005) observes that the tension that exists between professors with children and child-free professors over accommodations for children on campus such as day care centers, family leave, nursing spaces, and diaper changing areas in bathrooms might be reframed in terms of how family-friendly campuses are helpful to students:

> It seems to me that one way to get out of this childless women vs. women-with-kids pattern would be to think about the students, many of whom are also women, and many of whom also have kids. Work situations that are difficult for faculty with children are also, therefore, difficult for students with children. Faculty retention, productivity, and morale are strong arguments, as is the simple issue of equity and justice. But if I'm not mistaken, we often allow the inferred understanding that accommodations somehow compromise the institution, rather than strengthening it. Bringing into the argument the question of how institutional cultures that discriminate against women on the faculty also affect women in the classroom is something we should probably do a lot more of.

Like many feminists before me, I discovered that the personal issues that I myself had imagined regarding being a mother on my campus were in fact shared by others, in this case, the student parents at our university.

The reality I have come to grips with is that most of my students are not going to become professional postcolonial feminist literary critics. Actually, probably none of them are. The majority of my students are going to become parents, if population trends continue. Although I do think that my research on the intertwining of the familial and the imperial in the Caribbean and other African diaspora nations such as the United States is vitally important for students to understand, from another perspective, I think the way I can be most helpful to my students who are often the first in their families to attend a four-year college is to let them watch me try to parent and profess at the same time. In the classroom I enact being a professional with family obligations, even if that means allowing my students to see me fail. Since I often feel like being on the tenure track with small children is like climbing a mountain with no oxygen, it took me a long time to recognize that it was in my dual capacities as mother *and* professor that many of my students want to see me as a role model. I stumble, I get confused about which direction to go in, and people pass me on the way up. Even with all of this, I came to the conclusion that I needed to get past my graduate-school-instilled sense that I must appear to be omnipotent in the classroom. Like summiting, the attempt counts.

The second time I taught my mothers in popular culture class in my current position, I designated a class period for an in-class exercise of looking at parenting magazines for how they represented mothers. Since this was an assignment that did not involve class discussion but rather small group work answering questions on a handout, I invited student parents to bring their children. I also told the students that I would be bringing my daughter. I had first done this two years previously when my daughter was still in preschool. On this first occasion, I brought her on a day with no faculty meetings or office hours. I scheduled meetings in all of my classes about students' final projects. My daughter had been asking if she could come to work with me and was thrilled to meet my students and to see the classroom. She mostly wrote on the board or sat on my lap or listened to the students. The students' reactions to my daughter were immediate as they walked into the classroom. They seemed more relaxed in her presence and smiled at seeing me in a different role than the professor at the front of the class. Several students told me how cute my daughter was and that she looked just like me (a good strategy to win my approval?).

This first experience made me curious about how seeing me mother in the classroom struck my students. The second semester I taught the class, "Good Mother/Bad Mother: Interdisciplinary Approaches to Mothers in Popular Culture," I decided to bring my daughter but to make more formal my means for assessing students' reactions. Since there is little research on this topic, I created a short survey and got Institutional Review Board approval to get my students' reactions in writing.[8] I asked them for their general thoughts about the experience, if it made them "see me in a different way," without specifying what that way might be, if any of their other professors had ever done this, and if they had ever gone with a parent to work.[9] Although we had been talking about the contentious nature of mothering, feminism, work, and family in American culture all semester, I wanted to know what it would mean to my students to have me, my daughter, and them all in the same room engaged in a similar activity. All of the students surveyed had a general positive reaction to meeting my daughter. These reactions ranged from the more tepid "It was completely fine with me, it didn't interrupt the assignment or anything like that" to the more enthusiastic "I thought it was fun. I was impressed with how well spoken she is and how much she seemed to enjoy helping you pass out papers and doing whatever else . . . you should do it more often ☺." Five out of the nine students responding felt that seeing me with my daughter helped them integrate my two identities. One student commented thus:

> Yes, I saw you in a different way. You were being a mother. You were stopping to answer Elizabeth's questions. You didn't ignore her, she was there too. You were also being our professor at the same time. It was amazing to see the two together, it worked out nicely. The questions and comments she had were relevant to the classroom. She was interested in what you do and seemed excited to participate. Seeing you as a teacher and a mother did not make me think you were better or worse as either of those.

Another student wrote, "Although it allowed me to expand my thoughts about your being a mother, it did not make me see you in a different way, only to force me to think of a different side of you that I would otherwise not have be [sic] motivated to think about in a more detailed manner. I did enjoy the fact that you are an accomplished professional that is willing to integrate two completely separate parts of your life." While comments such as this made me feel as if this course on mothering and my experiment in bringing my daughter to class had achieved a refutation of the idea of the complete divide between professor and mother, another student commented that it did make her see me differently, but that "It would be the same if I had seen you at the bar."

In keeping with the findings of Cuddy, Fiske, and Glick (2004), who found the traits of softness to be in contrast to competence in terms of perceptions of mothers, two students used this wording to describe how their views of me changed because of our encounter. One student described it as being like the commercial for the department store, as she was "able to see the softer side of Sears," while another stated that "In some small way, I viewed you as more human, a softer person instead of an intimidating professor that life [sic] revolves around academia." Reactions such as this made me realize the extent to which I had internalized academic views about the necessity of separating the maternal and the professorial. I viewed my contributions in the class to be far more personal and to reveal my vulnerability more than in any other class I have taught before. Despite my perceptions of having "humanized" myself through personal revelation, there were still responses such as the ones just mentioned, or the student who agreed that although she saw me differently, much about my private life remained off limits to her: "I think your private life is understandably pretty separate from your public, teaching life." Perhaps for a generation raised on reality TV, their sense of private might be different than mine.[10]

Outside of breaking the norms of the classroom where I am the authority and they are the students, what benefits were there for my students? If we accept the statistic cited in Wilson (2005b), that 72 percent of women graduates go on to have children (and that a similar percentage of male graduates will have children), then it is reasonable to expect that the majority of our students will be confronting work/family balance issues in their lives (A16). Several students stated that this glimpse into my personal life was a refutation of two stereotypes that feed into each other: that professional women do not have children, and that mothers are not "serious." At a basic level, through parenting ("Good drawing on the board!") and mentoring ("Good idea for your presentation, but is this source a peer reviewed journal?") in the same space, I wished to demonstrate that my abilities in these areas lie on a continuum. One student noted, "This showed you in a mothering light and in a professional light. The two seemed synonymous with each other. It is not like you talk one way with your students and then a [sic] dumbed down way with your daughter. You showed her the same respect and attention you show any of us. I think that is great." Without lecturing, I think many of the students got the idea that public/private identities can be continuous. My hope is that students, both male and female and parents, parents-to-be, and child-free, will realize that their own capabilities for nurturing and analysis and that of their coworkers do not need to be dichotomized into workers here and having lives elsewhere.

In addition to the specifics of teaching a class on mothering, there are a few other ways I bring my mothering self into the classroom. I want to be clear at the outset that I am not recommending telling sentimental stories about one's children, handing around baby pictures every week, or bringing children to class (except in the limited circumstances I just discussed). My suggestions are more on the order of strategic modes for delivering knowledge to students about the role of mothers in society, in the workplace, and in the university setting. Emily Jeremiah's (2006) notion of maternal performativity is useful in teasing out how we might enact mother and professor in the same classroom moment. Jeremiah rejects essentialist notions of mother as origin and instead bases her work on Judith Butler's notions of drag and the performance of gender identity, in that there is no "original" self before cultural inscription—the self comes into being through public and private performance (26). Her work on this subject aligns clearly with the objectives of this collection, in that through advocating maternal performativity, she understands "mothering as a practice," which in its rejection of patriarchal notions of the passivity of mothers is "transformative, subversive" (25). Enacting maternal identities outside of patriarchal scripts "to vary the repetition of maternal practices" is to "exert maternal agency" (25). Thus the examples I offer next stem from my own positionality and are not meant to be prescriptive for other mothers. They are offered as suggestions in the hope that some of these ideas may be adaptable to different mothering identities, classroom practices, and disciplinary locations.

The examples I give of ways we might more effectively deliver new insights into the mothering experience might be categorized in three ways: Sharing Knowledge, Being Present, and Speaking from Your Perspective. While I have suggested that I do not advocate sharing inappropriate information with students, I do think that Sharing Knowledge gained from our lived experience as mothers can be beneficial to students. For example, when I experienced a sudden child care crisis, I did not share this with students. This was a personal issue that seemed irrelevant to classroom content. However, when discussing issues of women and work, I have shared local child care prices with students who are often surprised at how expensive it is. This information is contextualized by pointing out that the United States is one of the few industrialized nations not to offer free preschool. We also talked about the fact that the United States is one of a few nations worldwide not to mandate some form of paid maternity leave. In a post-feminist climate, where students think that battles for equality are won, it can be important to discuss parental leave policies at their college or institution. While pregnant, I was able to tell my students that although I had a right to a leave, it would be unpaid and my health insurance would no longer be paid after twelve weeks. This is a system-wide policy affecting faculty at seven universities and thirty-two community colleges in Minnesota.

In attempting to Be Present as both a parent and a professor within a context that is not disruptive to the course, I am employing Maori researcher Linda Tuhwai Smith's (2005) idea of *"kanohi kitea,"* or the importance of presenting people with your "seen face" rather than solely discursively (120). Smith's idea reinforces that our presence in the classroom is not just to facilitate the written content of the course but to enliven it through embodied engagement with our students.

Violating the academic mandate (especially for female faculty) of equating seriousness with disembodiment requires practice, as bell hooks (1994) reminds us: "Most professors must practice being vulnerable in the classroom, being wholly present in mind, body, and spirit" (21). I practiced this recently during a discussion of feminist legal theory, when I read with a group of graduate students Dorothy Roberts's (1999) essay "Mothers Who Fail to Protect Their Children: Accounting for Private and Public Responsibility." Roberts' essay about the legal ramifications of prosecuting women for failing to prevent the abuse of their children acknowledges that it is difficult to defend women who allow their children to be abused, but that we must understand women's choices in a "political context" of their relative power or powerlessness (38). In order to represent fully my own reading of this essay, I had to disclose the multiple ways my own life as a mother is legally determined in ways that non-parents are not, or even my own parents' lives were not: I cannot leave my children alone in a car, I cannot leave them at home alone, if I fail to put my children in a car seat correctly (or at all) I can be prosecuted for child endangerment, and so on. I needed to be "face-to-face" with my students about being legally liable for protecting my children, even if this made me seem to have more in common with child abusers than a neutral professor. I had to give up the illusion of neutrality and allow all of us to experience the resultant discomfort. Not doing so would have risked the danger Roberts alerts us to, of looking at mothers' choices through the eyes of a child, or through the male-dominated judicial system, and assuming mothers are all powerful. Like the mothers in Roberts's essay, I too am disciplined by the state.

Being Present in the classroom relates as well to my final idea of Sharing Your Perspective. This idea bridges both *kanohi kitea* and feminist standpoint theory, which argues that members of oppressed or excluded groups have unique and sometimes more objective knowledge of situations than that possessed by dominant groups. One of the gaps in Toth's notion of mothers being perceived as incompetent is that other women on campus are mothers as well. For example, the semester I was visibly pregnant with my son, I was never the only pregnant woman in my classes, and I was certainly not the only mother! In "Introduction to Women's Studies," there were two traditional-age undergraduate students who were pregnant, and two nontraditional undergraduate female students who had teenage children. The first time I taught the "Good Mother/Bad Mother" class at my current position, my graduate teaching assistant was pregnant with her second child and was also taking a graduate course from me. Having the two of us co-teaching while both being visibly pregnant added a dimension of reality and urgency to our discussions in "Good Mother/Bad Mother."

Perhaps the most salient example of my using my perspective as gestating mother was in our discussion of reproductive rights in "Introduction to Women's Studies." While the course discussion was based mainly on readings about feminist perspectives on the right to have children and the right not to be forced to do so, my pregnancy offered a unique opportunity for me to speak frankly about the realities of being pregnant—the expense, frequency of doctor's visits, physical symptoms, childbirth and recovery, and my belief that no woman should be forced by the state to endure this against her will. While I did not know ahead of time if the other pregnant women and mothers in the class would agree with me or not, I invited them first to share their experiences of the physical aspects of pregnancy and the emotional and financial consequences of raising children. This led to a very informed, detailed exploration of reproductive rights from a variety of viewpoints in a way that was respectful of individual differences. This discussion represents my hopes for an embodied, engaged feminist pedagogy: a thorough understanding of the theory from an academic perspective, coupled with the sharing of power and knowledge in a teacher decentered classroom.

Such examples about the benefits of deploying an embodied pedagogy as an academic mother might go a long way toward delivering what Hallstein (2006) calls "a feminist subject position on maternity that eschews matrophobia and its lingering vestiges" (104). Many of the sources I have discussed in this chapter have explicitly or implicitly demonstrated the prevalence of representing mothers from the outside rather than mothers' own views of their experiences and desires. "Motherist" descriptions and proscriptions, as I have called them, of mothers abound, and we cannot control these perceptions. In choosing to reject career advice that I should appear "natally dead" in the academic arena, as Morrison puts it, my attempts to perform the roles of intellectual and mother in the classroom are one way of challenging societal norms and expectations about mothers. In varying some of the United States' key gender scripts about mothering—that it is not mentally challenging, that it is to take place in private, and that we should expect no social support—by performing mothering in the workplace, I hope to provide students with one example, messy as it might be, of an embodied, engaged pedagogy and a blended life.

NOTES

Colleen O'Brien, Karin Spirn, and Pegeen Reichert Powell deserve effusive thanks for reading drafts of this essay and contributing their expertise on the discourses of race, gender, and sexuality in American culture, teaching personas and pedagogy, and mothering studies and rhetoric, respectively. Their help has been invaluable.

1. I want to emphasize that I am not speaking for all mothers in this chapter, and that in my discussion of strategies for creating and enacting mothers' teaching personas no unitary "mothering" perspective is implied. In addition, while I am speaking here of my own struggles with work life balance primarily from the perspective of a parent, I see caring for friends, partners, and one's own parents as part of this larger issue. See Jacobson and Rhoades (2004), "Who Cares?: A Tale of Two 'Good Daughters,' " for a description of caring for their dying mother while working as academics.
2. The forum boards on the *Chronicle for Higher Education* are filled with anxiety-ridden posts about the variety of ways in which the "no-uterus rule" is used against women. Besides their specific application to women who are mothers, these rules include, but are not limited to, ideas that women who have not "yet" had children are a liability, since they might need maternity leave, women with male partners are thought likely to put their partner's career first, and so might leave or neglect their job, and single women and lesbian, bisexual, and transgendered women (partnered or not) are thought to be a "flight risk" because of their assumed difficulty fitting into a small town or rural area.
3. Indeed, there are many potential explanations for these statistics, including the fact that many women do not desire to have children, and/or that given the possibility of a fulfilling career, some women may choose to focus on that rather than on motherhood. In addition, although motherhood may be socially sanctioned, actual mothers are given little social support or social status, something academics may be more likely to identify than the general population using the analytic skills of their disciplines (DiQuinzio

From Postcolonial to Postpartum 187

2006, 58). The choice to reject this identity may stem from these factors rather than from the difficulty of "doing it all."
4. Patrice DiQuinzio (1999) helpfully notes that "An account of mothering that begins with women's experiences . . . facilitates the representation of mothering from a maternal perspective" while bringing with it the danger that such reliance on experience will reify hegemonic notions of motherhood and femininity (207). I hope to provide here *a* maternal perspective without seeming to provide *the* maternal perspective.
5. See Basset (2005).
6. While issues of parenting as it relates to university faculty have been the subject of recent works such as an anthology by Bassett (2005); scholarly research by Wolf-Wendel and Ward (2006) and Stockdell-Giesler and Ingalls (2007); blogs such as "Bitch Ph.D."; and personal narratives about professing with children by O'Reilly (2006), there is no research, to my knowledge, about professors as role models of working and parenting for students. Much of the scholarship on academic parents laments the lack of role models for faculty parents, so it is perhaps not surprising that faculty parents do not see themselves as role models for others.
7. Natalie Wilson's ideas of an embodied maternal activism, in chapter 11 of this book, and Shope's (2005) ideas of embodied pedagogy and knowledge were helpful to me as I worked through the ideas in this section of the chapter.
8. The surveys were anonymous, and I told the students that I would not look at their responses until after grades were in. Given the small sample size (nine surveys were returned to me) and the fact that I was the instructor for the class, the results should be considered very preliminary and as part of a pilot study about student attitudes toward professors as parents, not as generalizable data.
9. Space considerations preclude me from discussing in detail all of the responses to the surveys. I find it interesting that all respondents stated that they visited their parents' workplaces while they were growing up—four students visited their mothers' workplaces, three students visited their fathers' workplaces, and two students remembered visiting both of their parents' workplaces. I would like to know more about how the shift in norms for mothers to be working outside of the home has affected students' expectations for their own lives and their perceptions of their professors. I can only speculate that my students might have a different perspective about women, work, and competence because of class and region than the undergraduates at Princeton. For example, two students remembered helping with their mothers' small businesses, and another discussed accompanying her mother to her job as a maid, which involved playing with wealthier children's toys as well as her pride in being able to help her mother with cleaning. Another student discussed wishing she could have visited her father's work, but that since he worked the 2 a.m. to 10 a.m. shift to be home with her during the day, she never could.

10. The July 2008 edition of *Working Mother* magazine identified this as an issue that separates "Generation Y" from my generation, "Generation X." Kelly Tharpe, a twenty-seven-year-old marketing representative, is quoted as saying about older women in her office: "Their families are private, their hobbies are private. We want to bring our whole selves to work . . . not to be somebody at work and then somebody different at home" (Holmes 2008).

REFERENCES

Bassett, R. H. 2005. Introduction. In *Parenting and professing: Balancing family work with an academic career*, ed. R. H. Bassett, 1–17. Nashville, TN: Vanderbilt University Press.

Bhabha, H. 1994. *The location of culture*. New York: Routledge.

Bitch Ph.D. [pseud.]. 2005. Moms in the Academy. *Bitch PhD*. April 5. http://www.bitchphd.blogspot.com/2005/04/moms-in-academy.html.

Coontz, S. 2000. *The way we never were: American families and the nostalgia trap*. New York: Basic Books.

Correll, S. J., S. Benard, and I. Paik. 2007. Getting a job: Is there a motherhood penalty? *American Journal of Sociology* 112:5: 1297–1338.

Cuddy, A. J. C., S. T. Fiske, and P. Glick. 2004. When professionals become mothers, warmth doesn't cut the ice. *Journal of Social Issues* 60:4: 701–18.

DiQuinzio, P. 1999. *The impossibility of motherhood: Feminism, individualism, and the problem of mothering*. New York: Routledge.

———. 2006. The politics of the mothers' movement in the United States: Possibilities and pitfalls. *Journal of the Association for Research on Mothering* 8:1, 2: 55–71.

Fogg, P. 2008. The 24/7 professor: What to do when home is just another word for the office. *Chronicle of Higher Education*, February 1. http://www.chronicle.com/ weekly/ v54/ i18/ 18b02701.htm.

Hallstein, D. L. O. 2006. Conceiving intensive mothering. *Journal for the Association for Research on Mothering* 8:1, 2: 96–108.

Holmes, T. 2008. Multicultural gen yers are redefining attitudes about race, work/life, and job advancement. *Working Mother*, July. http://www.workingmother.com/web?service=direct /1/ViewArticlePage/dlinkFullArticle&sp=S1308&sp=102.

hooks, b. 1994. *Teaching to transgress: Education as the practice of freedom*. New York: Routledge.

Jacobson, S.W., and K. A. Rhoades. 2004. Who cares?: A tale of two "good daughters." On Campus With Women. *Association of American of Colleges and Universities* 33:2. http://www.aacu.org/ocww/volume33_2/from whereisit.cfm?section=3.

Jeremiah, E. 2006. Motherhood to mothering and beyond: Maternity in recent feminist thought. *Journal for the Association for Research on Mothering* 8:1, 2: 21–33.

Kaplan, E. A. 1990. The case of the missing mother: Maternal issues in Vidor's *Stella Dallas*. In *Issues in feminist film criticism*, ed. P. Erens, 126–36. Bloomington: Indiana University Press.
Martinez, L. [pseud.]. 2006. Saying yes too often. *Chronicle of Higher Education*, November 8. http://www.chronicle.com/jobs/news/2006/11/2006110801c.htm.
Mayberry, K. J., ed. 1996. *Teaching what you're not: Identity politics in higher education*. New York: New York University Press.
McCaskill, B. 2005. At close range: Being Black and mentoring Whites in African American studies. In *White scholars African American texts*, ed. L. A. Long, 108–22. New Brunswick, NJ: Rutgers University Press.
McKay, N. 2005. Naming the problem that led to the question "Who shall teach African American literature"; or, are we ready to disband the Wheatley court? In *White scholars African American texts*, ed. L. A. Long, 17–28. New Brunswick, NJ: Rutgers University Press.
Morgan, J. 2004. *Laboring women: Reproduction and gender in New World slavery*. Philadelphia: University of Pennsylvania Press.
Morrison, T. 1987. *Beloved*. New York: Plume.
———. 1992. *Playing in the dark: Whiteness and the literary imagination*. London: Picador.
O'Reilly, A. 2006. *Rocking the cradle: Thoughts on motherhood, feminism, and the possibility of empowered mothering*. Toronto: Demeter Press.
Roberts, D. 1999. Mothers who fail to protect their children: Accounting for private and public responsibility. In *Mother troubles: Rethinking contemporary maternal dilemmas*, ed. J. E. Hanigsberg and S. Ruddick, 31–49. Boston, MA: Beacon Press.
Ropers-Huilman, B. 2004. Balancing, blocking, or blending?: Creating family and professional identities. On Campus With Women. *Association of American of Colleges and Universities* 33:2. http://www.aacu.org/ocww/volume 33_2/fromwhereisit.cfm? section=4.
Ruddick, S. 1983. Thinking about Mothering—and putting maternal thinking to use. *Women's Studies Quarterly* 11:1: 4–7.
Rusch-Drutz, C. 2006. Performing the good mother: Maternal identity, professional persona and theatre practice. *Journal for the Association for Research on Mothering* 8:1, 2: 270–81.
Said, E. 1978. *Orientalism*. New York: Vintage Books.
Segal, C. F. 2006. Having it all . . . Over all. *Chronicle of Higher Education* 52:19 (January 13): B5.
Shope, J. H. 2005. Reflections on the no-uterus rule: Pregnancy, academia, and feminist pedagogy. *Feminist Teacher* 16:1: 53–60.
Smith, L. T. 2005. *Decolonizing methodologies: Research and indigenous peoples*. London: Zed Books.
Spivak, G. 1991. Theory in the margin: Coetzee's *Foe* reading Defoe's *Crusoe/Roxana*. In *Consequences of theory*, ed. J. Arac and B. Johnson, 154–80. Baltimore, MD: Johns Hopkins University Press.

Stockdell-Giesler, A., and R. Ingalls. 2007. Faculty mothers. *Academe* 93:4: 38–40.
Toth, E. 1997. *Ms. Mentor's impeccable advice for women in academia.* Philadelphia: University of Pennsylvania Press.
———. 1998. Women in academia. In *The academic's handbook*, ed. A. L. Deneef and C. D. Goodwin, 38–47. Durham, NC: Duke University Press.
Wilson, R. 2005a. Keeping kids close: Campuses provide child-care centers to help professors cope. *Chronicle of Higher Education* (February 25): 51:25: A10.
———. 2005b. Marc Goulden: Crunches numbers on academics' family lives. *Chronicle of Higher Education* (July 15): 51:45: A16.
———. 2008. Bye, bye baby: Why doctors and lawyers out-reproduce professors. News Blog. *Chronicle of Higher Education*, April 17. http://www.chronicle.com/news/article/?id=4331.
Wolf-Wendel, L. E., and K. Ward. 2006. Academic life and motherhood: Variations by institutional type. *Higher Education* 52: 487–52.

NINE

Constrained Agency

British Heterosexual Mothers of Homosexual Sons

JANET PEUKERT

This chapter investigates the narratives that British heterosexual mothers use to shape their "mothering" and their understanding of themselves as mothers of homosexual sons. In the aftermath of my discovery of my son's sexual identity and my husband's concomitant crisis of masculinity, I turned to books on mothering and masculinity in an attempt to ascertain what I did wrong. I started to question the assumptions that informed the ways in which mothers are made to feel about their role in raising masculine sons. I had a healthy, kind, and intelligent son of whom I was immensely proud, so why did everything I read suggest that I failed as a mother? The books I came across mostly seemed to be written by experts who were telling women how to raise children and how to respond when things go wrong and a child turns out to be gay. None of these texts explicitly answered why I felt as guilty as I did, and I noted that mothers' own voices about how their sense of themselves is shaped by existing ideas of motherhood were conspicuously absent from the self-help books. When I then turned to academic research on motherhood, I also found a gap, in that mothers' articulations of their experiences were not represented. Turning to feminist critical literature on motherhood and masculinity has only helped me understand how this guilt is engendered, but even this has not enlightened me about the ways in which mothers

191

conceptualize the mother-son relationship. My thesis is an attempt to fill this gap. I start this chapter by exploring how motherhood is constructed in the nuclear family.

The nuclear, heterosexual family epitomizes an unspoken mandate of "heteronormativity" (Jackson 1999, 174). Richardson (1998, 11) argues that social life is informed by a "naturalized sexuality [which] is interpreted as heterosexuality," and this has led to the heterosexual couple becoming the raw material through which society interprets and imagines itself. Within this schema, the "good" wife-mother has historically been expected to be submissive and deferential to her male partner-husband and to bear the responsibility for the successful, "normal" upbringing of their children. Modern mothers are expected to nurture the full physical, social, and intellectual potential of the child until the child reaches adulthood. This system of beliefs and practices is called "intensive mothering" (Hays 1996). The "child-centeredness" of family life (Beck and Beck-Gernsheim 2002; Jenks 1996; Miller 2005) has brought about a discourse of the "child as project" (Beck and Beck-Gernsheim 2005). While the father may be required to fulfill certain roles in this project, it continues to be regarded as primarily the mother's job, and the mother is the one who takes the main responsibility for the child's success or failure.

Mothers are to raise "boys that will become men," or "normal" sons, where masculinity and normality are equated with heterosexuality. The centrality of heterosexuality as an unspoken "family value" has rarely been questioned. A woman's worth does, to a significant extent, continue to be based on her ability to conceive, give birth, and raise children. The concept of the mother as an individual or a "self" has been overlooked in the discourses of child development, socialization, definitions of masculinity, and the self-help genre. Socialization and individualization theories, child development psychology, and the self-help genre all perpetuate the notion that the good mother's task is to produce a good sexual citizen who will go on to marry and have children of his or her own. When a boy deviates from these expectations, the mother is regarded as a failure, and she then understandably feels tremendous guilt. Nowhere, however, does the literature explore how mothers of homosexual sons experience these ideologies and expectations. The goal of this chapter is to examine the variety of ways in which married, heterosexual mothers of homosexual sons "cope," or, in other words, how they construct narratives of mothering that can provide a space for themselves as "good" mothers. While these mothers accomplish this without abandoning traditional narratives of mothering, they engage with these narratives in new and creative ways in articulating their experiences. None of the mothers in my study see themselves as passive individuals. Rather, they consider themselves active agents struggling to effect positive change for their children and their families. All of the mothers focused on the rewards of seeing the benefits that their support brought their sons and their families. They regard themselves as the lynchpins of the traditional nuclear family. The most striking feature to emerge from my research is the strength of commitment these mothers have toward their sons and the ideal of the nuclear family.

My desire to research mothers of homosexual sons arose out of my individual dissatisfaction with the lack of existing literature on the subject. Until now, it has been the homosexual son's "coming out" story that has been privileged, with "mainstream" analyses drawing on this one voice to tell the whole story. As a mother of a homosexual boy, I did not see myself or my experiences of mothering represented in academic studies of this field. The rearing of a homosexual son has far-reaching implications for the way in which a woman sees herself both as a mother and as a gendered subject. Mothering is a gendered activity whereby the "characteristics of "good" mothers are also "feminine" characteristics" (Lawler 2000, 130; Phoenix and Woollett 1991). Motherhood is regarded as a mechanism through which women's "natural" femininity is confirmed, and, as a result, "the nexus linking marriage, sexuality and reproduction is also one which generates and reproduces gendered identities" (Morgan 1996, 76). As part of this investigation, this chapter will explore how mothers of homosexual sons attempted to "fit" their sons into hegemonic ideas of masculinity as they were growing up, and, when this failed, how they "explained" their sons to themselves and to their husbands.

METHODS

I conducted twenty-five interviews throughout Britain on a one-on-one basis with the assurance of total confidentiality, and I located my interviewees through Families and Friends of Lesbians and Gays (FFLAG).[1] A representative of FFLAG made it clear that the organization is wary of working with researchers, because most of the projects they get approached with tend to reinforce stereotypes that blame mothers. After careful scrutiny of my motivation and location as a mother of a homosexual son, FFLAG decided to support my project and put me in touch with other mothers. The interviews were semi-structured and carried out one-on-one. The topics covered in the interviews included everyday family life, parental roles and identities, relationships between the mothers and their sons and husbands, and the ways in which the sons' and their own coming-out stories were negotiated within the family and the community. These areas were chosen as they reveal not only the everyday lives of the mothers but also how their sense of themselves is impacted by finding themselves mothers of homosexual sons. My use of open questions such as "Could you please tell me about your current relationship with your son?" highlights my intention to focus on the "construction of contextual knowledge" by concentrating on "relevant specifics" during interviews (Mason 2002, 64). For instance, rather than asking interviewees about what they "would do" or what they "generally do," I encouraged the interviewees to tell their own stories by talking about specific experiences in their lives, prompted with questions such as: "Are there any episodes in your son's childhood which stand out in your memory?" My aim was to allow interviewees to talk throughout the entire interview. The telling of these stories accorded power to the mothers by making their lives visible, which was especially important to them as the experiences of mothers of homosexual sons have been traditionally omitted from the social narrative.

Before I continue, a note on my method of reporting the mothers' speech and the codes I am using. Extracts or quotation marks will indicate the mothers' own words, and, where necessary, the interviewer's question or prompt will be within parentheses, for example (Why?) or (umm). Pauses will be indicated by the use of [. . .], and emotional responses will be in italics, for example *(laughter)*.

The interviewees' personal narratives enable me to see how they construct an individual sense of self and locate the narratives in a historic and social context (Plummer 1995; Whisman 1996; Jackson 1998). The issue of my shared identification with the interviewees is meaningful, therefore, I was prepared to answer questions and provide support in an effort to forge what Oakley (1990) calls a "reciprocal relationship" (49). Although my "insider" perspective is useful to understanding these women's experiences on their own terms, I needed to merge this perspective with that of an "outsider" or a researcher who is critically analyzing the narratives.[2] We all tell ourselves and others stories or narratives about our experiences in order to make sense of and lead our lives. Throughout my work I keep in mind that personal narratives are not merely a transparent record of women's experiences but, rather, a source for comprehending how women interpret their life stories (Personal Narratives Group 1989).

CONSTRUCTIONS OF MOTHERS AND MOTHERHOOD

Modern psychological discourses fit into political ideologies about "the family," thereby rendering mothers who are not "good" as "deviant" (Phoenix and Woollett 1991). Most writing about motherhood takes the psychodynamics of the mother-child relationship as a starting point, while feminist texts tend to revolve around mother-daughter relationships (see Apter 1990; Chodorow 1978; Eichenbaum and Orback 1985; Gordon 1990; Rowbotham 1989). Despite the reality of family diversity, current ideologies maintain that children should be brought up in a nuclear family, with a traditional labor division of mothers at home, responsible for the children's primary upbringing, and fathers employed outside of the home, financially providing for their families. This means that "[i]t is the mothers who are seen to have the responsibility of ensuring that their children 'turn out right' " (Phoenix and Woollett 1991, 14).

At this stage it is useful to consider Lawler's (2000) Foucauldian analysis of the way in which current "knowledges" regarding mother and daughter relationships become a means by which mothers in particular are scrutinized, monitored, and regulated (23). Lawler draws on Foucault's theory about "subjectivation." Foucault argues:

> This form of power applies itself to immediate everyday life which categorizes the individual, marks him [*sic*] by his own individuality, attaches him to his own identity, imposes a law of truth on him which he must recognize and which others recognize in him. It is a form of power which makes individuals subjects. There are two meanings of the word *subject*, subject to someone else by control and dependence, and tied to his own identity by a conscience or self-knowledge. Both meanings suggest a form of power which subjugates and makes subject to. (Foucault 1982, 212, emphasis in original)

The application of Lawler's argument regarding mothers and daughters to mothers and sons shows that mothers and sons, through "subjectivation," become "tied" to identities through relationships of power and knowledge. Also, "they become subjected to the rules and norms engendered by a set of knowledges" about mothers and sons, their relationship, and, most importantly, the role of the mother in producing the son's self (Lawler 2000, 26–27). This self, then, is not "natural" but is a product of a system of social regulations that has at its core relations of power and knowledge. Therefore, "techniques of normalization" in the form of "expert" knowledges that promote ideas of "natural" motherhood, "normal" children, and "natural" families can act as a method of self-regulation for individual mothers (Lawler 2000). Despite the obvious fact that motherhood is a multifaceted and complex process, women's individual subjective experiences as mothers are rarely examined (Phoenix and Woollett 1991, 217). It is rare for anyone to ask mothers directly about their relationships with their children, and rarer still to take their responses seriously.[3] By making the mothers' narratives the object of analysis, what emerges is just how creative mothers are in constructing "new ideas about mothering and new forms of maternal activism" (Powell and Stitt 2010).

MOTHERING HOMOSEXUAL SONS: NARRATIVES AND STRATEGIES MOTHERS EMPLOY

It is difficult to imagine heterosexual mothers spending much time asking themselves how their sons developed into heterosexuals. Yet straight mothers of homosexual sons are greatly preoccupied with attempting to understand how their sons developed into homosexuals. According to my findings, the mothers in my study have considered their sons' sexuality, as well as their own roles in the development of their sons' gayness, in great depth.

The initial reactions to learning of their sons' homosexuality made it clear that these women had internalized social messages of the mother being to blame for the failure to raise "normal" (read heterosexual) sons to a considerable extent. All the mothers I spoke to expressed going through feelings of guilt. For example, when I asked Ruth about her feelings after her son "came out," she described

> feeling at first that I've done something wrong, that I haven't been tough enough on him to make him a real boy or whatever . . . you know so um that was probably the main guilt I mean you sort of think you encouraged it. I used to take him to the ballet and he was all into dancing I mean you know you sort of think gosh you know did I encourage this or anything you know.

The "good" mother is expected to avail herself of every possibility that can lead to the prevention of homosexuality in her son because, as Simonds (1992) argues, according to the popular psychology voiced by self-help authors, "though mothers may be seen as passive women in many ways, they are not considered passive *as* mothers" (189, emphasis added). Lawler (2000) reminds us that the "sensitive 'good enough mother' finds her 'other' in the bad, insensitive mother who fails to allow the real self to flourish; hence the boundaries of the 'normal' are marked by the 'bad mother and her offspring, the bad child' " (74). It seems that even if mothers exercise the "normal" motherly characteristics of sensitivity and femininity, these can become instruments of blame.

Despite her initial feelings that she has done something wrong, Ruth is conflicted: "I mean it's just sort of illogical thoughts really, I mean your head is telling you one thing, whereas your heart is telling you something else." I suggest that the contradiction in Ruth's narrative is related to a "certain tension in her experience" (Chase and Bell 1994, 69). On the one hand, Ruth has been informed by experts in child development, psychological writing, and child care manuals, which tend to blame mothers for behavioral or other problems with children due to their central role in child rearing (Phoenix and Woollett 1991, 216). On the other hand, she has her own mothering experiences, and, as she mentions further on in the interview, "his school was a grammar school so they played rugby . . . and I mean he was a Cub Scout for a long time and he certainly had a lot of male input from that, and he used to go camping with the Scouts and hiking." Ruth is attempting to resist the social discourse that would blame her for having inadvertently "caused" her son's homosexuality. According to Chase and Bell (1994), "Once we understand that women often work to achieve control over their lives in social contexts that make their desire for control problematic, such contradictions within a woman's narrative come as no surprise" (69).

Many works addressing the topic of raising boys start with the essentialist notion of "natural sex differences" to argue that boys and girls are innately dissimilar. Books such as psychologist Michael Gurian's (1999) *The Good Son* and (1996) *The Wonder of Boys* stress that boys should not be raised the same as girls because of their biological differences (see also Biddulph 1998; Pollack 1998). Gurian insists that children must be raised in a nuclear family format, because "learning about femininity and masculinity [is] absolutely essential" for healthy male development (Hoff 1996).[4]

This relates to a further interesting dimension of Ruth's narrative where she comments about her husband "but I have to say that [my husband is] not a big sports fan so he perhaps didn't give a particularly macho role model regarding sports at home." This remark suggests that even if there is a male presence in child rearing, boys do not necessarily learn the hegemonic ideals of masculinity. Although the mothers I interviewed all expressed going through "feelings of guilt" after their sons "came out," their sons' homosexuality per se was not the main issue of concern for any of them. Rather, they felt saddened that their sons were initially unable to come out to them, and thus the sons felt compelled to suffer alone for a period of time, until they were able to confide in their mothers. Their distress and anger were directed at social institutions (for example, the church) for instilling such a degree of homophobia in society at large that their sons feared that their mothers would reject them. These mothers thus felt that society's homophobia prevented them from fulfilling their role as "good," supportive mothers and created a situation where they were unable to be there for their sons.[5] Jenny told me about how her son had waited until he had his first gay relationship before coming out because it "really wasn't an issue for him." She was upset because "it was for me, and I know a lot of other mothers felt very badly that their children didn't tell them at the time, and that they weren't there for them." Catherine told me that although she "totally accepted" her son's homosexuality after he came out to her, "it devastated me for a couple of years. (Why?) Well I realized how desperately unhappy he had been and so much without the support (*begins to cry*) that I felt that I as a mother should have been able to give him because I had always supported everything else in his life." After reading about her son's homosexuality in his diary, Doris put it like this: "As far as I was concerned there was nothing changed [. . .] I loved him just as much, but I just wished he had told me because I was worried now about what he had gone through when I didn't know and how long had he known and so on."

The one exception to this line of responses came from Ruth, who claimed not to be bothered at all by the fact that her son did not tell her of his homosexuality until later. She explains:

> Well I am so proud of him because I realize now that he must have suffered a lot of turmoil as he was growing up and he admits this now (um huh). I mean he knew um certainly from about fourteen he knew he was gay and probably from a much younger age [. . .] Um and I feel very proud of the fact that he got through all of that on his own the turmoil that must of been going on in his head.

Upon closer consideration, however, Ruth's response does not represent any radical departure from that of the other mothers. The previous section examined the pressures on women to be caring, loving mothers who bring up boys to become men. What Ruth is praising is her son's ability to deal with his own pain and his display of strength of character. The characteristic of suffering in silence is traditionally regarded as a stereotypically masculine trait. It seems that all of these mothers are reaching for different aspects of the "good mother" formula to make sense of their experiences. While most of the mothers emphasize their willingness (though thwarted by larger social forces beyond their control) to play the role of loving, caring, and supportive mother, I interpret Ruth's narrative as a choice to focus on her success in raising a strong man who can deal with his feelings alone.

RETROSPECTIVE SENSE-MAKING: RECALLING THEIR SONS' CHILDHOOD

None of these responses indicates any significant reconceptualization of either motherhood or homosexuality. Other responses similarly reflect a deep-seated adherence to very conventional stereotypes of gender and sexuality. Witness, for example, Fiona's explanation of why she always felt that her son was gay:

> I knew from about this age [about five] that David was gay, but he didn't. (And how did you know?) I don't I really god it sounds stupid! (*emphasizes this*) but he (*laughs*) this is going to sound silly he had trousers, I um bought him some trousers and they were sort of plaid trousers, blue and green and cream checky things (um huh) and he hated them alright he didn't like them and he wouldn't wear, if it was blue and he wanted green and I would say, "Well you can either wear this one or you can go without," and he would go without, and he was um he was always very sensitive, this not liking to be shouted at, and it was it was just whole lots of little things.

These narratives seem to be indicative of the extent to which gender in general and femininity in particular become conflated with sexuality. Martin (2005) points out that "many advisors . . . entangle the development of sexual identity with the development of gender identity. Many make the assumption of this link, and most assume the development of heterosexuality" (467). She goes on to remark, "Especially from a psychoanalytic perspective, the development of a 'normal' sexuality coincides with the development of a 'normal' gender identity" (467).

When I asked Ruth if she had ever entertained the possibility that her son might be gay, her response was this:

> Yes! Yes! Because I have to say that I had my suspicions about Sean for a long time um even from when he was really tiny when he used to help me to hang the washing out on the line and it crossed my mind. (Why? Because he helped with clothes hanging?) Um erm well just because of his character, his character was so gentle. I can remember his grandma actually describing him as a "gentle" little man, and he was probably about ten at the time (um hum), and just his character was such that I knew he was never going to be particularly macho.

Beth's reason for not imagining that her son could possibly be homosexual is similarly revealing:

> Ummmmm I had no inkling with Michael at all because he had never shown any signs of [homosexuality], um you know, even as a child he used to play with cars and trucks, so ummmmm he just hit me with it and it completely gutted me because I wasn't expecting it.

All of these mothers engage in a retrospective interpretation of their sons' behavior as children in an attempt to account for their deviation from conventional norms of masculinity. The need to justify the difference of their gay sons prompts the mothers to scrutinize these indicators of homosexuality, even though similar behavioral traits in straight children would not invoke the same level of reflexive inquiry.

SEEKING SUPPORT

The mothers eagerly sought out established, albeit alternative, discourses on mothering within which they could situate their experiences. All but one of the mothers I interviewed turned to FFLAG meetings in order to gain an understanding of their roles as the mothers of gay sons. FFLAG played an important role in facilitating the emotional work that the mothers do in order to balance their sons' homosexuality and the normality of their families, and it provided them with a safe forum in which they could talk about their sons. After Ruth's son "came out" to her, she told me "that was quite a horrible first few days, but after the first few days things sort of started to simmer down, um but I did feel that I needed to be able to talk to other people that had been in this situation." At this point she located a FFLAG support group in her area.

When I asked Karen her reason for contacting FFLAG she told me this:

> The reason I rang FFLAG is because you like to talk to people because you want to be sure you are handling the situation correctly and saying the right things to your child.

Helen put it more succinctly: "It was just so important for me to speak to another mother because I felt I was a freak, I felt I was the only one in the world."

At the first meeting, Ruth "did nothing but cry through it all and go through all the emotions from the guilt and the trauma that most parents of gay children all go through." Feeling part of a community where everyone was "in the same boat" was a great help for Ruth as it was for my other interviewees. Doris put it this way:

> It was just a relief really to find um you tend to um you do tend to feel guilty yourself at first you feel um I did go through what is called this sort of thing is it something I've done is it something I've done in his upbringing is it something in me that's done this and to meet mothers and find that they are a perfectly normal bunch of people that you'd never guess they've got gay children nothing about them looked at all odd and it is very reassuring to know that it is nothing you've done that it is not in your upbringing or anything else it is just one of those things that happens.

Fiona's responses and the contradictions therein reflect the confusion she feels and make her need for some kind of guidance more understandable. When her son David told her he was gay, her reaction surprised her. She related:

> I just burst into tears, I don't know why, because I'd always known it wasn't a surprise in the least, and I knew what he was going to say before he said it [. . .]. I um I just I just cried and cried [. . .] I can't to this day explain why I just felt as if somebody had kicked me in the stomach, really it was a physical hurt. (Even though you had felt that this was coming?) I know I know I really cannot explain it, and I keep thinking oh I must have been disappointed, but I wasn't.

Later during the interview she said she felt exasperated by doubt as to how she should proceed with her son's sexuality. She said, "I didn't want to not mention it and then for [David] to think 'Oh she's pretending it's not happened' (um humm), but on the other hand I didn't want to keep asking about being gay, what's it like to be gay, what do you do there um he said 'for God's sake just leave me alone.' " Fiona's need for a protocol in a culture dependent on expert advice, which has provided very clear-cut guidelines as to what a good mother/bad mother is, is not surprising. In a society where women are judged as mothers and where mothers are judged by their ability to raise "normal" children who will perpetuate the existing patriarchal social structure of which the heterosexual nuclear family constitutes the building block, the scrutiny that the mother of a homosexual son faces cannot be overestimated. Representations of mothers and children have thus secured a place in the public as well as the private arena. Lawler (2000) notes that "abnormal" children are the subjects of moral panics and become barometers by which larger ideas of morality are defined (140). Mothers who "fail" are, in other words, accountable not only to their own families but also to society at large. According to Beck and Beck-Gernsheim (2002, 2005), nowadays women who choose to become mothers are, more than ever before, expected to ensure that their child reaches his or her full potential, emotionally, athletically, and intellectually. Gatrell's (2005) research confirms that the expectations society has of women and that women have of themselves concerning "good" mothering are at an all-time high (61).

NORMALIZING HOMOSEXUALITY

The outward appearance of masculinity seems to matter a great deal. Fiona acknowledges this when she talks about her sister-in-law's gay son and the reasons she felt badly for not being able to share David's coming out with her:

> Obviously David didn't want us to discuss it, so you know we had to respect that (Right), but I also felt as if I was betraying [my husband's] sister because through it they'd had a bit more of a traumatic time and her son is quite camp, whereas David isn't really at all, where you wouldn't say "oh God he's probably gay!" whereas Peter obviously is.

Later in her narrative, Fiona highlights how well her son David and two of his other gay cousins have been accepted into the family fold:

[We] had this big family do [. . .] and um one of the nieces had got this boyfriend that nobody likes very much and he's a bit full of himself (um hum) and um there was Joel, Peter and David, all the gay lads just in chinos and T-shirts or plain shirts, very ordinary looking shirts, just ordinary young men you know in regular clothes standing together, and this boyfriend of the girl came in and he had on tight leather trousers, and he's about forty, big heels and a purple velvety sort of patterned shirt and his hair was [. . .] all sort of spiked, there was gel over it, and my daughter came over and she says, "There's you three gays and look at that!" and they were all hysterical because there was this lad that looked so gay when he came in and the three of them in just shirts and trousers, it was just so funny!

Steven Seidman (2005) points out how a man who is

"normal" or ideal in every way other than his sexual identity [. . .] conventionally masculine, [. . .] is part of an extended close-knit family, [. . .] does not challenge a social order that assumes the division and complementarity of men and women is natural and right, and it does not question the ideal of heterosexual marriage and family; it only creates a space of social tolerance for gays, or, more correctly, for normal gays. (48)

Seidman's contention is reflected in Doris's current feelings about homosexuality in general when she says:

I don't like to see a gay pride, um you know I don't like all that dressing up, it's something I don't find particularly enjoyable to see people clowning up like that, um it's a sort of in your face [. . .], but that has nothing with being gay as such, I mean I'll fight to the end for people to be how they are made.[6]

Doris is accepting homosexuality per se, but she still finds "campness," in the sense of exaggerated femininity, problematic. While she will "fight" for people's right to be gay, she prefers it not to be in her "face." In Susan Sontag's (1994 [1966]) seminal essay "Notes on Camp," she describes camp as an aesthetic sensibility that is essentially "playful" and aims to "dethrone the serious" (275–92). Many theorists of camp, such as Meyer (1994), contend that camp is "both political and critical"

(1) and regard it as an exaggeration and a subversion of heterosexuality that attempts to highlight the unnaturalness of the social construction of heteronormativity. The mothers, however, do not consider camp's subversive potential. While they do regard it as more than merely disreputable, they tend to focus on the fact that camp can be unsettling for their sons' acceptance in society. When I asked Iris if her son was camp, she replied, "No he isn't!" I then asked her whether this made his gayness easier for her and if having a camp gay son would be problematic. She explained:

> Oh definitely! If you passed him in the street you wouldn't know James isn't like that [. . .] I think he would be ridiculed if he was camp, so obviously it makes it easier for him that he's not. If you were to talk to him he's not at all effeminate at all, and I'm glad! It makes it easier!

These mothers were also concerned about the lifestyles of their gay sons. In Seidman's (2005) analysis of 1990 film representations of gays, he found that

> the normal gay also serves as a narrow social norm. This figure is associated with specific personal and social behaviors. For example, the normal gay is expected to be gender conventional, link sex to love and a marriage-like relationship, [and] defend family values. [. . .] Although normalization makes it possible for individuals to conduct lives of integrity, it also establishes a moral and social division among gays. Only normal gays who conform to dominant social norms deserve respect and integration. (45)

Karen echoes these concerns when she says, "You worry, you know, you think I've got a gay son that um you worry about is he going to get a partner, will it last a long time, you know, everyone wants their children to be settled and loved." When I asked Iris what was most difficult about having a gay son, she replied:

> Things have changed now haven't they? He still could have children, I mean they adopt now don't they, so things change on that score, um worries about if he has a partner, I mean he has got one now but in two years he might not, um I just want him to have a partner and be happy.

My question to Fiona about what advice she would give to a mother who has just found out that her son is gay elicited the following response:

> I think you've got to sort of accept the way they are, but then I don't know how David how I might feel if David was promiscuous or was out um if he found out when he was thirteen or fourteen if he'd been sort of running away to Birmingham or something, so say I feel as if I've had a very easy sort of path through (um humm) as opposed to somebody whose son you know they're worried, they're out on Canal Street or something, you know, picking up older blokes.

Regarding an upcoming family wedding Jenny said:

> When Steve got married two years ago um Eric had been with William for less than a year, but we were sure they were going to stay together and we were absolutely determined that Eric and William would go as a couple (um hum) to the wedding.

Further in the interview when asked to summarize what is good about having a gay son, Jenny, discussing her son's partner, says, "Well having a son-in-law I think it is quite newsworthy, and I do love talking about it and seeing other people's reactions." Seidman (2005) has stressed the extent to which "[o]nly gays who are gender conventional, connect sex to romantic, quasimarital, and family values are considered 'normal' " (54).

The references to the "trauma" of having a gay child and the relief that other "normal" looking people are the parents of gay children serve as reminders of the ubiquity of the unspoken mandate of "heteronormativity" (Jackson 1999, 174).[7] The need for guidance becomes particularly acute when mothers have to enter a terrain where the "taken for granted" ideas of heterosexuality no longer suffice. Their sons' homosexuality places them in a situation where conventional expert advice does not apply, and, as a result, they feel adrift. This prompts them to seek a new community of meaning, and FFLAG provides a language and a set of meanings that are applicable to their circumstances. They seem to be engaged in a kind of "repair work" that will enable the integration of their sons into their own heteronormative worlds. FFLAG's discourse provides a template that helps these mothers make sense of their sons' gayness by normalizing both the sons and the mothers. We all draw on a number of narratives in the construction of our own identities and in attempts to make sense of our own experiences. While this project of normalization has limits, it represents a challenge to the discourse of homosexuality as deviance or illness.

There were differences in the mothers' narratives concerning their continued affiliation with FFLAG and how they currently saw themselves as mothers of gay sons. Some of the mothers felt it their duty to promote gay issues within their communities. As Jenny explains:

> One of my crusades is you know all parents of gay people should be out as well in relation to their child [. . .], you know, I think that parents can be a huge influence in this, really.

Or Helen, who said:

> I became a telephone contact for FFLAG, and you know I have never looked back. I got so many calls from parents, because you do think that you are the only one, you know, I mean now in hindsight I know I am one of thousands [of] millions! Well I started getting all of these phone calls, and I could tell my story, and I used to cry over the phone like I am to you now, but that helped the parents and when I said about my mum's death I said I thought that was the worst thing that could happen they all identified straight away "that's just what is was just like a bereavement for me as well!" and I was getting on so well with all of these parents and I was approached to start a group.

Both Jenny and Helen find great comfort in the reclamation of some measure of agency as mothers. The way in which their agency is, however, shaped by their involvement with FFLAG reminds one that agency is always played out within particular circumstances, and that these mothers can resist only within their specific contexts.[8]

Some of the mothers chose not to campaign for FFLAG. Although they have various reasons for not engaging in FFLAG activism, they all remain very positive about the impact that FFLAG has had on their lives. While Gina does not actively campaign for gay issues, she is a firm believer in FFLAG and asserts that it has helped her on a personal level. She continues to attend FFLAG meetings regularly. Like the other mothers, she is still in the process of fully coming to terms with her son's sexuality. Gina sees her inability to be more open about his gayness as a lack of courage on her part and finds support through FFLAG. She said:

> I think the parents' group is great, because you come away feeling stronger [. . .] it certainly helped me to be able to tell people and to be able to say it, but it's taken me a long time. When I first started going to the parents' group I used to come out feeling really strong and thinking I can do it, you know. But that feeling wore off, and I didn't want [my son's homosexuality] to come up in a conversation, because I didn't want to have to say it, I didn't have the courage. I am a lot stronger now. I don't find it easy, but I have learnt to recognize places in the conversation where I can get it in without making it a statement, erm, so that you don't deflect, erm, you don't kill the conversation stone dead.

Circumscribed and embedded in established structures, though, these mothers' agency is that they do seem to experience it as more empowering than other interviewees who chose to extract themselves emotionally from what they could not control. These mothers were content with just their small circle of family and friends knowing about their sons' homosexuality, and they reasoned that it was unnecessary to convince others, as it was not their problem to change the world.

CONCLUSION

The women's belief in themselves as good mothers was severely challenged, but they had all come to terms with their sons' sexuality and were engaged in managing the ensuing personal and social dilemmas. They restored their own self-image, managed their own and others' emotional responses, and had reintegrated their sons into their family circle. Over the course of my research I have become aware that my own desire to valorize these mothers' attempts to accept and engage with their gay sons' sexuality is inadequate. The contradictions and recourse to stereotypical notions of masculinity and femininity that characterize their narratives demand closer scrutiny of the assumptions underlying their acceptance and engagement. It is crucial to keep in mind that even when women are subjects in the telling of their own stories, they are still speaking within and from a space that is structured according to the privileging of masculinity at the expense of the degradation of femininity.[9] These realities cannot but affect their stories. As a researcher I also found myself struggling to avoid heteronormative assumptions. Indeed, the research process has greatly aided my understanding of my own position and experiences as a mother and a woman. I have found that there is a constant tension between these "taken-for-granted" attitudes as determinants and as resources. There has, in other words, never been a stage where either I or my interviewees have completely come to terms with our sons' homosexuality. Such a description is too linear and does not take into account the continuing emotional work that we do to integrate our sons in all the different areas of our social worlds. Exley and Letherby (2001, 125) note that "emotions are not internal to the individual but are found within relationships, and further to this are constituted and reconstituted in ongoing relational practices." New relationships thus necessitate renewed work to manage emotions. The "complex processes of managing and reconstructing their identities" (Exley and Letherby 2001, 129) demand continuous effort from these mothers as well as from myself. While I have been able to exercise agency, my actions are often shaped by such attitudes. On an intellectual level, I recognize that the problem lies in the way in which I see and conflate sexuality and masculinity. However, like my interviewees, I continue to find it difficult to integrate this knowledge into my everyday life and dealings with my son's homosexuality. For example, in new social circles and situations I still try to avoid the topic of having a gay son, and I never volunteer the information. I still fear that I will be judged as a failed mother, and I find myself focusing on my son's "straight" appearance and his "normal" interests and good friends. In thinking through these issues, I have found Chase and Bell's (1994) theorization useful:

> This subtle conceptual switch—from thinking about women as subjects of their experiences, to thinking about women as narrators of their experiences—preserves the feminist interest in empowerment that underlies the injunction to treat women as subjects. As a narrator, a woman has the power to speak as she chooses; she controls the telling of her experiences. At the same time, this conceptual switch makes room for women's experiences of subjection. (79)

Perhaps we need to look beyond the dichotomy of the good mother/bad mother and develop a notion of maternal agency, where agency is defined as a "reiterative or rearticulatory practice, immanent to power, and not a relation of external opposition to power" (Butler

1993, 15). That is, we should be open to the notion of maternal subjectivity as operative within institutions (which are in flux themselves) and as relational and communal in complicated ways. Upon closer consideration of these mothers' narratives, it becomes clear that they are forging new ways of incorporating their homosexual sons into families by creatively adapting and expanding traditional ideas of mothering and families. It is the mothers' stories themselves, rather than those of experts, that provide these insights.

It is crucial to keep in mind that my research focuses exclusively on mothers living in heterosexual nuclear families. Although their willingness to engage with their sons' homosexuality is laudable, they continue to be restricted by the desire to preserve the gendered framework of the traditional family in which they, as wives and mothers, have a vested interest. When I asked the mothers how having a gay son affected their relationship with their husbands, the general consensus was that it had brought the family closer together. For example, Doris told me, "It just helps the family feel close because we share this," and, regarding her current relationship with her son, "we're as close as we ever were when he was younger." The majority of the mothers felt that their sense of themselves as good mothers and their sense of family have become stronger by having a gay son. These women's creative negotiation of their roles as mothers of homosexual sons has enabled them to exercise a considerable degree of agency, albeit limited by the structure within which they find themselves. My dealings with my son's homosexuality have also been characterized by such continuous and creative struggles.

I embarked on this research project because of my sense of having failed as a mother and because of a gnawing feeling that there was something wrong with feeling this way. Initially, I was primarily interested in the internal workings of the family and in the relationships between mothers and fathers. These concerns resulted from my own experiences of feeling like a mother who had failed, despite doing all I could to be a good mother and devoting myself full time to giving my son the love and attention he deserved. I was in a position to do so because my husband was a good financial provider and I did not need to work outside of the home. All of these factors contributed to my shock when my son turned out to be homosexual and my husband insinuated that my closeness to our son was to blame. I was located in a society where heterosexuality is the expected outcome of "successful" mothering, and a homosexual child points to a fault with the mother. Before I started this project, I had never questioned heterosexuality and had assumed that homosexuality was somehow aberrant, although I did not believe that the failure lay in the mother-son relationship and that it might be genetic. Regardless of my assumptions and like all my interviewees, I viewed homosexuality as a "problem" that needed to be dealt with, and my research was partly an attempt to equip myself with the knowledge I would need for this endeavor. My data have not provided any conclusive answers to the question of the impact of the parental relationship, since my research focus shifted to the ways in which heterosexuality is privileged in both the assumptions of individuals and in the expectations of society.

My questioning of heterosexuality and the centrality of the nuclear family represents a major shift in my thinking. Like the other mothers, I had always accepted these institutions as the norm. Unlike the other mothers, however, I am no longer invested in the nuclear family, and this has given me much greater scope to question things that I used to take for granted. Even though I am intellectually aware that the problem lies with society's way of looking at homosexuality, I and my interviewees live in this society, and we must make our way in it as best we can. Like my interviewees, I have found ways to act positively and to "accept" my son's homosexuality. In a way, this thesis has been part of my therapy. Yet I know that my acceptance is partial at best. This has not been a linear process with a clearly identifiable beginning, middle, and end. For me, as for the other mothers, it is a continuing process and a struggle. Unlike the other mothers, I stepped out of the nuclear family, and the learning process has led me to question heterosexuality. Although my family no longer looks exactly like that of the other mothers, in that I have left my marriage, I still have a family and I am still determined for my son to be a fully integrated member of that family. I now realize that we regard homosexuality as a problem because we uncritically privilege heterosexuality.

My findings show that the value attached to conventional notions of "romantic coupling" is as strong as ever, even when the couple is made up of two men. The narratives of the mothers in my study demonstrate that nonheterosexual relations are as susceptible to the influence of heteronormative pressures as any more traditional relationship. The heteronormative assumptions that structure our society and confront me every time I turn on the television or watch a movie ensure that these issues are never out of my mind for very long. Ian Burkitt (1997) notes that "emotions are not 'things' internal to the individual and the biological constitution, but are to do with the social relations and interdependencies between people" (52). Homosexuality per se is not the problem; rather, the way in which it is perceived is problematic. Greater attention needs to be paid to the ubiquity of the heterosexist gaze and the pressures of heteronormativity that ensure that these mothers, like myself, will forever be engaged in emotional work in order to keep their sons integrated in their families and social worlds. Further research needs to be done on the way in which mothers who are not as heavily invested in the traditional nuclear family, such as lesbians and single mothers, deal with their sons' homosexuality.

NOTES

1. FFLAG is a British "national voluntary organization set up in 1993 in response to the needs of individual parents' support groups and telephone help lines throughout the country" (FFLAG 2007). It focuses on the needs of parents of lesbians, gays, and bisexuals.
2. For further explanation of the problematic concerning insider and outsider status, see Ribbens (1994) and Stanley and Wise (1993).
3. Steph Lawler's (2000) in-depth interviews with women who speak both as mothers and daughters are an exception to this rule.
4. Michael Gurian (1999) maintains the values of masculinity and femininity and explains how the education system is designed for girls and why boys and girls should be educated separately due to biological learning differences. In an interview with Burt H. Hoff, he discusses reasons for the "massive amounts" of male attention that he maintains boys require. Gurian argues that boys need men to take them hunting (or an equivalent such as backpacking) because of their high levels of testosterone. He concludes by emphasizing the need to train boys to be "sacred males" who, much like the hunter archetype, will learn to "feed women physically and spiritually," which will happen quite easily and "naturally" if we simply "allow males to be males" (Hoff 1996).
5. Emily W. Kane's (2006) qualitative interviews address parental responses to children's gender nonconformity, and her analysis indicates that parents have a complex relationship to gender nonconformity regarding their sons. Parents are often consciously aware of their own role in accomplishing gender with and for their sons. Heterosexual fathers are especially likely to be motivated to accomplish this by their own personal endorsement of hegemonic masculinity, while heterosexual mothers are more likely to be motivated by accountability to others in relation to those ideals. "In comparison to mothers, [fathers'] comments are less likely to refer to fears for how their son might be treated by others if he were gay and likely to refer to the personal disappointment they anticipate in this hypothetical scenario. . . . Many especially heterosexual mothers and gay parents expressed a sense that they felt accountable to others in terms of whether their sons live up to normative conceptions of masculinity" (165).
6. The notion that "sexual orientation is not chosen," or, in Doris's words, that people are "made" that way, is also featured in FFLAG's literature.

7. The "trauma" of having a gay child can also be traced back to these mothers' fears that they have done something wrong and thus damaged their children.
8. Over the course of these interviews, the recurrence of FFLAG jargon in the mothers' narratives has been striking. Examples of this include their insistence that homosexuality is not chosen, their response to the coming out that includes shock, bewilderment, and fear that it is not their fault and that it is not unusual. All of these phrases are also in the FFLAG (2007) booklet *A Guide for Families and Friends of Lesbians Gays*.
9. Julia Serano (2007), in her book *Whipping Girl: A Transsexual Woman on Sexism and the Scapegoating of Femininity*, looks at the abject status of femininity and its relationship to mothers' fears for their feminine sons.

REFERENCES

Apter, T. 1990. *Altered loves: Mothers and daughters during adolescence*. Hemel Hempstead: Harvester Wheatsheaf.
Beck, U., and E. Beck-Gernsheim. 2002. *The normal chaos of love*. Cambridge: Polity Press.
———. 2005. *Individualization*. London: Sage.
Biddulph, S. 1998. *Raising boys: Why boys are different—and how to help them become happy and well-balanced men*. New York: HarperCollins.
Burkitt, I. 1997. Social relationships and emotions. *Sociology* 31:1: 37–55.
Butler, J. 1993. *Bodies that matter: On the discursive limits of "sex."* New York and London: Routledge.
Chase, S., and C. Bell. 1994. Interpreting the complexity of women's subjectivity. In *Interactive oral history interviewing*, ed. E. Mahan and K. Lacy Rogers, 63–82. Hove: Lawrence Erlbaum.
Chodorow, N. 1978. *The reproduction of mothering: Psychoanalysis and the sociology of gender*. Berkeley: University of California Press.
———. 1989. *Feminism and psychoanalytic theory*. Cambridge: Polity Press.
Eichenbaum, L., and S. Orbach. 1985. *Understanding women*. Harmondsworth: Penguin.
Exley, C., and G. Letherby. 2001. Managing a disrupted lifecourse: Issues of identity and emotion work. *Health* 5:1: 112–32.
FFLAG. 2007. Friends and families of lesbians and gays: A guide for families and friends. http://www.fflag.or.uk/content/view/17/20/.
Foucault, M. 1982. The subject and power. In *Michel Foucault: Beyond structuralism and hermeneutics*, ed. H. Dreyfus and P. Rabinow, 208–26. Chicago, IL: University of Chicago Press.
Gatrell, C. 2005. *Hard labour: The sociology of parenthood*. Maidenhead and Berkshire: Open University Press.
Gordon, T. 1990. *Feminist mothers*. London: Macmillan.
Gurian, M. 1996. *The wonder of boys*. New York: Jeremy P. Tatcher/Putnam Press.

———. 1999. *The good son: Shaping the moral development of our boys and young men.* New York: Putnam.
Hays, S. 1996. *The cultural contradictions of motherhood.* London: Yale University Press.
Hoff, B. H. 1996. The wonder of boys: An interview with Michael Gurian. Men's Web-Men's Issues. http://www.menweb.org/guriboys.htm.
Jackson, S. 1998. Telling stories: Memory, narrative, and experience in feminist research and theory. In *Standpoints and differences: Essays in the practice of feminist psychology,* ed. K. Henwood, C. Griffin, and A. Phoenix, 45–64. London: Sage.
———. 1999. *Heterosexuality in question.* London: Sage.
Jenks, C. 1996. *Childhood.* London: Routledge.
Kane, E. W. 2006. "No way my boys are going to be like that!" Parents' responses to children's gender nonconformity. *Gender and Society* 20:2: 149–76.
Lawler, S. 2000. *Mothering the self: Mothers, daughters, subjects.* London: Routledge.
Martin, K. 2005. William wants a doll. Can he have one? Feminists, childcare advisors, and gender-neutral child rearing. *Gender and Society* 19:4: 456–79.
Mason, J. 2002. *Qualitative researching.* London: Sage.
Meyer, M. 1994. *The politics and poetics of camp.* London: Routledge.
Miller, T. 2005. *Making sense of motherhood: A narrative approach.* Cambridge: Cambridge University Press.
Morgan, D. 1996. *Family connections: An introduction to family studies.* Cambridge: Polity Press.
Oakley, A. 1990. *From here to maternity: Becoming a mother.* Harmondsworth: Penguin.
Personal Narratives Group. 1989. Forms that transform. In *Interpreting women's lives: Feminist theory and personal narratives,* ed. the Personal Narratives Group, 3–16. Bloomington: Indiana University Press.
Phoenix, A., and A. Woollett. 1991. Motherhood: Social construction, politics, and psychology. In *Motherhood: Meanings, practices, and ideologies,* ed. A. Phoenix, A. Woollett, and E. Lloyd, 13–27. London: Sage.
Plummer, K. 1995. *Telling sexual stories: Power, change, and social worlds.* London: Routledge.
Pollack, W. 1998. *Real boys: Rescuing our sons from the myths of boyhood.* New York: Random House.
Ribbens, J. 1994. *Mothers and children: A feminist sociology of childrearing.* London: Sage.
Richardson, D. 1998. Heterosexuality and social theory. In *Theorising heterosexuality: Telling it straight,* ed. D. Richardson, 1–20. Buckingham: Open University Press.
Rowbotham, S. 1989. To be or not to be: The dilemmas of mothering. *Feminist Review* 31: 81–93.
Seidman, S. 2005. From polluted homosexual to the normal gay: Changing patterns of sexual regulation in America. In *Thinking straight: The power, the*

promise, and the paradox of heterosexuality, ed. C. Ingraham, 39–62. London: Routledge.

Serano, J. 2007. *Whipping girl: A transsexual woman on sexism and the scapegoating of femininity.* Emeryville, CA: Seal Press.

Simonds, W. 1992. *Women and self-help culture: Reading between the lines.* New Brunswick, NJ: Rutgers University Press.

Sontag, S. 1994 [1966]. *Against interpretation.* London: Random House.

Stanley, L., and S. Wise. 1993. *Breaking out again: Feminist ontology and epistemology.* 2d ed. London: Routledge.

Stitt, J. F., and P. Reichert Powell. 2010. *Mothers who deliver: Feminist interventions in public and interpersonal discourse.* Albany: State University of New York Press.

Whisman, V. 1996. *Queer by choice: Lesbians, gay men, and the politics of identity.* London: Routledge.

TEN

Writing the Script

Finding a Language for Mothering

LYNN KUECHLE

After eight years of being a stay-at-home mom, I began course work for a master's degree in speech communication. I was given the opportunity and task in communication studies to think, write, and discuss many of life's processes that often go by without notice or mention. I was learning about stereotypes, perception, ways of knowing, identity, and self-concept, and how we use all of these strategies to navigate our place in society and to fill the roles we assume throughout our lives.

I began to think about my role and identity as a mother. I felt the pressures of being a mom to act a certain way and perform up to some undefined standard, but I could not figure out who was making these rules, who I was supposed to be measuring up to. Certainly I could not measure up to images in the media; intellectually, I knew these were unattainable images. I was not pressured by my family; they were always supportive and loving. I felt I was fighting against something, but it was more like boxing at shadows than an actual battle. In many ways I knew being home with my kids was the right thing for me and my family, but in so many other ways I felt like I was falling short. One of the first pieces of literature I read that captured the discontent I was feeling was Susan Maushart's (1999) *The Mask of Motherhood*. She explains: "The content of women's daily realities has changed enormously, as has the nature of the images to which we seek to conform.

But the identity crisis—the mismatch between expectation and experience, between what we ought to be feeling and how we do feel, between how we ought to be managing and how we do manage—remains as painful and as intractable as ever" (xi). I knew this feeling, and I had an idea that others had felt this too, but I was searching for the language to describe this part of my motherhood experience.

There were many times at home with my kids when I thought I must be doing this wrong, that there had to be an easier way: from the most efficient way to get a two-year-old dressed and out the door on a schedule that, in the child's eyes, is far from desirable, to the trepidation about how the childhood years will build the character of an eventual teenager who faces her or his own independence in a world that is full of less than desirable influences and circumstances. I often reached out to advice manuals written by people who clearly were better at accomplishing these tasks of motherhood than I. I do not think I ever made it to the end of any of the books that I purchased. I would always reach a point where I thought, "That is not the way I want to do it, or, I tried that and it did not work." Plus I had come up with many of my own solutions to problems that worked fine for me and my kids, but I never read, "Follow your own instincts, you know your child best." With the number of parenting books on the shelf and with more being published each year, I know I was not alone in looking for answers. I think it is safe to say that every mother adapts these suggestions and advice to fit her personal situation and value system. It is in this adaptation that mothers find little support or recognition and much judgment. I think the negotiation of this landscape of the motherhood experience is extremely interesting.

In my graduate work it became obvious that I needed to focus on some subject matter to study, and as I continued to follow the line of research on motherhood, my choice became clear. I did not want to write about parenthood, I wanted to write about motherhood. I wanted to write about me. I had read many insightful and powerful essays and studies to which I related, but I did not see an outlet for sharing the experience of being a mom. I felt like the only time I could talk about myself as a mom was when I wanted to share the moments of joy. There were many moments that were far from joyful, and I felt they needed a space to be shared. It seemed when I did allow myself to let those curtailed stories emerge, showing my dissatisfaction with motherhood, I was confronted with well-intentioned (or not) suggestions of how to restore my state of mind back to joyful. I did not want suggestions, I wanted validation, and I wanted to be validated on a stage similar in scope to the task at hand. The work I was doing, raising children, was on a public platform for the world to see. Everyone, from teachers to store clerks, was deciding whether I was up to the task of motherhood based on snapshots they saw of my life and how my children were performing in that moment. But they were not seeing or hearing the whole story—my story, my friends' story, a stranger's story; they all have value and are all an integral part of the novel of life we are all experiencing. The trenches of motherhood are filled with dirty diapers and interrupted sleep, they are filled with everyday challenges, both trivial and monumental, which women overcome or become overwhelmed by on a daily basis. The problem is that the trenches do not make a pretty magazine cover and if revealed may awaken the judgmental and the judged to rise up together to create a place where mothers could rise and fall, succeed and fail as human beings do, rather than to become infallible simply because a child has become part of their life.

For the past nine years and throughout the process of trying to explain and understand my own motherhood experience, I talked with many other mothers, but I felt that I was not getting the whole story. Either I was having some sort of mental block, or it was a lack of full disclosure from other mothers with whom I was sharing the experience. I was always comparing myself to these others without really knowing the full truth about their experience. I knew what I saw from the outside, and I knew what they chose to share with me about the experience, but I was skeptical that I really knew the whole truth. H. L. Goodall (1989), in *Casing a Promised Land*, explains my skepticism by stating that "our experience of meaning comes to us only in the stories we tell about them, and so the ways we read ourselves into those stories become the investigative means we need to articulate them if our aim is to tell the truth" (xxv). I do not think that other mothers purposefully tell half truths, but I do think that because we do not truly understand one another's experience, it is difficult to know what is acceptable to reveal and what is not. I felt that if my research was going to have any value then it needed to help me understand more fully the motherhood experience. Additionally, I was searching for a shared experience and understanding with other mothers to find validation and empowerment in a role that I would be in for the rest of my life.

Drawing on interviews with five women, my own story of motherhood, and the writing of mother scholars, I developed a script that was performed publicly as a reading. I have had the opportunity to perform "Extraordinary Ordinary: Mothering in the Face of Unattainable Social Norms" for a local moms' group, a college Women in History brownbag luncheon, a local Mamapalooza event, a radio show, and two national academic conferences. The first conference was the National Communication Association Conference in Chicago, Illinois, and the second was the Association for Research on Mothering symposium, part of the national Mamapalooza festival held in New York City.

In each of the cases where the reading was done and discussion followed, mothers in the audience were eager to share their own stories. It seemed those who shared felt some validation in their experience by telling it to others. Although they were not on stage, the attention of everyone in the room was upon them when they were talking, transforming them from spectator to actor. Many of the shared stories followed the themes of the reading. And while this type of activism is far from the drama of marches and protests, the simple act of sharing stories is where the change starts. We are recognizing that we, as mothers, have something to say, and it is time for a new script. We need a new vocabulary, and I think the stage and public performance is where new material begins to take shape and begins to enter into our consciousness.

In this chapter I will explain some of the background information I used in putting this performance together and will follow up with an abbreviated script and the past and future impact of this project.

REFLECTION, INSPECTION, AND UNDERSTANDING

Andrea O'Reilly (2004), in *Mother Outlaws*, warns that the language of motherhood, the stories passed down through generations through the mother line, "is rendered in a specifically feminine discourse or dialect that has been discursively and culturally marginalized by patriarchal culture" (255). However, there are those voices that see that motherhood is enriching. In my experience, I have come to understand that the circumstances surrounding motherhood are not the only components of an empowered, fulfilling experience, and I have come to believe that motherhood creates a bond not only between mother and child but between mothers, a type of sisterhood that I am trying to embrace and within which allow myself to be embraced. In her book *Don't Blame Mother*, Paula Caplan (1989) declares, "Women don't speak up enough, certainly not in defense of mothers. Let us vow that at every possible opportunity we will protest, we will educate, even interrupt—when anyone in any setting utters or implies any of the dangerous myths about mothers" (283). As I was putting this performance together I began to see mothers as a subculture for the first time. I realized when an inappropriate comment is made referencing the underprivileged that I am confrontational. When a mother is the butt of a joke or ridicule I am conciliatory. In fact, I find ridiculing myself and other mothers effortless. If we ever hope to internalize motherhood as a place of power and entitlement, then we first must stop verbalizing messages of inadequacy, diminished accomplishment, and guilt. In *Families on the Fault Line,* Lillian Rubin (1994) writes,

> for words are more than just words . . . they are the symbols that give meaning to our thoughts; they shape our consciousness. New ideas come to us on the wings of words. It's words that bring those ideas to life, that allow us to see possibilities unrecognized before we gave them words. Indeed, without words, there is no conscious thought, no possibility for the kind of self-reflection that lights the path of change. (90)

One way to use words constructively is suggested by Njoki Nathani Wane (2000) in her article "Reflections on the Mutuality of Mothering," where she suggests, "Mothering is a very complex institution; it is only by documenting our mothering experiences and by telling our stories that we can begin to understand and appreciate its complexity" (238). It was my intention to capture, with the script and the performance, the complexities of motherhood. I wanted mothers to describe their motherhood journey, free of the restraints of the typical talk of being a mom, but through the real stories about their experiences ranging from the ordinary to the extraordinary. I wanted to see mothers sitting together side by side and experiencing these stories and to feel empathy and celebration rather than judgment and jealousy.

It is my hope that by sharing many different experiences this project can start a dialogue about motherhood. Abigail Brooks (2007) writes in *Feminist Standpoint Epistemology,* "Constructing a space that is open to dialogue across women's different experiences and standpoints, a space where multiplicity of women's voices are granted equal air time, we actually build *community*" (75, emphasis in original). She continues, "[In] a community that serves as a gathering site on which multiple standpoints converge, and where respectful listening and dialogic interchange is encouraged, we can begin to imagine the potential for increased understanding among and between women from different backgrounds and cultures and from different life experiences" (75). That is what I felt was missing from my experience, community, a place where I and others shared a common experience but held different values, different ways of knowing, different ways of being. I felt this bridge toward community could be built through a sharing of stories based on common experiences of mothers everywhere.

I am aware that my experience and the experiences of other mothers around me do not represent the complete picture of motherhood. Factors like race, socioeconomics, cultural background, sexual orientation, and marital status play important roles in motherhood practice. I was struck by Brooks (2007) when she explained that

> feminist standpoint scholars understand and recognize differences between and among women—different experiences of oppression and different standpoints, or perspectives, based on those experiences—they also continue to emphasize the importance of dialogue between and among women, the need for empathetic understanding, and the potential for achieving alliances. After all, alliances between and among women are possible—*without risking the repression and difference*—and *necessary*, if we hope to fight for more just societies and to improve women's condition within them. (78, emphases in original)

A NEW VENUE AND CONTEXT

Ronald Pelias (1992), in *Performance Studies: The Interpretation of Aesthetic Text*, states that "all human communication is an act of performance" (3). It is true that stories people tell all have characters, a plot, a beginning, and an end—some have drama, some have humor, and some fail at both, but the elements of performance are present. Pelias explains further that "performance offers experiences for our lives. Doing performance is a way of producing understanding. It is a means for coming to know others" (ix). It seems to me that neither the act of mothering nor motherhood as an institution is explained very well. I know numerous mothers who have said "I didn't know it would be like this." If women have been mothers for as long as there has been life on earth, then why hasn't someone been able to explain motherhood in a way that is understandable and relatable to more people? I began to read about performance as a method of inquiry. I have often felt misunderstood by others as a mother. My sarcastic wit has often gotten me sideways glances from others. I have also had many encounters with mothers who did not seem to exist on the same planet as I did, let alone having a very common experience of raising a child. I wondered how mothers who were all so different could find commonality. The stage and theater historically has been a place where even taboo subjects can be openly talked about and considered, as in the *Vagina Monologues*. The *Vagina Monologues* is a play by Eve Ensler that has been performed in venues all over the world. The script was based on interviews with women about the sexual violence they experienced in their lives and anecdotes used to refer to women's vaginas. It has since become part of a movement to end violence against women. I thought it was incredible how the script, because it was based on real women, was able to speak to an audience and create a sense of connection among women and those who care about ending violence against women. I was so moved by this type of theater when I first saw it, and I immediately saw a correlation to what I was trying to accomplish with this project. Thus, a performance on stage was what I felt I needed to do—I needed to present the research in a way that could increase understanding for me and for others about what it meant to be a mother.

The idea that I needed to pull in other mothers to be part of the story was a thought from very early on. Although I had a great deal to say about my own experience, I was not egocentric enough to think that I was the only one who had something worth sharing. With trepidation, I approached mothers who were willing to be involved and to honestly share their experiences. I feared that I would hear the same stories that I had heard at the multitude of mommy groups and playground chats. "Isn't being a mom just the best?" I could not have been more wrong. The women shared stories that were heartwarming and heartbreaking; they used terms that busted every stereotype and myth, and they were eager to talk about their real experiences.

The stories collected during the interviews became the pieces of the script that I would construct for this staged reading. I organized the different stories into themes, which became the different sections of the script. Throughout the mothers' monologues I thought it was important to maintain their unique use of language, to keep the voices of the individual mothers as real as possible. As Pelias (1992) explains, "No two speakers will structure their communicative acts in exactly the same manner . . . each speaker has a voice, a personal signature, a style" (137). I believe it is important to hear the mothers' individual voices come through the actors as they perform the stories. Therefore, the narrative sections of the performance are virtually verbatim from the interviews.

I interviewed five mothers for this project. While many of their demographics were similar, I tried to select women with some differences who had a wide range of experiences. One mother was home full time and had one young child, one worked part time and was starting her own business and had one preschooler and one school-age child, one was a divorced mom and had two adult children and one grade-school child and shared custody of them with her ex-husband, one was a full-time working mom with a career and had two high-school-age children and one in grade school, and one had all adult children and had a full-time, home-based business and helped with child care for her grandchildren. The interviews took place at a variety of locations, from the women's homes, to a library, to a coffee shop. I asked the same questions at each interview but added some of my own stories on different occasions during the interview sessions. Each question invoked a story from the mothers, and through these stories themes began to emerge. I grouped the themes together, and they became the different sections or scenes of the script. Each woman was aware that the stories they shared would be put into a public performance and that I would be recording the conversation. All of the women were excited to share their stories and to help with this project.

I combined the five mothers into three different voices. The first mother is "the young mom." She is introduced to the audience as the mother who believes that she has choices, can work or stay home, and can handle it all. She has read many books that have prepared her for what lies ahead. She believes that she should look good, that her baby should look good, and that her home should look good. The second is "the middle mom." She is introduced as the mom who is trying to do it all, and she is running herself ragged. She has seen the implications of her choices, both personally and professionally. She knows she cannot do it all, however, she does not know what other options she has, and she is not sure which path to take next. She feels like she is always running behind and does not know if she will ever catch up. The third is the mother with "the most experience." Her children are grown and no longer live at home. She can reflect on the fruits of her labor. She can see the results of the choices that she has made in her own motherhood experience as she sees her children as adults and having children of their own.

The first section after the mothers are introduced and arrive on stage is *I thought it would be*. This section provides insight into how we think being a mom will be great, but it is really much more complicated and encompassing than "great" can describe.

> MIDDLE MOM: I thought it would be easier.
> YOUNG MOM: I didn't think I would be so busy.
> MIDDLE MOM: I didn't think it would be so hard.
> OLDER MOM: I thought it would end when they moved out of the house.

MIDDLE MOM: I thought I would get more help from my husband.
OLDER MOM: I thought it was the thing to do.
MIDDLE MOM: I thought it would be the fairy tale.
YOUNG MOM: It's really fun.
MIDDLE MOM: It's totally worth it.
OLDER MOM: It's wonderful, and I'll love them forever.

Having all of the mothers talk in succession allows the audience to hear the different voices very close together. It gives a wide range of experiences and expectations that everyone can relate to and in a contextual way. I wanted the audience to feel what it is like to be inside the thought process of a mother when thoughts come like gunfire and can be varied in scope and continuity.

It's important to me. This section gives each mother a longer narrative about internal feelings and thoughts about what she thinks are important elements of her mothering experience. The younger mother talks about how it is really important that she interacts and plays with her kids.

It's important to me that I read to my kids, with enthusiasm and animation . . . sit on the floor and play with them . . . go to the playground and run with them . . . sing to them . . . go for walks . . . explore nature . . . look at bugs . . . but at the same time let them have some independence . . . and I don't want to forget about their imagination . . . I really want to foster that . . . and I do . . . I'm pretty good at that.

The middle mother feels that communicating with her kids is really important, although difficult at times. The older mother thinks that it is important that she really listen and validate her kids and grandkids and also shares that she is worried about her daughter's eating disorder. This section shows the variety of concerns that mothers have, from building the foundation of respect and education to allowing them to go out on their own but still worrying about their well-being even when they are adults.

I want you to know. In this section mothers are presenting short stories giving insight into what they want their children and outsiders to know about them. The middle mother wants her kids to know that she is working really hard to give them what they want and hopes that someday they will realize how difficult it was for her. She shares the responsibility she feels as the major breadwinner for their family, yet she admits that she does not tell her children directly the trepidation she feels in this role. The young mom tells stories about how she is often overwhelmed and feels like she was not prepared for how difficult it would be.

> I want you to know. . . . It is so much more work than I thought, and I feel like such a loser. Where is my accomplishment, my house, have I painted, no have I done anything, no for two years if I think about it I can name stuff and then I look at him and I feel like I have done something. What they need changes. He needs my boob for the first months. It's always something new. . . . They say the stages are only going to last two weeks, but in those two weeks the days are so stinking long there are times where I was like oh my god I want to drop kick him I want to throw him out the window and I'd call my husband at work and say he won't stop crying. . . . I was completely overwhelmed . . . it seems like so long ago now.

In each of the stories the struggles are apparent, but the audience can also see how the mothers are proud of their abilities to deal with adversity and work through their insecurities. I think this is an important element of the script, as it gives the audience a chance to reflect on times when they felt they were overwhelmed and, in their minds, underperforming. Actually hearing people bravely admit, out loud and on stage, that they also have failures may give the audience a moment to let some of their own self-loathing rest.

Judging. This section creates the most conversation and discussion after the reading. Here, each of the mothers shares a time when she has been judged. The young mom talks about strangers making comments about what her child is wearing. The middle mom shares a story of being ridiculed by another mother because she did not know that her daughter had a boyfriend and shares the pressure she feels for her children to not fall through the cracks because she is working. She says, "The underlying factor is that you are working, and you have no idea what is going on with your children. If my children fail, then I have failed, because I was out of the house at work." The older mother recounts a time when she left her husband and kids. This is by far the most shocking of the revelations, because the entire audience knows how a woman who left her kids would be judged, even though she makes it clear that her husband was more than capable of taking good care of the children. I was excited to include this section because I wanted the audience to be very aware of their feelings of disapproval but also struggle with the feeling of empathy as this mother is standing there in person telling how she felt during this time in her life. The story ends with the woman sharing that she ended up back with her husband, but that she struggled for two years before finally being content with her decision. She also shares that she and her husband have been married for forty years and how this time of separation made their marriage stronger and made them better parents. I wanted to include the ending to the story to show the audience how often we make judgments based on a mere glimpse rather than knowing the full scope of a situation. In this section the audience is able to view the wide range of judgments placed on women and to consider how they have been judged in their own lives and how they have judged others. During the discussion of every performance, someone makes a comment about how women are their own worst critics and are guilty of holding one another back.

I'm not in your shoes. In this section the mothers attempt to look beyond the actions of other mothers and begin to question their preconceived ideas about right and wrong and good and bad and rather than placing judgment instead say, "I'm not in your shoes, so I don't know." The middle mother talks about a single mom who is dating and questions when it is appropriate for the new man to be introduced to the children. The older mother states that she has been in the place of being judged: "Up until the time I went through the separation from my husband and kids, there were a lot of times that I judged others . . . then you go through something like this [and] you figure they are walking in their shoes and I don't know what that feels like. And I know what it felt like, and it doesn't stress me anymore." I think this is an important time for the audience to consider the amount of information on which they are basing their judgments.

Maybe I shouldn't have done that. In this section the mothers all make confessions about actions they have taken that in retrospect they may have done differently. The older mother talks about crossing the lines of her son's privacy to find out if a questionable relationship had become physical. At the end she says, "It doesn't make me a bad mom, but I did go where I was not welcome in his private life." The middle mother starts talking about taking her family on vacation, which they hated. She then goes on to say that her anger turned into a rant about professional choices that she has made for her family and their lack of understanding about her being the major breadwinner for their family. She says, "I was putting this whole big thing on them, and even as teenagers they don't comprehend it at all . . . I feel like I am looking out for their future and their father looks out for tomorrow, and that's about it." In both of these stories the audience can see how mothers continually self-evaluate and reconsider their choices and actions, however, even when mistakes are made, they are often rooted in good intentions.

I'm afraid. In this section the mothers take turns stating a list of seventeen different fears.

> YOUNG MOM: I'm afraid that I won't like my kids.
> MIDDLE MOM: I'm afraid that my kids won't like me.
> OLDER MOM: I'm afraid that my kids won't like themselves.
> YOUNG MOM: I'm afraid that my child will die.
> OLDER MOM: I'm afraid that my child will want to die.
> MIDDLE MOM: I'm afraid that my choices will hurt my child.
> OLDER MOM: I'm afraid that my child's choices will hurt them.
> YOUNG MOM: I'm afraid that my child won't talk to me.
> MIDDLE MOM: I'm afraid that I won't talk to my child.
> OLDER MOM: I'm afraid that my child will be financially irresponsible.
> MIDDLE MOM: I'm afraid that my child will learn financial irresponsibility from me.
> YOUNG MOM: I'm afraid that my child will need me for everything.
> OLDER MOM: I'm afraid that my child will need me for nothing.
> MIDDLE MOM: I'm afraid that my child will fail.
> YOUNG MOM: I'm afraid that I will fail.
> MIDDLE MOM: I'm afraid that my kids won't respect others.
> OLDER MOM: I'm afraid that my kids won't respect themselves.

In this section I wanted the audience to feel overwhelmed by the amount of responsibility and anxiety that mothers face. The breadth of different fears, and hearing them one right after another, is a powerful moment in the script. I think it is also placed in the script at a time when the audience is getting used to hearing the longer narratives, so it provides a bit of shock in that aspect as well.

My mom. In this section each mother shares a short story about her mom. The younger mom shares that she is irritated with her mom for not telling her it would be so hard. The middle mom is in awe of her mom and impressed by her ability to be so organized and able to handle motherhood so well. The older mom is sympathetic toward her mother, as she feels she was not a good mom. She also shares that she and her mother are good friends now. I think this section challenges the audience to think about their own mothers and consider how their mothers have affected their own mothering experience.

My metaphor. At the end of each interview, I asked each mother to share a metaphor about what it was like to be a mom. The older mother's metaphor was about picking rocks and cracking eggs. What is underneath and inside is unknown—sometimes it is good, and sometimes it is yucky. The middle mother's metaphor was about her struggle and failure to grow a sunflower patch and how she hopes that as her children grow and move on that the sunflowers will remind her of them growing up on the farm. Although she has not been successful yet, she says she will keep trying. The young mom's metaphor is about the ripples in a pond caused by throwing a rock and how it is beautiful to look at, but if one is trying to swim against the waves, then it can be quite difficult. Although the metaphors are a bit silly and simple, they are also poetic. I wanted to include this section to allow the audience to think about how they could explain motherhood in different terms and use different examples to expand the ideas about motherhood and how mothers describe the experience.

Throughout the script I, as narrator, interject some of my personal stories and add quotations from some of the academic research. The quotations from the researchers are put up on multimedia slides, allowing the audience to read the quotations along with me. Audience members have commented on how they enjoyed seeing the text and hearing it at the same time. They also said they enjoyed the scholarly aspect of the performance. One group of mothers felt that the scholarly writings offered them the opportunity to really think about the information for themselves rather than having it already watered down by an author who is writing for a nonacademic audience, insulting their intelligence.

THE FUTURE

I have been immersed in the culture of motherhood for almost a decade. During that time I have had personal relationships with many different mothers whose stories of motherhood I have heard and with whom I have shared many of my stories. While I do not have field notes documenting the experience, I have memories that emerge as I read the writing and research of others and hear the stories and experiences of those who are also living in motherhood culture. I believe motherhood is a culture—it has a set of rules and norms; to recognize it as such will begin the process of change to make it a culture that will support rather than suppress.

I wanted to get across to the audience that we have a limited vocabulary to use to talk about motherhood. I did not want to place blame on men, society, or other women, but I wanted to show that we are all responsible for this limited vocabulary. I wanted the audience to see the commonalities of motherhood, and that while it seems that we are all raising kids individually, we are really all in the same boat. It is through our shared experiences that we can relate to one another rather than our individual experiences being our whole reality.

As difficult as it can be to be confident in our roles as mothers, it goes beyond our own self-esteem when becoming a mother affects a woman's equality as a worker and her ability to move through society with impartiality. Joan Williams and Holly Cooper (2004) write about these often unspoken issues in their article "The Public Policy of Motherhood." They contend that "if public policy offered mothers less brutal trade-offs between children's needs, economic stability and personal fulfillment, mothers' choices would likely change" (852). In her article "'Go Home!' When Discrimination Forces Moms Out of a Job," Kimberly Tso (2005) quotes from an interview with Faye Crosby, of the Cognitive Bias Working Group, who says, "We need to challenge people to view caregiving as highly skilled work" (4). Public performance can be a place to start. While it certainly has its limitations, I believe the foundation is there to make this into a training tool for companies as well as parenting groups. I have had the opportunity to present the reading in this context. I have presented for a local moms group and have been contracted by a local community college to present, as part of their diversity training, to seven campuses. It seems to relate well in these settings as well as the theater venue. However, some mothers approached me after the reading and said they wished there had been some marginalized mothers' voices included in the script. As I continue this work, my hope is that mothers will continue to share stories, and that the script can evolve to include all mothers.

So far this project has been a fantastic experience. I learned a lot and, most importantly, I accomplished what I set out to do. I feel my role as a mother goes outside of the walls of my home. Elena Joseph (2006), in her essay "Crack Your Shackles, Martyred Mom!," expresses her vision thus:

> Without social action, we have no hope of expanding the buffet. But, without internal change, we will not be able to eat. To become a feminist mother, I learned to disobey the guilt.

Guilt informs me that I am not enough; I need to do more, be more, before I can take what I need. I now say, it is enough to be not enough. I am flawed and I am adequate. I will eat. A feminist mother is an UnMartyred Mom, a woman who shows her children by example that a woman can experience fulfillment, can have an excellent life. A feminist mother joins with other mothers to embrace the full splendor of our varied lives and to improve our world. Let us face ourselves, come together, and dance the mothers' movement toward freedom.

This performance is about bringing those stories of empowered mothering to life, bringing them to a public venue for people to hear, to reflect on, and to be encouraged to take the time to share their mother stories with others. Through these narratives we might get a more realistic picture of motherhood. A picture of an airbrushed mother in a magazine or a fairy-tale ending in a Disney film might be more of what we want motherhood to look like, but fantasy does not lead to change. We need a society that supports women to reach their full potential rather than setting the bar so high and out of reach that all energy is wasted trying to measure up. Changing societal views is never easy, and it does not begin with legislation and corporate policy. People are swayed to take a look at old issues in a new way by hearing stories, real stories from real mothers about real-life challenges and triumphs. Real stories from mothers are beginning to emerge on blogs and in the media, but they are often met by those who are resistant to change. Many repressed groups have come before and have stood together to make our world more fair and just, so mothers too must unite and stand together. If I can, I will make sure my daughter does have choices, real choices that she can make with confidence, and that she has the language to talk about her choices without condemnation.

REFERENCES

Brooks, A. 2007. Feminist research practice. In *Feminist standpoint epistemology: Building knowledge and empowerment through women's lived experience*, ed. S. N. Hesse-Biber and P. L. Leavy, 53–82. Thousand Oaks, CA: Sage.

Caplan, P. J. 1989. *Don't blame mother: The mother-daughter relationship*. New York: Harper & Row.

Goodall, H. L. 1989. *Casing a promised land: The autobiography of an organizational detective as cultural ethnographer*. Carbondale: Southern Illinois University Press.

Joseph, E. T. 2006. *Crack your shackles, martyred mom!* The Mothers Movement Online. http://www.mothersmovement.org/essays/ 06/11/taurke_joseph.html.

Maushart, S. 1999. *The mask of motherhood: How becoming a mother changes our lives and why we never talk about it.* Toronto: Penguin Books.

O'Reilly, A., ed. 2004. *Mother outlaws: Theories and practices of empowered mothering.* Toronto: Women's Press.

Pelias, R. J. 1992. *Performance studies: The interpretation of aesthetic text.* New York: St. Martin's Press.

Rubin, L. B. 1994. *Families on the fault line.* New York: HarperCollins.

Tso, K. 2005. *"Go home!" When discrimination forces moms out of a job.* The Mothers Movement Online. http://www.mothersmovement.org/features/05/go_home.html.

Wane, N. N. 2000. Reflections on the mutuality of mothering: Women, children and othermothering. *Journal of the Association for Research on Mothering* 2 (Fall–Winter): 105–16.

Williams, J. C., and H. C. Cooper. 2004. The public policy of motherhood. *Journal of Social Issues* 60 (December): 849–65.

ELEVEN

From Gestation to Delivery

*The Embodied Activist Mothering of
Cindy Sheehan and Jennifer Schumaker*

NATALIE WILSON

From Mary Wollstonecraft's famous message that female children deserve equal education to Mother Mary Jones's emphatic call for workers' rights, mothers around the world have delivered various activist messages. Until the last several decades, this message was usually delivered through a maternalist frame—a frame that relied on what the introduction of this volume refers to as "the mythology of motherhood," or, the institutionalized beliefs surrounding mothering as natural, desirable, and good for women, and mothers as nurturing, caring, and honorable.[1] Earlier activists often drew on these institutionalized beliefs in order to frame their arguments and justify their right to protest. However, by essentializing motherhood, this maternalist framing sometimes tied women to the very things they were trying to protest—to their socially constructed, second-class status as mothers and women. Yet in the past twenty or so years, activist mothers have shorn the limiting maternalist frame. This shift certainly owes a debt to the feminist analysis of mothering specifically, as well as to the growing interest in the subject of mothering over the past thirty years more generally. In order to assess this shift, this chapter will focus on mothers' agency, political engagement, and activism in the early years of the twenty-first century. In particular, the discussion will explore the activism of Cindy Sheehan and Jennifer Schumaker as practiced during the period 2003–2008.

Cindy Sheehan, an anti-war activist who was spurred into action via her son Casey's death in the early days of the Iraq war, and Jennifer Schumaker, a lesbian activist who was concerned with ending homophobia and securing equal marriage rights, both utilized three key practices in their activism: first, they performed a "just a normal mom" or what I will call an "everymom" identity in order to manipulate this status into what Andrea O'Reilly (2004) (drawing on Adrienne Rich) defines as a "mother outlaw" identity;[2] second, they invoked a "personal is political" methodology that not only reconsidered and expanded mothering practices but also built on the long traditions of women's protests surrounding concepts of nationalism and "the good citizen"; and third, they enacted what I call "embodied activism," a form of activism that resolutely refuses "abstract rationalism" and instead foregrounds the ways in which national and international policies and institutions affect mothers and their families. Each of these practices coincides with what I read as a continuum from the maternalist framing of earlier activist movements to the embodied activist mothering of the early twenty-first century.

FROM MATERNALISM TO ACTIVIST MOTHERING

The "trope of motherhood" has been utilized in various ways by activist movements (Cockburn 2007, 209). Yet as Cynthia Cockburn (2007) notes in her recent assessment of women's activism, feminists "remain divided, and sometimes unsure, as to whether the political activation of motherhood is a help or a hindrance" (209). What Cockburn's discussion of this debate fails to illuminate is that the "trope of motherhood" is not monolithic but extremely varied, heterogeneous, and contextual. While deploying this "trope" to suggest that mothers are *essentially* peace loving, nurturing, or empathetic is problematic from a feminist perspective, utilizing this "trope" in order to disrupt dominant discourses and practices allows for the exertion of maternal agency—an agency that can instigate societal changes and paradigm shifts. For despite what Cockburn's argument suggests, motherhood need not be delivered as a static trope that ties women to outdated essentialist notions of motherhood. In fact, while mothers have historically been associated with home and hearth, a feminist look at history reveals that motherhood often radicalizes women, prompting them to want to change the world for their families and children. For example, women such as Elizabeth Cady Stanton and Mother Mary Jones were emboldened to fight for social justice through their experience as mothers.[3] As

Kristin Rowe-Finkbeiner (2004) argues in her polemic, *The F Word: Feminism in Jeopardy*, for many women "motherhood brings to the fore social inequalities that must be addressed politically" (150). This "bringing to the fore" to which Rowe-Finkbeiner refers has inspired political engagement, or, in my terminology, activist mothering, on the part of Sheehan, Schumaker, and many others.

"Activist mothering," which has variously been called feminist mothering, other mothering, maternal thinking, and outlaw mothering by scholars such as Adrienne Rich (1976), Sara Ruddick (2001), and Andrea O'Reilly (2004, 2006), is a politically aware and engaged type of mothering. It forms a continuum with earlier forms of maternal activism such as "maternalism" or "maternalist feminism." While maternalism draws on essentialist notions of women as "natural" caretakers of children and thus is problematic from a contemporary feminist perspective, it nevertheless gave many women an activist voice in society.[4] It allowed mothers to move beyond the "private sphere" and gave them a public voice, albeit a voice that limited the ways in which they could speak. Through this framework, women were given voice *as mothers* and thus had to play the patriarchal game that constructed them as domestic and nurturing, as women who put their families, and particularly their children, first. As an extension of maternalism, activist mothering is aimed at social injustices at all levels and in all places but does not necessarily focus on or emphasize women *as mothers*. While maternalist-based movements chained women to their status as mothers by reifying "motherhood" and all of its attendant associations as "natural," activist mothering moves beyond this limiting frame by using motherhood as a launch point rather than a base. For example, activist mothers of the early twenty-first century such as Sheehan often instigated their activism through reference to their role as mothers, but they did not tend to use this status as the entire grounding for their aims. Thus while Women Strike for Peace used what Amy Swerdlow (1993) calls a "maternalist standpoint" in order "to speak to the American people in a language they believed would be understood and expected" (235), Cindy Sheehan, who has similar anti-militarism aims, refused the "compliant" voice of the mother. She did not attempt to speak in "accepted mother language" that appeals to people's expectations of mothers as caring, soft-spoken, or domestic. On the contrary, she proved herself to be argumentative, confident, angry, and rather fond of the f-word. She explicitly argued that mothering is not private, domestic, or apolitical, as has so long been claimed, but that mothering is, as O'Reilly (2006) argues, "explicitly and profoundly political and public" (15).

While activist mothering in the first decade of the twenty-first century did not tend to be framed along maternalist lines in the explicit ways earlier activism was, it nevertheless can be read as an extension or a growth of the long, fruitful history of activist mothers. From Julia Ward Howe to Anna Jarvis and their fight to institute a Mother's Day for Peace, to Code Pink, an activist collective that calls "on mothers, grandmothers, sisters, and daughters, on workers, students, teachers, healers, artists, writers, singers, poets, and every ordinary outraged woman willing to be outrageous for peace," many activist mothers have used any and all means possible to birth the just world they envision (Benjamin and Evans 2005, 233). Often doing so under inhospitable, hostile conditions, activist mothers have utilized their culturally acceptable status as mothers as a platform from which to speak. Drawing on the general respect that mothers are granted in society (even if this respect is mainly symbolic and does not afford real power), women have historically utilized acceptable mothering practices (such as a bear-like tendency to protect their children and to be devastated over their loss) to protest war, poverty, child labor, and myriad other social injustices. However, sometimes this activism has (necessarily) been delivered through a maternalist framework that entrenches motherhood as a necessary component of womanhood, on the one hand, and defines motherhood in very specific ways, on the other. For example, as noted by Gibbons (in this book), the American group Another Mother for Peace framed its protest within traditional notions of motherhood and protested the Vietnam War using images of mothers as peaceful. As Gibbons further notes, both the Argentine Madres de la Plaza de Mayo and Another Mother for Peace insisted on their apolitical aims and tried to frame their arguments within traditional and culturally specific tropes of motherhood and maternalism. In contrast, mothering activists of the early twenty-first century were able to more radically depart from traditional ideas of motherhood. In a sense, the maternalist framework employed by earlier activists can be read as a gestation period in which mothers nourished various budding forms of female activism in order to eventually deliver a full-fledged activist agenda. Hence, maternalism and activist mothering should not be read as two disparate modes but rather as a continuum of activism.

This continuum of maternalist activism to activist mothering is also marked by the fairly consistent tendency toward what I call "embodied" activism, or activism that emphasizes the fact that we all live in and through our bodies. As mothers, women are often forced into a keen awareness of the embodied nature of existence. As Rich (1976) explores in *Of Woman Born*, the body often becomes a trap for women, and especially mothers, as they are forcibly tied to the body side of the mind-body duality. Not only do woman occupy the disparaged side of this duality *as women*, they also are quite literally tied to the body in mothering—not only to their own bodies through pregnancy, birth, and breastfeeding, but also to the body care of their children. Thus, as Rich (1976) notes, "The body has been made so problematic for women that it has often seemed easier to shrug it off and travel as a disembodied spirit" (40). Hence, women have been encouraged to forget their bodies, to deny the bodily realities of pregnancy and birth, to hide the embodied practices of breastfeeding, and to deny the profound ways in which they, and their children, are shaped through the undeniable corporeality of existence. However, many maternalist activists and activist mothers staunchly refuse the call for bodily forgetting.

Like Rich (1976), who refers to her "determination to heal—insofar as an individual woman can, and as much as possible with other women—the separation between mind and body," activist mothers such as Sheehan and Schumaker specifically highlight the embodied nature of existence (40). Moreover, by carrying out what I call embodied activism, both Sheehan and Schumaker deliver a form of activism that utilizes embodiment to further particular political causes. In so doing, they take their place in a long history of embodied activist mothers. Whether using the body as a sort of weapon to blockade factory entrances or as manifestation of powerlessness and injustice (as when the body is purposefully rendered weak during a hunger strike so as to literally *materialize* various political injustices in ways that are visibly embodied), mothering activists have consistently refused to disembody their activism. From Julia Ward Howe's focus on war as destroying and maiming bodies in late 1800s America to the women of the Chipko movement in India who, in the 1970s, prevented the felling of trees in a 12,000 square kilometer area of sensitive watershed by surrounding the trees with their bodies, activist mothers have focused on how bodies are harmed by various social injustices while utilizing the body itself to prevent these injustices from happening.[5] The Argentine Madres de la Plaza de Mayo, for example, used their bodies as walking billboards, *embodying* their grief while carrying massive posters of their disappeared children and marching "with life-sized silhouettes, giving a very physical presence to the bodies of the disappeared" (see Gibbons, in this volume). This practice of making use of the physical presence of the body in public spaces to protest has been key to activist mothers historically, as has the practice of using visual representations of other bodies (as with the posters of the disappeared) to call attention to the fact that far more bodies than those specifically involved in the protest need to be taken into account. As when suffragettes in the United States printed pictures of their children to argue that voting was a maternal duty, activist mothers have often used images of their children to further their cause (Ellison 2005, 218). More recently, Sheehan used her corporeal form as a sort of screen from which to deliver pictures of her son Casey, of statistics of war atrocities, or to manifest the exhaustion brought about from protesting outside Bush's Crawford ranch in 100–plus-degree weather. Likewise, Schumaker enacted embodied activist mothering through both her mode of delivery (walking) and her insistent foregrounding of the body in her writing and speeches. Thus activist mothers have a well-established tradition of corporeally based political engagement, or, to use a sporting phrase co-opted by Sheehan, of "putting their skin in the game" (2005, 115). However, this does not necessarily mean that for activist mothering to take place the bodily presence of the orator is required. Rather, it requires a cognizance of the *embodied* nature of humanity, a delivery of a message that injustices are not abstract wrongs that hurt a particular nation but literal wounds that injure living, breathing bodies.

One of the most well-established traditions of activist mothers, protesting war, markedly draws on embodied activism. In a sense, such protests have been condoned through the notion that it is only natural for mothers to grieve children who have been killed in battle, wounded in service, or disappeared by militarized government practices. This acceptable form of protest fits into motherhood as an institution in which the selfless mother is to efface herself (and her body) in order to live her life through and for her children. Yet when "acceptable grief" moves into a more public, politicized enactment of grief, and when bodily denial turns into embodied protest, the story changes profoundly. As Gibbons attests in her chapter in this book, a certain amount of grief is condoned (as it was with both the Madres and Another Mother for Peace), but once this grief is politicized, it is no longer viewed as acceptable. This is also the case in relation to Sheehan, a woman whose activist mothering helped jump-start in 2004 an anti-war movement. This success is undoubtedly informed by her role as a mother, and, moreover, by her status as the mother of a dead soldier. While drawing on traditional concepts of motherhood and the trope of the grieving mother to further her cause, Sheehan also expanded the notion of what a mother can and should be. Likewise, Jennifer Schumaker translated her own personal frustration concerning the ways that she and her children are disenfranchised by society due to heteronormative mandates into a profoundly public activist movement in 2006. While drawing on her status as an everymom (and in particular on tropes such as soccer mom and carpool mom), Schumaker expanded the definition of mothering to include LGBTQ (lesbian, gay, bisexual, transgendered, and queer) activism.

FROM PEACE MOM TO ACTIVIST, FROM PATRIOT TO MATRIOT: CINDY SHEEHAN

For Cindy Sheehan, a large part of her success was no doubt related to her "peace mom" status. As part of a long-standing tradition of peace-activist mothers, Sheehan delivered her anti-war messages through public speaking tours, peace rallies and marches, various Internet media (such as CommonDreams.org and TruthOut.org), and numerous books, and, in 2007, she announced that she planned to run for Congress against Speaker of the House Nancy Pelosi on a pro-peace platform. While at first she was respected as a grieving mother questioning the costs of war, her galvanization of the peace movement in the United States was increasingly met with harsh criticism. Reporting on the less than positive response to her peace activism in *The Nation*, Karen Houppert (2006) notes how Sheehan evolved "from the darling of the press (in the early days, when she was portrayed, Rosa Parks-style, as a grief-stricken mom who simply materialized on Bush's doorstep) to a less trustworthy spokesperson of the left's antiwar message (once her connections to a more radical peace agenda were exposed)." In addition to being criticized for being too political, the perception of Sheehan as a sympathetic, grieving mom to crazy, radical leftie undoubtedly also came about due to her transgressing the supposedly normal time limits of grief and the normally privatized role of mother. Mothers, like widows, are supposed to mourn for a certain amount of time, and then they *should* get on with their lives, which usually means attending to the living children or spouse. Expectations such as these were made patently clear regarding Sheehan through the increasingly loud outcry that she should "go home and take care of her kids" (Sheehan 2005, 118). Sheehan has responded to this chorus of disapproval by noting that her activism is a profoundly important form of mothering, that "what I am doing is for my children, and the world's children," that "I *am* taking care of my kids, and yours, too" (118, emphasis in original). Here Sheehan refuses the individualized script of motherhood and insists on a more expansive concept of mothering that involves caring for the world and all of its children, expanding, in effect, the idea of mothering into a global, activist one. Moreover, her comments emphasize that although she is framed as one woman against the world by the mass media, she represents many women and mothers who care not only for their own children but also for the entire world and its inhabitants. Sheehan further notes that the directive "go home and take care of your kids" offends her "because it is so blatantly sexist. Would anyone think of e-mailing George Bush when he is out and about . . . telling him to go and take care of his kids? Does anyone write to *any* man and tell him to go home and take care of his kids?" (118, emphasis in original) Here Sheehan emphasizes unequal gendered expectations—moms are supposed to care for kids, while dads are free to run the corporation, the country, or the world. Referring to "the load of misogynistic crap" that children need their mothers' "constant presence in their lives so they can thrive and grow," Sheehan reveals an incisive awareness of the damaging dictates of motherhood as institution (119). In so doing, she represents the progression of activist mothering—critical of the maternalist stance, she framed herself as a mother and an activist but did not ground her entire agenda on her "maternal duties" as many earlier mothering activists did.

Sheehan's criticism of the ways in which motherhood as an institution is based on a system of gendered inequality also links particularly well with scholar Anne McClintock's (1993) assessment of nations as gendered:

> Women are represented as the atavistic and authentic "body" of national tradition (inert, backward-looking, and natural), embodying nationalism's conservative principle of continuity. Men, by contrast, represent the progressive agent of national modernity (forward-thrusting, potent, and historic), embodying nationalism's progressive, or revolutionary principle of discontinuity. (66)

McClintock argues that nations and concepts of nationalism are configured in very gendered ways. In relation to Sheehan's activist mothering, she is moving beyond being the traditional inert female national body into the area of (male) potency and thrust. As McClintock (1993) notes, women are "excluded from direct action as national citizens" and thus "subsumed symbolically into the national body politics as its boundary and metaphoric limit" (62). Thus women are not meant to be *active* citizens but symbolic ones—they are supposed to symbolize patriotism through the birthing of future citizens, through revering national law, and through acquiescing to the mandates of the nation-state. As symbols of nationalism, they are to function like Lady Liberty or Lady Justice, as beautiful, inert icons representing the nation's ideals. This symbolic nationalism allies to the maternalist framing of women that is often enacted during wartime when women tend to be framed not as active soldiers, policy makers, or global ambassadors but as weeping widows, tearful girlfriends, and bereft mothers endlessly standing by disembarking ships or mourning graveside.

Yet Sheehan (2005) refused this symbolic nationalism and maternalist framing. Instead, she insisted on being an active, potent mother who ceaselessly delivers her message to the world. Noting that her story exemplifies that "One mom has shown that we can be the change in our government," Sheehan emphasized to (m)others that they too could be the change (20).[6] In fact, she went so far as to argue that those not doing anything are accessories to the crimes of war; Sheehan (2006a) encourages "everyone in America to move away from the comfortable complacency that allows Bush Co to kill people with impunity." However, she has also been careful to emphasize that it is difficult to move beyond the apathy, acknowledging, "What kept me from speaking out in the beginning was the sense that I couldn't make a difference" (Houppert 2006). She further notes, "I think the people in power want you to feel helpless, because if we all find our voice, our power, we really can make a lasting difference in this country" (Houppert 2006). Here, using an everymom stance, Sheehan characterizes her previous sense of powerlessness as *induced,* as one that those in power purposefully manifest in order to keep the populace under control. As such, she seems dedicated to motivating the masses and does so through a purposeful use of everymom language. Specifically avoiding complex jargon or vituperative rhetoric, Sheehan (2005) spoke in the voice of the mom next door, making very clear points such as "as long as moms are having to hold bake sales to buy their sons body armor . . . military service should be opposed" (31) and asking simple questions such as the one she has repeatedly posed to George W. Bush: "If it's such a noble cause, have you asked your daughters to enlist? Have you encouraged them to go take the place of soldiers who are on their third tour of duty?" (98). Sheehan further enacts this type of everymom status by her (often criticized) refusal to dress up or to wear makeup, regardless of whether she is appearing on national television or speaking to a group of thousands.

Refusing to hide her grief or pretend that it will go away after the allotted mourning time, Sheehan also astutely drew on her status as an everymom as a justified platform from which to air her grievances while simultaneously transgressing this role by being too sad, too angry, too political, and too public. Additionally, she has directed her condemnations of the war very specifically to George W. Bush, often roundly accusing him of murdering her son. This personalization allies in intriguing ways with the feminist mantra "The personal is political." In statements such as, "I often get introduced as a mother who lost her son in Iraq. I didn't lose Casey. I know right where he is. He is in a grave in Vacaville, and I know who put him there: George Bush" (Sheehan 2005, 52), Sheehan refuses to play the good, grieving mom proud of her son's patriotism. Instead, she angrily rejects the notion that her son was "lost" and instead insists he was murdered due to the president's criminal war.

She further brings the politics of language to the fore in her analysis of the word "matriotism" as opposed to patriotism. Referring to matriotism as a "new paradigm for true and lasting peace in the world," Sheehan (2006a) argues that "A true Matriot would never drop an atomic bomb or bombs filled with white phosphorous, carpet-bomb cities and villages, or control drones from thousands of miles away to kill innocent men, women, and children."[7] Here her conception of matriotism implicitly emphasizes the need to *personalize the political*—to realize that the bombs we drop from afar have very real, personal consequences on individual bodies. Thus unlike patriotism, matriotism emphasizes individual embodiment and interhumanity rather than the depersonalized allegiance to a nation-state that patriotism calls for. This places Sheehan in a long line of feminist activists who have worked to reveal, in various ways, the ways in which women have been codified as "eccentric subjects" that "have had a problematic relationship to the modern nation-state and its construction of subjectivity" (Alarcon et al. 1999, 1). Sheehan's use of the word matriotism gestures toward this problematic relationship, emphasizing the ways in which subjectivity has been constructed along pater or male lines. Calling attention to the fact that women are linguistically and otherwise left out through words such as patriotism and concepts such as nation, Sheehan insists, as many have before her, that we must consider the gendered implications of defining citizens, nations, and patriotism as if gender did not matter. By foregrounding gender in her reclamation of patriotism into matriotism, Sheehan emphasized that we are not homogenous citizens but humans shaped by gender, race, class, geopolitical location, and many other axes of identity. More specifically, in her meditation on the implications of the word matriotism, Sheehan calls upon the mothers of the world to "never send her child or another mother's child to fight nonsense wars," and, in so doing, she turns the "power over ideology" of patriotism into a "solidarity with" paradigm for peace (2006a, para. 9). In so doing, Sheehan not only stresses the need to be active *at the level of language*, she also reveals a profound understanding that in order to change the world, we must change not only the words we use but also the ideologies they represent and perpetuate. Here, her birthing of the word matriotism is analogous to what I am arguing in regard to the continuum of maternalism and activist mothering. Within the maternalist frame, mothers often emphasized themselves as "good patriots" who wanted to protect the sons of the nation (as with the Women Strike for Peace slogan "Not Our Sons, Not Their Sons, Not Your Sons"), while within contemporary activist mothering, women are delivering the more radical message that allegiance to any nation-state is problematic, and that not only sons but daughters, lovers, animals, and the planet itself deserve protection.[8]

Sheehan delivers matriotism by questioning male dominance and refusing to deify political leaders/fathers. Unlike earlier maternalist activists who tried to work within the frames of patriarchy and the nation-state, Sheehan refuses to play by these rules and, in so doing, delivers a new matriotist message. In addition to delivering speeches across the United States, Sheehan has also delivered her message in numerous books and essays. Further, through her practice of calling President Bush "George," Sheehan delivers the message that ordinary mothers (and their soldiering children) deserve as much (or more) respect as government leaders. Here she refutes the institutionalized respect that government leaders are supposed to be afforded and declines to see the president as father of the nation. In fact, the basic rationale behind Camp Casey (2004–2007), that Bush should not be on vacations when soldiers and civilians are being maimed and killed everyday in Iraq, suggested that the president be held accountable not only as a figurehead but also in his private, everyday life. He should, she argued, not be allowed vacations or rest when his actions continue to cause atrocities across the globe. Here Sheehan delivered a radical message—that the president is human, too, and that he should not be held in high esteem simply because he is president. This tenacity with which she refused her "patriotic duty" of respecting one's nation and its leaders extends to Sheehan's criticism of Laura Bush as well who, she insists, is neglecting to be an activist mother. More specifically, Sheehan (2005) implies that Laura should be supportive of the pro-peace cause, that she should "come down to Camp Casey with some brownies and lemonade" (83). By using George, rather than Bush or the president, and by using Laura, rather than "the first lady," Sheehan, at the level of language, emphasizes that these two figureheads are no better, no more important, and no more deserving than any other citizen.

This linguistic activism has the effect of framing George and Laura as bad parents who are neglecting the (nation's) children. Thus her plea that Bush talk with her and answer a few questions is predicated on a matriotic methodology of personalization—one that encouraged thousands of (m)others that opposing the war needs to be a *personal* issue undertaken by all who do not support it, and that not opposing war will lead to *personal* cost. While those in power attempt to depersonalize the war with statistics and euphemistic jargon such as collateral damage, Sheehan (2006a) repeatedly emphasizes the personal dynamics of war, emphasizing that death tolls do not account for the fact that "for those of us who have lost a son or a daughter or a brother or a sister or a father or a mother in this war, the number one is more than enough." Here Sheehan's matriotism insists that all human loss counts and refutes the patriotic notion that it is noble to die for one's country. By personalizing grief in this way and making public (and political) the palpable pain and suffering that war brings, Sheehan put matriotism into action. For example, when she asks "How many more mothers are we going to watch sobbing over their children's flag-draped coffins before we get out in the streets and demand an end to the immoral and illegal occupation so no other mothers will have to be plunged into a pool of pain?" Sheehan (2006a) publicizes the coffins the government tries to keep hidden, politicizes the pain caused by war, and specifically calls for action—to get out in the streets to demand an end to war.[9] Thus her brand of matriotism calls for action rather than compliance, for being critical of the government rather than reverential, and for actively protesting societal wrongs.

Through her activism during the period 2004–2007, Sheehan delivered and nurtured the continuation of activist mothering. As Thom Hartmann (2005) argues in "Cindy: An Historic Perspective," "Cindy Sheehan stepped forward in the great tradition of the mothers of Chile and Argentina, the women who have protested against war from the times of ancient Greece through every one of America's wars, and of Julia Ward Howe" (xv). Sheehan built on this collective tradition in keeping with the activist mothering groups of Chile and Argentina by attempting to forge dedicated groups of activists through the founding of Camp Casey and the Crawford Peace House. In 2007, her campaign for Congress carried on the tradition of Jeannette Rankin, the first female congresswoman who after only four days in office made history by voting against U.S. entry into World War I. Moreover, she delivered her activism in ways that move beyond the limiting confines of maternalism. While she initially grounded her protest through her status as the mother of a dead soldier, she ultimately transcended this maternalist stance by rejecting the notion that she was "only a mother" and insisting on herself as a human citizen disgusted by the actions of her government.

THE EVERYDAY ACTIVISM OF A LESBIAN EVERYMOM: JENNIFER SCHUMAKER

While Sheehan may be one of the most famous early twenty-first century activist mothers from the United States, many other activist mothers worked to right a number of social wrongs during this time frame. Many of these activist mothers utilized the same parameters as Sheehan, such as the everymom stance, performing outlaw mothering, explicitly making the personal political and the political personal, and enacting embodied activism. For example, in San Diego, Jennifer Schumaker carried out the *500 Mile Walk for Togetherness* in the spring of 2006 to create dialogue about LGBTQ rights and issues specifically and to emphasize human togetherness and interconnection more generally. According to the *Walk for Togetherness* Web site, Schumaker envisioned the walk as a way to deconstruct the entrenched "us and them" way of thinking that dominates both public and private discourse, especially in relation to sexuality. As noted on the Web site, Schumaker (2005) believes that "any discussions or debates that use the words 'we' and 'they' to polarize communities are erroneous and destructive." Thus her vision of togetherness was not aimed at merely dismantling the hetero/non-hetero binary but at moving beyond binary, judgmental thinking altogether and making all humans visible. As the Web site reads, "Jennifer is not only walking for LGBT people and their families, but also for anyone who feels invisible in our society." Schumaker (2005) dedicated her walk to a twelve-year-old boy named Dakota, who has cerebral palsy. When Dakota was seven, Jennifer heard him call himself "the Invisible Man." Schumaker often invokes Dakota's story when writing or talking about her activism, emphasizing that no one, regardless of race, sexuality, disability, or any other difference, should be rendered invisible by society.

Like Sheehan, Schumaker regularly evokes her status as an everymom in order to create a sustainable link between forces that wish to "other" her. For example, she often emphasizes her everymom identity in interviews and speeches, referring variously to herself as a lesbian soccer mom, a carpool mom, and a suburban matriarch. Like Sheehan, Schumaker is aware of the power of this stance. As she notes, "There's a certain respectability with being a mom that gives me privilege that some of my LGBT sisters and brothers don't have" (Sherman 2006). However, as Schumaker explains, she realized that she did not "want to rest on that privilege" (Conlan 2006, para. 16). This realization is, as she puts it, really the crux of this walk. I'm very aware that I have a lot of privilege in this society, and if I can share that with people who maybe wouldn't get received the same way I have, hopefully I can open some dialogue that will include people who do feel more invisible than I do, people who don't necessarily have the confidence or the privilege to speak up. (Conlan 2006)

Emphasizing the need to use everymom privileges to help others, Schumaker is nevertheless acutely aware that being a lesbian ejects her from the everymom club. However, the fact that she has four children, lives in suburbia, and "does not look like a stereotypical lesbian" gives her a "normal" edge. Recounting the tendency of people to not hear the lesbian part when she introduces herself, Schumaker notes, "My physical appearance seems to elicit certain recognitions and activate 'comfort' stereotypes" (personal communication 2006). As she explains, her "normal" appearance is not used to trick people into a comfort zone; rather, she uses this appearance privilege as a bridge toward open, nondiscriminatory communication. According to her, "The privilege comes in being white, extroverted, feminine, mom-like (whatever that means), dressed decently, etc." (personal communication 2006) and allows her, like Sheehan, to successfully enact outlaw, activist mothering. Because Sheehan and Schumaker occupy a number of privileged social identities, they are able to, in effect, deliver their messages to a much wider audience by drawing upon these privileges. However, as Schumaker emphasizes, the way she enacts this type of activist mothering is through drawing on her personal identity/appearance as a means through which to change the other (and as a result, society as a whole), or, as she puts it, "It is very important that outlaw mothering be seen in terms of the 'mother other' outlook—that just by quietly revealing simple facts about my life and personhood, there can be a revolution in the thoughts and categories *in the other*" (personal communication 2006). Here Schumaker reveals that her quiet mode of delivery functions as a deliberate attempt to change others in a nonconfrontational way. This type of delivery has the effect of making people who would otherwise be disinclined to consider the merits of a nonheterosexist society to hear the message of inclusiveness, equality, and togetherness rather than to hear "lesbian" and shut their ears.[10]

Schumaker is particularly committed to what feminists call "everyday activism." In her explanation of these everyday activisms, Schumaker reveals that activism is not only about walking 500 miles but also about the little daily steps of promoting awareness and togetherness:

> I would buy my groceries and I would say, "Remember, a Lesbian spent money here today." I would get my car towed, and I would say, "Hey, guys, remember you helped out a Lesbian today." I would leave a plane, and I would look at the crew and say, "Hey, remember, 10 percent of your passengers are Gay, Lesbian, Bisexual, or Transgender." It was never easy. Sometimes my face would get a little red. Sometimes I had to ask myself if I could really do this.... But if it isn't easy for an extremely hyper, extroverted person like me, how are other people doing it? (Conlan 2006)

As such, she is an everyday activist for LGBTQ rights and visibility. While this concept of everyday activism is well known within the feminist community, Schumaker is helping to bring this conception of activism to a much wider audience. Her approach to activism emphasizes that everyday acts that may happen in the line at a grocery store or while picking up the kids at school are just as important as the "big acts" of marching, picketing, or petitioning. Championing this mode of everyday activist delivery seems a crucial move in terms of expanding the parameters of what it means to be an activist in a way that makes activism an activity open to all mothers rather than just those who can travel to D.C. or Crawford, or who have the time/money privilege to be able to picket, petition, lobby, run for office, and so on. By showing that activism can be delivered at the Boy Scout meeting, at the park, or during the lunch break, Schumaker brings to the fore a mode of activist delivery open to all. Or, to put it in her own words, she is a "pioneer." She explains:

> In some ways, I feel like this big pioneer. I even looked up "pioneer" in the dictionary one day. It means someone who goes into new territory or brings a new idea to a new area. I can say that being backstage at your kid's junior theatre production and helping with the other moms and having a button on that says "I'm much Gayer than I look" probably fits the pioneer definition. (Conlan 2006)

Here, akin to Sheehan's retooling of patriotism into matriotism, Schumaker redefines what it means to be a pioneer. While the word traditionally calls to mind notions of male settlers who colonized "new" sections of land in order to expand U.S. power and profit, Shumaker's use of the word emphasizes doing things not for personal or national gain but for the betterment of all humanity. As a pioneering activist,

Schumaker continually breaks new ground with her activist goals and, like other contemporary activist mothers, does not limit her purview to one group, issue, or platform. She is active in groups such as Scouting for All, San Diego Family Matters, Marriage Equality U.S.A., and Equality California. She regularly attends political protests and rallies and frequently lobbies Governor Schwarzenegger to pass inclusive legislation. In addition to her extensive activism surrounding LGBTQ issues, Schumaker emphasizes her solidarity with all people who are rendered invisible by society, whether due to their race, age, body size, health, and/or immigrant status. As she explains, "I frame my need for inclusion in the wider issue of what barriers exist to full inclusion and respect for anyone" (personal communication 2006).

PUTTING YOUR SKIN IN THE GAME: EMBODIED ACTIVISM

In addition to manipulating everymom status for activist purposes and revealing that with activist mothering the personal is political, activists such as Sheehan and Schumaker also emphasized the physicality of mothering and the inherently *embodied* nature of our human condition. In Sheehan's case, the body was deployed as a visible reminder of injustice, grief, and injury, both through the living, present bodies of protestors at Camp Casey, Crawford Peace House, in front of the White House, and so on, and through the pictorial/oral reminders of those bodies killed/injured in Iraq, Afghanistan, and Guantanamo. In Schumaker's case, the normal bodily act of walking was juxtaposed with what some would see as a radical request to be treated as equally human, regardless of one's social positioning, sexuality, or (dis)ability. Such enactments of embodied protest are by no means new to feminist activist traditions—from the Women of Greenham Common in the United Kingdom to the Madres de la Plaza de Mayo in Argentina to Grannies for Peace in the United States, feminist activism has been a profoundly embodied practice. From the dancing and holding of hands around nuclear silos that the Women of Greenham Common practiced, or the chaining of oneself to old growth trees that ecofeminists have enacted, or the lying nude en masse to call for peace as the women of Baring Witness do, female activists the world over use their bodies to enact protest. Such acts also draw attention to the way social injustices harm individual bodies. Perhaps the particularly embodied emphasis of female activism is in large part due to the fact that, as Rich (1976) puts it, "The woman's body is the terrain on which patriarchy is erected" (55). However, as the activism of Sheehan makes clear, militarization is also erected against male bodies. And, as Schumaker's activism emphasizes, homophobia is damaging to female, male, and transgender bodies in that it defines some types of bodies and bodily practices as abnormal.

Akin to the hunger strikes of the suffragettes or the cross-country female activist walkers "Peace Pilgrim" and "Granny D," the activism of Sheehan and Schumaker emphasized physicality. Sheehan, for example, often placed large pictures of her son Casey around her neck that hung (deliberately?) at womb height, as if to emphasize that the son she housed in her womb, gave birth to, raised, and cared for now forms a wound on her own body—a wound of grief that will not go away.[11] Like the Mothers of the Plaza de Mayo, who carry placards with large faces of their missing children as they protest, Sheehan insisted that the face (and the body) of her son not be forgotten by offering a pictorial replacement of his now-dead body. Likewise, at Camp Casey, crosses were put in the ground as visual, material reminders of those killed. Unlike the practice of bringing dead and wounded soldiers back to the United States under the cover of darkness, placing tangible reminders of those killed allowed people to visualize the number of dead in the fields outside where Bush vacations. Moreover, the choice to *camp* outside Bush's ranch was in itself an embodied form of activism. While there, Sheehan and her supporters serve as embodied reminders of the lack of public support for this war, as material proof of the growing numbers of people who are calling for an end to the escalation of the military industrial complex. These activist bodies, laboring under the 100–plus-degree August weather in Texas, could not be erased by one of Bush's smirks or smarmy platitudes—they were there, in all their materiality, sweat, sun block, and thirst, squinting into the blazing sun, reminding the world not only of the bodily cost of war but of the bodily ways one can *protest* war and other social injustices.

In another instance of embodied activism, in the summer of 2006, Sheehan participated in the "Troops Home FAST" hunger strike, which launched on July 4. Offering a rationale for the fast, Sheehan explained, "While others are celebrating July 4 with barbeques, we'll be showing our patriotism by putting our bodies on the line to bring troops home" (Troops Home Fast 2006). Her choice of words here brings to mind the front lines that put soldiers' bodies at extreme risk of death and injury, the very lines that the media and the government put under erasure by acting as if war is a strategy far removed from the actual bodies that must fight and die. In addition to drawing attention to the bodily costs of war, Sheehan (2005) also continually emphasizes the ways in which war has damaged her own body by regularly emphasizing the ways in which her son's death manifests itself physically on her body. As she relates, she has been forced to learn "to live with a pain that is so intense that sometimes I feel like throwing up, or screaming until I pass out from sorrow" (96). Not only is she putting her own skin in the game, Sheehan (2006b) also calls attention to the way *all bodies* are harmed by the militaristic mentality that currently reigns supreme, that, as she writes, "chews up . . . flesh and blood to spit out obscene profits."

Schumaker's Walk for Togetherness, as well as her regular emphasis on the physical nature of existence, also serves as embodied activism. Noting that she purposefully chose a physical form of activism through which to deliver her message, Schumaker recounts the physical terror she felt before the walk, a terror that she says caused her to wake up repeatedly at 3 a.m. in the weeks leading up to the walk. Linking this embodied fear to the fear that pregnant women often experience before delivery, Schumaker associates the feeling of pressure women feel as the baby's head presses on the cervix to the pressure she felt to be an activist. She relates:

> The deeper I get into my activism, the more I actually remember the physical feeling of the baby's head beginning to push down in my pelvis; this is something that I could never really feel before unless it was actually happening the four times, nor could I recall the feelings in any real way between births or in the years following. Now, the feelings I have about the potential for peace and change and my place in those births are so near to the imminent signs of childbirth that I am at times simply blown away, at times on my knees in wonder. (personal communication 2006)

Explaining that when people told her not to do the walk, she felt they "might as well tell me not to have the baby," Schumaker links her activism to birth, to a physical eventuality that cannot be stopped (personal communication 2006). However, she also emphasizes that, as with birth, "it's about pushing when the time is right," that the birthing of particular activist movements will not be as healthy or productive if one "pushes too soon" (personal communication 2006). This notion of "pushing too soon" seems a useful way to read earlier incarnations of maternalist activism. In previous eras, women could only "push so much" and found ways to be activists through manipulating their accepted (and respected) status as mothers. However, now that many women have broken away from the chains of domesticity, mothering activists are able to push a lot harder and push in a lot of different directions and ways.

THE POLITICS OF THE POSSIBLE:
DELIVERING ACTIVIST MOTHERING INTO THE FUTURE

If the work of activist mothers such as Sheehan and Schumaker is any indication, then the twenty-first century will deliver many new conceptions of activist mothering. In spite of this boom in deliveries, though, there is still a cultural tendency to give mothers very little credibility and to sentimentalize their actions to, in effect, use the maternalist frame to limit and belittle activist mothering. For example, as Karen Houppert (2006) reveals, activists such as Sheehan are belittled in the mainstream media: "Sheehan has been lambasted for a host of infractions, ranging from charges that she has politicized her grief to rebukes for naïvely weighing in on foreign policy decisions best left in the hands of the big boys in Washington." Schumaker analyzes this disempowering sentimentalization of mothers, noting that while Sheehan has been unbelievably successful considering she is just "a single woman fighting the war machine," that the press and public often still respond to her as if "she were a Hallmark card" (personal communication 2006). Much of the criticism, as Houppert (2006) notes, is predictable: "She speaks as a mother, and her mothering comes under fire. There are the scoldings she gets—typically from other women—for protesting the war instead of staying home to cook her family dinner. A tiresome charge dredged up for decades against any woman who takes to the streets for a political cause." Schumaker comments that she was privy to the same sort of attacks while planning and carrying out her Walk for Togetherness. In fact, the press coverage of her walk almost never failed to consider who was taking care of her children while she was gone, if she missed them, and how they were faring—as if her status as a mother was more important than the activism she was carrying out. Thus as analyst Ahmed (2005) indicates, for activists such as these women to succeed, "we need a sudden outbreak of journalism in America." Although Sheehan and Schumaker are undoubtedly making changes and delivering activism in new ways, the waves of change would come all the faster and bigger if the press offered analytical coverage that actually took to task the issues upon which they focus—war, imperialism, homophobia, poverty, and prejudice.[12] Instead, as Sheehan (2005) points out, "The right-wing media . . . assiduously scrutinize the words of a grief-filled mother and ignore the words of a lying president" (74). In effect, it is as if the media hold steadfastly to a staunch maternalist frame that refuses to see women as activists or to give the stories of activist mothers the coverage they deserve.

However, as (m)others, we cannot wait for the corporate media to wake up. Instead, we must take it upon ourselves to seek out independent media, to follow the blogs and Web sites and writings of activist mothers such as Sheehan and Schumaker, to vocalize our support for an inclusive, peaceful world at the polls, the PTA meeting, and the school pickup. If all of us activist mothers offer vocal and visible support, then we can change the tide, for, as O'Reilly (2006) notes, "It will be mothers, empowered and united, who will create the just and caring society, that feminist new world, we seek for ourselves and our children" (50). Drawing inspiration from the fact that this century opened with the Million Mom March, we must embrace "the politics of the possible" and look forward to a better tomorrow (Frazer 1998, 56). Whether through walking, talking, camping, educating, blogging, or other activist means, we must continue to deliver activist mothering in order to give birth to a better tomorrow, for ourselves, our children, and the world.

NOTES

1. For examples of this maternalist frame, see Swerdlow (1993).
2. See, for example, O'Reilly (2004).
3. For a discussion of motherhood as a radicalizing (and an intellect-inducing) experience, see Ellison (2005) and MacDonald Strong (2008).
4. For further discussion of maternalism and its place within feminist activism, see Gibbons, chapter 12, in this volume.
5. For a discussion of the Chipko movement, see Warren and Cady (1994).
6. I purposefully use the term (m)other here to indicate that Sheehan's message, along with the message of many contemporary mothering activists, is not only aimed at literal "mothers" but at all people, mothers and others, who care about ending war, homophobia, and so on.
7. For more on the use of white phosphorous in the Iraq War, see Manning's (2005) *Caught in the Crossfire: The Untold Story of Falluja*.
8. See Swerdlow (1993, 4–5).
9. For a discussion of the government directive that prohibits photographs of soldiers' coffins, see Carter (2004).
10. I personally witnessed this effect on listeners when Schumaker spoke in 2007 to my "Introduction to Women's Studies" students.

11. For photo, see Sheehan (2005, 92).
12. Part of this continuing activism includes running for Congress, on Sheehan's part, and working on a book manuscript documenting her activism, on Schumaker's part.

REFERENCES

Ahmed, A. 2005. Counteroffensive: Bush launches "Operation Cindy Sheehan." *Palestine Chronicle*. August 28. http://www.palestinechronicle.com.

Alarcon, N., C. Kaplan, and M. Moallem, eds. 1999. *Between woman and nation: Nationalism, transnational feminisms, and the state*. Durham, NC: Duke University Press.

Benjamin, M., and J. Evans, eds. 2005. *Stop the next war now: Effective responses to violence and terrorism*. Maui: Inner Ocean.

Carter, B. 2004. Showing U.S war dead: Coffin pictures published despite ban by Pentagon. *New York Times*. February 17.

Cockburn, C. 2007. *From where we stand: War, women's activism, and feminist analysis*. London: Zed Books.

Conlan, M. G. 2006. Lesbian activist starts walk for togetherness. *San Diego Indymedia*. April 8. http://www.sandiego.indymedia.org.

Ellison, K. 2005. *The mommy brain: How motherhood makes us smarter*. New York: Basic Books.

Frazer, E. 1998. Feminist political theory. In *Contemporary feminist theories*, ed. S. Jackson and J. Jones, 50–61. New York: New York University Press.

Gibbons, M. 2010. Political motherhood in the United States and Argentina. In *Mothers who deliver: Feminist interventions in public and interpersonal discourse*, ed. J. F. Stitt and P. Reichert Powell. Albany: State University of New York Press.

Hartmann, T. 2005. Cindy: An historic perspective. In *Not one more mother's child*, ed. C. Sheehan, xiii–xvi. Kihei, HI: Koa Books.

Houppert, K. 2006. Cindy Sheehan: Mother of a movement? *The Nation*. June 12. http://www.thenation.com.

MacDonald Strong, S. 2008. *The maternal is political: Women writers at the intersection of motherhood and social change*. Berkeley, CA: Seal Press.

Manning, M., producer/director. 2005. *Caught in the crossfire: The untold story of Falluja*. [Motion picture]. Concept Media.

McClintock, A. 1993. Family feuds: Gender, nationalism, and the family. *Feminist Review* 44: 61–80.

McReynolds, J. 2006. Walking the walk, talking the talk. *Lompoc Record*. May 9. http://www.lompocrecord.

O'Reilly, A., ed. 2004. *Mother outlaws: Theories and practices of empowered mothering*. Toronto: Women's Press.

O'Reilly, A. 2006. *Rocking the cradle: Thoughts on feminism, motherhood, and the possibility of empowered mothering*. Toronto: Demeter Press.

Rich, A. 1976. *Of woman born: Motherhood as experience and institution.* New York: W. W. Norton.
Rowe-Finkbeiner, K. 2004. *The F word: Feminism in jeopardy.* Emeryville, CA: Seal Press.
Ruddick, S. 2001. Making connections between parenting and peace. *Journal for the Association for Research and Mothering* 3:2: 7–20.
Schumaker, J. 2005. Walk for togetherness. http://www.walkfortogetherness.org/about.htm.
———. 2006. Love, loss, and lots of walking. *The Advocate.* May 31. http://www.advocate.com.
Sheehan, C. 2005. *Not one more mother's child.* Kihei, HI: Koa Books.
———. 2006a. 2,500 dead: How many more? *The Progressive.* http://www.truthout.org.
———. 2006b. Matriotism. *Truth out.* http://www.truthout.org.
———. 2006c. Starving for attention: Troops home fast, day one. Common Dreams News Center. July 5. http://www.commondreams.org.
Sherman, P. 2006. A mother's message. *San Diego Union Tribune.* June 25. http://www.signonsandiego.com.
Swerdlow, A. 1993. *Women strike for peace: Traditional motherhood and radical politics in the 1960s.* Chicago, IL: University of Chicago Press.
Troops Home Fast. 2006. Cindy Sheehan, Dick Gregory, Diane Wilson, and hundreds more launch the "Troops Home FAST." *YubaNet.* July 3. http://www.yubanet.com.
Warren, K. J., and D. L. Cady. 1994. Feminism and peace: Seeing connections. *Hypatia* 9:2: 4–20.

TWELVE

Political Motherhood in the United States and Argentina

MEGHAN GIBBONS

The revelation that much of the natural world could be approached through scientific study was the hallmark of the Enlightenment. As people discarded the superstition and mythology of the Middle Ages, they embraced positivism across diverse disciplines. The study of human behavior, especially as it related to gender, became the subject of investigation in biology, chemistry, and psychology. For a combination of social and economic reasons, women were described as having certain essential characteristics—that is, qualities that were "most irreducible, unchanging, and therefore constitutive of a given person or thing" (Fuss 1989, 250). Women, and particularly mothers, were portrayed as being closer to nature, dependent, emotional, and self-sacrificing. Although the twentieth century has awarded women/mothers considerable freedoms and advances, these characterizations have continued to limit their political power. These "essential" qualities in women/mothers are the antithesis of patriarchal qualities that are rewarded in twentieth-century capitalist cultures: reason, independence, public action, and competitiveness. Within this patriarchal paradigm, women's voices are relegated to the "private" sphere and have no legitimate place in the "public" affairs of the state.

Despite this, two twentieth-century groups of mothers have wielded extraordinary political power in times of national crisis. During the Argentine military dictatorship, from 1976 to 1983, the *Madres de la Plaza de Mayo* (mothers of the Plaza de Mayo) took to the streets to protest the disappearances of their children by the regime. They were the only group that was able to publicly decry the violence of the era without being largely silenced. They successfully drew the attention of international journalists and human rights groups to the issue of the *desaparecidos* or "disappeared people." They defied bans on public gatherings, marching in front of the state house on a weekly basis. Similarly, Another Mother for Peace spoke out during the Vietnam War (1959–1973) in the United States. They worked at draft resistance centers, marched on the Pentagon, and sent campaign contributions to the "doves" in Congress. They organized at the grassroots level to get "hawks" out of office and to make the military responsive to citizens' voices. They publicly demonstrated their solidarity with Vietnamese mothers.[1]

Both of these groups used their identities as mothers to authorize themselves to speak publicly about unpopular state policies: the kidnapping and murder of Argentine citizens without charges or trials was a practice that many believe left close to 30,000 Argentines dead by 1983 (Comisión Nacional por la Desaparición de Personas 1985, 29).[2] The drafting of U.S. soldiers into an unpopular war in Vietnam left over 58,000 young Americans dead by the time U.S. troops withdrew in 1973. The actions of these two groups of mothers against their governments disrupted several binaries upon which state power rested and profoundly changed the way we think about motherhood as a political identity and about political action itself. National circumstances inspired women to take private "familial" concerns into the public arena; they justified the use of emotion in the traditionally reason-based public arena; they demonstrated that the identity of "mother" does not have to be dominated by the state; they modeled how mothers can work across national difference, even in the face of repressive state forces; and they showed how "strategic essentialism" can be used to strengthen mothers' claims and to authorize them to speak for their children. Both of these groups had surprisingly similar impacts on the construction of motherhood as a political identity, despite their origins in distinct cultures.

While both of these groups acted against traditional, limiting essentialist models of motherhood, they did not discard essentialism entirely. Instead, they created new paradigms of motherhood and redefined essentialism itself. Based on the experience of mothering and of their states' refusal to recognize their political voices, a new force was born—what I call "experiential essentialism." These women were driven by something that was the product of their experiences as mothers (based in the biological and the social) and their treatment as mothers by the state (as citizens whose subject positions in the nation were manipulated to serve nationalist ends). Both groups of mothers showed great sophistication in dealing with the powerful force of essentialized motherhood. At times they rejected essentialism, but at other times they played on the power that it conferred upon them as mothers. In the end, the mothers rejected this binary and constructed a paradigm that reflected their social and political identities as well as their lived experience.

FROM PRIVATE TO PUBLIC

The movement of mothers from the "private" sphere of the home to the "public" arena of protest is the most obvious shift marked by these two groups. That womanhood and, particularly, motherhood have been constructed as private roles closely linked to the domestic sphere and to morality was not lost on these mothers. The Argentine mothers played on the cultural paradigm of *marianismo,* a Catholic model of ideal womanhood based on the Latin American cult of the Virgin Mary (Taylor 1997). In her image, good, Catholic Argentine women were constructed as pious, self-sacrificing, obedient, and devoted to their families. Most importantly, women/mothers were morally superior to men, and spiritually stronger, praying patiently for the redemption of their men from their sinful natures (Stevens 1973, 91). The archetypal image of the *mater dolorsa,* mourning the loss of her son Jesus, is one that the *madres* in the Plaza regularly evoked. The earliest mothers wore a single nail attached to their jackets to show their identification with the mother of Jesus and "to remember the sacrifice of Christ, nailed to the cross. We also have our Christ and we relive the pain of Mary" (Bousquet 1980, 47).[3] Their appearances also suggested humility and their maternal connection to the missing children: they wore white headscarves made from their children's old cloth diapers. Originally meant as a way to identify each other in crowds, the scarves also made them appear more traditional and pious.

The madres also made it a practice to pray publicly, especially in confrontations with the police and military. This unique and baffling protest strategy had several interesting effects. Such performances increased their credibility in the eyes of witnesses who were most likely Catholic and sometimes paralyzed the officers who were sent to arrest them or break up their meetings (Asociacíon Madres de Plaza de Mayo 1999). In open letters to the dictatorship—which were also printed in newspapers—the women regularly framed their arguments in terms of their identities as Catholic mothers, whose protests obeyed a culturally sanctioned devotion to their children. Since the dictatorship was obsessed with the concept of duty, the mothers argued that they were only fulfilling the maternal obligations assigned to them by their nation and the Church. The regime's penchant for framing its political agenda in terms of Catholic nationalism only helped the mothers, who continued to play the role of the obedient, mournful mother. The powerful construction of motherhood as being essential to the new nation under Juan and Evita Perón in the early 1950s undoubtedly helped the madres' argument that they were fulfilling a sacred mission.

The dictatorship's reactions to the mothers' piety revealed their frustration that the women were manipulating the maternal paradigm that was supposed to control them. One Monsignor Quarracino rebuked the madres publicly with, "I can't imagine the Virgin Mary yelling, protesting, and planting seeds of hate when her son, our Lord, was torn from her hands" (Taylor 1997, 196). Bishop Carlos Mariano Péres of Salta was quoted in Mignone (1988) as saying, "The Mothers of the Plaza de Mayo must be eliminated" (6). The regime tried various strategies to silence the madres, clearly disturbed that they had disrupted the public/private divide that was supposed to keep them quietly in the home. The military formally dismissed the issue of the disappeared people as the imaginings of a bunch of hysterical women and even passed a law in 1976 that prohibited the mention of the subject in newspapers (Fisher 1989, 25). The regime went on to try to discredit the mothers of the Plaza de Mayo by publicly labeling them "las locas" (a bunch of crazy women). Meanwhile they arrested and detained dozens of the mothers and disappeared at least three, who were later found murdered.[4]

While the regime tried to appear nonchalant about the madres' protests, it went to great lengths to keep the madres' voices out of the public sphere. It tried to force the mothers back into the private sphere by attacking their integrity and respectability, calling them crazy, prostitutes, and bad mothers. The Church even backed up the military in arguing that the disappearances were a private matter that should not be handled in public. In contrast, the mothers argued that their connections to their children, although nurtured in the private sphere, authorized them to speak in the public sphere. The fact that the military had violated the sanctity of the private sphere—62 percent of the *desaparecidos* were taken by force from their homes—meant that the mothers could also step over that barrier and enter the public sphere (Comisión Nacional por la Desaparición de Personas 1985, 29).

The mothers of Another Mother for Peace experienced a similar invasion of their private spheres. The institution of the draft during the Vietnam War took hundreds of thousands of young American men out of their homes and into a distant conflict that was poorly understood by

Americans. As their sons began dying in increasing numbers, the mothers of AMP charged into the public sphere with a confidence that surprised many of the women themselves. Like the Argentine women, they had been raised to respect the private/public divide. In fact, the history of Protestantism in the United States had made the nuclear family particularly patriarchal in nature.[5]

Another historical trend helped the mothers in the United States justify their participation in the anti-war drive: the female moral reform movement in the United States, which had championed abolition, temperance, and suffrage for women. These campaigns had argued successfully that women (and particularly mothers) were more naturally qualified to make judgments about issues of morality. This legacy was continued by the AMP mothers, who highlighted their essentialist connections to the natural world in the imagery of their protests: flowers, children, and doves. They even crafted a slogan that linked their identities to their abilities to bear children: "We who have given life must be dedicated to preserving it" (AMP Archives 1967).

At the same time the AMP mothers emphasized their femininity and domesticity, knowing that these qualities contained important social capital for their audiences. Numerous articles, by AMP members and by outside writers, focused on how these women were still adequately feminine in their attitudes and aesthetics, despite their recent public participation in demonstrations against the war. AMP itself stressed that its average recruit was a mother who had never been involved in politics and had done so only reluctantly when the war had invaded her home. Human interest pieces on AMP mothers were frequent in the media, with headlines that reified women's/mothers' supposedly "naturally" pacifist politics and gentle temperaments. Typical of this approach is the 1967 article "Gentle Reminder by Two Doves," published in the *San Francisco Chronicle*. The piece describes how "blond, pretty Whitney Blake" was drawn to the movement "by the cute little cards" that AMP produced. The article focuses on how Whitney "wanted to see the fighting stopped, but I didn't really want to get involved" (Craib 1967).

Beneath all of this attention to femininity and domesticity was a growing anxiety that women/mothers who moved into the public sphere would be somehow masculinized or corrupted. The second-wave feminist movement, which challenged Americans to question their facile acceptance of traditional gender roles, disrupted the equilibrium that patriarchal tradition had established. The arrival of the birth control pill and more liberal attitudes toward sexuality loosened the dominance of traditional mores. Betty Freidan's groundbreaking book *The Feminine Mystique* epitomized the challenges to middle-class domestic existence, explaining it as intellectually limiting and socially and psychologically isolating for women (Evans 1979, 18). All of these factors combined to make the 1960s and 1970s a time in which the public and the private were increasingly blurred for many Americans.

AMP rightly sensed that disguising their protests with femininity and domesticity would have a settling effect on their audiences. They sought to project that the private and the public were still in their proper places. The mothers argued that they did not want a revolution. In fact—much like the Argentine mothers—they were only protesting because they wanted so badly to protect their children, whom they had nurtured in the private sphere. A 1970 Mothers' Day AMP newsletter captures this posture with: "We labor to bring children into the world . . . we sacrifice to raise them" (AMP Archives 1970). On the surface, AMP's promotion of a traditional image of motherhood was reassuring to their audiences, who knew they could trust the traditional mother to defer to patriarchal authority. They could tolerate mothers in the public sphere if their political motives were properly maternal.

But the distinctly feminine nature of the mothers' protests was not only for show. Their inclusion of gentle, domestic imagery was a conscious reaction against the violence that they perceived was inherent in the patriarchal politics that threatened their children. They linked their identities as mothers to a kind of politics that was distinct—nonviolent, inclusive, and emotional. They sought to counter the competition, individuality, and exclusive rationality of traditional politics. This is evident from the strategies and tone of much of their recruitment material. AMP's existence was spread primarily through individual women meeting in their homes with other women or writing about their own experiences for the AMP newsletter. One newsletter, published March 19, 1970, advertises, "We are having coffee with some of our Another Mothers from your community and hope you will be able to come. . . . We look forward to meeting with you, mother to mother, and brainstorming together about our mutual problem" (AMP Archives 1970). Another 1970 letter mailed on AMP stationery and signed by actress Donna Reed Owen explains, "We work on a person to person basis . . . we need responsible, caring people like yourself who can reach out to friends to make our association known" (AMP Archives 1970). The emphasis on private, individual relationships as well as "public" politics enacted in the domestic sphere are certainly characteristics not common to patriarchal politics and were an outgrowth of the participants of AMP's unique subjectivities.

Despite these qualities, at times the mothers' public protests became impossible to ignore, and patriarchal forces showed their discomfort with the blurring of the private/public divide. In 1967, the American women sent 1,000 Mother's Day cards to Congress, urging it to work for peace, a campaign that was covered widely in the press. A May 8, 1967, *Los Angeles Times* article by Lynn Lilliston ("Mothers Campaign for Peace Talks"), for example, excerpted part of the women's message to legislators, explaining that "This mothers [sic] day I don't want candy or flowers. I want an end to war" (AMP Archives 1967). The response to this campaign from other Americans was overwhelming, and 200,000 more cards were printed in the next two months to keep up with the demand.

But as AMP and other maternalist organizations became increasingly outspoken, government officials responded with puzzlement and irritation. One political cartoon surrounding the 1962 hearings of the House Un-American Activities Committee had one male senator demanding of another maternalist group: "What's bugging those 'Strike for Peace' women? Why aren't they at home looking after their children's welfare?" (Swerdlow 1993, 97). One AMP mother, Peg Mullen, who lost her son in Vietnam, took her protest to the military brass, where she received a chilly reception by Pentagon officials. They were clearly uncomfortable with Mullen's connection of her private grief to U.S. public policy in Vietnam. By Mullen's account, U.S. officials who were expecting the *mater dolorosa* were surprised by her anger and persistence at investigating her son's death. She comments in her memoir that the Pentagon officials must have been asking each other, "Why isn't this woman behaving like a grieving mother's supposed to?" (Mullen 1995, 28). Finally, a 1965 propaganda film starring President Lyndon Johnson explained to these anxious mothers that their approach was misguided, and that "weakness doesn't bring peace" (Department of Defense 1965). In a paternalistic narration heavily slanted toward continuing U.S. involvement, Johnson assures the mothers that: "I do not find it easy to send the flower of our youth . . . into battle" (Department of Defense 1965). But the United States continued to send troops for ten years after the film was made.

The extent to which the U.S. government has tried to shape twentieth-century American paradigms of motherhood is, at times, subtle. Its propaganda is less transparent than that of the Argentine military dictatorship, which enjoyed almost complete hegemony over popular discourse. The establishment of the American Gold Star Mothers, however, is an example of attempts by U.S. administrations to win mothers' allegiance away from the nuclear families and into the camp of the national family. Formed in 1929, the American Gold Star Mothers were honored for their sacrifices, having lost sons in conflicts involving the U.S. armed forces. The growth of the group, which was dedicated to patriotism and allegiance to the United States, strategically channeled maternal grief into support for the state.

EMOTION IN POLITICS

In addition to blurring the public/private divide, both of the mothers' groups changed political activism by basing their campaigns on emotion. From the time of the Enlightenment, reason has been the episteme most respected in patriarchal politics (Elshtain 1981; Jordanova 1993).The mothers challenged this claim by foregrounding their emotions. They loved their children and feared for their safety. Through their campaigns both groups demonstrated that emotion could be a powerful motive for political struggle. Emotion transformed the mothers, some of whom were timid housewives before their tragedies, into bold public actors who defied violent state apparatuses. Many of the mothers remarked in testimonials that they experienced a kind of rebirth, drawing on courage that most of them did not know they had. As one madre put it, "Nothing could stop us, nothing could paralyze us. Our safety wasn't important" (Mellibovsky 1997, 75). One AMP mother describes her transformation upon hearing of her son's death in Vietnam: "I became the angriest mother in the world. That's when my protest began" (MacDonald 1968). A 1967 newspaper article on AMP, published in *The Herald Tribune*, describes the intense devotion that these politicized mothers seem to possess when it comes to their children: "A lioness protecting her cub is merely a cuddly, purring pussycat by comparison to these mothers" (Bigelman 1967).

But using emotion in public discourse around political topics was a tricky move. Since emotion has been traditionally constructed by patriarchy as unreliable and destabilizing, the mothers' emotionality was often used against them. Wanting to discredit the madres, the dictatorship called them *las locas*, or "hysterical," women. The Greek origin of the English word "hysterical" is "womb." Sigmund Freud popularized the term as a medical one for women with a variety of psychological and physical symptoms that he attributed to a "wandering uterus" (Wright 1992). While Freud's theory has long been debunked, the stereotype of women as being overly emotional still lingers. Some mothers in AMP found their public emotions the object of their communities' scorn. One mother recounts: "They repeatedly accused us [politicized mothers] of . . . acting like crybabies . . . they argued, thousands of other mothers had lost sons, and they weren't going on talk shows to criticize our government and its policies" (Mullen 1995, 62).

The question of where maternal devotion to children originates is certainly important here, as it is closely bound up with the powerful emotions that mothers feel toward their children, which have inspired their daring protests. Various cultures have tried to naturalize maternal devotion—either through religious myth, like the Catholic figure of the Virgin Mary, or through evolutionary biology, in which women nurture their children because they are genetically programmed to work for their offsprings' survival. A third possibility, which is given less attention than it deserves, is that emotional interaction is learned through the practice of mothering. Sara Ruddick (1989) writes that young mothers come to value emotion as a primary episteme because they have to learn to read the emotions of their young, nonverbal children. Why is a child crying? Is it from fear, hunger, fatigue, or pain? Since mothers must interact with young children on this level, they come to see much of the world through this lens. Ruddick argues that the inclusion of emotion in problem solving is one of the disciplinary practices of motherhood and not something innate to women or divinely inspired. In this view, the mothers' privileging of emotion in their political protests grows directly out of their experiences as mothers. This may explain, in part, why mothers' groups all over the world—in El Salvador, Sri Lanka, Ireland, and Israel—have crafted campaigns that highlight emotion as being fundamental to their organization.

In the case of U.S. and Argentine mothers' groups, the two not only grounded themselves in emotion (love for their children, anger at their governments), but they tried to evoke emotion in their audiences through a variety of dramatic techniques. The Argentine mothers carried enormous photos of their children, putting distinctly human faces on the very intangible status of the *desaparecidos*. They also marched publicly with life-size silhouettes, giving a very physical presence to the bodies of the disappeared. AMP staged "die-ins," carried flag-draped coffins, and wore provocative signs as they marched. One mother's poignant placard read: "My Son Died in Vain in Vietnam" (Swerdlow 1993, 158–59). Few observers could witness such displays without experiencing some kind of emotion, a dynamic that led the Argentine military to dub the madres "emotional terrorists" (Taylor 1997, 200).

Both groups of women sensed that their own bodies and the bodies of their children (or representations of them) had the power to demand attention. Few humans can ignore the presence of another human being—a lesson, perhaps, that these mothers learned over years of contact with demanding toddlers. In using their own bodies to this same end, the mothers delivered their arguments to witnesses in very visceral, tangible ways.[6] Although the patriarchal powers in these cases have argued that emotion has no place in politics, both governments selectively used carefully controlled emotion themselves to try to marginalize the mothers' groups. The nationalist rhetoric of the Church and state in Argentina named any dissenters subversives and terrorists, labels that had high emotional content. The dictatorship even launched a public relations campaign during the 1978 World Cup that affirmed that "Argentines are right and human," a retort to charges by the madres that the junta was violating "Argentine human rights" (Taylor 1997, 79). (The Spanish phrase is *los Argentinos somos derechos y humanos*, a play on the violation of *derechos humanos*.) The regime emphasized that citizens who did not embrace its values were not real Argentines, whipping up a patriotic fervor that ultimately resulted in the disastrous invasion of the British Falkland Islands (*Islas Malvinas* to Argentines) in 1982. The fact that emotion was such an essential part of the Catholic, nationalist campaign reveals that the emotion/reason binary was not exclusive to women's campaigns. Nationalist governments tend to oppose the use of emotion when they feel that their political enemies—such as mothers, in this case—may have the upper hand. They broadly conflate (uncontrolled) emotional expression with weakness and reactivity, not a difficult argument to sell when audiences already feel the insecurity of a national crisis. At the same time, such regimes employ carefully controlled emotions—embedded in familiar paradigms of national identity, patriotism, and duty—to promote their own narratives. The Argentine regime, for example, readily encouraged fear in their citizenry, an emotion that could be quelled only by stringent measures (including the imprisonment of certain "dangerous" elements), which were enacted by the state (Taylor 1997). The dictatorship was not averse to emotion as long as it fit into narratives that the junta had constructed. It was not emotion, per se, that was censored but emotion outside the control of the state, such as the madres' grief and anger, which the women exhibited dramatically in the public sphere. The regime realized that such uncontrolled emotions had an unsettling effect on audiences: these emotions provided no "solution" and increased the public's feelings of instability. As Sara Ahmed (2004) cogently explains, "Being against something is also being for something, but something that has yet to be articulated or is not yet" (175). What threatened the dictatorship most was an alternative imaginary, such as the madres would come to represent. Thus the madres' emotions were labeled unreasonable and irrational, while Argentines were flooded with national propaganda that manipulated their emotions to a calculated end.[7]

The mothers of AMP were similarly derided for using emotion in their campaigns. While they argued that their motives could not be more pure—"It is because we cherish life that we are here today"—they were portrayed as dangerous elements by the cold warriors of the Vietnam era (Swerdlow 1993, 172). Their use of emotion was considered risky, as it broke the boundaries of ordered reason that was the patriarchal legacy of the Enlightenment. Women in particular were perceived as being especially vulnerable to such deception, as they did not have as much experience in the public sphere and were thought to be more trusting than male citizens. For example, Amy Swerdlow (1995) notes that participants in Women Strike for Peace were described in 1962 in the *San Francisco Examiner* as "being made dupes of the Communists" (218). Likewise, according to Swerdlow, a commentary in the *New York Journal American* by Jack Lotto that same year argued that mothers' demonstrations against their own government proved that "the pro-Reds have moved in on our mothers and are using them for their own purposes" (Swerdlow 1995, 217–18).

REMAKING MOTHERHOOD AND POLITICS

In breaking the public/private divide and including emotion in their campaigns, the mothers revolutionized politics. They revealed the hegemony in the patriarchal construction of motherhood and in the definition of politics, which had kept them from realizing their potentials. The first step was seeing clearly the extent to which traditional politics courted mothers into very narrowly defined roles. The madres only needed to look to the history of Peronism to see how social maternity was designed as a tool in service to larger economic and political plans.[8] More immediately, the dictatorship of the 1970s and 1980s used mothers and the very real anxieties of motherhood in a dangerous era to draw women into the narrative of Catholic nationalism. An open letter to mothers in a popular Argentine women's magazine, *Para Ti*, embodied the military's recruitment efforts:

> We insist that mothers have a fundamental role to play. In this criminal time that we live in, in the face of this subversive war that threatens to destroy everything, one of the objectives of the enemy is your child, the mind of your child. And you all, the mothers, with more strength and effectiveness than anyone,

are the ones who can break down this strategy, if you dedicate more time than ever to the care of your children.[9] (Blaustein and Zubieta 1998, 130)

In this paradigm, as in many other nationalist models, mothers are given a place of honor rooted in their roles as domestic caregivers. The discovery by the madres that they could reject this narrative—albeit at great psychological and spiritual cost—was a watershed in their movement. They realized that they could define motherhood in their own terms. Mothers could organize and shout in public places, experiences that were unimaginable to most of the housewives before the repression. Mothers could channel their anger into action, as well as prayer, in contrast to the mournful but passive model of the Virgin Mary. Mothers could question their governments but still be patriotic Argentines. Finally, mothers could argue that their rights to protect their children's well-being trumped all other claims on their identities—religious, familial, and national. In short, the trauma of their losses and their abandonment by the Catholic Church and by the state allowed them to view motherhood and the space of political action through new eyes: "The fact that such a tragedy did not paralyze us, but on the contrary, stimulated us, is amazing. It gave us strength to set out on a path that we never thought we were going to take" (Mellibovsky 1997, 77–78).

They learned quickly that fighting the regime meant that they had to take control of the language that allowed political action and movement. Words such as "patriot," "subversive," "crazy," "Christian," "mother," and "terrorist" worked together to construct paradigms that reified the power of the regime. Where they could, the madres deconstructed these terms—in newspapers, in interviews, on film. Where they could not—in the face of overwhelming military force and heavy censorship—they publicly performed the role of mourning, submissive *mater dolorosa*. This guise at least allowed them a modicum of protection from the repression and sympathy from Catholic audiences who were undecided on the issue of the *desaparecidos*.

The madres were also purposeful in their use of the term *desaparecidos*, new in the Argentine lexicon, but evoking the recent Chilean practice of disappearing political rivals under Augusto Pinochet and the Nazi doctrine of "Night and Fog."[10] The madres made sure audiences knew that their children had been disappeared by someone. As Hebe de Bonafini explains: "They've tried to convert us into the mothers of dead children and put an end to the problem of the *desaparecidos*. We will never accept they are dead until those responsible are punished" (Fisher 1989, 158).

Maternal activist Cindy Sheehan, according to Wilson in her chapter in this volume, adopted a similar strategy with George W. Bush during the period 2005–2006. Instead of saying that her son Casey died in the conflict with Iraq, she says that he was murdered. Sheehan's use of "matriotism" (as a form of maternal patriotism) also echoes the madres' insistence that they were still loyal Argentines, despite their protests. Many maternalist groups recognize the importance of maintaining their identities as loyal citizens in the context of protest; in part, this is because so many nations have a history of maternalist roles embedded in nationalist frameworks. To resist these images, protesting mothers must perform their own allegiance to the nation or risk being cast aside as traitorous to the community. Romania, Argentina, and Yugoslavia are just a few sites among many in the late twentieth century in which motherhood has been woven into a nationalist narrative to promote specific nationalist objectives such as ethnic dominance or submission to dictatorship. That some women embrace these roles should be seen within individual cultural contexts, particularly those of war and violence, in which women/mothers may gain protection for themselves and their children from nationalist forces. Even in times of peace, however, some women may choose to perform nationalist roles in patriarchal societies because they provide privileges that they may otherwise not enjoy.[11] In addition, some mothers' groups may embrace nationalist models because they provide national identities that they have been historically deprived of (by forces of racial or ethnic oppression).[12]

Another Mother for Peace experienced a less physically repressive nationalism in the U.S. government but still one that sought to promote a specific ideology. Groups such as the American Gold Star Mothers and the Women's Section of the Navy League in World War I were evidence that the U.S. government had also worked to shape womanhood/motherhood as an important national identity. Constructed on self-sacrifice, patriotism, and service, a mother's duty to her country was a sacred one. Mothers continued to play an important social role in the Vietnam era, as shown by President Johnson's 1965 propaganda film *Why Vietnam?* (addressed specifically to them). But white, middle-class mothers at least were beginning to see that they had relatively more choices than their mothers had. Although not without complexities, many women saw that they could choose to work or stay home, that they could choose how many children to have, and that they could choose to see that "the personal is the political." All of these choices shaped the environment into which AMP was born and made it relatively easier for women/mothers to see how the paradigm of traditional motherhood was being constructed by patriarchal powers. Perhaps this is why many members of AMP were young women who did not yet have sons fighting in Vietnam. Many members had children who were still young but they feared might be drafted in a future conflict.

Many AMP members were also rural mothers who tended to be more traditional in their values. These members were rarely involved in the bourgeoning feminist movements that were gaining momentum in urban centers of the country (Katz 2006). A good example of an AMP member was Mrs. Billie Backer, whose son was killed in Vietnam at age nineteen. An article in the *New York Post* in June 1970 described how "the shock radicalized Mrs. Backer, who had never before been politically active, had seldom read a newspaper, and had never even voted" (Damski 1970). A profile such as this mother's served AMP well, as members could distance themselves more easily from the machinery of formal politics. They could argue, as celebrity AMP member Joanne Woodward did in 1969, that they were "more maternally oriented than politically" (Radcliffe 1969). The more distant a mother was from any hint of formal politics, the better her story played.

While the political climate in the 1960s and 1970s does not seem to have revolutionized the rhetoric of AMP, it most likely influenced the way the group was seen by outsiders. White, middle-class Americans were facing challenges to constructions of gender and sexuality that disrupted traditional paradigms. Members of AMP positioned their antiwar stance within the familiar space of traditional motherhood, assuring audiences that they were still domestic and feminine mothers. While many in AMP probably reflected in private on issues of gender construction in their personal lives, their public rhetoric was purposefully free of such themes.

Another hallmark of both groups was their claim to being apolitical. AMP's slogan was merely a maternal observation: "War is not healthy for children and other living things." However, at the same time, AMP members acted on multiple political channels to end the war. They raised money to support the reelection campaigns of "doves," wrote letters to the president and Congress, and contacted the wives of the "hawks" in Congress, asking them to sway their husbands toward peace. In fact, they created a liminal space between the political and the apolitical, and they could shift into either space, depending on the needs of the setting. They also made a point, like the madres, of defining terms themselves, a powerful discursive weapon in their fight to end the war. Words such as "patriot," "Communist," "terrorist," and "American" were reframed within the context of motherhood, which trumped all other identities. As grieving mother Backer wrote to AMP in 1970: "I love my son more than I love my flag or my country, and I would lie down and die for any of my children before I would let them give up their lives for President Nixon and the other politicians who are asking us to survive through this tragedy" (Backer 1970). Only a mother could make a statement like this and be forgiven by a thoughtful audience. The AMP members knew this, and they played it to the hilt.

An interesting contrast to this dynamic is the relationship of the father to the state. While citizenship in women is defined by reproduction—bearing and raising citizens for the nation—male citizenship is defined by a willingness to serve the state in military conflict. Men who have aged out of military service must be willing to sacrifice their sons in a war. A father who protested his son's draft would not only be considered unpatriotic but insufficiently masculine himself. In addition, he would rob his son of the chance to prove his own masculinity through military service.[13]

TRANSNATIONAL MOTHERHOOD AND ESSENTIALISM

Another revolutionary component of these motherhood campaigns was the successful alliances that they built across national boundaries. In a 1969 editorial in *Harper's Bazaar*, one AMP member explained that "Each child who dies . . . in the final obscenity of war is lost by every woman who has ever borne a child" (Gittleson 1969). Their devotion went beyond their own children and to the more universal notion of life: "The reverence for life must live especially in female loins" (Gittleson 1969). The AMP members' rhetoric directly avoided imagery that suggested race or nationality, cognizant that they would benefit from alliances with Vietnamese mothers as they pushed for an end to hostilities. It also avoided placing specific blame for the conflict, anticipating that this could create tensions between Vietnamese and American mothers. Their campaign "Not Our Sons, Not Your Sons, Not Their Sons," which several mothers took to Vietnam in person, successfully avoided these tropes (Swerdlow 1993, 96–97). At the same time the group was careful to minimize any hint of the second-wave feminist politics that might have crept into their membership. Many of the social issues addressed in the second wave, including women's sexuality and changing gender roles, would certainly have problematized the U.S.-Vietnamese alliance. Instead, AMP members such as Angie Brooks (1970) focused on what mothers share: "No mother is the enemy of another mother."

In Argentina, the madres grew more gradually into their associations with foreign mothers'/women's groups. The madres had always petitioned foreign embassies for assistance, but with limited success. Fortuitously, the madres' weekly marches were discovered by a group of Dutch women who were traveling to Argentina in 1978 and who returned home to form SAAM (Support Group for the Mothers of the Plaza de Mayo in Argentina). The group held fund-raisers and solidarity events in the Netherlands, inspiring the formation of still other groups in Western Europe. France, Germany, Switzerland, Denmark, and Norway all organized support groups. SAAM also sent money back to the madres, which enabled them to found an office in Buenos Aires (Bouvard 1994, 86–87). To this day, surviving madres still remember those other mothers and assert that they never would have survived without their support (Madres 2005).

Their successful interactions with foreign mothers'/women's groups inspired the madres to take their stories abroad, and they began traveling in pairs and small groups. Always emphasizing their maternal orientation, the madres approached heads of state, the pope, the United Nations, the Organization of American States—anyone who would receive them. Their maternal status allowed them to circumvent the traditional diplomatic requirements and present their cases in their own voices. They had no representatives, no lawyers, and no media relations people, and yet they had an unwavering faith that their bodily presence, as mothers, would overcome all of these hurdles. What might be called naïve optimism turned out to be a stroke of genius. They were right! The corporeal mother had an authority that was not easily questioned and a determination that was not easily thwarted. The purity of their motives and the social capital inherent in their identities proved a powerful combination.

The madres were particularly creative in not only using their own bodies in protest but those of their missing children as well. The women are internationally known for carrying large photos of the faces of their missing children and representing the bodies of the *desaparecidos* in life-size figures.[14] In a provocative 1989 protest in Buenos Aires, the madres carried thousands of life-size cardboard cutouts to represent the bodies of the missing. At other times, life-size silhouettes of the *desaparecidos* have appeared painted on walls and sidewalks in Argentina. These strategies conjure up the physical presence of an actual human being as closely as possible in their absence. The highly emotional content of these protests speaks to the unique approach to protest that the madres developed, unconstrained by traditional notions of practicality or decorum, and their desire to place discourse around the *desaparecidos* on a plane that privileged an emotional episteme.

What is striking about the success of these two groups' alliances across national difference is that each performed very culturally specific models of motherhood within its country. The Argentine mothers played the mournful, submissive Catholic mother required by *marianismo*. The mothers of AMP played the domestic, feminine mother to distance themselves sufficiently from the second-wave feminist movement. Despite these local constructions of motherhood, each group sensed that its campaigns abroad should be cloaked in appeals to more universal images of motherhood. Because of their bond to their children, the groups asserted that mothers around the world also share a bond with each other. As a 1970 AMP Mother's Day newsletter asserted, "Every mother all over the world rears her young with the same love and concern" (AMP Archives 1970). The AMP members argued through their alliances that the experience of motherhood, despite differences in race, nationality, and class, gives mothers a particular essence. I use the term *essence* in a nontraditional manner here. This essence is not one that is born in nature or evoked by religious narrative. Instead, it is based on the experience of mothering—what I call "experiential" essentialism. Ruddick's (1989) descriptions of the discipline of mothering describe this same phenomenon in different terms: All mothers come to share certain skills that mothering demands of them—patience, flexibility, reading emotions, and nurturing. The experience of mothering contributes to a common episteme, from which mothers can approach political action.

The distinction between experiential essentialism and what I will call traditional or "proscriptive" essentialism is a crucial one for understanding the actions of mothers' groups across difference. In the cases of the madres and AMP, both groups used pointedly essentialist language in their rhetoric. As celebrity AMP mother Woodward claimed in a 1967 newsletter to supporters, "A Mother's dream of peace is older than time" (AMP Archives 1967). Similarly, one of the Argentine madres, Enriqueta Maroni, asserted, "*el amor por los hijos nos llevaba a desafiar todo el aparato represivo*" [Our love for our children made us defy their repressive system] (Mellibovksy 1997, 96).

These arguments were remarkably similar to nationalist constructions of motherhood that had kept mothers isolated, mourning, and prayerful in Argentina and self-sacrificing and obedient in the United States. So how were the mothers' groups able to employ this rhetoric without being confined to these roles? First, the blurring of the private/public spheres in each case was a central factor. The argument that the mothers only entered the public domain of politics to defend something that was intrinsic to their private lives—their children's welfare—was very persuasive to audiences. It allowed audiences to sympathize with the mothers' causes without questioning their own fundamental beliefs about proper political action and traditional gender roles. And it also gestured to archetypal images of motherhood that are present in most patriarchal cultures. As Sherry Ortner (1974) explains, the location of women (and, I would add, mothers) in the intermediate space between nature and culture puts females in a position of "greater symbolic ambiguity" (85). The tendency of diverse cultures to cast women in polarizing roles is easily observed. Women are frequently goddesses, exalted, dispensers of salvation, and transcendent, or evil, witches, castrating mothers, and whores. Ortner explains this tendency through women's inability to occupy either space fully from the perspective of patriarchy, which has historically defined such terms. A mother's "natural" sphere—giving birth, breast-feeding, caring for young children—is so foreign to the male experience that it is mythologized as Great Mother, self-sacrificing, spiritual. Her contributions to the "cultural" sphere are judged only in terms of her ability to produce loyal, obedient subjects for the state and patriarchal powers. If she deviates from behaviors that are thought to accomplish this—challenging male authority, spending too much time in the public sphere, and thinking too independently—then she is vilified as a whore, home wrecker, and witch (with the social effect of bringing her "back into line"). While Ortner focuses primarily on women, mothers are even more vulnerable to being cast into these polarizing categories because of their childbearing experiences. Their bodies speak to the physicality of childbirth, which is perhaps the female experience from which men feel most distant, and thus is the most powerful determiner of their gender. It is directly inaccessible to them. At the same time, mothers, in their daily care of children, play a central role in the construction of culture (through the production of citizens for the state), which is undeniably powerful. This background helps explain why political motherhood is such a powerful space, why it is viewed with such suspicion by patriarchal powers (which may include nationalist women), and why women/maternal activists are often attacked so aggressively.

Building on Ortner's notion of the symbolic ambiguity of women, the success of these groups is also rooted in their ability to create a new space for political action. Both mothers' organizations stressed that they were not political groups, and yet they undertook campaigns that were distinctly political. They lobbied formal political bodies, demonstrated publicly, and courted the media. Despite this, they were able to maintain a discourse that they labeled nonpolitical because they framed it in terms of their identities as mothers. They took advantage of the traditional construction of mothers as private, nonpolitical subjects, and they occupied a space in which they could speak with unique authority.

In this way, traditional patriarchal constructions of mothers actually helped these groups in the long run. The association of mothers with the private sphere (family is a private matter), with morality, and with emotion authorized mothers to speak out about their children with a moral authority and pathos that are rare in formal politics. In the end, these factors raised their visibility and their discursive power. They cashed in on the social capital that patriarchal powers had planted in the societies around them.

Neither of these mothers' groups had intended to disrupt traditional gender roles or patriarchal paradigms. In fact, the madres are adamant about distancing themselves from the term *feminist* and strongly reject their portrayal by some scholars as gender-role reformers (Madres 2005). The AMP members include similar disclaimers in their testimonies, widely eschewing feminism in interviews and newspaper accounts. Both groups sensed—perhaps unconsciously—that the power they could extract from the social capital of traditional motherhood could only be preserved if they stayed within the constructions created by patriarchal powers. While many of them came to question the more fundamental bases of several models of national identity and of gender roles within the nuclear family, for example, they sensed that such narratives might risk the communication of their central message to average citizens. To stay relevant to populations whose support they needed and to continue to undermine the state's rhetorical construction of motherhood as being subservient to the nation's, they kept their arguments carefully within the bounds of traditional mores.

On one level they performed motherhood by rules with which their audiences would be familiar. The Argentine women were pious, Catholic, loyal citizens who turned obediently to their paternal state for help finding their children. The Americans were patriotic mothers whose passion for their sons—and for moral reform—motivated their opposition to the Vietnam War. On a less visible level, the members of these groups had been transformed in ways that problematized their relations to the state and the family in profound ways. Their tragic losses and disappointments (in the Church and the state) forced them into new subject positions, from which they discovered new strengths. From these vantage points, they saw how they had formerly truncated their own power by accepting state constructions of motherhood, and how reclaiming this power could have a significant effect. They used their voices to shout down giants of violence and authoritarianism with the very weapons of their oppressors: rhetoric. In the end, they redefined motherhood in their own terms as a political force that called powerful patriarchal states to accountability.

The popularity of these mothers' protests in their wider communities suggests several lessons about the performance and experience of motherhood. First, audiences are smarter than the media often assume. Nationalist constructions of idealized motherhood are weakened in the light of real mothers and their desperate, tangible devotion to their children. Paradoxically, these mothers' protests may have been strengthened by essentialisms that portrayed women as emotional, domestic, prayerful, and self-effacing. This allowed the mothers to perform such characteristics when necessary, while they also marshaled the weapons of reason, public action, and competitiveness to oppose their states.

Second, the notion of essentialism is not stagnant. It evolves, as human experience and human representation do. A richer "experiential" essentialism was born through these groups' struggles and informed the powerful political identities that they inhabited. In two distinct cultures these forces overcame the two-dimensional proscriptive essentialisms deployed by the states and won significant public attention for groups with no formal political training or traditional capital.

Most importantly, by privileging their identities as mothers, both groups had profound impacts on national discourse around their respective issues. The madres' campaign brought international attention to a brutal dictatorship whose atrocities had been hidden, even to many Argentines. That the group accomplished this without being decimated was a combination of cultural norms that protected mothers and the women's own savvy, persistence, and courage. Another Mother for Peace added a uniquely powerful element to the growing anti-war movement, which eventually halted the Vietnam conflict. In the process, AMP enlisted hundreds of thousands of women in the United States, many of whom were inspired by their first taste of political participation. They also showed women outside of the United States that many women/mothers in North America were opposed to the war, an important transnational effect.

It is difficult to judge fairly what these groups could have done to improve the outcomes of their campaigns. Both were remarkably daring, inventive, and persevering. Despite their different cultural and political locations, several similar patterns emerged from their protests, some of which could be useful models for future mothers' movements. AMP and the madres both displayed an unwavering focus on their children's welfare, resisting the urge to be distracted by attacks on their mothering, sexuality, sanity, or patriotism. They also resisted the urge to partner with political parties or to combine their agendas with other advocacy groups. They seemed to intuit that their voices were clearest and their authority was strongest when rooted in the experience of mothering. The mothers were diligent in assessing the power structures of their societies, alert to cultural capital that could strengthen their positions and the traps that could undermine them. They repeatedly confronted cultural and religious paradigms that had disempowered them and endured the discomfort of challenging familiar identity structures. Finally, both groups actively sought international collaborations through the media, diplomatic channels, celebrities, sports events, and other creative avenues, using international embarrassment as a weapon against their nations.

Employing some of these strategies may help future mothers circumvent some of the challenges they will encounter. Some of their hurdles, however, like some of their triumphs, may be rooted in cultural constructions unique to their geopolitical location. For the madres it was *machismo* and Catholic nationalism, and for AMP it was the second wave of feminism and the Protestant character of patriarchy in U.S. politics. Whatever their unique circumstances, future groups may find inspiration and strength in places where the madres and AMP discovered them: their devotion to their children will energize them; their solidarity with other mothers will comfort them; and their discovery of their own public, political voices will embolden them. In the process, they will become different people, recreating themselves, motherhood, and political action along the way.

NOTES

1. Evidence of this group can be found in the Another Mother for Peace (AMP) archives: My reference to these archives is to a collection of boxed letters, newsletters, and newspaper and magazine articles about the group, as well as two films and a taped radio program. The materials (none on microfilm) are all loose and span the period 1964–1985. The materials were donated by AMP, which is housed in Beverly Hills, California. The archives are maintained in the McCabe Library at Swarthmore College, Pennsylvania, and were originally funded by a grant from the Ford Foundation.
2. Although the official number of confirmed disappeared persons, as reported by the Commission on Disappeared Persons (CONADEP), is 8,960, the investigative body acknowledges that the real figure is probably much higher. It admits that fear of reprisals probably kept many people from reporting their relatives as disappeared. Human rights groups such as the Madres de la Plaza de Mayo estimate that closer to 30,000 people

disappeared during the repression. Many texts use the 30,000 number (see Bouvard 1994, 31; Fisher 1989, 10; Acuña and Smulovitz 1996, 14).
3. "para recordar el sacrificio de Cristo, clavado en la cruz. . . . Nosotras también tenemos nuestro Cristo, y revivimos el dolor de María." No one madre/mother is named here by Bousquet, but the words are taken from direct interviews that Bousquet conducted with various madres.
4. Azucena Villaflor, Esther Ballestrino de Careaga, and María Eugenia de Bianco disappeared in December 1977.
5. The movement of Church authority under the Reformation from the parish priest to the household patriarch has been cited, in combination with the shift in economic production to the home, as a significant influence on the strongly patriarchal nature of the U.S. nuclear family (Stone 1977).
6. In AMP's case, some of these protest methods could also have been learned from the U.S. civil rights movements, out of which some of the anti-Vietnam War leaders sprung.
7. Sara Ahmed's (2004) *Cultural Politics of Emotion* is an excellent reference for the Kantian distinction of emotion as "an obstacle to good judgment" (195) and for the productive role of anger in reimagining social and political circumstances (174).
8. Evita Perón, the wife of Argentine leader Juan Perón, championed the role of mothers as being central to the success of the Argentine nation. The first Peronist period (1946–1955) encouraged increased birth rates and promoted the maternal figure as being vital to the stability of the home and of future Argentine citizens. Motherhood was a sacred duty to the nation. While some of Peron's policies appeared progressive toward women—the right to vote in 1947 and increased political participation—Peron's propaganda constructed women and mothers as subjects in service to the larger scheme of Peronism. For more, see Calvert (1989); Di Liscia et al. (2000); Rock (1993).
9. "Insistimos: Las madres tienen un papel fundamental que desempeñar. En este tiempo criminal que nos toca vivir, ante esta Guerra subversiva que amenaza destruirlo todo, uno de los objetivos claves del enemigo es su hijo, la mente de su hijo. Y son ustedes, las madres, con más fuerza y efectividad que nadie, las que podrán desbaratar [to break down] esa estrategía si dedican más tiempo que nunca al cuidado de sus hijos" (my translation).
10. Under Pinochet, thousands of Chilean citizens disappeared and thousands more were jailed. The Nazi regime used the term *noche y niebla* to refer to its practice of disappearing enemies "nacht und nebel," which means "night and fog" (Feitlowitz 1998, 49). "The prisoners will disappear without a trace. It will be impossible to glean any information as to whence they are or what will be their fate" (Marshall Keitel, qtd. in Feitlowitz 1998, 51).
11. Cynthia Cockburn (2007) discusses this phenomenon more thoroughly with respect to Serbian nationalism and Hindu communalism in *From Where We Stand: War, Women's Activism, and Feminist Analysis* (197). There is a wide body of literature on the dynamics of nationalist mother-

hood in a host of nation-states. For more, see Werbner and Yuval-Davis (1999); Steinson (1980); Wright (2001); Ortner (1974); Strange (1990).
12. See Cockburn (2007, 193) for more on this.
13. Several interesting narratives explore the disruption of this paradigm of masculine identity as experienced by fathers whose sons are called to war. One particularly insightful story in the documentary *Another Family for Peace* (1971) juxtaposes a veteran who is also the father of military-age sons. Already having lost one son in Vietnam, he claims that he will take his family to Canada rather than risk losing another.
14. It is one that is still imitated in contemporary maternal protest, such as that of Cindy Sheehan, who often carries a large picture of her son Casey.

REFERENCES

Acuña, C., and C. Smulovitz. 1996. Adjusting the armed forces to democracy: Successes, failures, and ambiguities in the Southern Cone. In *Constructing democracy: Human rights, citizenship, and society in Latin America*, ed. E. Jelin and E. Hershberg, 13–38. Boulder, CO: Westview Press.
Ahmed. S. 2004. *Cultural politics of emotion*. New York: Routledge.
AMP Archives. 1967–1986. Peace Collection. Swarthmore College, Pennsylvania.
Another Family for Peace. 1971. Film. Dir. Donald MacDonald. Cambridge, MA: Library of the American Friends Service Committee, Films Inc.
Another Mother for Peace. 1970. *Mother's Day newsletter*. AMP Archives, Peace Collection, Swarthmore College, Pennsylvania.
Asociación Madres de Plaza de Mayo. 1999. *Historias de las Madres de Plaza de Mayo*. Buenos Aires, Argentina: Ediciones Asociación Madres de Plaza de Mayo.
Backer, B. 1970. Letter to AMP. June 6. In AMP Archives, Peace Collection, Swarthmore College, Pennsylvania.
Bigelman, N. 1967. "Mothers for Peace" map gigantic mailing. Woodland, California, *Herald Tribune*. May 11. In AMP Archives, Peace Collection, Swarthmore College, Pennsylvania.
Blaustein, E., and M. Zubieta. 1998. *Decíamos ayer: La prensa argentina bajo el Proceso*. Buenos Aires, Argentina: Ediciones Colihue.
Bousquet, J. P. 1980. *Las locas de la Plaza de Mayo*. Buenos Aires, Argentina: El Cid Editor.
Bouvard, M. G. 1994. *Revolutionizing motherhood: The mothers of the Plaza de Mayo*. Wilmington, DE: Scholarly Resources.
Brooks, A. 1970. *Another Mother for Peace newsletter*. In AMP Archives, Peace Collection, Swarthmore College, Pennsylvania.
Calvert, S., and P. Calvert. 1989. *Argentina: Political culture and instability*. Pittsburgh, PA: University of Pittsburg Press.
Cockburn C. 2007. *From where we stand: War, women's activism, and feminist analysis*. New York: Zed Books.

Comisión Nacional por la Desaparición de Personas. 1985. *Nunca más: Informe de la Comisión Nacional sobre la Desaparición de Personas.* Buenos Aires, Argentina: Editorial Universitaria de Buenos Aires. Translated as *Nunca más (Never again): A report by Argentina's National Commission on Disappeared People* (Faber and Faber, in association with Index on Censorship, 1986).

Craib, R. 1967. Gentle reminder by two doves. *San Francisco Chronicle,* April 15. In AMP Archives, Peace Collection, Swarthmore College, Pennsylvania.

Damski, M. 1970. Ritual of peace at grave. *The New York Post,* May 13. In AMP Archives, Peace Collection, Swarthmore College, Pennsylvania.

Department of Defense. 1965. *Why Vietnam?* [Motion picture]. National Audiovisual Center.

Di Liscia, M. H., M. E. Folco, A. Lluch, M. Morales, A. M. Rodríguez, and M. Zink. 2000. *Mujeres, maternidad y Peronism.* La Pampa, Argentina: Fondo Editorial. Pampeano.

Elshtain, J. B. 1981. *Private man, public woman: Women in social and political thought.* Princeton, NJ: Princeton University Press.

Evans, S. 1979. *Personal politics: The roots of women's liberation in the civil rights movement & the new left.* New York: Vintage Books.

Feitlowitz, M. 1998. *A lexicon of terror: Argentina and the legacies of torture.* New York: Oxford University Press.

Fisher, J. 1989. *Mothers of the disappeared.* Boston, MA: South End Press.

Fuss, D. 1989. *Essentially speaking: Feminism, nature, and difference.* New York: Routledge.

Gittleson, N. 1969. Needles and pins: How to win the human race. *Harper's Bazaar.* May. In AMP Archives, Peace Collection, Swarthmore College, Pennsylvania.

Jordanova, L. 1993. Natural facts: An historical perspective on science and sexuality. In *Women's studies: Essential readings,* ed. S. Jackson et al., 374–78. New York: New York University Press.

Katz, G. 2006. Telephone interview by author, March.

MacDonald, D., director. 1968. *And another family for peace* [Motion Picture]. Available from the Library of the American Friends Service Committee in Cambridge, Massachusetts, #529.

Madres. 2005. Interviews by author, Buenos Aires.

Mellibovsky, M. 1997. *Circle of love over death: Testimonies of the Mothers of the Plaza de Mayo.* Translated by M. Proser and M. Proser. Williamantic, CT: Curbstone Press. Originally published as *Círculo de amor sobre la muerte* (Buenos Aires: Ediciones del Pensamiento Nacional, 1990).

Mignone, E. 1988. *Witness to the truth: The complicity of church and dictatorship in Argentina 1976–1983.* Translated by P. Berryman. Maryknoll, NY: Orbis Books.

Moses, C. G., and H. Hartmann, eds. 1995. *U.S. women in struggle: A feminist studies anthology.* Chicago: Board of Trustees of the University of Illinois.

Mullen, P. 1995. *Unfriendly fire: A mother's memoir.* Iowa City: University of Iowa Press.
Ortner, S. B. 1974. Is female to male as nature is to culture? In *Woman, culture, and society,* ed. M. Z. Rosaldo and L. Lamphere, 67–87. Stanford, CA: Stanford University Press.
Owen, D. R. 1970. Letter to AMP supporters. In AMP Archives, Peace Collection, Swarthmore College, Pennsylvania.
Radcliffe, D. 1969. Mothers stump for peace. *The Evening Star,* February 6. Washington, DC. In AMP Archives, Peace Collection, Swarthmore College, Pennsylvania.
Rock, D. 1993. *Authoritarian Argentina: The nationalist movement, its history and impact.* Berkeley: University of California Press.
Ruddick, S. 1989. *Maternal thinking: Towards a politics of peace.* Boston, MA: Beacon Press.
Steinson, B. J. 1980. The mother half of humanity: American women in the peace and preparedness movement in WW I. In *Women, war and revolution,* ed. C. R. Berkin and C. Lovett, 259–84. New York: Holmes and Meier.
Stevens, E. 1973. *Marianismo:* The other face of *machismo* in Latin America. In *Female and male in Latin America,* ed. A. Pescatello, 89–102. Pittsburg, PA: University of Pittsburg Press.
Stone, L. 1977. *The family, sex, and marriage in England, 1500–1800.* New York: Harper Row.
Strange, C. 1990. Mothers on the march: Maternalism in women's protest for peace in North America and Western Europe, 1900–1985. In *Women and social protest,* ed. G. West and R. L. Blumberg, 209–44. Oxford: Oxford University Press.
Swerdlow, A. 1993. *Women strike for peace: Traditional motherhood and radical politics in the 1960s.* Chicago, IL: University of Chicago Press.
———. 1995. Ladies day at the Capitol: Women strike for peace versus HUAC. In *U.S. women in struggle: A feminist studies anthology,* ed. C. Moses and H. Hartmann, 214–39. Chicago: Board of Trustees of the University of Illinois.
Taylor, D. 1997. *Disappearing acts: Spectacles of gender and nationalism in Argentina's "Dirty War."* Durham, NC: Duke University Press.
Werbner, P., and N. Yuval-Davis. 1999. Introduction: Women and the new discourse of citizenship. In *Women, citizenship, and difference,* ed. P. Werbner and N. Yuval-Davis, 1–39. New York: Zed Books.
Wright, E., ed. 1992. *Feminism and psychoanalysis: A critical dictionary.* Cambridge, MA: Blackwell.
Wright, S. 2001. *International human rights, decolonization, and globalization: Becoming human.* Routledge Studies in International Law. London: Routledge.

Epilogue

Power in a Movement

JUDITH STADTMAN TUCKER

It was a typical Friday morning—at least as typical as any weekday morning in our eclectic household. My children were up and getting ready for school. I was preoccupied with my weekend travel plans—in a few hours, I would depart for suburban New York and the National Association of Mothers Centers *Mothers '08* Conference (April 4–6, 2008). In the midst of checking backpacks and clearing the debris from the kids' breakfast, I realized I had not mentioned to my soon-to-be-eleven-year-old son that I was heading out of town, or that I would be 250 miles away when he came home from school that afternoon. The boy has a long memory for slights and rarely misses an opportunity to torment me about my maternal shortcomings: *Hey mom, don't forget to sign my permission slip today. You know, like the time you FORGOT TO TELL ME YOU WERE GOING AWAY FOR THREE WHOLE DAYS.*

Of course, I felt absolutely rotten about letting him down (I may be a forgetful mother, but I am not a heartless one). The truth was that attending out-of-town meetings and conferences to hold forth on the future of the mothers' movement had become, well, not a grind exactly but a reflexive routine, like putting away the milk carton someone left out on the kitchen counter, or reminding the kids to brush their teeth before bedtime. Let me be clear: I still look forward to motherhood conferences as an opportunity to meet up with old friends and colleagues and connect with new ones. And until quite recently, there was nothing I relished more than the prospect of getting together with a bunch of like-minded women (and whenever possible, a few feminist men) to brainstorm about mobilizing mothers for change.

Reader, I must tell you that a change has come over me. After six rewarding and highly productive years as the editor and publisher of a popular Web site on the motherhood problem and what to do about it (http://www.mothersmovement.org/), I am no longer satisfied to write and talk about the goals of the mothers' movement when there is no sign of purposeful action on the horizon. I am still dedicated to articulating the values and policy priorities of a caring society and what it will take to move the United States in the right direction. But I am tired of dissecting the relationship between motherhood ideology, conflicts in feminism, and the politics of organizing mothers for change (Stadtman Tucker 2008, 205-206)—so tired of it that just writing this down makes my head hurt. I am moving on to the next stage. I am ready to get the job done. And I have a few ideas about how to get started.

THINKING BEYOND OURSELVES

The theme of the *Mothers '08* conference was "thinking beyond ourselves and beyond today"—and the organizers deserve credit for inviting a wider circle of advocacy and support groups to join the national mothers' organizations with a permanent place at the table.[1] The weekend offered an inviting range of creative and action-oriented programming, including a rabble-rousing keynote by Ellen Bravo, former executive director of the 9to5 working women's association and author of *Taking on the Big Boys* (2007), a handbook on organizing for gender equality and workplace rights. In an effort to connect movement leaders and identify action issues for future collaboration, the conference program included a half-day, professionally facilitated roundtable discussion with representatives from a dozen prominent mothers' organizations. But as is true for the vast majority of professionally run social movement projects, the members and leaders of the organizations at the forefront of the mothers' movement are predominantly white, college-educated, and relatively affluent (DiQuinzio 2006, 56), and motherhood conferences and interorganizational meetings are notoriously poor forums for promoting inclusion and a diversity of viewpoints. Good intentions aside, the *Mothers '08* conference was no exception.

Looking back on early motherhood conferences and events—beginning with the 2001 Mothers & More National Conference, where our advocacy team presented one of the first mother-centric workshops on work-life policy, and the October 2002 Symposium on Maternal Feminism at Barnard College (which was particularly memorable due to several panelists' open hostility toward "mainstream" feminists) (Charen 2002)—there is little doubt that the movement has matured in both vision and substance, as have several of the leading organizations affiliated with it. The discussion during the *Mothers '08* leadership roundtable suggested that groups seeking to improve the lives of mothers are becoming more specialized in their services and message delivery and more amenable to forming coalitions to work on advocacy initiatives.

Despite such promising developments, it was difficult to sustain any optimism about the *Mothers '08* conference as a watershed event. As the weekend wore on, the burning question was whether organizational leaders would use the conference as an opportunity to improve the movement's signal-to-noise ratio by balancing the volume of talk with a clear transition toward pragmatic change work, or whether the mothers' movement—like the contemporary progressive movement in general—would get stuck in the process of endlessly elaborating on the nature of the problem, with no realistic action plan in sight.

WORDS AND DEEDS

The tension between talk and action surfaced early during the leaders' roundtable session, where representatives from several stakeholder groups agreed that lobbying the federal government to collect better data on caregiving and mothers' patterns of employment should be the movement's top priority. If we just had more detailed information about mothers' lives and livelihoods, these advocates proposed, then the media and the public would take mothers' grievances more seriously, and pressure groups would be in a better position to persuade employers and legislators to do the right thing. (Roundtable participants included representatives from Mothers & More, the National Association of Mothers Centers, Welfare Warriors, National Advocates for Pregnant Women, MomsRising, Family and Home Network, Mothers Acting Up, the Motherhood Project, the Mothers Movement Online, NOW Mothers & Caregivers Economic Rights Committee, and The MotherHood social networking Web site.)

It is tempting to imagine that the solution to the motherhood problem (or any persistent injustice in American society) lies in more targeted research, accurate mass media coverage, an in-depth understanding of national opinion, and a more skillful framing of the public conversation—in other words, a solid base of expertise that would contribute to more persuasive communication about motherhood and caregiving as political issues. But here is the thing: we already have all the information we need to mobilize the mothers' movement. Indeed, we have a surplus of high-quality studies linking maternity to women's inequality in public and private life. We have thirty-plus years of peer-reviewed social research on the causes and consequences of the motherhood penalty and reams of expert findings on policy models and labor standards that are known to have broad social benefits and reduce mothers' economic vulnerability. If the latest research has anything critical to tell us, it is that the situation for working women and families in the United States has not improved significantly in the last thirty-five years—and by many social and economic measures, it is getting worse (Heymann 2005, 89–91).

While economic and time pressures on middle-income working parents are approaching unsustainable levels, mainstream media and political attention to the nation's "care crisis" (Rosen 2007) has improved. Overwork, flexible work, work-family conflict, and parenting as a gender issue attracted more frequent—and better balanced—news coverage and commentary in mass media outlets in the five-year span between 2003 and 2008 than the total number of work-life articles published between 1980 and 2000 (although lifestyle reporting and opinion essays reheating the legendary "Mommy Wars" continue to generate the highest readership) (Graff 2007). Early in the 2008 Democratic primary race, front-running candidates announced a commitment to expanding policies to support caregivers and working families—a move that four years earlier would have amounted to political suicide. Three states—California, Washington, and New Jersey—have passed paid family and medical leave legislation, and more than a dozen states and municipalities are currently considering legislation to guarantee workers a minimum number of paid sick days. Mothers who want social change do not need more facts and figures to get a movement off the ground. We need to get on the train before it leaves the station.

THE LETTERHEAD BRIGADE

To be completely fair, mothers' movement sympathizers are not alone in the conviction that producing and disseminating the right kind of information is key to shifting the balance of political power in the United States. According to conventional thinking, if we could just get our hands on unassailable data that prove, once and for all, that our nation's spending and policy priorities reinforce historic inequalities, are directly harmful to children and families, and are otherwise antithetical to core democratic values, then how could any self-respecting lawmaker possibly fail to act?

It may be true that mothers' advocates are struggling to find a plain-spoken, compelling way to talk about what we feel and know is wrong (Stadtman Tucker 2008, 208), but it is a mistake to think that progress has stalled because our current arsenal of studies and statistics is inaccurate, inconsistent, or incomplete. If we want to create the social conditions necessary for truly equal opportunity and shared prosperity—for middle-class mothers and everybody else—then we need to invest in less talk and a lot more action.

Since the mid-1980s, the progressive movement has concentrated its resources in the production and distribution of ideas and information, primarily through funding public interest research organizations and progressive media outlets. (I use the term *funding* loosely, since it is common knowledge that progressive organizations and media projects are perpetually strapped for cash.) Today, the most prominent actors in the progressive change community are media professionals, academically trained analysts, communication specialists, and heads of labor and non-profit organizations. In various capacities these experts interact with the press, other non-profit executives, the research community, legislators, and the informed public to build opposition to social and economic policies that fly in the face of progress or otherwise diminish the general welfare. Day-to-day work in the progressive research industry involves data collection and analysis, writing reports, providing expert testimony, developing policy models, and organizing events, meetings, forums, symposia, press conferences, and panel discussions where academically trained policy wonks, professional advocates, allied journalists, labor movement leaders, liberal lawmakers, and other masters of the progressive universe come together to exchange ideas about how to solve our country's most pressing problems. Sometimes non-expert stakeholders are invited to participate—particularly when information is delivered through blogging or other online sources, or when emotional personal testimony is needed to bring a policy platform to life. But most of these projects and programs exist to enlighten political elites and movement professionals about the effects of bad policy making on American communities, not to mobilize ground-level activists.

The professionalization of the progressive movement (including mainstream elements of the women's rights, civil rights, economic justice, and peace movements) was a strategic and necessary response to the catastrophic breakdown of mid-twentieth-century change movements and the massive growth of the right-wing thought industry (Alterman 2004). It has also contributed to an explosion of professionally staffed, quasi-civic, non-profit organizations headquartered in the nation's power centers (Putnam 2000, 50). In *Bowling Alone*, Robert Putnam defines these groups' "mailing list" or "letterhead" organizations—groups founded to represent the public interest but having limited interaction with people outside of the politicized professional sphere, and no meaningful programs or structure for mobilizing ground-level volunteers. Although the "new associations" often sustain their projects through cash contributions and membership dues from concerned citizens, Putnam notes, "The newer groups focus on expressing policy views in the national political debate, not on providing regular connection among individual members at the grass roots" (51).

The professional activities of the Letterhead Brigade have been fabulously helpful to intellectual activists (like yours truly, for example) who do the work of interpreting and rebroadcasting research validating a given cause for the benefit of a non-expert audience. In building the case for a mothers' movement, advocates have cited reports and resources produced by a legion of progressive research institutes, "grasstops" advocacy organizations, and academic centers, including the Institute for Women's Policy Research, Economic Policy Institute, Center for Economic and Policy Research, Families & Work Institute, Center for WorkLife Law, Center for Law and Social Policy, National Women's Law Center, Project on Global Working Families, National Partnership for Women & Families, Sloan Work & Family Research Network, National Center for Children in Poverty, New America Foundation, Demos, projects funded by the Annie E. Casey Foundation, and numerous others. Experts who work in the progressive research industry also tend to write a lot of books, opinion columns, and magazine articles, expanding the dominance of intellectual activism as the favored model for progressive problem solving.

Frankly, I love this stuff. I love the notion that information and power are essentially interchangeable, and that knowing the truth will set us free. On the other hand, we have accumulated a mountain of knowledge—sound knowledge based on solid research and fair, accurate analysis—in the form of books, studies, reports, briefing papers, and public commentary, all of it written by brainy people with top-notch credentials who do a fine job of explaining what is wrong and what to do about it. Yet in the past twenty-five years, the progressive movement has had few unqualified victories in the area of policy and regulatory reform. To be perfectly honest, we suffered some significant defeats. The post-Reagan-era rise of new conservatism and a thirty-year partisan stalemate in Congress clearly contributed to the progressive agenda's failure to thrive. But another salient factor in the moribund state of the progressive movement is the lack of a stable, community-based infrastructure to organize a diverse population of individual, non-professional activists for ongoing change work.

The academic model of progressive activism rests on the theory that: (1) intellectual activists—either by the force of overwhelming evidence or by wording an appeal the correct way—can overcome historic patterns of resistance and move powerful decision makers to act for the common good; and (2) when societal conditions become unbearable— or when ordinary folks absorb enough information about how and why they are getting the raw end of the deal—this will result in a spontaneous uprising of a critical mass of self-organized citizen activists. (In social movement lingo, this is referred to as "the tipping point.") But what happens in the real world is that social movement professionals, progressive media celebrities, and freelance intellectuals (like me) go to meetings and conferences to let off steam and scratch our collective heads, because—given the urgency of the present situation—we cannot figure out why so many Americans are more fired up about the next episode of *American Idol* than working to change the unfair, unhealthy, and unsustainable conditions that beset us.

The assumption that we can talk our way into meaningful social change diverges from classic community and labor organizing models, which aim to interrupt the status quo by amplifying conflict and contention between the "haves" and those who have a little and want more (Alinsky 1989, 18–19). When this in-your-face, people-powered approach to action works well, it fosters solidarity in the activist community and establishes an urgent context for negotiation and resolution. In a knowledge-driven society with super-educated elites on both sides of the bargaining table, organized efforts to catalog and publicize negative fallout from flawed policy decisions and unchecked ideological forces overshadow community-based organizing as an avenue for giving ordinary people more clout. When other channels for political activism are unavailable, naming and framing our common grievances becomes the last, best option for achieving a sense of engagement—at least until new opportunities arise.

BUILDING ON-RAMPS TO ACTIVISM

The professionalization of the progressive movement has also produced dozens of non-profit groups dedicated to training and leadership development for social justice advocates, young activists, political party activists, and community organizers. But few communities outside of major metropolitan areas have access to low-cost, continuing programs for building and sustaining grassroots capacity on a local scale, leaving most would-be activists with limited opportunities to acquire basic change work skills from more experienced organizers. As civic engagement in the United States continues to erode, non-partisan community groups that at one time facilitated grassroots networking—including voluntary associations, membership groups, and service organizations—are rapidly succumbing to attrition (Putnam 2000, 43), creating a void for those in search of entry-level on-ramps to political activism. Needless to say, the disintegration of the labor movement in the United States has also closed off pathways to collective action for millions of middle- and lower-income Americans.

Based on firsthand observation, my impression is that the average middle-class mom is not underinformed or ambivalent about the persistence of gender inequality, or apathetic about employer practices and policy gaps that constrain women's opportunities and put every mother—and her dependent children—at greater risk for hardship. On the contrary, a 2004 national survey found that 90 percent of U.S. mothers believe the government can do more to support children and families (Erickson and Aird 2005, 5). But short of one-click action campaigns launched by net-roots ventures such as MomsRising and MoveOn.org, mothers and others who want to take part in collective action are hard pressed to find ready-made opportunities in their home communities. Starting a social movement organization from scratch *is not* a feasible solution for would-be activists with real jobs and family responsibilities—meaning just about everyone between the ages of thirty and sixty-five—and in any case, examples of productive (or even unproductive) grassroots organizing are so rare in most localities that millions of would-be activists who thirst for change are missing crucial background knowledge about what really works and where to begin. To shift the mothers' movement from talk to action, we must begin to fill in the blanks.

THE HEART AND SOUL OF SOCIAL MOVEMENTS

Successful change movements require more from social activists than inspiration, passion, and commitment to a shared ideal—there is real, time-consuming work involved in organizing for change, which (like other kinds of work) can be done effectively, or not.

The single most important thing to know about social movement work is that organizing for change is a *social process*. The heart and soul of social activism is making a connection with other people who care about the future of the community, whether the practical definition of "the community" is everyone in your neighborhood, or everyone on the planet. Working for change is not an abstract, academic endeavor. It requires working with people you know, and people you will get to know. The time we spend writing, deliberating, and consciousness-raising is a critical step in the change-making cycle, because it helps us refine our claims, clarify mutual goals, and identify others who are sympathetic or opposed to our cause. As sociologist Charles Tilly (2002) observes in *Stories, Identities, and Political Change*, political activists invest significant effort in "the creation and broadcast of collective standard stories that will facilitate communication, coordination, and commitment on the part of allies, bystanders, and even objects of collective claims" (9). Yet as Michael Gecan (2002), a community organizer with the Industrial Areas Foundation, explains, on-the-ground activism that gets results is fundamentally relational. Organizing for change is about understanding how people in a community experience real-world problems, "to hear their interests and dreams and fears." Even action involving public confrontation, he writes, "is at bottom an attempt to engage and relate" (21, 54).

But change work that works is also a *political process*. Successful social movements involve planning, resource mobilization, and strategic interaction with allies and power holders representing the systems or institutions we intend to transform. If we want the mothers' movement to flourish as a change movement, then at some point we must add a pragmatic layer to all the chatter and take action to achieve the progress we hope to see. Making change is not rocket science. In addition to sharing stories about who you are and listening with empathy when others tell *their* stories, most of the hands-on work of grassroots activism involves things many moms already know how to do—such as breaking down big tasks into small, concrete steps, setting priorities, being flexible when flexibility is called for, and keeping channels of communication open. Everything else you need to know can be learned.

Finally, scholars who study political activists and the birth and demise of social movements agree that working for change is an *identity process* (Meyer 2002, 9–10). Becoming a social activist means stepping into the stream of change, as an individual and as a member of your community. Change is defined as "passing from one place, state, form, or phase to another," which, on a personal level, means feeling and thinking differently about the world and our role in it, and acting out of that new awareness. Working for change is about taking your personal politics public; there can be a palpable sensation of crossing a boundary, or finding a calling (Teske 2009, 42). Unless you happen to be an extraordinarily uninhibited or self-actualized person, working for change will force you to step out of your comfort zone. (If it does not, then you should check out whether your change work is having the impact you would like to see.)

Social change, however, is not just a happy by-product of random acts by isolated individuals who feel strongly identified with a cause. Some kind of organizing structure is necessary to get a meaningful chunk of the activist community heading in the same direction. As an emerging and (so far) unstructured enterprise, the mothers' movement is in a perfect position to take advantage of new models of working for change. For example, the innovative organizing paradigm of the 2008 Obama for America campaign successfully mobilized millions of volunteers with a hybrid model fusing the culture and values of community organizing with a conventional electioneering ground plan and paired conventional, labor-intensive outreach techniques with sophisticated online networking tools to streamline communication and organizing tasks.

If we hope to grow our movement in a way that will empower mothers and others to act for change, then we must invest in the development of new structures and capacities. (This challenge applies equally to proponents of revitalizing the broader progressive movement.) The following is a short list of needs and opportunities:

1. Invest in new organizing structures, including new, community-centered programs for grassroots training and leadership development. Instead of trying to restore or recreate the voluntary networks and organizational structures that supported feminist, labor, and social justice activism thirty-five years ago, we need to develop and fund new projects and organizations that can sustain the work of grassroots activists at the community level and beyond.

2. Develop and invest in inclusive organizing structures. Working for change is not just for young people, people in marginalized communities, or people with advanced degrees. Our social movement organizations, programs, funding priorities, and actions can do a better job of bringing together stakeholders from diverse communities and backgrounds to develop collective capacity, instead of splitting people who share progressive values into competing narrow-interest camps. Today's top-heavy progressive movement is ill equipped to foster truly inclusive organizing structures; sadly, there may be a grain of truth to the caricature of progressive leaders as latte-drinking snobs who are desperately out of touch with the values of "real" Americans. The mothers' movement does not have to repeat this mistake—and we do not have to design our social movement organizations based on existing, non-inclusive models.

3. Do what works. For activist mothers, time and energy are precious resources. We need to be realistic and smart about evaluating our objectives and whether our collective actions are bringing about the change we want to achieve. (A good rule of thumb is "use common sense." Wearing a T-shirt with a slogan on it is a nice way to show your support for a candidate or cause, but it is not going to change the world unless you are doing some kind of pragmatic political work while you are wearing it.) What works will depend on the specific goals of an action campaign, but it is important to match the organizing approach and tools to the problem you want to solve. For example, if you are concerned about reducing maternal poverty in your community, then you might be better off joining a grassroots coalition that is fighting for paid sick days or a living wage ordinance, rather than volunteering at the local soup kitchen. Mothers' movement organizations can play an important role in modeling and facilitating effective change work by focusing on what really works instead of resorting to conventional modes of activism that have little measurable impact on resolving unhealthy, unsafe, unfair, and unsustainable social conditions.

4. Plan action campaigns with multiple entry and exit points for first-time volunteers and seasoned activists. Some volunteers are so fired up by an issue that they are prepared to devote days or months to a political cause. Others activists may only have a few hours to spare but still have something valuable to contribute to a campaign. It is possible to make room for everyone by breaking down tasks into smaller components. Organizers need to build as much flexibility as possible into when and where tasks are performed and provide ongoing training and coaching so volunteers can use their time productively, learn new skills, and come away with the feeling that they have made a difference.

5. Use technology with an eye toward its limitations, and cultivate multiple communication streams. As a campaign volunteer and lead organizer of an active grassroots organizing network in New Hampshire, I have encountered a number of situations where overreliance on electronic communication creates barriers to participation. In the local context, I work with volunteers who do not like to read or send e-mail (my preferred mode of communication by far), and several who do not have home computers or Internet access but want to stay informed. I have also volunteered for Get Out The Vote campaigns in low-income communities where the majority of households do not have Internet access. The fantastic thing about computer-mediated communication is that it is fast and cheap and can move huge volumes of information to millions of recipients at the same time. The downside is that it does not reach everybody, and high-frequency Internet users tend to be concentrated in

younger, more educated, and more affluent demographic groups (Pew Internet and American Life Project 2008). In using new technologies, we need to think carefully about who we are actually empowering (information consumers or the people who produce and distribute information) and who gets left out altogether.

6. Think bigger. Strategically, mothers' movement organizations have resisted the language of systematic exclusion as being too strident for the college-educated, professional-class moms they hope to engage, preferring the softer platform of securing recognition for the economic value of unpaid caregiving and expanding mothers' opportunities for self-determination (Stadtman Tucker 2008, 211–12). But if we continue to envision the movement's political capacity only in terms of problem solving—and without addressing the durable relationship between gender, race, class, and power—then even our best efforts are unlikely to bend the arc of history closer to justice (DiQuinzio 2006, 57).

THE REASON

A week after I returned form the *Mothers '08* conference, I took another trip—a journey that led me away from my family and the comforts of home for fourteen days, the longest I have ever been apart from them. In April 2008, I organized a group of New Hampshire volunteers to travel to Philadelphia, Pennsylvania, for a Women for Obama weekend to fire up support for the candidate before the state's primary election. From there I traveled to the far southwestern corner of the state to volunteer in a bare-bones field office in Uniontown. When social scientists and investigative journalists write about grinding poverty and once-thriving, middle-class communities destroyed by the disappearance of manufacturing and industrial jobs, they are describing places like Uniontown, Pennsylvania.

My job there was to talk with local voters about their personal hardships and hopes for the future. Suffice it to say, these folks did not feel that the system was working for them—*or that it ever could*—and they had good reasons for feeling left behind. Spending time in Uniontown permanently altered my awareness of my own privilege in a painful and profound way; it changed my worldview on a deep-tissue level. In Uniontown, I learned that thinking and talking about the change we need is not enough, because people in power already know about the widespread despair and human suffering in the hidden corners of America, *and they do not care*—in the real, raw world as it is, the "haves" are experts at using their political clout to make sure the "have-nots" remain isolated and powerless. And that is why I have decided to organize for change, full time.

Mothers and others who want to tap into the power of their inner activist do not need to go to Uniontown, or someplace like it, to discover the will to make a meaningful difference. Decide what is worth fighting for, and take a stand. Start small—think about one action you can take today, tomorrow, or next week to move your personal politics into the public square, something that will force you to step out of your comfort zone (as Bernice Johnson Reagon [1983] remarked in her classic commentary on coalition building and the future of the women's movement, "If you feel the strain, you may be doing some good work"). Set a goal. Figure out what you need to know, who you need to talk to, and who can help you get there. Then go out and do it. Then, take a deep breath—and go out and do it again.

NOTE

1. Full disclosure: As a movement leader with a history of criticizing the lack of diversity in mothers' movement organizations, I was asked by the organizers of the *Mothers '08* conference for recommendations regarding who to invite and how to plan the conference program to make the event more inclusive.

REFERENCES

Alinsky, S. D. 1989. *Rules for radicals.* New York: Vintage Edition.
Alterman, E. 2004. Think again: Ideas have consequences, and so does money. Center for American Progress, October 24. http://www.americanprogress.org/issues/2004/10/b222111.html.
Bravo, E. 2007. *Taking on the big boys, or why feminism is good for families, business, and the nation.* New York: Feminist Press.
Charen, M. 2002. Mothers unbound. Barnard News Center, October 25. http://www.barnard.edu/newnews/news110402.html.
DiQuinzio, P. 2006. The politics of the mothers' movement in the United States: Possibilities and pitfalls. *Mothering and Feminism: Journal of the Association for Research on Mothering.* 8:1, 2: 55–71.
Erickson, M. F., and E. G. Aird. 2005. Motherhood survey annotated questionnaire. *The motherhood study: Fresh insights on mothers' attitudes and concerns.* New York: The Institute for American Values. (Separate appendix.) http://www.motherhoodproject.org/wp-content/themes/mothe2/pdfs/annotatedquestionnaire.pdf.
Gecan, M. 2002. *Going public: An organizer's guide to citizen action.* New York: Anchor Books.

Graff, E. J. 2007. The opt out myth. *Columbia Journalism Review* (April–May). http://www.cjr.org/essay/the_optout_myth.php.

Heymann, J. 2005. Inequalities at work and home: Social class and gender divides. In *Unfinished work: Building equality and democracy in an era of working families*, ed. J. Heymann and C. Beem, 89–121. New York: New Press.

Meyer, D. S. 2002. Opportunities and identities: Bridge building in the study of social movements. In *Social movements: Identity, culture, and the state*, ed. D. S. Meyer, N. Whittier, and B. Robnett, 3–21. New York: Oxford University Press.

Pew Internet and American Life Project. 2008. Demographics of Internet users [table]. December. http://www.pewinternet.org.

Putnam, R. D. 2000. *Bowling alone: The collapse and revival of American community*. New York: Touchstone.

Reagon, B. J. 1983. Coalition politics: Turning the century. In *Home girls: A black feminist anthology*, ed. B. Smith, 356–68. New York: Kitchen Table: Women of Color Press.

Rosen, R. 2007. The care crisis. *The Nation* 284:10 (March 12): 11–16.

Stadtman Tucker, J. 2008. Rocking the boat: Feminism and the ideological grounding of the 21st century mothers' movement. In *Feminist mothering*, ed. A. O'Reilly, 205–18. Albany: State University of New York Press.

Teske, N. 2009. *Political activists in America*. University Park: Pennsylvania State University Press.

Tilly, C. 2002. *Stories, identities, and political change*. Lanham, MD: Rowman & Littlefield.

Contributors

LEE BEHLMAN is an assistant professor of English at Montclair State University, where he teaches courses on Victorian poetry and prose, gender studies, and classical and biblical literatures in translation. He received his Ph.D. in English language and literature at the University of Michigan and has taught at Kansas State University. Much of his published work has focused on the way in which nineteenth-century writers received the classical past, in such journals as *Nineteenth-Century Prose* and *Victorian Poetry* and in the recent book collection *Antiquity Recovered: The Legacy of Pompeii and Herculaneum* (2007). He is currently completing a book project on nineteenth-century stoicism and masculinity that focuses on such authors as Matthew Arnold, Walter Pater, and A. C. Swinburne. His current research on mothering studies addresses several late Victorian women poets, and he is completing an article on one of these figures, Augusta Webster, and her unfinished 1895 sonnet sequence *Mother and Daughter*.

JILLIAN M. DUQUAINE-WATSON received her Ph.D. in women's studies with a disciplinary concentration in feminist anthropology from the University of Iowa. She is currently a senior lecturer I at the University of Texas at Dallas, where she teaches in the School of Interdisciplinary Studies and the School of Natural Sciences and Mathematics. She holds a certificate in non-profit management and has been actively involved in non-profit and non-governmental organizations for the past decade. Her research interests include motherhood and reproduction, rhetoric of public policy, social change/activism, and educational policies and practices. An award-winning educator, she has taught undergraduate and graduate courses in women's studies, sociology, anthropology, history, American studies, and communications. Duquaine-Watson's work has appeared in a number of journals and edited volumes, including *Equal Opportunities International*, *The Journal of the Association for Research on Mothering*, *Equity & Excellent in Education*, and *Pedagogy and Student Services for Institutional Transformation: Implementing*

Universal Design in Higher Education. Her book, *Mothering by Degrees: Single Mothers and the Pursuit of Postsecondary Education*, is currently under contract with Rutgers University Press and will be published in 2010. She is a member of several professional organizations, including the Association for Research on Mothering, the American Anthropological Association, and the Association for Feminist Anthropology. In her free time, she can most likely be found behind the lens of her camera, volunteering at her local elementary school, or making memories with her two wonderful daughters and her husband.

MEGHAN GIBBONS received her Ph.D. in comparative literature from the University of Maryland, with a specialty in women's testimonial accounts in the Americas. Her scholarly work explores the representation of "truth" in testimonial forms, including oral histories, written narratives, and film, particularly within human rights struggles. She has written extensively on the activism of mothers against their nation-states in times of national crisis in the Americas, and she is completing a book that profiles politicized mothers' groups in the United States, El Salvador, and Argentina. Her interests are in the organizational and rhetorical similarities of the groups and how distinct cultural, political, and religious environments influenced differences in their formations and protest strategies. Gibbons's research on politically active mothers has been published in *The Washington Post* and *The Nation*. Her most recent project is on testimonial accounts of Guantánamo Bay, published as "Representing the Real on the *Road to Guantánamo*," in *The Curious Knot: The War on Terror and Post 9/11 Popular Culture*. Gibbons currently works as a speechwriter. She is continually inspired by her own parents' engagement with international politics and devotion to their children.

LISA HAMMOND is professor of English at the University of South Carolina Lancaster, where she teaches first-year composition and a wide range of literature and women's studies courses. Her research focuses on American women writers, composition and technology, and gender issues in culture; her work has appeared in the *National Women's Studies Association Journal, Biography,* and *Kairos: A Journal of Rhetoric, Technology, and Pedagogy*. Much of her recent scholarship focuses on representations of maternal identity online, including her article, " 'Work It Out with Your Wife': Gendered Expectations and Parenting Rhetoric Online." In addition to her academic writing, Hammond is also a poet. Her collection *Moving House* (Texas Review Press, 2007) won the Robert Phillips Chapbook Prize. She has published poems in *Southern*

Poetry Review, storySouth, River Oak Review, North Carolina Literary Review, South Carolina Review, Literary Mama: A Literary Magazine for the Maternally Inclined, and *English Journal,* among others. She lives in a small southern town with her husband and two children.

LYNN KUECHLE is an instructor of speech communication at Minnesota State University, Mankato, where she teaches courses in public speaking and interpersonal communication. She received her M.A. in speech communication from MSU, Mankato. Kuechle became active in the research on mothering when she returned to get her M.A. after being a stay-at-home mother for eight years. Since then she has spoken to area mom groups and has been part of the diversity program for a local community college. She is a board member for the Motherhood Foundation and an advisor for small-market Mamapalooza Festivals. She produced the first Mamapalooza festival in the state of Minnesota in 2007. She is a member of the Association for the Research on Mothering (ARM) and in 2008 presented at their conferences in New York City and Toronto. She has also been the director of a volunteer organization that provided volunteers to the elderly, helping them retain their independence by providing non-medical services, and she ran a support group for women who were caring for their husbands suffering from Alzheimer's disease. Kuechle is the mother of two school-age children.

NAN MA is a Ph.D. candidate in the Department of English at the University of California, Riverside. Her research interests include twentieth-century American literature, Asian American literary and cultural studies, film studies, minority discourses, and feminist theory. She is currently completing her dissertation, "Suspended Subjects: The Politics of Anger in Asian American Literature." She also writes creatively in Chinese.

ANDRA MCCARTNEY is an associate professor of communication studies at Concordia University, Montreal, Canada, where she teaches courses on sound production, reflexivity studies, and sound theory. She received her Ph.D. in music from York University in Toronto. She is well known internationally for her research on issues of gender, creation, sound, and technology. She has published writings with the *Electronic Music Foundation, Leonardo Music Journal, Musicworks, Axis Voor de Kunsten V/M, Contact!, Array, Resources for Feminist Research,* and *Borderlines,* as well as several edited volumes on gender, technology, and creation: *Gender and Music, Ghosts in the Machine, Canadian Music: Issues of Hegemony and Identity,* and *With a Song in Her Heart.*

She edited in 2002 an issue of the journal *Organised Sound* on the topic of soundscape composition. She coedited with Dr. Ellen Waterman in 2006 a special issue of *Intersections Journal of Canadian Music*, based on papers presented at the In and Out of the Sound Studio Conference on gender and sound technologies, which she directed at Concordia University in July 2005. She is also a practicing soundwalk artist, leading public walks and creating gallery installations and radio works. She is the mother of two children and the grandmother of one.

GRETCHEN PAPAZIAN is an assistant professor of English at Central Michigan University, where she teaches courses in children's literature, cultural studies, multiculturalism, and writing. She received her Ph.D. in English from the University of Wisconsin-Milwaukee. She has presented work on mothering in academia at the conference of the Midwest Division of the Modern Language Association, and her work on representations of mothers in picture books found its first audience at the Popular Culture Association/American Culture Association Conference. Her publications include "Anorexia Envisioned," in Anne Bower's collection *Reel Food*, "Feed My Poor Famished Heart," in *American Transcendental Quarterly*, and "Razing Little Houses, or Re-envisionary History," in Brajesh Shawney's collection *Louise Erdrich: New Essays in Criticism*. She is the mother of two children, Nicholas and Alice.

SHELLEY PARK is an associate professor of philosophy at the University of Central Florida in Orlando, where she teaches courses in contemporary epistemology and social and political theory (including a course on family values). Her recent scholarship analyzes the activities of mothering through the lenses of feminist theory, queer theory, and cybertheory. The author of several essays in feminist anthologies (e.g., *Mothers against Racism, Adoption Matters, Fragment by Fragment*) and scholarly journals (e.g., *Hypatia, Journal of Popular Culture, Florida Philosophical Review*), she is currently working on a book-length manuscript on "Real Mothering." She is the mother of two teenage daughters who test her theories daily.

JANET PEUKERT has recently completed her Ph.D. in women's studies at the University of York in the United Kingdom. Her research focused on the emotion work that mothers of homosexual sons have to continually engage in to keep their sons integrated in their families and social worlds. Her major research interests include the ways in which existing ideologies of motherhood and masculinity and femininity affect a mother's identity and relationships. Her experiences raising a homosexual son led her to question why she blamed herself, why she so readily accepted "expert knowledge" about what a good mother is supposed to achieve with her children, why it is assumed that they will be heterosexual, and why if they are not it is assumed that in all likelihood it has something to do with the mother-child relationship. Peukert is also interested in questions of morality and sexuality: Why is a mother responsible for the "moral self" of her children, and why must a moral child be sexually moral, in other words, heterosexual? She is currently working toward qualifying to practice as a counseling psychologist in New Mexico.

PEGEEN REICHERT POWELL received her Ph.D. in English from Miami University (Oxford, Ohio) and is currently a faculty member in the English Department at Columbia College, Chicago. In addition to feminist mothering studies, Reichert Powell's research includes work on pedagogy, basic writing, and critical discourse analysis. She has published articles in *College Composition and Communication* and *JAC: Journal of Advanced Composition*, as well as chapters in edited collections in the fields of composition studies and rhetoric. Her recent work in the field of composition studies focuses on the relationship between writing instruction and retention in higher education. Reichert Powell came to the field of mothering studies through her mothering activism at Duke University in Durham, North Carolina, where she founded Parents@ Duke. This organization pushed for policies and practices that enabled people to be simultaneously good employees and good caregivers, for example, paid family leave, lactation rooms, flex time, and improved child care. Her work with Parents@Duke earned her the "Maverick Mom of the Year" award in 2004 from *Working Mother* magazine. Reichert Powell has presented on the topic of mothering activism at conferences and she has published a chapter on the discourse of work-life "balance" in *Feminist Mothering*, a collection edited by Andrea O'Reilly (State University of New York Press, 2008). Reichert Powell is the mother of two school-age children.

Jocelyn Fenton Stitt is an associate professor of women's studies at Minnesota State University, Mankato, where she teaches courses on global feminism, postcolonial culture and theory, and feminist mothering. She received her Ph.D. in English and women's studies from the University of Michigan and has held fellowships at the Institute for the Humanities at Michigan and the International Museum of Women. Her publications investigate the intertwining of the familial and the imperial in Britain and the Anglophone Caribbean from the nineteenth century to the present, in journals such as *Small Axe: A Journal of Caribbean Criticism* and *ARIEL*. She coedited with Pallavi Rastogi *Before Windrush: Recovering an Asian and Black Literary Heritage within Britain* (2008). Stitt has been active in mothering studies since she first began teaching in 1999 a course on mothers in popular culture. She has been a member of the Association for Research on Mothering (ARM) for several years and has presented at its international conferences. Her current research explores how familiar postcolonial literary themes such as diaspora, decolonization, immigration, education, nation building, and globalization look different through the eyes of mothers, rather than through the more common figure of the child or the coming-of-age novel. Stitt is the mother of an elementary-school-age daughter and a preschool-age son.

JUDITH STADTMAN TUCKER is a writer and an activist. From 2003 to 2009, she was the editor and publisher of *Mothers Movement Online*, an internationally read Web site featuring resources and reporting on women, work, family, public policy, gender equity, and economic justice. Tucker's essays on feminism, maternal activism, social movement organizing, and the political ethic of care have been published in numerous academic collections and in the popular anthology *The Maternal Is Political* (edited by Shari MacDonald Strong, Seal Press, 2008). She also contributed a chapter on advancing workplace rights for pregnant and parenting women to the *Our Bodies, Ourselves Pregnancy and Birth Book* (Boston Women's Health Book Collective, Touchstone, 2008), and her political commentary has appeared in various online media outlets, including the *Huffington Post, The American Prospect Online, AlterNet*, and *Talking Points Memo*. After working as a full-time volunteer field organizer for the 2008 Obama for America campaign, Tucker became the lead organizer for the Seacoast for Change Grassroots Network, a locally grown, community-directed resource for political volunteers and citizen activists in search of purposeful collective action. Tucker lives in Portsmouth, New Hampshire, with her husband and two school-age sons.

NATALIE WILSON is a lecturer in the women's studies program at Cal State, San Marcos, where she teaches courses in feminist theory, feminist activism, popular culture, literature, and engaged pedagogy. She holds an M.A. in English from San Diego State University and a Ph.D. in literature from the University of London, Birkbeck College. Her research interests include feminist theory and pedagogy, corporeal theory, feminist activism, popular culture, militarization, and mothering studies. She has published essays in journals such as *Feminist Media Studies, Women and Performance,* and *The International Journal of Gender and Sexuality Studies.* Wilson has been interested in mothering studies and representations of mothers and mothering in literature since writing a dissertation that examined motherhood in relation to feminist theory and the literature of the grotesque. Her most recent paper in this area is "Womb Fiction: Late Twentieth Century Challenges to the Woman as Womb Paradigm," published in *Womanhood in Anglophone Literary Culture* from Cambridge Scholars Press. Wilson is currently writing a feminist analysis of the *Twilight* cultural phenomenon entitled *Seduced by Twilight.* Planned for release in 2010, this work will include analysis of the representation of motherhood in the texts as well as how motherhood plays out in the fandom. She is the mother to two budding feminist activists, a son and a daughter.

Index

academia
  Job market, 163, 172
  Negative attitude toward mothers, 153, 155, 156
  Stigma of being a mother in, 165–166, 170
  Working within, as a mother, 165
active citizens, 238
activism, 282–291
  goals of, 246
  intellectual, 284–285
  lesbian, 243–249
  linguistic, 241–242
  mothering and, 13, 14, 218, 231–250, 287–290
  movements, 248
  political, 260, 286, 287
  women's, 232
  See also anti-war activism, embodied activism, everyday activism, grassroots activism, LGBTQ activism, maternal activism, maternalist activism, social activism
activist voice, 233
Africanist representation, 174–175
agents of discourse, 6–7, 9
American culture, 78, 128, 181
American Gold Star Mothers, 259, 265
Anderson, David, 121, 128
Angel of the House, 102–103
Another Mother for Peace (AMP), 14, 234, 254, 256–261, 263–273
anti-war activism, 13, 231–232, 237–242, 257, 265–266, 272

Armstrong, Heather, 79, 80, 83, 91
Association for Research on Mothering, 1, 13, 172, 218
Austin, Linda M., 99, 107
autobiography, 82–84, 101
Awakening, The (Chopin), 78

babies, sounds of, 22–23, 28, 31, 33
balancing work/life, 176, 178, 182
Bang, Molly
  Ten, Nine, Eight, 127
Barbauld, Anna Letitia, 100
Baring Witness, 246
Beloved (Morrison), 175
Berger, Barbara Helen
  Lot of Otters, A, 126
binary
  constructions of mother, 10, 42, 44, 53, 255
  cyborg, 61
  emotion/reason, 262
  hetero/nonhetero, 243
"Bitch Ph.D.," 179
Black Feminist Thought (Collins), 2
BloggingBaby (blog), 93
BlogHer conference, 85–87, 93–95
Blogs, 11, 77–95, 145, 229, 250
  maternal narratives in, 80
  readership, 84, 104
bond
  between mothers, 218, 269
  between mothers and child, 108, 218, 269
  between mothers and daughters, 42, 47, 48

301

Bowling Alone (Putnam), 283
Bradley, Alice, 77, 79, 86–89, 90, 91–92, 95
breadwinner for the family, mother as, 58, 69, 223, 225
breeder identity, 62
Brooks, Abigail, 219–220
  Feminist Standpoint Epistemology, 219
Brown, Margaret Wise, 125–127
  Runaway Bunny, The, 125
Buchanan, Andrea J., 79, 94
  Mother Shock: Loving Every (Other) Minute of It, 90
  But Enough about Me: Why We Read Other People's Lives (Miller), 82
Butler, Judith, 8, 183, 208–209

call-and-response, 28
campaigns based on emotion, 260–263
campaigns
  motherhood, 267
  political, 8
  women's, 262
Camahort, Elisa, 77, 86–87
camp (gay pride), 202–204
Camp Casey, 241, 242, 246, 247
Caplan, Paula, 124, 125
  Don't Blame Mother, 218
Cardoso, Patricia, 10, 41–54
carpool mom, 236, 243
Casing a Promised Land (Goodall), 217
Cather, Willa
  Sapphira and the Slave Girl, 175
Caulfield, Mina Davis, 49
cell phones. See technologies of co-presence
change
  as a condition of modern life, 107
  definition of, 287
  social, 286–290
childbirth, 7, 27, 32
child care, 150, 152, 153, 155, 179, 183

affordable, 5
devalued, 3, 37
child care manuals, 197
child development, 21, 24, 37
  experts in, 197
Childhood (Meynell), 99
childhood, 105
  idealized, 104
  individuality of, 105
  as a special condition, 105
  looking back as an adult, 108
  reimagining, 129
childless, passing as, 163, 165, 166
child, redefining, 101
Children, The (Meynell), 99
children
  aesthetic sensibility of, 106
  enjoyment of fantasy, 106
  modes of treating, 104
  normal, 196–197, 202
  upbringing of, 192, 195, 201
children's literature, 120–122, 125, 129
  adult reading of, 121, 135
  instruction on how to be a child in, 122
  instruction on how to be a parent in, 120, 122
  learning-to-read process, 121
children's picture books, 11, 119–135
  African American, 131–134
  classic, 126
  representation of children, 135
  representations of girls, 123
  representations of mothers, 124, 135
  representations of women, 123–125
  shaping notions of parents, 135
child's voice, 24–25, 28–31, 38–39
Chipko movement, 235
Chocolate, Debbi
  On the Day I Was Born, 133
Chodorow, Nancy, 123, 125, 128–129
  Reproduction of Mothering, The, 2, 195
Chopin, Kate
  Awakening, The, 78

Index 303

citizenship for women, 267
civil rights movements, 283
Cockburn, Cynthia, 232
Code, Lorraine, 24, 35, 37–38
Code Pink, 234
Cognitive Bias Working Group, 228
Collective decision-making process, 148
Collins, Patricia Hill
  Black Feminist Thought, 2, 43–44, 129–130
comfort stereotype, 244
Coming on Home Soon (Woodson), 131–132
coming out of the closet
  LGBTQ, 193, 194, 196–198, 200–202
  mothers in academia, 169–170
commonality, 220, 228
CommonDreams.org, 237
community, 286–287
  among mothers, 11, 80, 81, 83–95, 219–220
  commuting parents, 58, 69
computers, 64–65, 145
Contratto, Susan, 123, 125, 128–129
Coontz, Stephanie
  Way We Never Were, The, 2, 174
Cooper, Holly, 229
consciousness-raising, 12, 146, 287
contrapuntal, 21–22, 25
counterpoint, 21, 25
Crawford Peace House, 242, 246
Crittenden, Ann
  Price of Motherhood, The, 2, 5
Crosby, Faye, 228
cult of the apron, 127
cultural contradictions in narratives, 13
cultural contradictions in motherhood, 100, 170
Cusick, Susan, 27
cyberfeminist, 59, 60
cyber mother, 57, 60, 63, 67, 69–73
Cyborg Mommy: User's Manual, The (Hastings), 62–63

Dash, Julie, 173
daughters, 41–54, 58–60, 69–70, 195
Daughters of the Dust, 173
Day, Alexandra
  Good Dog, Carl, 127
day care. *See* child care
devotion to children, 255, 260–261, 267, 272–273
diaper changing areas, 179
diary, 81–84
die-ins, 261
digital communication technologies, 64–65. *See also* technologies of co-presence
DiQuinzio, Patrice, 186–187, 280, 290
  The Impossibility of Motherhood: Feminism, Individuality, and the Problem of Mothering, 2, 7, 15, 100, 167
disability rights, 13, 243
disappeared people, 254, 256, 264, 267
discourse
  community, 85, 91
  family values, 5
  feminine, 218
  feminist, 3, 44
  mothering, 7, 9, 111, 174, 200
  nonpolitical, 260, 270–271
  scholarly, 1, 3, 165–166
divorced parents, 58
domesticity, 59, 110, 249, 257–258
domestic violence, 4
Don't Blame Mother (Caplan), 218
Dooce (blog), 79, 80, 83, 91
"Dooced," 91
Douglas, Susan
  Mommy Myth: The Idealization of Motherhood and How it has Undermined all Women, The, 2, 5, 71, 124–125
Doves in Congress, 254, 257, 266
Drake, Jennifer
  Third Wave Agenda: Being Feminist, Doing Feminism, 53

duty
  maternal, 236, 256, 263, 265
  parent's, 133
  patriotic, 241, 262
dystopian anxieties, 66–67

ecofeminists, 246
economic justice movements, 283, 298
Edin, Kathryn, 2
e-mail. *See* technologies of co-presence
embodied activism, 14, 232, 234–236, 243, 246–248
empowerment, 44, 134, 155, 208, 217
Ensler, Eve, 221
essentialism, 37, 171, 253, 254–255, 269, 272
  experiential, 254, 269, 272
  strategic, 14, 254
everyday activism, 243–245
everymom, 232, 236, 239, 242
  identity, 14, 232, 243
  privileges, 244
  status, 246
Everywhere Babies (Meyers), 127

Facebook accounts, 58, 63
face-to-face interaction, 11–12, 81, 89, 145, 160, 184
  with children, 71, 78
familial power relations, 24
Families and Friends of Lesbians and Gays (FFLAG), 13, 193, 200–201, 205–207
Families on the Fault Line (Rubin), 219
Family and Home Network, 281
family leave, 179, 282, 297
fathers
  expressing anger, 128
  mothers and, 93, 209
  parenting experience of, 34
  representation of, 121
  role of, 127, 195
  working, 166, 168, 169, 195

female power, 31, 36
Feminine Mystique, The (Friedan), 63, 64, 257–258
feminism, 2, 36, 181, 271
  activists for, 240, 246, 288
  conflicts in, 6, 14, 280
  mothers and, 228, 229, 233
  unfinished business of, 3
feminist movement, 3, 43, 173, 266
  Second wave, 42, 53, 123, 257, 269, 273
  Third wave, 53–54
feminist new world, 250
feminist perspective, 185, 232, 233
feminists, 1–3, 6, 43, 57–58, 179, 244
  divisions amongst, 42, 67, 68, 232
  ecofeminists, 246
  mainstream, 42–43, 280, 283
  postfeminists, 53–54
  technology and, 57–58, 62
Feminist Standpoint Epistemology (Brooks), 219
Feminist theory about motherhood, 2–3, 6–7, 24, 43, 57, 173, 175
film theorists, feminist, 10, 172–173
Finslippy (blog), 77, 79, 86–87, 91
500 Mile Walk for Togetherness, 243, 248, 249
Flossie and the Fox (McKissack), 133
Fox, Mem
  Harriet, You'll Drive Me Wild, 127–128
Franklin, Cynthia, G.
  Writing Women's Communities: The Politics and Poetics of Contemporary Multi-genre Anthologies, 84
Friedan, Betty
  Feminine Mystique, The, 63, 64, 257–258
Fussy (blog), 79, 87
F Word: Feminism in Jeopardy, The (Rowe-Finkbeiner), 233

gay sons, 12–13, 200, 209
  accepting, 210
  incorporating into families, 209

lifestyles of, 204–205
  normal, 203–205
  sexual identity of, 191, 199, 206
gender
  denaturalizing, 61
  divide, 42
  scripts, 186
Getting a Life: Everyday Uses of Autobiography (Smith and Watson), 84–85
Get Out the Vote campaigns, 289
Gilbert, Sarah, 93–94
Gilligan, Carol, 35
Gilman, Charlotte Perkins
  "Yellow Wallpaper, The," 78
Glenn, Evelyn Nakano, 44, 129–130
Goodall, H.L.
  Casing a Promised Land, 217
Good Dog, Carl (Day), 12
good housekeeping, 64
good mothering, 64, 82, 202
Good News (Greenfield), 133
Good Son, The (Gurian), 197
Gore, Ariel, 94
grassroots
  activism, 254, 285–286
  activists, 288
  networking, 286, 289
  training, 288
Grannies for Peace, 246
Granny D, 247
Great Mother, 36, 270
Greenfield, Eloise, 133
grief
  maternal, 235–237, 247, 250, 259–260
  politicized, 236–242, 246, 249, 260
  grown-up child, 107–108
Guess How Much I Love You (McBratney), 127
Gurian, Michael
  Good Son, The, 197
  Wonder of Boys, The, 197

Halberstam, Judith, 59–61, 67
Hamilton, Mykol, 121, 128

Hample, Stoo
  I Will Kiss You (Lots & Lots & Lots), 126
Hansen, Elaine Tuttle, 3
Haraway, Donna, 59–63, 67
Harriet, You'll Drive Me Wild (Fox), 127–128
Harrington, Emily, 108
Hastings, Pattie Belle
  Cyborg Mommy: User's Manual, The, 62–64
Hawks in Congress, 254, 266
Hays, Sharon, 100, 192
Hemans, Felicia, 100
heteronormativity, 12, 192, 204–205, 208, 211
heterosexist, 2, 13
  gaze, 210
  non-, 244
heterosexuality, 13, 43, 62, 192, 199, 205
  questioning, 209–210
  rejection of, 6
  subversion of, 204
Heywood, Leslie
  Third Wave Agenda: Being Feminist, Doing Feminism, 53
Hip Mama, 94
Hirsch, Marianne
  Mother-Daughter Plot: Narrative, Psychoanalysis, Feminism, The, 48
Hochman, David, 85, 90–93
Honest-to-Goodness Truth, The (McKissack), 133
Hollywood, 29, 43, 44, 47–50, 53
homicide, maternal, 4, 15
homophobia, 167, 169, 198, 210, 232, 247
hooks, bell, 3, 72, 155, 176, 184
  Bone Black, 35
Howe, Julia Ward, 234, 235, 242
Huff, Cynthia
  Women's Life Writing and Imagined Communities, 85
Hunt, Peter, 121–122

identity, 8–9, 36, 170, 215, 240
  activist mother's, 232, 244, 258, 265, 270–273
  categories of, 42
  communal, 83, 85
  construction of, 24, 32, 42, 206
  crisis, 127, 216
  defining, 84, 94
  feminine, 34, 37
  gender, 183, 199
  maternal, 67, 77–95, 169
  mother's, 32–33, 170, 173, 215, 270–273
  of mothers of gay sons, 13, 194, 207
  national, 262, 265, 271
  personal, 72, 85, 88, 93, 244
  political, 149, 165, 171–173, 254, 287
  professional, of academic mothers, 165, 167, 177
  See also breeder identity, everymom identity, LGBTQ identity
If I Were a Lion (Weeks), 127–128
I Have Heard of a Land (Thomas), 132
immigrant mothers, 43, 45
immigrant women, 49, 246
  exploited by traffickers, 4, 15
  victims of crime, 4
Immigrant Acts: On Asian American Cultural Politics (Lowe), 44
interpersonal discourse, 11–12
insider, cultural/racial/gender, 157, 171, 194
instant messaging, 57, 58, 63, 68
integration of work and family, 177, 178
internet, 9, 42, 45
  as a way to communicate between family, 10, 63–65, 68
  as a way to communicate between strangers, 77–95, 237, 289
  intimacy between family members, 10, 59–60, 63, 68
  physical proximity and, 64–65
  technology transforming, 10, 63–65, 71

invisible by society, people rendered, 243, 244, 246
I Will Kiss You (Lots & Lots & Lots) (Hample), 126

James, Stanlie, 129–130
Jarvis, Anna, 234
Jeremiah, Emily, 8, 183
Johnson, Angela
  When I Am Old With You, 132–133
Johnson, Dolores
  My Mom Is My Show-and-Tell, 132–133
Joseph, Elena, 228
journals, personal, 82–83
June Cleaver, 174
less-than-, 79

Kaplan, E. Ann, 10, 43–44, 49–50, 173, 174
Karlsson, Lena, 81, 88
Kefalas, Maria
  Promises I Can Keep: Why Poor Women Put Motherhood before Marriage, 2
Kelly, Mary
  Post-partum Document, 31, 37
Kennedy, Eden Marriott, 79, 87–90
Kingfisher, C.P., 153, 155
kin networks, extended, 68
Kristeva, Julia, 22–24, 27

Laboring Women: Reproduction and Gender in New World Slavery (Morgan), 2, 175
Labor movement, 283, 286, 288
Lady Justice, 238
Lady Liberty, 238
Lamar, Michelle, 79
Lamott, Anne
  Operating Instructions: A Journal of My Son's First Year, 78, 90
language
  of child, 23, 29
  as a method for delivering information, 101, 146, 158
  of motherhood, 12–13, 215–229

as a political act, 155–156, 240, 264
Latinas in film, 41–54
La vitesse de liberation, 66–67
Lawrence, Jen, 92–93
Leighton, Angela, 110–111
lesbian activist, 232, 243–249
Letterhead Brigade, 282–284
letterhead organizations, 283
LGBTQ
  activism, 237, 243–249
  identity, 12–13
  rights, 13, 245, 246
  visibility, 245
Literary Mama: A Literary Magazine for the Maternally Inclined, 94
Lot of Otters, A (Berger), 126
Love You Forever (Munsch), 126–127
Lowe, Lisa
  Immigrant Acts: On Asian American Cultural Politics, 44

Madonna image, 33
Madres de la Plaza de Mayo, 14, 234–236, 246–247, 253–256, 260–273
Mailing list organizations, 283–284
mainstream media. *See* media
Mamapalooza, 13, 217–218, 295
Marianismo, 255, 269
deMarneffe, Daphne
  Maternal Desire, 2
marriage, 13
  contract, 150
  equal rights in, 232, 246
  ideal, 203, 204
  sexuality, reproduction, and, 193
  as sole purpose of woman's life, 46, 49
masculinity, 191, 192–193, 208, 267
  femininity and, 197, 207
  ideals of, 197, 200
  outward appearance of, 202–203
Mask of Motherhood, The (Maushart), 215
Maternal Desire (deMarneffe), 2
mater dolorosa, 255, 259, 264
maternal activism, 1, 13, 14, 196, 233

See also activism
maternal activists, 265, 270
maternal devotion, 261
maternalism, 233–234, 241, 242
maternalist activism, 14, 234, 248
  See also activism
maternalist feminism, 233
maternalist framework, 231–232, 234, 239, 241, 249–250
maternal love, 10, 57, 59, 60, 71, 110
  over love of the state, 260, 261, 266, 269
maternal subjectivity, 71, 209
  See also subjectivity
maternal thinking, 38, 165, 233
Maternal Thinking (Ruddick), 2, 165, 233, 261, 269
maternal warmth, 43, 105, 109
maternity, 8–9, 61
  feminist position on, 185
  modern, 111
  rewriting of, 95
  social, 263
  and women's inequality, 281
matriot, 237, 240
matriotic, 242
matriotism, 240–242, 245, 265
Mayberry, Katherine
  Teaching What You're Not, 171
Maus, Fred, 30–31
Maushart, Susan
  Mask of Motherhood, The, 215
McBratney, Sam
  Guess How Much I Love You, 127
McClintock, Anne, 238
McKay, Nellie, 171, 173
McKissack, Patricia
  Flossie and the Fox, 133
  Honest-to-Goodness Truth, The, 133
media, 9, 229, 257, 270, 272
  independent, 250
  mass, 215, 237–238, 249–250, 281, 282
  portrayal of Latinos, 42
  portrayal of mothers, 5, 32, 80, 85, 87
  progressive, 283, 285

memoirs, 82, 83
mentoring, 163, 168, 169, 172, 178
Meyers, Susan
  Everywhere Babies, 127
Meynell, Alice, 11, 99–111
  Childhood, 99, 106
  Children, The, 99, 101–104, 105, 107, 108
Michaels, Meredith
  Mommy Myth, The, 2, 5, 71, 124–125
Midwest Modern Language Association, 1, 8
Mildred Pierce, 173
Miller, Nancy K.
  But Enough about Me: Why We Read Other People's Lives, 82
Million Mom March, 250
mirror, 45–46, 50, 53, 54, 131
Moments of Laughter (Westerkamp), 9, 21–39
momism, new, 71
Mommybloggers (blog), 82
Mommyblogging, 77–95
Mommy Dearest, 174
Mommy Myth: The Idealization of Motherhood and How it has Undermined all Women, The (Douglas and Michaels), 2, 5, 71, 124–125
Mommy Needs Coffee (blog), 79
mommy wars, 2, 123, 282
MomsRising, 281, 286
moral reform movement, 257
"More More More," Said the Baby (Williams), 127
Morgan, Jennifer
  Laboring Women: Reproduction and Gender in New World Slavery, 2, 175
Morrison, Toni, 171, 186
  Beloved, 175
  Playing in the Dark, 174–175
mortality rate, maternal, 4
mothers
  absence of, as an opportunity for child's growth, 132

accountable to society at large, 202
African American, 130–134
alienated, 110
anxieties of, 111, 226, 263
bad, 82, 196–197, 207–209
confident, 131–134, 228, 233
connection to child, 23, 25, 70, 110–111, 218, 255–256
definition of bad, 175, 202
definition of good, 149, 175, 192, 202
empowered/empowering, 6, 120, 131, 218, 229, 250
failure as, 5, 192, 196208–210, 224
of gay sons, 191–211
good, 174, 196, 197, 199, 207, 209
Latina, 41–54
mythic, 11, 119–134
new, 77, 83, 86, 122, 127, 135
redefining, 91, 218, 228, 264
separation from, 43, 46
status in society, 5, 170, 231
working, 5, 123, 132, 166
  as seen by colleagues, 168
mother-child relationship, 195, 297
Mother-Daughter Plot: Narrative, Psychoanalysis, Feminism, The (Hirsch), 48
mother-daughter relationships, 41–54, 175, 195
  conflicts, 47, 50
  impact of race/ethnicity and class on, 42, 44
mother figure, 14, 42, 103, 174
  Four paradigms, 50
motherhood
  culture of, 78, 227
  idealized, 48, 82, 134, 272
  ideology, 14, 280
  image of, 126, 258
  institution, as an, 3, 58, 220, 236, 238
  judgment of, 79, 216–217, 224–225
  kinds of, 125
  paradigms of, 254, 259, 265
  penalty, 5, 282
  political, 14, 253–273

popular notions of, 32, 111, 256
public, 11, 99–111
radicalizes, 170, 232
redefined, 94–95, 272
redefining, 264
reimagining, 129
traditional notions of, 2, 170, 234, 271
universal images of, 269
writing about, 78, 83, 85, 94–95, 216
Motherhood Project, 281
MotherHood, The (Web site), 281
mothering, 95, 134, 181, 186, 219
act of, 170, 220
cyborg, 10, 57, 60, 63, 69–72
difficulties of, 168, 176
double bind of, 92
embodied activist, 13–14, 232, 235, 236
new definitions, 11, 80, 87, 94, 108
racialized, 44
reinvented, 6, 71, 81
romanticized notions of, 81
tied to the body through, 235
mothering activist. *See* activism
mothering experience, 12, 13, 183, 219, 223, 227
mothering literature, 78–79
mothering relationships, 63
mothering studies, 1–2, 6, 165
motherist representations, 174–175, 185–186
Mother Mary Jones, 231, 232
Mother Outlaws (O'Reilly), 14, 130, 218, 232
Mothers '08 Conference, 279–281, 290
Mothers & More National Conference, 280–281
Mothers Acting Up, 281
Mother's Day for Peace, 234
Mother Shock: Loving Every (Other) Minute of It (Buchanan), 90
mothers' movement, 272, 279–290
Mothers Movement Online, 14, 280, 281
mother-son relationship, 192, 210

mother status, 4, 166, 177
Mothers Who Think features in *Salon Magazine*, 94
MoveOn.org, 286
Mrs. Kennedy. *See* Kennedy, Eden Marriott
Ms. Mentor, 166–167, 177
MUBAR (Mothered Up Beyond All Recognition) (blog), 92
Mulvey, Laura, 173
Munsch, Robert
Love You Forever, 126–127
My Mom Is My Show-and-Tell (Johnson), 132–133
My Space accounts, 58, 63
myths of motherhood, 124–125, 127–133, 170, 231
busting, 221

narratives
of capitalism and colony, 175
in the classroom, 176
in film, 43, 46
mother's, 25, 77–95, 173
of mothers of homosexual sons, 13, 191–211
National Advocates for Pregnant Women, 4, 281
National Association of Mothers Centers, 279, 281
National Communication Association Conference, 13, 218
National Organization for Women (NOW), 148
Newman, Catherine
Waiting for Birdy, 80
Nilsen, Alleen Pace, 127
No, David! (Shannon), 127–128
normalization, 195, 204, 206
Not Our Sons, Not Their Sons, Not Your Sons, 241, 267
"no-uterus rule," 165–166
NOW Mothers & Caregivers Economic Rights Committee, 281
nuclear family, 195, 197, 257, 271
abandoning for national family, 259
decontextualized, 48

nuclear family (*continued*)
  heterosexual, 13, 67, 192, 202
  ideal of, 150, 193,
  outside of, 60, 68, 72, 130, 210–211

Obama for America, 288, 298
Of Woman Born: Motherhood as Experience and Institution (Rich), 1–2, 42–43, 78, 111, 232–235, 246
Oliver, Kelly, 60, 70, 72, 73
Oliveros, Pauline, 30–31
On the Day I Was Born (Chocolate), 133
Operating Instructions: A Journal of My Son's First Year (Lamott), 78, 90
oppression
  racial, class, and gender, 130–131, 265
  women's, 3, 49–50, 68, 170
O'Reilly, Andrea, 6, 14, 130, 218, 232, 233, 250–251
  Mother Outlaws, 14, 130, 218, 232
Orleck, Annelise, 129–130
organizing mothers for change, 14, 280
Ortner, Sherry, 270
other mothering, 233
Other Side, The (Woodson), 133
outlaw mothering, 218, 232–233, 243, 244

pagers, 68
paid leave, 5, 179, 183
paradigm
  heteronormative, 58, 60
  motherhood, 254–256, 259, 265
  patriarchal, 253, 271
  for peace, 240
parenting, 21, 58, 135, 159, 182
  as a female occupation, 120, 122, 125, 127
  as a gender issue, 282
  and working, 165, 178,
parenting advice, 79, 93

parenting and professing, 165, 176, 182
parenting blogs. *See* blogs
parenting books, 216
parenting groups, 228
parenting magazines, 77, 79, 86–87
parenting manuals, 197, 216
parents, new, 121–123, 126–127
passing, 169–170
patriarchal authority, 258, 262
patriarchal construction of motherhood, 263, 265, 271
patriarchal culture, 218, 270
patriarchal game, playing the, 233
patriarchal oppression, 49
patriarchal politics, 258, 260, 265
patriarchal society, 174
patriarchal values, 42
  mother as mouthpiece for, 10, 42, 48
  rejection of, 183
patriarchy, 43–44, 47, 49–50, 241, 270
patriotism, 238, 240, 247, 260, 262, 265
peace movements, 237, 259, 283
Peace Pilgrim, 247
Pelias, Ronald
  Performance Studies: The Interpretation of Aesthetic Text, 220, 221
Performance Studies: The Interpretation of Aesthetic Text (Pelias), 220, 221
persona
  feminine, 102, 103
  mother, 100, 101
  professional, 99, 100, 170
personal is political, the, 87, 232, 240, 246, 265
personalization of political issues, 241–242, 281
personalize the political, 240, 243
Personal Responsibility and Work Opportunities Reconciliation Act of 1996 (PRWORA), 153
Peskowitz, Mirian
  Truth behind the Mommy Wars, The, 2, 5

picture books. *See* children's picture books
Pinkney, Myles
    Read and Rise, 133
Playing in the Dark (Morrison), 174–175
Post-partum Document (Kelly), 31, 37
Poster, Mark, 63–67
potential of the child, 104, 192, 202
poverty, 153, 234, 250, 290
    maternal, 289
    in old age, 5
powerlessness, 184, 235
    as induced by those in power, 239
Price of Motherhood, The (Crittenden), 2, 5
professional women and mothering, 100, 103, 111, 177, 182
professor/mother, 12, 164–167, 176
progressive movement, 281, 283–285, 288
Promises I Can Keep: Why Poor Women Put Motherhood before Marriage (Kefalas), 2
public discourse, 9, 94, 260
public performance, 13, 39, 218, 222, 228
public and private spheres, 25, 43, 67–68, 111, 253
    blurred through activism, 233, 255–257, 258–260, 263, 269
Putnam, Robert
    Bowling Alone, 283–284, 286

Rankin, Jeannette, 242
Rape Victim Advocacy Program, 148
Read and Rise (Pinkney), 133
Read to Your Bunny (Wells), 119–122
Reagon, Bernice Johnson, 291
Real Women Have Curves, 10, 41–54
reproduction, 46, 59, 61–62, 66, 193, 267
Reproduction of Mothering, The (Chodorow), 2, 123, 125, 128
reproductive rights, 4, 185
"response-ability," 10, 60, 70

Rich, Adrienne
    Of Woman Born: Motherhood as Experience and Institution, 1–2, 42–43, 78, 111, 232–235, 246
right-wing thought industry, 283
Roberts, Dorothy, 184
role models, 12, 43, 46, 168–169, 177
roles
    maternal, 79, 82, 84, 87, 91, 265
    mother's, 45, 95, 100, 122, 131–132, 228
    narrowly defined, 85, 263
    stereotypical, 25, 199, 207, 244
    traditional, 22, 257, 269, 270
    within the nuclear family, 78, 271
romantic coupling, 13, 210
Rose, Jacqueline, 121–122, 129
Rowe-Finkbeiner, Kristin
    F Word: Feminism in Jeopardy, The, 233
Rubin, Lillian
    Families on the Fault Line, 219
Ruddick, Sara, 165, 233
    Maternal Thinking, 2, 261, 269
Runaway Bunny, The (Brown), 125–126

Sapphira and the Slave Girl (Cather), 175
salaries, lower for mothers, 166
Satterwhite, Jean, 79, 89, 90
Save the Children's Mothers' Index, 4
Savoca, Nancy, 173
scholar, and mother, 9, 177, 217
scholar, and woman, 168, 169, 172
scholars of color, 172
Schaffer, Talia, 102–103
Schumaker, Jennifer, 13, 231–232, 236–237, 243–250
second wave feminism, 1, 2, 42, 123, 267, 273
    third wave criticism of, 53–54
self-sacrificing mother, 236, 253, 269–270
self-sacrificing mothering, 71, 125, 127
self-sacrificing parents, 93

self-sacrificing women, 255
Sendak, Maurice
  Where the Wild Things Are, 127–128
sexism, 167, 174
  challenging, 148
Shannon, David
  No, David, 127–128
Sheehan, Cindy, 13, 231–232, 237–242, 249–250, 265
  refusing the compliant voice of the mother, 233
  using her body in her activism, 236, 246, 247–248
single motherhood, 145–160
  political nature of, 149, 152
  stereotypes, 22, 80
sisterhood, between mothers, 218
Sleep Tight, Little Bear (Waddell), 127
S.M.A.R.T.: Single Mothers Achieving and Reflecting Together, 12, 145–160
Smartypants, Mimi
  World According to Mimi Smartypants, The, 80
Smith, Sidonie
  Getting a Life: Everyday Uses of Autobiography, 84–85
soccer mom, 85, 237, 243
social activism, 130, 286–287
social change, 6, 15, 82, 282, 285, 288
social justice, 232, 285, 288
social movements, 286–288
social networking sites, 10, 57, 63, 73
social spaces, 65–67
sons
  gay/homosexual. *See* gay sons
  masculine
    failure to raise, 191
    normal, 192, 203
    failure to raise, 196
Sontag, Susan, 203–204
sound making, childhood, 21–22, 24
sounds, domestic, 25
Spillers, Hortense, 2
Stanton, Elizabeth Cady, 232
Stay-at-home mothers, 5, 123
Stella Dallas, 43, 49–50, 173

stereotypes, 215, 244
  of gender, 52–53
  of gender and sexuality, 199
  of motherhood, 10, 22
  of women, 260
  of working mothers, 168, 182
  stereotypical notions of masculinity and femininity, 207
stereotyping, 31, 37, 170
Stone, Allucquére Rosanne, 64–66
Stories, Identities, and Political Change (Tilly), 287
student, mother and, 12, 145–160, 163
student parents, 145–160, 178–180
Students for a Democratic Society (SDS), 148
subculture, mothers as, 218
subjectivity
  of mother and child, 60,
  of mothers, 42, 71, 167, 175, 209
  of single mothers, 145–146, 155
Suburban Bliss: Birth Control via the Written Word (blog), 77–81, 88, 92
suffragettes, 236, 247, 257
Summers, Melissa, 77–78, 81, 87–90, 92
support groups, 12, 13, 145–160, 280
symbolic citizens, 238–239
Symposium on Maternal Feminism, 280

teacher decentered classroom, 185
Teaching What You're Not (Mayberry), 171
technologies of co-presence, 10, 57–73
  cell phone, 9, 10
  e-mail, 10
  telephone, 65–66
Ten, Nine, Eight (Bang), 127
Third Wave Agenda: Being Feminist, Doing Feminism (Heywood and Drake), 53
third wave feminism, 53–54
Thomas, Joyce Carol
  I Have Heard of a Land, 132
Thomas, Trudelle, 130
Thurer, Shari, 124, 125

Tilly, Charles
  Stories, Identities, and Political Change, 287
Toth, Emily. *See* Ms. Mentor
Troops Home FAST, 247
trope of motherhood, 232, 234, 236, 237, 267
Truth behind the Mommy Wars, The (Peskowitz), 2
Truthout.org, 237
Tso, Kimberly, 228
24 Hour Woman, 173

unequal gender expectations, 238
UnMartyred Mom, 229

Vagina Monologues, 221
validation as mothers, 91, 216–218
violence against women, 4, 221, 258
Virilio, Paul, 66–68
virtual space, 58, 70

Waddell, Martin
  Sleep Tight, Little Bear, 127
Waiting for Birdy (Newman), 80
Wall, Barbara, 121
Wane, Njoki Nathani, 219
Watson, Julia
  Getting a Life: Everyday Uses of Autobiography, 84–85
waves of feminism, 15. *See also* second wave feminism; third wave feminism
Way We Never Were, The (Coontz), 2, 174
weblogs. *See* blogs
web sites, 145, 250
Weeks, Sarah
  If I Were a Lion, 127–128
welfare recipients, college enrollment amongst, 153
welfare reform, 146, 152–153
Welfare Warriors, 281
Wells, Rosemary
  Read to Your Bunny, 119–122, 133
Westerkamp, Hildegard
  Moments of Laughter, 9, 21–39

When I Am Old With You (Johnson), 133
Where the Wild Things Are (Sendak), 127–128
White Trash Mom (blog), 79
Williams, Joan, 228
Williams, Linda, 46, 52, 173
Williams, Raymond, 126, 134
Williams, Vera
  "More More More," Said the Baby, 127
  Working Cotton, 131
Wollstonecraft, Mary, 231
woman's work, 46–47
woman's worth, 192
Women of Greenham Common, 246
Women's Liberation Front, 148
Women's Life Writing and Imagined Communities (Huff), 85
women's rights movements, 266, 283
women's studies, 6, 171, 185
Women's Studies Quarterly, 165
Women Strike for Peace, 233, 241, 263
women who have children, percent of, 3, 163, 169
Wonder of Boys, The (Gurian), 197
Woodson, Jacqueline
  Coming on Home Soon, 131–132
  Other Side, The, 133
Working Cotton (Williams), 131
working fathers, 166, 168–169, 195
working mothers, 5, 123, 132, 166, 168
working women, 111, 167, 280, 282
World According to Mimi Smartypants, The (Smartypants), 80
World Economic Forum, 4
WRAC (Women's Resource and Action Center), 145–160
writing mother, 80, 94, 102–103, 106, 111
Writing Women's Communities: The Politics and Poetics of Contemporary Multi-genre Anthologies (Franklin), 84

"Yellow Wallpaper, The" (Gilman), 78